# A History of Habit

# A History of Habit

## *From Aristotle to Bourdieu*

Edited by Tom Sparrow and Adam Hutchinson

LEXINGTON BOOKS
Lanham • Boulder • New York • Toronto • Plymouth, UK

Published by Lexington Books
A wholly owned subsidiary of The Rowman & Littlefield Publishing Group, Inc.
4501 Forbes Boulevard, Suite 200, Lanham, Maryland 20706
www.rowman.com

10 Thornbury Road, Plymouth PL6 7PP, United Kingdom



British Library Cataloguing in Publication Information Available

**Library of Congress Cataloging-in-Publication Data**

A history of habit from Aristotle to Bourdieu / edited by Tom Sparrow and Adam Hutchinson.
p. cm.
Includes bibliographical references and index.
ISBN 978-0-7391-8198-0 (cloth : alk. paper) — ISBN 978-0-7391-8199-7 (electronic)
ISBN 978-1-4985-1129-2 (pbk : alk. paper)

1. Habit (Philosophy) I. Sparrow, Tom, 1979– editor of compilation.
B105.H32H57 2013
128'.3—dc23

2013010683

∞™ The paper used in this publication meets the minimum requirements of American National Standard for Information Sciences Permanence of Paper for Printed Library Materials, ANSI/NISO Z39.48-1992.

Printed in the United States of America

For George Yancy, both the Monongahela
and Allegheny to our little Ohio.

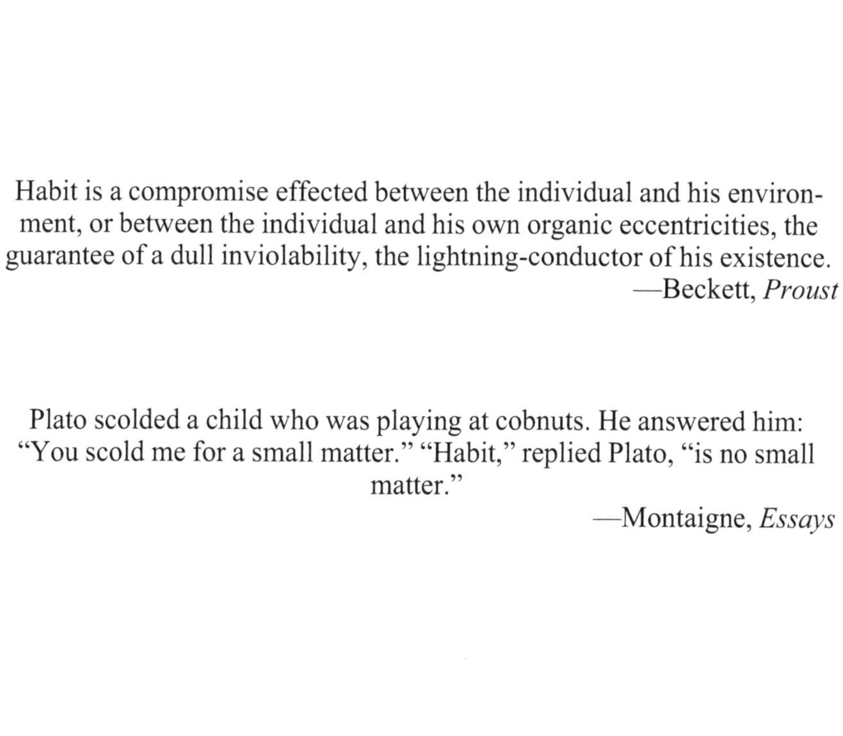

Habit is a compromise effected between the individual and his environment, or between the individual and his own organic eccentricities, the guarantee of a dull inviolability, the lightning-conductor of his existence.

—Beckett, *Proust*

Plato scolded a child who was playing at cobnuts. He answered him: "You scold me for a small matter." "Habit," replied Plato, "is no small matter."

—Montaigne, *Essays*

# Contents

# Acknowledgments

Despite careful preparation, the task of compiling an edited collection leads editors into unforeseen difficulties. At every turn, from the preparation through the detours, George Yancy helped us navigate this endeavor with his bottomless practical knowledge and enthusiasm. It is his guidance to which we are most indebted. Since contributors ultimately provide the contours of a book such as ours, we are incredibly grateful to them for providing this book with its distinct shape and conceptual rigor. We thank all of you for your faith, diligence, and dedication to our project. Along the way we also solicited aid from Jennifer Bates, John Fritz, Ron Polansky, Anthony Steinbock, Jim Swindal, and Nick Warcholak. Their strategic help enabled us in major ways; we thank each of you for it. Last, but not least, we must thank Jana Hodges-Kluck, our editor at Lexington Books, for readily acknowledging the philosophical merits of our project and for taking it on at the press and seeing it to print.

# Introduction

## *Reflections on the Unreflected*

Tom Sparrow and Adam Hutchinson

### 1. ABOUT THE PHILOSOPHY OF HABIT AND THIS BOOK

René Descartes believed common sense to be the most equitably distributed thing in the world. The essays collected here contest Descartes' assessment by affirming that habit enjoys a more generous distribution, for it is detectable not only in the minds of humans, but also in the behavior of non-human animals, the dynamics of populations, the growth patterns of plants, and the tendencies of systems. Under the influence of C. S. Peirce and Charles Darwin, William James went even one step further when he claimed that the laws of nature are nothing more than habits.[1] Even if this sort of brash speculation cannot in the end be substantiated with empirical evidence, it is at least the case that habit is universally acknowledged as basic to human thought and action. Quite often the detection of habit in human behavior is also charged with a moral valuation, as when we chastise someone for their bad habits or praise them for cultivating healthy ones. Occasionally habit calls attention to its existential valence, as when in *Waiting for Godot* one of Samuel Beckett's most well-known characters soberly proclaims that "habit is a great deadener."[2] The metaphysical weight of this pronouncement is as palpable as Vladimir's ambivalent tone. The reach of habit, however, cannot be confined to the behavioral, moral, or existential spheres. It admits of biological, sociological, psychological, neurological, epistemological, phenomenological, and ontological dimensions among many others.

When you peek beyond the popular discourse familiar to everyone what you find is a rich philosophical discussion of the role that habit plays in our personal, political, spiritual, and intellectual lives. Countless questions arise in the history of habit. Is it simply a psychological phenomenon, easily manipulated by positive and negative reinforcement? Are customs and passions different in kind or degree? Are personality and character habitual? How do habits help or hinder our attempts to solve problems? Does habit function at the transcendental or empirical level (or both)? Do inanimate objects possess habits, or can only sentient creatures act habitually? What about plants? Do habits constitute our first or second nature? Can we exist without habits? Can we be sure that the laws of nature are more (or less) than physical habits? What is the metaphysics of habit? If only one thing is agreed upon between anyone who has offered a reflection on these questions, it is that habit solicits contradictory evaluations. It remains an elusive concept, but one with great explanatory power. This, as much as its enduring significance and ambivalent interpretation, provoked us to assemble a text that would exhibit the plurality of ways that habit has been used to explain, understand, and regulate the world.

The idea for this book grew out of a series of informal discussions on the history of philosophy which took place—habitually, it should be noted—at Hanlon's Café in Pittsburgh, Pennsylvania, not far from the campus of Duquesne University. It owes just as much to our respective research into theories of embodiment and, especially, a common interest in the naturalistic philosophy of the pragmatists, for whom habit is a basic mechanism of human nature. Adding to this a mutual affection for David Hume and a longstanding familiarity with the account of virtuous individuals outlined in the *Nicomachean Ethics*, we began to regard habit as one of the most recurrent and useful concepts at work in the history of Western philosophy. We suspect that many readers will see this as a truism, which is why we were surprised to find a text on the history of habit unavailable. We have therefore sought to assemble one that would make explicit the largely unheralded, yet readily acknowledged, role that habit plays in the history of philosophy, while at the same time demonstrating its privileged importance for many prominent thinkers, for example, Aristotle, Thomas Aquinas, Descartes, Hume, Maurice Merleau-Ponty, Pierre Bourdieu, and entire schools of thought, such as Roman Stoicism and American pragmatism. Most of the chapters focus on how a particular thinker engages the concept of habit in his or her work. Some of them dig deeply into the question of what constitutes a habit—the metaphysics of habit, as it were—while others, instead of asking *what* a habit is, examine *how* the concept can be applied—to ethical practice, social problems, or intellectual endeavor—to better understand and change the order of things. As editors we asked each contributor to explore either or both of these dimensions, and to do so with a view toward demonstrating the historicity of their figure's mobilization of habit. This is achieved to a greater or lesser degree, contingent upon the contributor's discipline, tradition, and methodological approach. The variability resulting from this pluralism, rather than constituting a weakness, is one of the collection's chief virtues. It reflects the pluralistic history of habit itself and is why we committed ourselves as editors to soliciting, as well as preserving, the multiple sensibilities of our contributors.

Taken as a whole the book aims to show how and in what sense philosophers and other thinkers of habit are engaged in a broad, multifaceted dialogue concerning the nature and meaning of habit, its function in human affairs, and its appropriation by speculative thought—a dialogue that is perhaps only today garnering critical recognition. Toward this end, *A History of Habit: From Aristotle to Bourdieu* offers a heterogeneous history of the philosophy of habit through a series of critical interventions which continue to push the dialogue forward. At the same time, these essays attempt to provoke a dialogue between philosophy and other disciplines. Like many of our contributors we contend that the many discourses of habit found in philosophical texts have vast import for a panoply of other fields as well.

So, it was not the indiscriminate or quotidian use of the concept of habit—which take habit's meaning and applicability for granted—that generated the idea for this book. It was our common recognition that the discourses of philosophy, psychology, and sociology (just to name a few) are littered with offhand references to, and technical engagements with, the fundamentality of habit. Assertions of its efficacy as well as strong ascriptions of its role in the formation of subject identities, social relationships, and ways of comporting oneself or representing one's world are distributed across disparate fields of study. Habit is identified as the basis of knowledge, perception, and aesthetic pleasure. Casual references abound, and more often than not these occur at crucial moments in an author's argument or analysis. It is a ready-made concept that is difficult to resist when another is lacking. Hume famously reduces causality to customary association, that is, habit, when he cannot locate the necessary connection between cause and effect, and yet needs to account for their universal association. Aristotle and James appeal to habit when they need to explain the persistence of actions that are sometimes active, sometimes dormant. More recently one influential film theorist has argued that the masculinist gaze, which is built into so many films, conditions women to see like men. How does this happen? This conditioning, she concludes, is "a *habit* that very easily becomes *second nature*."[3] The explanatory power of habit is immense. And yet, with some exceptions its ontological constitution is rarely investigated, or it is overshadowed by its physical description.[4]

Habit complicates our understanding of what it means to act. This is perhaps what makes it so fascinating and why it continues to serve as a useful conceptual, as well as rhetorical, device for explaining behavior. It is a liminal concept, occupying a space at the border between several of the binaries that organize the philosophical discourse of action. In this respect it tends to mingle oppositional concepts like freedom/determination, natural/artificial, active/passive, cause/effect, spontaneity/instinct, and agent/patient. In one way or another each of our contributors renders salient this aspect of habit. Or, more precisely, they make it clearer insofar as they color the edges of a liminal space, occupied by habit, that resists our usual conceptual framework. As such, habit marks a certain indecision about the cause of action; this indecision repeats throughout the history of philosophy, and suggests that habit is not merely a cog in the determinist's machine. The dual nature of habit, therefore, makes trouble for our ideas of moral choice, autonomy, culpability, and so forth. Félix Ravaisson referred to this as the "double law of habit," a phrase which indicates habit's repetitive and generative aspects and, once again, confirms its paradoxical status as an explanatory concept.[5] This is, perhaps, the reason for its enduring relevance and manifold interpretation.

But habit is not just a concept that makes trouble and steers us into paradox. It is true that these critical attributes make for intellectual intrigue and are important insofar as they disturb familiar ways of thinking. More than that, what we see emerging in the history of habit—with notable intensity in the French context—is a viable alternative to the Cartesian picture of subjectivity much maligned in the nineteenth and twentieth centuries. If Cartesianism trades in a dualist metaphysics that regards mind and body, spirit and matter as distinct substances, and then assumes this basic dualism in its accounts of thought, passion, behavior, and action, then by contrast the philosophy of habit encourages us to conceive these phenomena as occurring *between* mind and body, spirit and matter. Habit becomes indispensable for constructing a nondualist metaphysics along with new accounts of subjectivity. Proponents of the ongoing critique of Cartesian subjectivity will no doubt find resources in this book.

Our collection is designed to be read in a couple ways. Reading the text cover-to-cover provides a narrative of habit's history in the Western philosophical tradition and a window onto its application in contemporary social theory. It is not necessary, however, to read each chapter in succession. Although each chapter makes reference to figures and ideas elaborated at length in other chapters, each stands alone and encourages readers to dip selectively into the collection. Some chapters are more general than others; they lay the groundwork for the discussion. Many chapters make critical interventions into the discussion, focusing on specific conceptual, historical, and/or social issues.

Every historical narrative includes gaps in the story, interpretive distortion, and unforgivable omissions. Every text suffers the constraints imposed upon it by time, space, and word counts. Ours is no exception. Although a generous selection of figures is covered, with a project of this scope—and given the interpretive apparatus outlined above—a number of thinkers who deserve more attention could not receive exclusive treatment. The necessity of these omissions, we contend, only demonstrates the ubiquity of habit in the history of ideas. To be sure, many of the excluded are operating at the margins of the included or are discussed explicitly, if only for comparison or contrast. Several (likely more) glaring omissions warrant some justification.

First, the nineteenth-century British Utilitarians arguably deserve inclusion in any collection exploring the history and future of habit in philosophy. Both Jeremy Bentham and J. S. Mill (not to speak of Henry Sidgwick) argued that much of what we consider either good or bad—pleasurable and painful—is a matter of historically established habit; that the best of laws are themselves attempts to habituate behaviors that previous generations found to promote the greatest happiness for the greatest number. Bentham was especially active in calling attention to how many seemingly "static" social and gendered notions of his day were just the accumulation of historical habit: we ignore the obvious suffering of animals not because it is somehow "natural" for us, but because the habit of thinking of them as non-rational mechanisms has been so firmly ingrained in our thought. As Richard Rorty later pointed out, Mill was especially influential among early American jurists and philosophers of a certain pragmatic bent; he is in large part responsible for the attention that such thinkers pay to habit as a social force. It would certainly be a little too much to say that Dewey's and James's robust developments of the concept of habit are a direct result of their reading of utilitarian philosophy, but it would also be wrong to dismiss such an obvious historical influence.

Our next painful omission also represents a powerful influence upon American pragmatism and the social psychology of George Herbert Mead, among more recent philosophical views of habit. We have not included any essays that focus exclusively on the major German idealists. This omission does not imply that German Idealism has nothing of worth to say about habit. Indeed, at the very least, Immanuel Kant, J. G. Fichte, and G. W. F. Hegel all make interesting contributions to the development of habit, not to mention F. W. J. Schelling, who may have had direct influence on Ravaisson's thinking.[6] The influence of German idealism is probably most easily seen cashing out in Karl Marx's theory of ideology and Dewey's later rendering of the social as a habituated organic unity. This is not to say, of course, that German idealism's contribution to the philosophy of habit can only be gleaned from those who were influenced by the movement. Implicit in Hegel's famous philosophy of history, for instance, is the idea that habit has some sort of greater metaphysical or ontological basis within spirit and *is not* something fully explicable within the mechanistic framework favored by so many in his day. By the same token, Kant's ethics seems to stand as a great critique of the role of habit within moral thought. In his *Critique of Practical Reason* and associated works, Kant argues that the distance of the moral law from something like habit is precisely what distinguishes the ethical from other forms of thought. After all, in order to act ethically I must appeal only to a law that I give myself, which finds its origin in reason alone and never in my desires or normative social rules. That is to say, an appeal to habit—whether in the form of automatic action or the historical fossilization of experience in common law—is always foreign to the true ethical standpoint that is found in reason alone.

Friedrich Nietzsche memorably advocated for the efficacy of what he called "brief habits." In *The Gay Science* he draws a memorable contrast between habits that stick around for a lifetime and habits that linger for a short while, then flee the scene. His ambivalence toward habit is not aimed at habit as such; he instead prepares a critique of habit on the basis of its temporality and purpose. Brief habits are seen as healthy, for they allow knowledge to expand and deepen through diverse experiences. Enduring habits, by contrast, are a hindrance to self-overcoming. "*Enduring* habits I hate," he writes. "I feel as if a tyrant had come near me and as if the air I breathe had thickened when events take such a turn that it appears that they will inevitably give rise to enduring habits."[7] A more thorough exploration of Nietzsche's writing on habit and its relation to the theme of health is certainly called for.

A full treatment of Martin Heidegger's pragmatism and hermeneutics is missing here.[8] Although he does not frame his analysis in terms of habit, early Heidegger (and Merleau-Ponty after him) understands Dasein's worldhood as principally a matter of habitual tool use. In its everyday mode Dasein (Heidegger's stand-in for the human being) is a being entangled in equipment and working to achieve a set of tasks which are enabled by a sedimented historical and practical knowledge. It is on the basis of this knowledge that Dasein navigates its historical situation, and it is from this perspective that Dasein establishes an interpretive framework upon which to understand and operate in the world. Insofar as Heidegger is a thinker of historical rootedness and practical knowledge, or, put otherwise, a thinker of *habitus* and habitat, his philosophy of habit demands further treatment—especially given the shadow it casts over the entirety of twentieth-century continental philosophy.

John Locke's 1693 educational treatise, *Some Thoughts Concerning Education*, no doubt deserves a place in the history of habit. An influence on Jean-Jacques Rousseau's *Emile*, Locke's text treats explicitly the habits to be inculcated in students. The case is easily made that the function of habit in Michel Foucault's analyses of disciplinary societies and biopolitics deserves sustained study as well. There is no doubt, given that he writes: "the soldier has become something that can be made; out of formless clay, an inapt body, the machine required can be constructed; posture is gradually corrected; a calculated constraint runs slowly through each part of the body, mastering it, making it pliable, ready at all times, turning silently into the automatism of habit."[9] Finally, it is more than apparent that a keystone in the history of habit is the translation of the Greek *hexis* into the Latin *habitus*. A proper linguistic study of this important transition is absent from our collection, and bridging this gap would require a close inspection of the work of Quintillian and Cicero, among others.

Despite these lacunae—born of necessity rather than neglect—readers will find in these pages a representative tour of the philosophy of habit. While it is inevitable that some reviewers will find our omissions scandalous (such is the fate of endeavors such as this), we are confident that the rough texture of philosophical thinking about habit has not been smoothed out. In other words, we hope to help generate a more historically informed discussion of habit, *not* provide a definitive history of it as a subject.

## 2. THE CHAPTERS

The book is divided into three historical periods. Part I showcases some classical thinking on the role that habit plays in the determination of character. A concern with the cultivation and maintenance of ethical integrity (taken in the structural sense) is the real thread that runs through this set of essays. The opening chapter by Thornton Lockwood lays the groundwork for each of the chapters that follow it by providing a close textual analysis of the concept of *hexis* in Aristotle, who forms a central reference point for virtually every philosophy of habit that comes after him. In an attempt to contest the view that what Aristotle bequeaths to us is a non-philosophical, mechanistic view of character formation Lockwood explores the Greek vocabulary of habit which attends Aristotle's thinking of ethical character. Lockwood works to dissociate the repetitive interpretation of habituation from Aristotle's less mechanistic understanding of ethical character. He argues that Aristotle's notion of ethical excellence is best formulated in terms of *hexis*, rather than *techne* or *ethos*, precisely because the former bears a moral connotation lacking in the latter. The ethically virtuous person is not defined by the skills she possesses, but by the habits she embodies and, with a certain virtuosity, summons in the appropriate circumstances.

In chapter 2, William O. Stephens turns his attention to the teaching of the Roman Stoics Seneca, Musonius Rufus, and Epictetus, whose ethics prescribe a way of life organized by the rigorous rejection and cultivation of habits of thought, action, and emotion. The advantageously organized life only results from careful attention to the metaphysics of human action, and consistently sound judgments about the good, the bad, and the indifferent. Consistency of judgment leads to consistent—that is, habitual—actions, which ultimately pave the way to happiness. Not unlike Aristotle, who understood virtue and, consequently, happiness to be a product of long-established habit, the Stoics regard happiness as something achievable for most people only after a lifetime of training (*askēsis*). In addition to outlining the accounts of habit provided by three major figures in the history of Roman Stoicism, Stephens surveys the diverse habits to be shunned or adopted by the Stoic who aspires to live a life of virtue, that is, to live a life in accordance with nature and reason.

Robert Miner's essay on Aquinas (chapter 3) explores the supposed contradiction between habituation and freedom of the will, a topic that arises again and again in the essays that follow. Miner demonstrates how, for Aquinas, *habitus* actually conditions "freedom in its most desirable form." He provides readers with a non-technical presentation of the Scholastic's analysis, proceeding in four steps which clearly articulate the principle, subject, cause, and distinction of habit as Aquinas understands it. He helpfully contrasts habit and its cognate, disposition, and concludes by comparing Aquinas with Nietzsche's remarks on habit in *The Gay Science* §295 (referenced above) in order to evince the compatibility of habit and freedom, as conceived by both philosophers.

Margaret Watkins (chapter 4) closes Part I with a close look at the *Essays* of Montaigne, a figure who synthesizes ancient and medieval thinking on habit in a subtle ideal of personal integrity. Watkins picks up on Montaigne's suspicion of habit as an artificial and settled custom, a "second nature," before going on to adduce Montaigne's ambivalent reflections on the reliability of character. She argues that what Montaigne calls "custom" bears a complex relation to the late-medieval (Aristotelian) understanding of "habit," one that raises certain paradoxes of freedom and necessity. Montaigne does not settle with a paradox, however, but prescribes a paramodern form of self-stylization that strives for excellence by balancing the force of habit with the force of reflection freely undertaken. Liberation from custom as second nature, Watkins shows, is perhaps achievable via the self-cultivation of a virtuous character or, alternatively, via an engagement with Montaigne's *Essays* themselves.

Part II considers some of the many ways that habit is taken up in modernity, sometimes for intellectual and sometimes for practical purposes. Toward the end of the modern period the concept of habit is systematically and famously mobilized by the American pragmatists, who find habits at work in every domain of existence. This is not surprising given that their predecessors had already articulated the place of habit in methodology (Descartes), epistemology and moral philosophy (Hume, Adam Smith), educational theory (Locke, Rousseau), as well as metaphysics (Maine de Biran, Ravaisson, and Bergson). Dennis Des Chene (chapter 5) examines the consequences of the replacement of the late-medieval notion of *habitus* with that of "trace" in the early modern period. Specifically, Des Chene is keen to demonstrate that, for Cartesian psychology, in partial contrast to Suárez's, habits are material traces of physical encounters mechanistically lodged in the brain. This is an idea that is taken up centuries later in James's *The Principles of Psychology*, as well as one that continues to influence the neuroscientific theory of habit today. The story of how habits are accumulated in the mind, however, is not straightforward and, suggests Des Chene, contemporary philosophy of mind would do well to heed the account of habit given by Suárez and Descartes after him.

It is Hume who more often than not springs to mind when the word habit is uttered in philosophical circles. The centrality of habit, custom, and history in what might be called Hume's "critical philosophy" is adduced in Peter Fosl's essay (chapter 6). Fosl conceives Hume as a critical philosopher not only in the Kantian sense—as someone concerned with drawing the limits of reason and the conditions of thought and action—but also in the sense of "critical" as it is employed in contemporary aesthetic, textual, and social criticism. In addition to prompting a comparison with Montaigne's account of custom, and drawing important contrasts with Kierkegaard, Wittgenstein, and others, Fosl engages the secondary literature on Hume to argue that the Scotsman is not best understood by an analogy with the conservative politics of Edmund Burke; instead, Hume should be seen as a political progressive whose position is best articulated through more recent figures like Deleuze, Gadamer, and Mouffe.

In chapter 7 Clare Carlisle gives thorough treatment to Ravaisson's account of habit as it is found in his 1838 essay *Of Habit*. Looking at habit primarily as it pertains to moral practice, she contrasts Ravaisson's view of habit with the Aristotelian and Kantian views. Kant remains hostile to habit in his moral philosophy, but only, argues Carlisle, because he maintains a dualistic perspective on mind and body, freedom and necessity, a perspective that is overcome in Ravaisson's philosophy of habit. In this way Ravaisson anticipates the turn to habit made in the twentieth century by phenomenologists like Merleau-Ponty and Paul Ricoeur. In addition to cataloguing his debt to Maine de Biran, Carlisle offers an overview of Ravaisson's unique interpretation of habit and what it can teach us about traditional Aristotelian theories of virtue.

David Leary (chapter 8) explores with the eyes of an historian the intellectual path William James traveled as he sought to negotiate a passage between the deterministic understanding of behavior he favored in physiology and the nascent field of psychology, and the voluntarism commanded by his moral sensibility. James's motivation is a familiar one shared by Aristotle, Aquinas, Montaigne, and many others who have sought to reconcile freedom and determinism. Using habit to enact such a compromise may not be an idea original to James. Nevertheless, it is habit, argues Leary, that allows James to mediate between his naturalistic and moral sympathies, first toward psychological, then toward metaphysical, ends. While he echoes some of the same worries about behavior that troubled his predecessors, James is a pivotal figure in the history of habit insofar as he anticipates the intense focus on the brain (neural plasticity in particular) that habit research exhibits today.

Edward Casey's classic essay (chapter 9) builds a bridge between the modern and contemporary periods by juxtaposing Bergson's subtle analysis of memory with the phenomenology of habit adduced by Merleau-Ponty. Casey's essay challenges many of our usual ideas about the function and place of memory, while also presenting a theory that squarely contrasts with Cartesian/dualistic theories of habit, memory, and action. For Bergson, Casey shows, memory does not reside *either* in the mind *or* in the matter of the body. By the same token, and following Bergson, Merleau-Ponty argues that habit need not be located either in the mind or in the body. Habits are embodied and enacted somewhere *between* body and world. This way of thinking, which is present in the work of pragmatists like Dewey as well, shifts the locus of habit and forces us to rethink habit formation, the ontology of memory, and the dynamics of freedom and necessity.

The chapters of Part III present some of the ways that habit has been applied to the analysis of contemporary society, culture, and thought. They each share a common focus on the materiality, or embodied nature, of our habits and their influence on the relationships we forge. They likewise exhibit the versatility and continuing fertility of the concept of habit for thinking about problems in contemporary social theory. Terrance MacMullan and Shannon Sullivan both work in the tradition of American pragmatism and have recently penned important books that use the concept of habit to interrogate whiteness, racial privilege, and the societal norms that allow racism to function today. MacMullan's offering here (chapter 10) continues this line of thinking by drawing upon resources in the pragmatist tradition to argue that we can alleviate social problems like racism by attending to the habits that unconsciously perpetuate racist attitudes and actions. He first provides a helpful historical review of habit in the work of key pragmatists like Peirce, James, and especially, Dewey. Dewey is critical, according to MacMullan, because he uses habit to both dissolve classical dualisms (mind/world, freedom/determinism) and analyze the persistent social problems that plague democratic communities. He acknowledges that the pragmatists often evade questions about the metaphysics and epistemology of habit, favoring as they do the question of use value. He then makes a case for the continuing meliorist potential of habit—as it is conceived by twentieth-century figures like Jane Addams, W. E. B. DuBois, and Shannon Sullivan—for addressing social issues, including sexism, racism, and homophobia. Partly though a critical engagement with Sullivan's work, MacMullan makes the case that careful attention to habit is indispensable for reconstructing the discriminatory and oppressive habits that persist in the United States.

In her chapter (chapter 11) Sullivan takes up Dewey's transactional model of embodiment with a view to highlighting the neglected biological dimension of, especially, sexist and white racist habits. Instead of evading the ontological question Sullivan investigates the psychosomatic dimension that underlies the constellation of habits that comprise white-racist domination. In critical dialogue with fields as diverse as feminism and gastrointestinal science, she contests the idea that habits admit of only phenomenological or psychoanalytic analyses. On the contrary, these analyses are at their best when appropriated by pragmatism *and* attentive to the biological basis of habit, to which Dewey's naturalism is already attuned. Sullivan's view acts as a corrective (which is not to say replacement) for the apparent dualism that emerges when someone like Merleau-Ponty distinguishes between the lived body and objective (i.e., physiological) body in order to outline his own theory of habit. Dewey's philosophy of habit does not land us in biological reductionism, however, but offers a transactional conception of habit that draws upon the hard sciences and lends a hand to feminists and critical philosophers of race trying to build an ethics of social justice.

Jeffrey Bell (chapter 12) offers a reading of Gilles Deleuze that draws together thinkers in the analytic and continental traditions in order to reconceive what it means to have ideas, conceive things, and create concepts (the task of philosophy), as well as the role that habit plays in thinking. He brings to the fore the influence of Hume on Deleuze in order to show that, as with Hume, Deleuze sees both the association of ideas and the determination of identities as the result of habit or custom. This does not mean, however, that the mind is the origin of the identity of things or ideas. It means instead that ideas and things can only be understood by examining the metaphysics of thought and the "profound life" of things which generates the habits of thinking and action. Bell applies the concept of habit in such a way that includes human and nonhuman activities, and argues that habit, as refracted through the lens of Deleuze's metaphysics, is required to understand the determination of identities and the dynamics of a reality which harbors within it the capacity to break our habits, move us to create new concepts, and to "tear us apart."

*Habitus* is a concept that has become synonymous with the sociological theory of Pierre Bourdieu; it continues to exert influence in the social sciences. Bourdieu, like many of the figures examined in this volume, works to dismantle the Cartesian picture of agency by drawing our attention to the role of habitual social practices in the constitution of subjectivity. Nick Crossley, a sociologist himself, closes our volume (chapter 13) by demonstrating the significance of Bourdieu's rehabilitation of the classical *habitus* by contrasting it, on the one hand, with its cognates in Weber, Mauss, and Lévi-Strauss;

and on the other, by pinpointing its relationship to philosophers like Aristotle, Heidegger, Merleau-Ponty, and Wittgenstein. In a broad exposition of Bourdieu's *habitus*, analogous to Lockwood's opening essay on Aristotle, Crossley evinces the way in which the philosophy of habit has fertilized research in the social sciences and, conversely, how this research feeds back into contemporary philosophy. He offers a clear and concise introduction to the set of concepts surrounding Bourdieu's *habitus*, as well as a critical appraisal of Bourdieu's contribution to our understanding of agency.

## 3. THE FUTURE OF HABIT

As we see it the mission of this volume is to chart some of the key moments in the Western philosophical history of habit, and to offer the intrepid reader something of a conceptual cartography of the way habit is utilized to explain everything from routine behavior and morality to the construction of reality itself. We would be remiss, however, if we did not at least offer some indication of where research into the concept of habit is currently heading. While a full exploration of habit's future would require another volume (if not several), a couple of noteworthy directions ought to be mentioned. These trends are not strictly speaking philosophical, although the way in which habit fits into them will soon require a great deal of philosophical inquiry and clarification. We think they show that philosophical investigation into the concept of habit—like so many burgeoning fields of research—is ongoing and will ultimately call for a thoroughly interdisciplinary inquiry into its meaning and use.

First, we should call attention to the quickly developing and very promising notion within neuroscience of "neuroplasticity." This term is everywhere, even in television commercials. The philosophical use of the concept of plasticity, which is probably most associated today with the French philosopher and student of Jacques Derrida, Catherine Malabou, can be traced back to the Anglo-American nineteenth century. It is there in Darwin, Peirce, and James.[10] It is taken up and carried into the early twentieth century by Dewey. The idea that after a certain age (typically corresponding to the physical maturation of the individual) brains achieve a static form was once a kind of orthodoxy among psychologists, philosophers, and brain scientists. However, research over the last several decades seems to indicate the opposite. The brains of adults, no less than those of children, are constantly on the move, responding to the repetitive or habitual behavior of persons and literally restructuring themselves accordingly. That is to say, the neural structures of fully mature brains rearrange themselves in response to repeated actions. Or, as Nicholas Carr puts it: "As the same experience is repeated, the synaptic links between the neurons grow stronger and more plentiful through both physiological changes, such as the release of higher concentrations of neurotransmitters, and anatomical ones, such as the generation of new neurons."[11] The behaviors we engage in on a routine basis then create or reinforce certain neural structures within our brains. At the same time behaviors we engage in rarely or sporadically leave few neural traces. In a manner of speaking, then, the neural structure of our brain may be viewed as a collection of fossilized habits, as the crystallized physical remainder of the seemingly unconscious[12] behaviors that sustain a large part of our day-to-day lives.

While such a theory is interesting on a number of different levels, it ought to be noted that it also implies that habit is never simply a "mental" activity: every habit has a corresponding physical deposit within the structure of the brain. Even the activity of sustained and solitary engagement with a text—the very habit that the success of this volume is predicated upon—is not a fundamental feature of the human brain, but is just another historically contingent practice that requires constant reinforcement. Like all texts ours is built upon a habit that has roots in the history of Western literary development as well as the neural infrastructure of the brain. Without the various social habits that make solitary reading possible (with the introduction of new information technologies, political toleration of free thought and expression, and the economics of book publication) and the continued reinforcement of such habits in the neural structure of individuals (such as the accepted research methods of contemporary higher education), the habit of reading as we understand it could be very different.

Second, and in conjunction with the concept of neuroplasticity, the ways in which contemporary information systems present themselves raise several interesting philosophical questions, not the least of which concerns how they shape the behaviors of their users. This is especially apparent if we take into account how the Internet—including the so-called Web 2.0—has fundamentally changed both our habits of thought and communication. As Carr ominously notes, the very practice of solitary reading discussed above is threatened by the habits acquired by habitual Internet use, which offers constant distractions and interruptions (in the form of hyperlinks, pop-ups, tabbed browsing, and so on, and the constant blending of different media) that make sustained engagement with longer texts a much more difficult activity. If the Internet in its current form continues to be the dominant venue for the distribution of information, then the habits it engenders in its users—one of which Carr helpfully calls "skimming"—will fundamentally shape the future of human habits.

As philosopher and futurist Jaron Lanier notes, the very way in which the Internet is currently structured is due to certain early design choices that have been reinforced by repeated use. That is to say, the way that browsers navigate the Internet, how websites choose to present information, and how software applications display and store information is on account of habit. To

Lanier this is nowhere more apparent than in the way that the notion of a "file"—in which different bits of information are organized and stored—has become an apparently indispensable facet of Internet use. However, as Lanier points out, this was not always the case: one of the earliest designs of the Internet by Ted Nelson (his *Xanadu*) organized all information into one, global source. Nelson's design, however, lost out and the *habit* of thinking that information can only be stored in discrete bits won out. This is a great illustration of the way that habits truly become second nature for us. As Lanier well notes, "The idea of the file has become so big that we are unable to conceive of a frame large enough to fit around it in order to assess it empirically."[13]

In short, if the notion of neuroplasticity presents us with the idea that habit takes a physical form (and needs constant reinforcement to be structurally maintained), then the design habits of information systems present us with the prospect of fully digitalized habits. Indeed, it is difficult to keep these notions apart; the neural structures of fossilized habit within our brains can be changed by the digital habits of information systems. And, of course, the opposite is also possible: the habit (displayed by certain early designers of the Internet) of conceiving of information as something best organized into highly individuated bins or files has become a digital habit of the Internet itself. Now, every time we open or close or save a file we are all habituated into thinking of information in this way.

There is much more to be said about all of this, and certainly far more that we can say about where habit research is headed. We have certainly left much unsaid about the role that habit will continue to play in our understanding of the myriad concepts dealt with and not dealt with in the present volume. Nevertheless, our hope is to impart to the reader a sense of just how indispensable the concept of habit has been, and will continue to be, in the history of Western culture. The future of a volume on habit—which no doubt depends on the habit of solitary, prolonged reading, open democratic communities, and the renewed promise of free discourse—is itself wrapped up in the future of the concept of habit itself.

Even though we have singled out two specific directions for the future of thinking about habit (brain science, information systems/digital media), we do not want to leave the impression that these are the most promising or even the most important lines of research, even if they are the most obvious at this historical moment. Our collection will have built a case *against* the idea that the brain is the exclusive locus of habit or that human behavior is merely the result of an individual's placement within an information system—claims like this are reductionist in the sense that they restrict the scope of habit to one domain, namely, the human body in its physicality. In this way many contemporary approaches to habit and habituation are less advanced than they are narrow in view. This is not to say that the progress of neuroscience, for instance, has not and will not continue to yield valuable new insight into the nature and function of habit in the human body. (Indeed, it will.) It is to say instead that habit is never simply an aspect of what people do or what occurs in their bodies, and it is much more than a name for what happens when humans mimic machines.

## NOTES

1. William James, *The Principles of Psychology*, vol. 1 (New York: Dover, 1918), 104.
2. Samuel Beckett, *Waiting for Godot* (New York: Grove Press, 1994), 105.
3. Laura Mulvey, "Afterthoughts on 'Visual Pleasure and Narrative Cinema' Inspired by *Duel in the Sun*," in *Visual and Other Pleasures* (Bloomington: Indiana University Press, 1989), 33.
4. See, for example, the recent book by Charles Duhigg, *The Power of Habit: Why We Do What We Do in Life and Business* (New York: Random House, 2012), which continues this tradition.
5. Félix Ravaisson, *Of Habit*, trans. Clare Carlisle and Mark Sinclair (London: Continuum, 2008), 37, *passim*. See also the editor's Introduction for a useful overview of the philosophy of habit.
6. See, for instance, the second chapter of Markus Gabriel and Slavoj Žižek, *Mythology, Madness, and Laughter: Subjectivity in German Idealism* (London: Continuum, 2009). See Clare Carlisle's contribution below (chapter 7) on Schelling and Ravaisson.
7. Friedrich Nietzsche, *The Gay Science*, trans. Walter Kaufmann (New York: Vintage, 1974), Book IV, §295.
8. See, however, the work of Mark Sinclair (Manchester Metropolitan University), who is engaged in important research on both Heidegger and habit, as well as the so-called pragmatic reading of Heidegger contained in Mark Okrent, *Heidegger's Pragmatism* (Ithaca, NY: Cornell University Press, 1991).
9. Michel Foucault, *Discipline and Punish*, trans. Alan Sheridan (New York: Vintage, 1977), 135.
10. For plasticity in Darwin, Peirce, and James see chapters 8 and 10 in the present volume, along with John Dewey, *Human Nature and Conduct*, ed. Jo Ann Boydston (Carbondale: Southern Illinois University Press, 1988), Part 2.
11. Nicholas Carr, *The Shallows* (New York: W. W. Norton, 2011), 27.
12. "Unconscious" should not be taken as entailing an allegiance to the Freudian model of mind. Instead, we just mean something like "explicitly unrecognized" or unreflected in consciousness.
13. Jaron Lanier, *You Are Not a Gadget* (New York: Vintage Books, 2010), 13.

## BIBLIOGRAPHY

Beckett, Samuel. *Waiting for Godot*. New York: Grove Press, 1994.
Carr, Nicholas. *The Shallows*. New York: W. W. Norton, 2011.
Dewey, John. *Human Nature and Conduct*. Carbondale: Southern Illinois University Press, 1988.
Duhigg, Charles. *The Power of Habit: Why We Do What We Do in Life and Business*. New York: Random House, 2012.
Foucault, Michel. *Discipline and Punish*. Translated by Alan Sheridan. New York: Vintage, 1977.
Gabriel, Markus and Slavoj Žižek. *Mythology, Madness, and Laughter: Subjectivity in German Idealism*. London: Continuum, 2009.
James, William. *The Principles of Psychology*. Vol. 1. Mineola, NY: Dover, 1918.

Lanier, Jaron. *You Are Not a Gadget*. New York: Vintage Books, 2010.
Mulvey, Laura. "Afterthoughts on 'Visual Pleasure and Narrative Cinema' Inspired by *Duel in the Sun*." In *Visual and Other Pleasures*. Bloomington: Indiana University Press, 1989.
Nietzsche, Friedrich. *The Gay Science*. Translated by Walter Kaufmann. New York: Vintage, 1974.
Okrent, Mark. *Heidegger's Pragmatism*. Ithaca, NY: Cornell University Press.
Ravaisson, Félix. *Of Habit*. Translated by Clare Carlisle and Mark Sinclair. London: Continuum, 2008.

# I

# Classical Accounts of Moral Habituation

## *Chapter One*

# Habituation, Habit, and Character in Aristotle's *Nicomachean Ethics*

Thornton C. Lockwood

The opening words of the second book of Aristotle's *Nicomachean Ethics* are as familiar as any in his corpus:

> Excellence of character results from habituation [*ethos*]—which is in fact the source of the name it has acquired [*êthikê*], the word for "character-trait" [*êthos*] being a slight variation of that for "habituation" [*ethos*]. This makes it quite clear that none of the excellences of character [*êthikê aretê*] comes about in us by nature; for no natural way of being is changed through habituation [*ethizetai*].[1]

Equally familiar, unfortunately, is the depiction of Aristotle's notion of character formation as a form of habituation or repetition of actions which results in a "habit." As a nineteenth-century commentator remarked on the passage above, "a mechanical theory is here given both of the intellect and the moral character."[2] From a Socratic perspective, such a view of becoming good seems hopelessly rigid and unconnected to the intellectual development which knowledge of the good requires.[3] Habit and habituation in Aristotle seem eminently familiar and eminently non-philosophical.

Such a view would be mistaken on at least three counts. First, the notion of character formation (to use the broadest possible term for the phenomenon of habituation) in Aristotle is significantly more complicated than the notion that through habituation one develops good habits which are what we mean by ethical virtue. Although character formation includes the development of proper emotional responses, such as taking pleasure in what is fine and being repulsed by what is shameful, it is equally concerned with cognitive development independent of the intellectual virtues. Second, although Aristotle's terms for "ethics" (*êthica*), character-trait (*êthos*), and habituation (*ethos*, *ethismos*, or *ethizetai*) are linguistically and conceptually interrelated, his notion of "ethical state" (*hexis*) is both linguistically and conceptually quite distinct from the notion of "habit," at least as we use that term today. As one Aristotle translator has put it, "A *hexis* is not only not the same thing as a habit, but is almost exactly its opposite."[4] For Aristotle, a *hexis* is a dynamic equilibrium which, although always productive of virtuous actions, is nonetheless the basis for being virtuous in varied circumstances. Third, once Aristotle's notion of a character state is retrieved from its false association with "habit" and repetitive habituation, one sees both that its apparent divorce from practical reason is more a fixture of Aristotle's analytical method and that its connotations of inflexibility or fixedness are in fact antithetical to Aristotle's description of ethical virtue. Rather than view ethical "character" in its Greek etymological sense as an indelibly fixed or engraved mark or stamp (*charactêr*) upon one's soul,[5] Aristotle's notion of ethical character (*êthos*) or virtue (*aretê*) captures the notion of a virtuoso who is responsive in an excellent fashion to what reason perceives in particular and changing circumstances.

To support these claims, in my chapter I elucidate three core notions—the nature of character development, an ethical state, and ethical virtue or character—primarily following the expository order of the second book of Aristotle's *Nicomachean Ethics*[6] (in which chapters II.1–4 examine the origins of ethical virtue, chapter II.5, the notion of an ethical state, and II.6–9, the general and specific nature of ethical virtue).[7] But before exploring the notions of "habituation," "habit," and ethical virtue textually, it is necessary to say a word about the use of Greek terms in my chapter. For clarity's sake, going forward in my text I transliterate the terms *êthos* (and its cognate adjective *êthikê*), *ethos* (and its cognate noun and verbal forms *ethismos*/*ethizetai*) and *hexis*. Admittedly, transliteration merely postpones conceptual clarification—which is what the three sections of my chapter aim at. But thinking through Aristotle's notion of character development in terms foreign to his thought seems destined to confuse. The most striking difficulty is that contemporary English uses the term "habit" in two distinct senses whereas Aristotle's Greek makes use of two different and etymologically unrelated terms for both senses. In English, one may speak about a person's "habits" (e.g, "punctuality is a good habit") but also their means of acquisition (e.g, "I learned to swim by habitual practice"). Aristotle, by contrast, uses the term *hexis* (derived from the verb *echein*—to have or possess) for the first sense of habit in English, but he uses *ethos* (and cognates *ethizein* and *ethismos*, all ultimately derived from the verb *ethein*—to be wont or accustomed) for the second sense of habit. Aristotle points to an etymological connection between *êthos*/*êthica* (things of character) and *ethos* (habit or custom), but there is no etymological connection between either of those two terms and *hexis* (ethical state) like there is between the English terms habit and habituation.

## 1. *ETHOS* AND THE DEVELOPMENT OF CHARACTER

Character development for Aristotle transforms what scholars have characterized as our "first nature" (for example, our congenital endowments, immature beliefs, natural virtues or temperaments) into a "second nature," namely, our mature dispositions, beliefs, and full-blown virtues or vices.[8] Aristotle articulates the point well in a quote from the poet Evenus in his discussion of the possibility of character change. After noting that incontinence (*akrasia*) comes about both by nature (*phusis*) and through *ethos* and that *ethos* is easier to change than nature, he then blurs the distinction and claims this is why *ethos* itself is hard to change—because it resembles nature; as Evenus puts it, too:

> [*Ethos*] comes, my friend, by practice year on year—and see:
> At last this thing we practice our own nature is. (1152a30–33)[9]

The process Aristotle has in mind has several developmental stages, but he is also clear that it never ceases and statesmen should continue the character development of their citizens throughout adulthood (1180a1–5). To even commence mature ethical reflection—the sort occasioned by a reading of the *Nicomachean Ethics*—one must first develop an attraction toward what is fine and a repulsion from what is base "just as," Aristotle puts it, "one has to prepare soil if it is going to nourish the seed."[10] What is the nature of *ethos* such that it is able to prepare such a person?

Aristotle regularly presents *ethos* as a mode of human development in contrast to other forms of human development.[11] For instance, Aristotle considers how well-being (*eudaimonia*) comes about, and his candidates include learning, fortune, divine dispensation, and "*ethos* or some other form of training" (*askêton*) (1099b9–11); elsewhere, he considers how people become good, and his candidates include nature, *ethos*, and teaching (1179b20–21). Several character states, for example, bestiality or weakness of will, can come about either through *ethos* or nature (1148b27–31, 1152a27–33).[12] Perhaps most relevant to the understanding of *ethos* and ethical virtue is Aristotle's claim that although intellectual virtues come about through learning or teaching, virtues of character come about through *ethos* rather than through nature (1103a14–18).

The likening of *ethos* to *askêsis* (the source of our term "ascetic") captures the standard notion of "habituation" expressed by Aristotle's repeated claim that we develop ethical virtue through the repetition of virtuous actions (1103b14–22, 1103b31–32, 1114a7–13). Although *askêsis* has a decidedly martial sense—for instance, the famed *agôge* or military training of the Spartans is an instance of such *askêsis* (*Politics* II.9.1271b6; cf. VII.14.1333b39, VIII.6.1341a8)—it is also the term that Aristotle uses to describe gymnastic training and even, in one instance, child care (*Politics* IV.1.1288b13, VII.17.1336a21). As I will discuss below, a *hexis* (which is the genus of moral virtue) is precisely the state that arises from repeated activities (*energeiai*) and thus is something that cannot come about by nature but only through repetition (1103b21–22). Precisely because such proper training is the difference between virtue and vice, Aristotle praises Plato for insisting on habituation from youth onward and, in his own account of becoming good, he gives the family and the political community fundamental roles in the establishment of virtuous character traits (1104b12–14, 1103b23–25, 1179b30–80a6).

Although *ethos* clearly includes a notion of what we mean by "habituation," Aristotle also uses *ethos* to describe an aspect of character development which includes a cognitive component. As Hardie points out, Aristotle himself undermines the dichotomy between learning and habituation in that he describes the process of habituation as including verbal instruction, exhortation, and protreptic.[13] But further, when discussing the acquisition of ethical principles (*archai*), Aristotle notes that we "study" (*theôrein*) principles by means of induction, sensation, and the process of habituation (1098b3–5). Such "habituation" produces what Aristotle calls "the knowledge that" (*to hoti*) rather than "the knowledge why" (*to dioti*) and such knowledge consists of a broad array of learned or cultivated behaviors about what is noble and shameful, about what one should take pleasure in and what one should be repulsed by.[14] Although Aristotle juxtaposes habituation and teaching, the notion that the desiderative or appetitive elements of moral development are distinct from its cognitive elements is a view foreign to Aristotle's notion of rational and non-rational desire as is the Humean notion that reason and desire are distinct and independent of each other.[15]

Aristotle scholars often contrast two different models of ethical habituation.[16] The first model of ethical habituation consists in what Hursthouse has characterized as "horse training" (or even horse breaking), according to which habituation consists of the disciplining and breaking of an unruly natural wildness. For instance, in the *Politics* Aristotle discusses how to habituate children to withstand extremes of temperature; he writes that

> It is beneficial . . . to accustom (*sunethizein*) children to the cold right from the time they are small, since this is very useful both from the point of view of health and from that of military affairs. That is why many non-Greeks have the custom (*ethos*) of submerging newborn children in a cold river, whereas many others—for example, the Celts—dress them in light clothing. For whenever it is possible to create habits (*ethizein*), it is better to create them right from the start, but to do so gradually. (*Politics* VII.17.1336a12–20)[17]

Certainly there are times when Aristotle's model looks non-cognitive, especially insofar as the recipient is younger.

By contrast, Aristotle also presupposes as his model a form of concerted cultivation in which individuals develop specific likes and dislikes through the prescriptions and models which parents provide, including verbal descriptions, weighing of costs and benefits, and delayed gratification.[18] Hursthouse imagines the following example concerning training for temperance which is involved with the right attitude to the pleasure of food:

> Surely this starts at least far back as saying to toddlers "You don't want that nasty thing." Such a remark can hardly be construed as merely "descriptive," for the howls of frustration that follow the removal of the bit of cat food, or mud, or what have you show that literally the remark is plainly false; the child precisely does want that thing; it appears pleasant to her. But it does not profess to be purely descriptive; it is, accompanied by the act of removing the thing, normative and descriptive. The child is being taught not to want that sort of thing, and also being taught that the nasty and dirty is as such the undesirable and bad.[19]

As I will examine in the discussion of the nature of ethical virtue, on a very deep level habituation takes the form of persuasion and exhortation because the ethical part of the soul stands in relationship to reason like a child stands in relation to a parent. Ultimately, Aristotle's notion of *ethos* avoids both Socratic intellectualism that views becoming good as a kind of teaching or acquisition of knowledge and a shallow behaviorism that views humans as creatures of simply negative or positive conditioning.[20] *Ethos* incorporates both cognitive and emotional elements and ultimately develops a specific kind of psychic phenomenon, what Aristotle calls a *hexis*.

## 2. *HEXIS* AND PSYCHIC ETHICAL STATES

Aristotle illuminates the core notion of *hexis* (*hexeis* in the plural) in the *Ethics* with a minor pun. He defines *hexis* as "that according to which, with respect to emotions, 'we are having' (*echomen*) either well or badly" (1105b25–26). The pun plays on the fact that the word *hexis* derives from the intransitive use of the Greek verb "to have" (*echein*) and a *hexis* is a kind of "having" or possession, albeit one which predisposes one adverbially, as it were. *Hexeis* determine not only how we act, but even what we feel.[21] To determine whether one acts from virtue depends on "how an agent holds himself when he acts" (*ho prattôn pôs echôn prattê(i)* 1105a30–31). A *hexis* is simply the reification of such "holding" into a persistent psychic phenomenon. *Hexis* is Aristotle's generic term for an entrenched psychic condition or state which develops through experience rather than congenitally. *Hexeis* include not only the psychic state of ethical virtues and vices, but also those of the intellectual virtues and vices and continence and incontinence. Thus, not only is ethical virtue a *hexis proairetikê* or "a state disposed to choosing" (1106b36), but art or *technê* is a *hexis poiêtikê* ("a state disposed to producing" (1140a7–8)), and practical wisdom is a *hexis praktikê* ("a state disposed to acting" (1140b4–5)). Although Aristotle ultimately distinguishes the notion of an ethical *hexis* from other *hexeis*, throughout the second book of the *Ethics* he makes use of the parallels between ethical virtue and the arts—since as *hexeis* both have their origins in experience and practice—and the parallels between ethical virtue and medical states such as health—since as *hexeis* both determine how we are disposed toward actions.[22] What is a *hexis*?

Linguistically, the translation of *hexis* as "habit" arises from the etymological parallel between the Greek term *hexis*—which is derived from the Greek verb *echein*, "to have"—and the Latin term *habitus*—which is derived from the Latin verb for "to have," namely *habeo*. Although one often finds in nineteenth-century translations and commentaries the term *hexis* translated as habit, more contemporary translations favor the terms "state" (as in mental state) and disposition. Aristotle's doctrine of *hexis* is one of his most significant and novel doctrines and no English term—whether habit, state, or disposition—will adequately convey its sense of meaning.[23] But habit seems especially problematic insofar as in contemporary English it conveys the notion of a tendency to act in a certain way (e.g., the habit of punctuality). Although one who possesses the *hexis* of justice always acts justly, it does not follow that he always acts in the same way. As Socrates put it in the *Republic*, just because the general rule of justice requires returning what one has borrowed, it does not follow that a just person returns a borrowed weapon to a madman (*Republic* 331b–332a). Although *hexeis* are distinguished from other mental states by their enduring, permanent, or entrenched nature, their permanence is paradoxically dynamic or kinetic rather than static.

Aristotle provides extensive discussion of the general notion of *hexis*, discussing it in the philosophical lexicon of the *Metaphysics* (V.20), the account of quality in the *Categories* (VIII), and the *Physics*; further, he regularly juxtaposes it with other psychic phenomena or faculties such as activities (*energeiai*), emotions (*pathê*), dispositions (*diatheseis*), and capacities (*dunameis*).[24] Several features stand out by means of juxtaposition:

**1)** *Hexeis* are individuated by spheres of activity: Although a *hexis*—either in the case of an ethical or intellectual *hexis*—is not identical with an activity, a specific *hexis* arises from the repetition of a specific kind of activity.[25] Both the *hexeis* of justice and *technê*, for example, arise from the way one acts within a certain sphere, for instance in the exchanges of goods or the navigation of a ship, and only the *hexeis* of justice/injustice or art/artlessness arise from such activities.[26] In the case of ethical *hexeis*, the sphere of activity includes both a domain of action and specific feelings. For instance, the *hexis* of courage concerns how we act in the face of death in battle and what feelings of fear or confidence one has toward such death (1115a33–35, 1115b18–21).

**2)** Individual *hexeis* give rise to specific pleasures: In the same way that ethical *hexeis* arise with respect to a sphere of activities, each sphere of activity gives rise to a specific kind of pleasure the right feeling of which derives from a virtuous ethical *hexis*; thus, the pleasures and pains which one feels are indicative of one's *hexeis*.[27] Pleasures supervene on *energeiai*, but *energeiai* are specific to *hexeis*.[28] Thus, different pleasures are connected to different *hexeis*, and habituation concerns the development of proper pleasures and pains in different domains of activities.

**3)** Ethical *hexeis* are unidirectional: Aristotle distinguishes ethical *hexeis* from what the *Metaphysics* calls "rational capacities" (*dunamis meta logou*): whereas the latter admit of opposites (for instance, possession of a *technê* like medicine allows one either to heal or diminish health), the former can only produce one kind of action (1129a11–17; cf. *Metaphysics* IX.2.1046b5–28).[29] Thus, only just actions stem from the virtue of justice and only unjust actions stem from the virtue of injustice.[30] Even in adversity, the virtuous individual will never do unvirtuous actions and always do the most fine actions (1100b34–1101a3).

**4)** Ethical *hexeis* ground moral responsibility: Since *hexeis* arise from activities, they differ from capacities (*dunameis*)—such as the ability to see or hear—which according to Aristotle exist by nature (1103a26–1103b2, 1106a6–14). Whereas no one is praised for something possessed congenitally, we are praised and blamed for characteristics the development for which we are responsible (1106a6–10, 1114a25–30). Ethical *hexeis* arise through the repetition of actions and according to Aristotle we are ultimately responsible for those actions. "Only an utterly senseless person can fail to know that *hexeis* concerning specific things arise from activities" (1114a9–10, 1114b21–25). Thus, we can be praised and blamed for our ethical *hexeis* because their development is ultimately up to us.[31]

**5)** Ethical *hexeis* ground the permanence of well-being: A *hexis* is more entrenched and permanent than either a disposition (such as a bad temper or a moment of elation) or a feeling (such as pity or anger).[32] For example, although liking (*philêsis*) is a positive feeling or disposition which one may have toward either animate or inanimate objects, friendship (*philia*)—as an enduring part of one's self—is a *hexis*, one which persists as long as one participates in the activities of friendship with a friend (1157b28–32, 1171b33–1172a8).[33] Aristotle rejects the claim that one's well-being is dependent upon fortune or chance because he defines happiness as activity of the soul in accord with virtue, and "of all of human functions, none are more firm (*bebaiotês*) than those activities in accord with virtue"; the virtues—as *hexeis*—are the basis of enduring and stable activities almost impervious to external impediments (1100b11–12).

All five marks together indicate why Aristotle claims that virtuous people are praised for their ethical *hexeis* (1103a8–10). The contrast which Aristotle makes between the amoral *dunamis* of cleverness (*deinotês*) and the praiseworthy *hexis* of practical wisdom illustrates how the various threads fit together. In his defense of the unity of the virtues in *EN* VI.12–13, Aristotle juxtaposes natural virtue with complete virtue and cleverness with practical wisdom. Both natural virtue and cleverness are proto-virtues (the former is a natural propensity to act in a way that appears virtuous and the latter is the capacity to conduct means/ends reasoning regardless of the end). But unlike complete virtue, natural virtue can be detrimental to its possessor (1144b9–14); unlike practical wisdom, cleverness as a rational *dunamis* can equally determine the best way to rob a bank and to protect against such robbers. Practical wisdom and complete ethical virtue mutually entail each other, and practical wisdom cannot exist without cleverness (1144a28–29), but to become practical wisdom the faculty of cleverness requires a sense of the fine. If the aim which cleverness seeks to promote is fine—something established by the presence of ethical virtue—then cleverness is transformed into the praiseworthy virtue of practical wisdom; if the aim which cleverness seeks to promote is base, then cleverness is simply unscrupulousness (1144a26–28). Habituation, by inculcating a love of what is fine through doing fine activities, transforms simultaneously both the amoral *dunamis* of cleverness into the intellectual *hexis* of practical reason and the natural virtue—for instance natural courage—into complete courage.[34] One can analytically separate the two forms of inculcation, but they are mutually dependent upon one another.

What Aristotle seems to have in mind in the contrast of cleverness and prudence is the paradoxical nature of the "wise villain." Although Aristotle stands within the Socratic tradition that sees knowledge as invincible and wrongdoing as a kind of ignorance (1147b9–19), his account of cleverness makes clear that ignorance is not the same thing as stupidity. The master assassin or master criminal personify cleverness—and thus personifies what is "*deinos*" or awe-some (in the sense of awe-inspiring) in the capacity of *deinotês*—in that they can find the means to accomplish through careful planning and execution the most evil of goals. Further, their cleverness is, as it were, value neutral like a rational capacity—it is precisely the same sort of faculty of ends/means reasoning which the virtuous person possesses, except that they choose to use it for bad rather than fine ends. Although the virtuous person possesses such ends/means cleverness, precisely because practical wisdom is a *hexis* can it not be used in a value-neutral fashion. The sense of fineness which the person of practical wisdom possesses can only come about through the process of moral habituation and the simply clever person is ignorant in the sense that he or she has no sense of what is fine.

Although the five marks I have identified distinguish *hexeis* from other states of soul, they do not explicitly address my claim that *hexis* ought best be understood as a dynamic rather than a static disposition of soul. A central text which has led readers to think of *hexis* as a static state is *Ethics* II.4, wherein Aristotle distinguishes ethical virtue from art (*technê*). As noted above, Aristotle claims that both intellectual and character virtues are *hexeis* and often Aristotle makes use of their similarities—especially with respect to their acquisition—to explain the nature of ethical virtue through analogies to the arts.[35] Although as *hexeis* both art and virtue arise through the practice of activities, Aristotle claims that whereas artistic or technical productions are judged on the basis of the object produced, ethically virtuous actions are judged on the basis of how one who does them "holds" himself (*ho prattôn pôs echôn pratté(i)*, 1105a30–31). More specifically, for an action to be judged as virtuous or done in accord with virtue, it must possess three characteristics: the agent doing the act does so (1) knowingly (*eidôs*), 2) choosing the act for its own sake, and (3) if he does so in a "firm and unchangeable" way (*bebaiôs kai ametakinêtôs echôn* (1105a30–33)).[36] Although all three criteria have generated considerable scholarly literature, I would like to focus upon the third claim and probe its relationship to the notion of ethical virtue as a *hexis*.[37]

Aristotle's third criterion generates a dilemma. On the one hand, the phrase "*bebaiôs kai ametakinêtôs*" conveys a sense of fixedness or permanence. The first adverb, *bebaiôs*, derives from the perfect tense of the Greek verb "to stand" (*bainô*), and means something like "steadfast" (for example, like a virtue friendship rather than an association based on convenience) or stable (like the law of non-contradiction or the foundational principles of demonstration).[38] The second adverb, *ametakinêtôs*, is rather rare in Aristotle's writings (it is used only once in the ethical corpus), and etymologically it is close to a transliteration of "unchangeable" or "immovable" (*akinêtôs*), but the insertion of the prefix "*meta*" gives the sense of "moved away from."[39] Given that Aristotle has described virtue as a *hexis* that results from a repetition of actions and that the virtuous person will always act in a virtuous way, the third criterion has been taken by some commentators to convey that acting from virtue implies an element of fixedness.[40]

On the other hand, throughout the *Ethics* Aristotle emphasizes that virtue provides what Broadie calls an "unconditional preparedness to act," namely, an ability to act in a way which is responsive to the particular circumstances involved in any particular action.[41] Although Aristotle's doctrine of the mean entails that the virtuous person hits the mean between excess and deficiency with respect to actions and feelings, specifying that mean is always context dependent. He notes that

> it is possible to feel fear and boldness and desire and anger and pity and in general pleasure and distress to a greater or lesser extent, and to go wrong in either direction; but to feel such things when one should about the things one should, and in relation to the people one should, and for the sake of things one should, and as one should, is the mean and the best, which belongs to virtue. (1106b16–23)[42]

A person responsive to so many circumstances does not act virtuously by mechanically reproducing the same action in different circumstances based on a fixed rule. The person who does the same thing in every case falls under the description of what Aristotle entitles (with opprobrium) "stubbornness" (*ischurognômonoi*), namely those unwilling to listen to persuasion and unwilling to change their beliefs or behavior, even standing fast against reason (1151b5–17).

By contrast, the *hexeis* of the virtuous person are characterized by their ability to move and change as circumstances dictate. Aristotle suggests a compelling analogy for such a person in his account of the virtue of *eutrapelia*, which is usually translated as "wittiness" but which literally means "turning readily from one direction to another."[43] The virtue of wittiness consists in the mean between the buffoon, who seeks to make a joke in every situation, and the boor, who finds nothing funny. It almost goes without saying that such a person is a master at finding something funny in every situation—much like an improvisational comedian—but as important is the person's tact or discretion (what Aristotle calls *epidexiotês*) in sensing when the joke he has arrived at is worth stating. Aristotle explains further:

> Those who are playful in a fitting way are called witty (*eutrapeloi*)—or supple-witted (*eutropoi*), as it were; for supple moves like these are thought to be ones that belong to character (*êthos*), and just as we judge bodies by their movements (*kinêseis*), so too do we judge people's characters (*êthê*). (1128a9–12)

Character is judged by the way one's *hexeis* allow one to move and respond to particular circumstances. Although *hexeis* are not fleeting or transitory like a mood or a feeling, their permanence does not imply an immovability or inflexibility. Although the *hexis* of justice only produces a just action, what that just action consists in will depend entirely on the circumstances of the action, and a *hexis* needs to be sufficiently supple to allow for that range of receptivity or preparedness.

## 3. *ÊTHOS* AND ETHICAL TRAITS

Having surveyed the senses in which Aristotle uses *ethos* and *hexis*—the two terms sometimes translated as "habit"—we are now in a position to consider their relationship to *êthos* and more generally the nature of *êthikê aretê*. Aristotle claims that *êthos* arises from *ethos*, and *êthikê aretê* is a *hexis proairetikê* (1103a17–18, 1106b36). These two claims mean that, first, repeated experience with different situations within a specific sphere of activity produces an enduring trait and, second, that such a trait makes one responsive to the variability of action and prepared to act virtuously across a broad range of particular circumstances.[44] To that extent, *êthos* is the sum of one's character traits and *hexis* is an enduring but flexible state or disposition of soul that predisposes its possessor to act and feel a certain way in specific contexts. What remains to be explained is first what it means to call this sort of virtue *êthikê* or "ethical," and second, how ethical virtue in general relates to the notion of the virtuous person. The first goal requires discussion of Aristotle's soul division but the second may help to explain why Aristotle's notion of "ethical virtue" is sometimes misleadingly depicted as a habit deriving from habituation.

Although the title of Aristotle's *Ethics* derives from the adjectival form of the word *êthos*, the adjective *êthikê* is used almost exclusively to modify the term *aretê* and usually in distinction to *dianoêtikê aretê*, or "intellectual virtue"; never in Aristotle's writings does he use the term as a plural substantive adjective corresponding to our word "ethics."[45] To that extent, the title of Aristotle's "Ethics" is too narrow: *ta êthikê* means literally "the things concerning ethical character traits" without leaving room for the intellectual character traits that come to the fore in the sixth book of the *Ethics* (and which are elevated as the highest forms of virtue in the last book of the *Ethics*). The ethical virtues are perfections of the "character-bearing" (to use Rowe's translation) part of the soul, namely that part which although strictly speaking is non-rational, is nonetheless capable of "listening" to reason or being receptive to the guidance which the intellectual virtue of *phronêsis* provides.[46] The "character-bearing" part of the soul is the source of human desires and motivations—both pleasures and aversions—and as we have seen, an ethical *hexis* is one which allows its possessor to feel or experience such pains and pleasures in a fashion consistent with the mean.

Focus upon Aristotle's account of the "character-bearing" part of the soul—which takes up the first half of the *Ethics*—can mistakenly influence how we understand the relationship between ethical virtue and the virtuous person—or the very notion of Aristotelian ethics in general. Although methodologically, Aristotle separates ethical virtue from intellectual virtue and examines them in two different parts of the *Nicomachean Ethics* (ethical virtue in books II–V and intellectual virtue in VI), both of those analyses operate in a kind of abstraction foreign to the nature of the virtuous person. As Broadie puts it, although Aristotle divides virtue into two kinds, "this division is misleading if it gives the impression that the two can occur apart—an impression unfortunately aggravated by the fact that Aristotle deals with them in separate parts of the *Ethics*."[47] Aristotle's doctrine of the unity of virtue claims that it is impossible to possess ethical virtue—at least in the fullest sense of the term—without also possessing the intellectual virtue of *phronêsis* (1144a29–31, 1144b13–17). Although there are approximations of full ethical and intellectual virtue which can exist in isolation of each other, namely natural virtue or cleverness (which we examined above), there is no such thing as a fully ethically virtuous person who in any way lacks the intellectual virtue of *phronêsis*.

Thus, when Aristotle examines the courageous person or the temperate person, analytically his focus is upon that aspect of the person's virtue which perfects the appetitive or "character-bearing" part of the soul. Most familiar are the claims that such courage is the result of a non-cognitive habituation process, like an army private being screeched at by a drill sergeant. But the notion that that person's courage could exist in the absence of intellectual virtue is simply false and the belief that such courage could be developed in isolation from intellectual engagement is seriously misleading. At the least, the truly courageous person possesses practical reason; but since courage perfects a non-rational part of the soul capable of responding to reason, the "character-bearing" part of the soul itself, independent of the rational part, must have a cognitive component. The notion that Aristotle's "ethical" teachings consist of a doctrine about the acquisition of ethical habits through ethical habituation is not even half of the story; omitting that those ethical "habits" themselves possess a cognitive receptivity to the rational part of the soul and imply the existence of the intellectual habit of *phronêsis* makes that half of the story a fable.

## NOTES

1. Rowe trans., slightly adapted (*Aristotle Nicomachean Ethics* [Oxford: Oxford University Press, 2002]). Aristotle's etymology most likely derives from Plato's *Laws*, VII: 792e. My analysis is based on Bywater's Greek text (*Aristotelis Ethica Nicomachea* [Oxford: Clarendon, 1894]). Although translations in this chapter are my own, they are informed by the translations of Rowe, Taylor, and Irwin.

2. Alexander Grant, *Aristotle's Ethics*, 4th ed. (London: Longmans, Green, 1885), vol. I, 482.

3. For instance, in the myth of Er in the *Republic*, Socrates claims that one who becomes good "through habit without philosophy" (*ethei aneu philosophias*) is destined to fail (*Rep.* X.618cd).

4. J. Sachs, "Three Little Words," *St. John's Review* 44 (1997): 2.

5. Aristotle uses the Greek term *charactêr* only in the sense of "impression" or "stamp" (e.g., *Pol* I.9.1257a40–41, *Gen Anim* V.2.781a28; cf. *Oec* II.1347a10, 1349b31), although his student Theophrastus composed a work entitled *Characters* which captures our sense of character as a certain way of life (for instance, the bore, the cheapskate, the cheater). By contrast, one finds in Epictetus's *Enchiridion* both the Greek term *charactêr* and its notion as a fixed and unchanging state exemplified by a stubborn and unyielding Socrates. See, for instance, *Encheiridion*, 33.

6. Although there are passages in the *Eudemian Ethics* which parallel the discussions of *ethos*, *hexis*, and *êthos*, scholars have argued that Aristotle presents significantly different notions of the desiderative part of the soul and the stages in ethical development in the *Eudemian* and *Nicomachean Ethics*. See further H. Lorenz, "Virtue of Character in Aristotle's *Nicomachean Ethics*," *Oxford Studies in Ancient Philosophy* 37 (2009): 193, and A. J. London, "Moral Knowledge and the Acquisition of Virtue in Aristotle's *Nicomachean* and *Eudemian Ethics*," *Review of Metaphysics* 54 (2001): 553–54.

7. As several commentators point out, Aristotle's procedure in the second book of the *Ethics* violates the Socratic claim made in the *Meno* (71ab) that one must know what something is (e.g., arrive at its definition) prior to determining its characteristics (e.g., how it is acquired). See, for instance, M. Pakuluk, *Aristotle's Nicomachean Ethics: An Introduction* (Cambridge: Cambridge University Press, 2005), 95. If so, it would hardly be the only Aristotelian quibble with the Socrates of the *Meno*; *Politics* I.13 (1260a24–26) rejects the Socratic claim from the *Meno* that virtue is the same for men, women, and slaves.

8. For the language of "first" and "second" nature, see M. Burnyeat, "Aristotle on Learning to Be Good," in *Essays on Aristotle's Ethics*, ed. A. Rorty (Berkeley: University of California Press, 1980), 74–75; I. Vasiliou, "The Role of Good Upbringing in Aristotle's *Ethics*." *Philosophy and Phenomenological Research* 56 (1996): 779–81; P. M. Morel, "L'habitude: une seconde nature?" in *Aristotle et la notion de nature*, ed. Morel (Pessac: Presses Universitaires de Bordeaux, 1997), 131–48; and R. Kraut, "Nature in Aristotle's *Ethics* and *Politics*," *Social Philosophy and Policy* 24 (2007): 207–9, 212–17. McDowell's influential "Two Sorts of Naturalism" is self-consciously influenced by Aristotle's discussion of character development and his account of "second nature" naturalism captures well the sense in which Aristotelian moral development is transformative. See especially J. McDowell, "Two Sorts of Naturalism," in *Mind, Value, and Reality* (Cambridge, MA: Harvard University Press, 1998), 169–73.

9. See further cf. *De Mem* 452a27–8, *MM* 1203b31–2, *Rhet* 1370a6–7, *Prob* 879b36–880a5, 949a28–9.

10. *EN* 1179b30–31, 1179b24–26. Aristotle repeats several times that the *Nicomachean Ethics* presupposes a specific audience or "auditor" (or listener). See further 1095a2–11, 1095b4–13.

11. *Ethos* is cognate with *ethismos* (usually indicating the process of *ethos*), the verbal adjective *ethiston*, and the verb *ethizein*. A survey of Aristotle's use of these four terms in the *Nicomachean Ethics* shows no differences in meaning, thus throughout this section I will refer to *ethos* including passages that make reference to other cognates of the term.

12. Although Aristotle acknowledges a form of "natural virtue"—certain congenital endowments which resemble virtue—such characteristics fail to consistently produce virtuous actions and can even be detrimental to their possessors (1144b3–9, 1117a4–5).

13. W. F. R. Hardie, *Aristotle's Ethical Theory*, 2nd ed. (Oxford: Clarendon Press, 1980), 99–100; see further *EN* 1103b12, 1180a1–10. Note that Aristotle also claims that the intellectual virtues of *nous*, *gnomê*, and *sunesis* come about by nature, although *sophia* and *phronêsis* do not (1143b6–9, 1142a13–21).

14. See further Burnyeat, "Aristotle on Learning to Be Good," 73. Curzer argues, contra Burnyeat, that more important than taking proper pleasure is developing pain at doing what is wrong (H. Curzer, *Aristotle and the Virtues* (Oxford: Oxford University Press, 2012), 340–41).

15. Aristotle recognizes both rational desire (which he calls *boulêsis* or "wish") and two kinds of non-rational desire (*thumos* or "spiritedness" and *epithumia* or "appetitive desire"). See *EE* 1223a26–27, 1225b24–26; *MM* 1187b37; *DA* 414b2, 421b5–6, 433a22–26; *de Motu* 700b19; *Rhet* 1369a1–4; *Pol* 1334b17–25; see further S. Broadie, *Ethics with Aristotle* (Oxford: Oxford University Press, 1991), 106–8, and G. Pearson, *Aristotle on Desire* (Cambridge: Cambridge University Press, 2012), 170–98. Although Aristotle analytically separates the rational and non-rational parts of the soul, that separation is an analytical contrivance. The fully ethical person is precisely the integration of the two parts into an interconnected whole. See, for instance, P. Gottlieb, *The Virtue of Aristotle's Ethics* (Cambridge: Cambridge University Press, 2009), 106–11. For Aristotle's rejection of a Humean divide between reason and desire, see R. Hursthouse, "Moral Habituation: A Review of Troels Engberg-Pedersen, *Aristotle's Theory of*

*Moral Insight*," *Oxford Studies in Ancient Philosophy* 6 (1988): 203, 206–210, and Broadie, *Ethics with Aristotle*, 70–72.

16. See, for instance, Hardie, *Aristotle's Ethical Theory*, 104; R. Hursthouse, "Moral Habituation," 210–12; I. Vasiliou, "The Role of Good Upbringing," 779.

17. For further discussion of this passage, see P. J. Bartok, "Aristotle on Habituation and the Development of Moral Virtue" (lecture delivered at St. John's College (Santa Fe), March 30, 2005, 11–12).

18. I take the term "concerted cultivation" from Annette Lareau's *Unequal Childhoods: Class, Race, and Family Life* (Berkeley: University of California Press, 2003). Although Lareau does not ascribe the term to Aristotle, she does develop it within the framework of Pierre Bourdieu's notion of *habitus*, a concept developed from Aristotle's notion of *hexis*. Curzer contests that Aristotle endorses such a model on the basis that "there is no textual evidence for [such a combination of instruction and habituation] and a fair amount of evidence against it" (Curzer, *Aristotle and the Virtues*, 339–40).

19. Hursthouse, "Moral Habituation," 213. Although a recent article has lamented that contemporary scholars neglect "the process through which an ethically undeveloped human becomes a virtuous person" (N. Bowditch, "Aristotle on Habituation: The Key to Unlocking the *Nicomachean Ethics*," *Ethical Perspectives* 15 (2008): n. 3, 339), there is extensive discussion of Aristotle's notions of ethical education (several of which Bowditch fails to identify in his bibliography). In addition to the previously cited articles by Burnyeat, Hursthouse, Bartok, and Vasiliou, see also N. Sherman, *The Fabric of Character: Aristotle's Theory of Virtue* (Oxford: Clarendon Press, 1989), chapter 5; G. Verbeke, *Moral Education in Aristotle* (Washington, DC: Catholic University of America Press, 1990); M. Homiak, "Politics as Soul Making: Aristotle on Becoming Good," *Philosophia* 20 (1990): 167–93; C. D. C. Reeve, "Aristotelian Education," in *Philosophers on Education*, ed. A. O. Rorty (London and New York: Routledge, 1998), 51–65; R. Kraut, "Aristotle on Method and Moral Education," in *Method in Ancient Philosophy*, ed. J. Gentzler (Oxford: Clarendon, 1998), 271–90; and H. Fossheim, "Nature and Habituation in Aristotle's Theory of Human Development," *Acta Humaniora*, no. 166, Oslo, 2003.

20. For the contrast between Aristotle's method and behavioralism, see further Bartok, "Aristotle on Habituation," 13–14.

21. See further L. A. Kosman, "Being Properly Affected: Virtues and Feelings in Aristotle's Ethics," in *Essays on Aristotle's Ethics*, ed. A. O. Rorty, 103–16 (Berkeley: University of California Press, 1980). For a description of the process by means of which *hexeis* produce *pathê* or emotions, see M. Oele, "Passive Dispositions: On the Relationship between *pathos* and *hexis* in Aristotle," *Ancient Philosophy* 32 (2012): 351–68.

22. For parallels between ethical *hexis* and the arts, see 1103a31–32, 1103b6–14, 1105a8–10, 1106b9–14; for parallels between ethical *hexis* and medical states, see 1104a14–18, 29–30, 1105b12–18. One can find precedents for both uses of *hexis* in Plato's work (see *Theaetetus* 153b, *Laws* 650b, *Republic* 591b) and in the Hippocratic corpus. Burnet (followed by Jaeger) goes so far as to claim that Aristotle's notion of *hexis* derives from medical writings. See J. Burnet, *Aristotle's Ethics* (London: Methuen, 1900), 133; W. W. Jaeger, "Aristotle's Use of Medicine as a Model of Method in his *Ethics*," *Journal of Hellenic Studies* 77 (1957): 58; and H. Bartos, "Aristotle and His Hippocratic Precursors on Health and Natural Teleology," *Rhizai* 7 (2010): 41–62.

23. Pakaluk claims that the term "state" does not capture the notion of *hexis*, because *hexis* implies a condition more stable than a "state" conveys, one which is present even when not in use, and which has a persistent orientation (*Aristotle's Nicomachean Ethics*, 107–108). Irwin, by contrast, claims that "disposition" does not capture the notion of *hexis* because it is too transitory and habit fails because a *hexis* is not merely a tendency to behave (*Aristotle's Nicomachean Ethics*, 349). Among modern translators, Taylor, Irwin, and Grant translate *hexis* as "state"; Rowe and Rackham translate it as "disposition"; Sachs translates it as "active condition"; and Stewart and Apostle translate it as "habit."

24. My discussion here follows—in an inevitably more concise fashion—D. S. Hutchinson's *The Virtues of Aristotle* (London and New York: Routledge and Kegan Paul, 1986), chapters 2, 4, and 6.

25. Aristotle's separation of *hexis* and *energeia* lies at the root of his criticism of his predecessors in the Academy, such as Xenocrates and Speusippus, who claimed that *eudaimonia* was a *hexis* or possession (1098b31–1099a3).

26. See 1098b31–1099a7, 1152b33–1153a1; 1103b21–25, 1103b29–31, 1114a9–10, 1115b20–21, 1121a35–1122b2; 1104a27–29, 1104b18–21. For a good discussion of the "spheres" of virtue, see M. Nussbaum, "Non-Relative Virtues: An Aristotelian Approach," *Midwest Studies in Philosophy* 13 (1988): 32–53.

27. See 1104b3–8, 1113a31–1113b2. As Hutchinson puts it, "virtues and vices are dispositions to find certain things pleasant and certain other things unpleasant. In other words, they are each a disposition to like some courses of conduct and dislike other courses of conduct. What this amounts to is that a trait of character is a taste in an area of conduct" (*The Virtues of Aristotle*, 78).

28. The *Nicomachean Ethics* presents two accounts of pleasure. The clearest articulations of the relationship between pleasure, *hexis*, and *energeia* from *EN* VII are 1153a13–16 and 1153b10–14; cf. X.4.1174b33–35.

29. There is debate about the extent to which Aristotle's account of the unidirectional nature of *hexis* maps on to the discussion of rational potentialities in the *Metaphysics*. See further Hardie, *Aristotle's Ethical Theory*, 101, and C. Freeland, "Moral Virtues and Human Powers," *Review of Metaphysics* 36 (1982): 3–22.

30. Commentators generally note that identifying virtue as an ethical *hexeis* responds to the classical Socratic dilemma of how to guarantee that the expertise of the virtuous person cannot—like a *technê*—be used to do something unvirtuous. See, for instance, *Rep.* 334bc.

31. Aristotle's claim that we are individually responsible for our character states has generated much scholarly debate. For a recent overview, see P. Destrée, "Aristotle on Responsibility for One's Character," in *Moral Psychology and Human Action in Aristotle*, eds. M. Pakaluk and G. Pearson (Oxford: Oxford University Press, 2011), 285–318.

32. See 1105b28–1106a2. Although *Categories* VIII clearly distinguishes *hexis* and *diathesis*, Aristotle will often use them synonymously in the *Ethics*. See, for instance, 1107b16, b30, 1108a24.

33. For similar reasons, Aristotle denies that shame (*aidôs*) is a virtue because it is a reaction to circumstances rather than the psychic state according to which those reactions take place (1128b10–14).

34. Aristotle's discussion of the interconnectedness of intellectual and ethical virtue in *EN* VI.12–13 has generated substantial scholarly discussion. See, for instance, R. Sorabji, "Aristotle on the Role of Intellect in Virtue," in *Essays on Aristotle's Ethics*, ed. A. Rorty (Berkeley: University of California Press, 1980), 201–20; P. Gottlieb, *The Virtues of Aristotle's Ethics*, chapter 5; and N. Bowditch, "Aristotle on Habituation."

35. For further discussion, see T. Angier, *Technê in Aristotle: Crafting the Moral Life* (New York: Continuum, 2011), chapter 5.

36. Aristotle's notion of "acting from virtue" has affinities with Kant's notion of "acting from duty" (*aus Pflicht*). See further R. Audi, "Acting from Virtue," *Mind* 104 (1995): 449–71.

37. For helpful discussion of the problems generated by the first two conditions, see Broadie, *Ethics with Aristotle*, 82–89, and Taylor, *Aristotle Nicomachean Ethics II–IV* (Oxford: Clarendon Press, 2006), 84–92.

38. The most common usage of *bebaiôs* in *EN* is found in Aristotle's description of permanent friendships (see, e.g., 1159b8, 1162a15; cf, *EE* 1236b19, 1238a11, 1239b15). For the claim that the law of non-contradiction is "the most stable" of principles, see *Meta* IV.7.1011b13; cf. *Meta* 1005b11, 1008a16–17.

39. Sachs suggests that the term means "in a condition from which one can't be moved all the way over into a different condition" ("Three Little Words," 4). In his translation of the *Ethics*, Sachs renders the phrase "being in a stable condition and not able to be moved all the way out of it"; in a note he writes, "The last eleven words of the sentence translate A's marvelous adverb *ametakinētōs*; *akinētōs* would mean in the manner of someone immovable or rigid, but the added prefix makes it convey the condition of those toys that can be knocked over but always come back upright on their own, a flexible stability or equilibrium" (Sachs, *Aristotle Nicomachean Ethics*, 26). Another instance of the term is found in *Physics* IV.4, where place is

said to be immovable with respect to something else—for instance, in the sense that one can say that with respect to a river's current, a boat is "immovable" (if it is not under power), but nonetheless the boat is still moving (212a15).

40. See, for instance, Burnet, *Ethics of Aristotle*, 87, and Grant, *Ethics of Aristotle*, vol. I, 486, 495. By contrast, Taylor takes the third criterion to mean that acting from virtue implies that one's character state cannot be lost (Taylor, *Nicomachean Ethics Books II–IV*, 93). At 1152a30, Aristotle claims that *ethos* is easier to alter (*metakinêsai*) than nature, which appears to support Taylor's claim that *ametakinêtôs* marks out that character change is what Aristotle rules out with his criterion. See further G. Lawrence, "Acquiring Character: Becoming Grown Up," in *Moral Psychology and Human Action*, eds. M. Pakaluk and G. Pearson (Oxford: Oxford University Press, 2011), 271.

41. Broadie, *Aristotle Nicomachean Ethics*, "Philosophical Introduction" (Oxford: Oxford University Press, 2002), 19. In *Ethics with Aristotle*, she expands on the concept as follows: "every such response at the same time carries the claim that under no manageable circumstances would one voluntarily act otherwise than as the one who in this particular case responds like this. The claim does not assume knowledge of how one would act in other circumstances, but it does assume that a response different from the present one would be different for a reason" (90).

42. Aristotle's claim that action is context dependent is repeated at 1104b25–26, 1109a24–30.

43. Taylor, *Nicomachean Ethics Books II–IV*, 234. For further discussion of the virtue of wit which shows that its domain is far more than simply telling jokes, see S. Collins, *Aristotle and the Rediscovery of Citizenship* (Cambridge: Cambridge University Press, 2006), 147–65.

44. The exception to this claim is Aristotle's account of "natural character" (*êthos*) which he attributes to different geographical or racial groups in *Politics* VII.7. See further M. Leunissen, "Aristotle on Natural Character and Its Implications for Moral Development," *Journal for the History of Philosophy* 50 (2012): 507–30.

45. See 1103a4–7, 1103a14–15, 1139a1; 1104b9, 1109a20, 1138b13–14, 1139a21, 1144b32, 1152b5, 1178a16–17. The only exception to the claim that Aristotle uses the adjective *êthikê* in opposition to intellectual virtue is the juxtaposition of *êthikê* and *nomikon* ("legal") friendship in *EN* VIII.13.

46. At 1144b14–15, Aristotle identifies the non-rational part of the soul which is capable of listening to reason as "ethical"; see also 1102b13–14, 1102b25–27, 1102b29–1103a1, 1138b35–1139a1, 1144b14–15. The extent to which the ethical part of the soul is rational (insofar as it is capable of being receptive to the rational part of the soul in the strict sense) has generated considerable recent scholarship. See further J. Cooper, "Reason, Moral Virtue, and Moral Value," in *Reason and Emotion* (Princeton: Princeton University Press, 1999), 253–80; G. Grönroos, "Listening to Reason in Aristotle's Moral Psychology," *Oxford Studies in Ancient Philosophy* 32 (2007): 251–72; and H. Lorenz, "Virtue of Character in Aristotle's *Nicomachean Ethics*," *Oxford Studies in Ancient Philosophy* 37 (2009): 177–212.

47. Broadie, *Aristotle Nicomachean Ethics*, "Philosophical Introduction," 17. Sorabji puts the point well: "Someone who reads in isolation *NE* 2.1 could be forgiven for concluding that Aristotle thinks habituation sufficient to make men virtuous. It is tempting to combine this with the further assumption that habituation is itself an unthinking process" (Sorabji, "Role of Intellect," 214).

## BIBLIOGRAPHY

Angier, T. *Technê in Aristotle: Crafting the Moral Life*. New York: Continuum, 2011.

Audi, R. "Acting from Virtue." *Mind* 104 (1995): 449–71.

Bartok, P. J. "Aristotle on Habituation and the Development of Moral Virtue." Lecture delivered at St. John's College (Santa Fe), March 30, 2005.

Bartos, H. "Aristotle and His Hippocratic Precursors on Health and Natural Teleology." *Rhizai* 7 (2010): 41–62.

Bowditch, N. "Aristotle on Habituation: The Key to Unlocking the *Nicomachean Ethics*." *Ethical Perspectives* 15 (2008): 309–42.

Broadie, S. *Ethics with Aristotle*. Oxford: Oxford University Press, 1991.

Broadie, S. and Christopher Rowe. *Aristotle Nicomachean Ethics: Translation, Introduction, and Commentary*. Oxford: Oxford University Press, 2002.

Burnet, J. *The Ethics of Aristotle*. London: Methuen, 1900.

Burnyeat, M. "Aristotle on Learning to Be Good." In *Essays on Aristotle's Ethics*, edited by A. O. Rorty, 69–92. Berkeley: University of California Press, 1980.

Collins, S. *Aristotle and the Rediscovery of Citizenship*. Cambridge: Cambridge University Press, 2006.

Cooper, J. M. "Some Remarks on Aristotle's Moral Psychology." In *Reason and Emotion*, edited by J. M. Cooper, 237–250. Princeton: Princeton University Press, 1999.

———. "Reason, Moral Virtue, and Moral Value." In *Reason and Emotion*, 253–80. Princeton: Princeton University Press, 1999.

Curzer, H. *Aristotle and the Virtues*. Oxford: Oxford University Press, 2012.

Destrée, P. "Aristotle on Responsibility for One's Character." In *Moral Psychology and Human Action in Aristotle*, edited by M. Pakaluk and G. Pearson, 285–318. Oxford: Oxford University Press, 2011.

Fossheim, H. "Nature and Habituation in Aristotle's Theory of Human Development." *Acta Humaniora*, no. 166 (2003).

Freeland, C. "Moral Virtues and Human Powers." *Review of Metaphysics* 36 (1982): 3–22.

Gottlieb, P. *The Virtue of Aristotle's Ethics*. New York: Cambridge University Press, 2009.

Grant, A. *The Ethics of Aristotle*. 4th ed. revised. London: Longmans, Green, 1885.

Grönroos, G. "Listening to Reason in Aristotle's Moral Psychology." *Oxford Studies in Ancient Philosophy* 32 (2007): 251–72.

Hardie. W. F. R. *Aristotle's Ethical Theory*. 2nd ed. Oxford: Clarendon Press, 1980.

Homiak, M. "Politics as Soul Making: Aristotle on Becoming Good." *Philosophia* 20 (1990): 167–93.

Hursthouse, R. "Moral Habituation: A Review of Troels Engberg-Pedersen, *Aristotle's Theory of Moral Insight*." *Oxford Studies in Ancient Philosophy* 6 (1988): 201–19.

Hutchinson, D. S. *The Virtues of Aristotle*. London: Routledge and Kegan Paul, 1986.

Irwin, T. H. *Nicomachean Ethics*. 2nd ed. Translation with introduction and notes. Indianapolis: Hackett, 1999.

Jaeger, W. W. "Aristotle's Use of Medicine as a Model of Method in His *Ethics*." *Journal of Hellenic Studies* 77 (1957): 54–61.

Kosman, L. A. "Being Properly Affected: Virtues and Feelings in Aristotle's Ethics." In *Essays on Aristotle's Ethics*, edited by A. O. Rorty, 103–16. Berkeley: University of California Press, 1980.

Kraut, R. "Aristotle on Method and Moral Education." In *Method in Ancient Philosophy*, edited by J. Gentzler, 271–290. Oxford: Clarendon, 1998.

———. "Nature in Aristotle's *Ethics* and *Politics*." *Social Philosophy and Policy* 24 (2007): 199–219.

Lareau. A. *Unequal Childhoods: Class, Race, and Family Life*. Berkeley: University of California Press, 2003.

Lawrence, G. "Acquiring Character: Becoming Grown Up." In *Moral Psychology and Human Action in Aristotle*, edited by M. Pakaluk and G. Pearson, 233–83. Oxford: Oxford University Press, 2011.

Leunissen, M. "Aristotle on Natural Character and Its Implications for Moral Development." *Journal of the History of Philosophy* 50 (2012): 507–30.

London, A. J. "Moral Knowledge and the Acquisition of Virtue in Aristotle's *Nicomachean* and *Eudemian Ethics*." *Review of Metaphysics* 54 (2001): 553–83.

Lorenz, H. "Virtue of Character in Aristotle's *Nicomachean Ethics*." *Oxford Studies in Ancient Philosophy* 37 (2009): 177–212.

McDowell, J. "Deliberation and Moral Development in Aristotle's *Ethics*." In *Aristotle, Kant, and the Stoics: Rethinking Duty and Happiness*, edited by S. Engstrom and J. Whiting, 19–35. Cambridge: Cambridge University Press, 1996.

McDowell, J. "Two Sorts of Naturalism." In *Mind, Value, and Reality*, 167–97. Cambridge, MA: Harvard University Press, 1998.

Morel, P. M. "L'habitude: une seconde nature?" In *Aristote et la notion de nature*, edited by P. M. Morel, 131–48. Pessac: Presses Universitaires de Bordeaux, 1997.

Nussbaum. M. C. "Non-Relative Virtues: An Aristotelian Approach." *Midwest Studies in Philosophy* 13 (1988): 32–53.

Oele, M. "Passive Dispositions: On the Relationship between *pathos* and *hexis* in Aristotle." *Ancient Philosophy* 32 (2012): 351–68.

Pakaluk, M. *Aristotle's Nicomachean Ethics: An Introduction*. Cambridge: Cambridge University Press, 2005.

Pearson, G. *Aristotle on Desire*. Cambridge: Cambridge University Press, 2012.

Reeve, C. D. C. "Aristotelian Education." In *Philosophers on Education*, edited by A. O. Rorty, 51–65. London and New York: Routledge, 1998.

Sachs, J. "Three Little Words." *St. John's Review* 44 (1997): 1–22.

———. *Aristotle Nicomachean Ethics*. Newburyport, MA: Focus Publishing, 2002.

Sherman, N. *The Fabric of Character: Aristotle's Theory of Virtue*. Oxford: Clarendon, 1989.

Sorabji, R. "Aristotle on the Role of Intellect in Virtue." In *Essays on Aristotle's Ethics*, edited by A. O. Rorty, 201–20. Berkeley: University of California Press, 1980.

Stewart, J. A. *Notes on the Nicomachean Ethics of Aristotle*. Oxford: Clarendon, 1882.

Taylor, C. C. W. *Aristotle Nicomachean Ethics Books II–IV*. Oxford: Clarendon, 2006.

Vasiliou, I. "The Role of Good Upbringing in Aristotle's *Ethics*." *Philosophy and Phenomenological Research* 56 (1996): 771–97.

Verbeke, G. *Moral Education in Aristotle*. Washington, DC: Catholic University of America Press, 1990.

Walker, A. D. M. "Virtue and Character." *Philosophy* 64 (1989): 349–62.

Walker, S. "The Natural Condition of the Soul and the Development of Virtue." *Dialogue* 29 (1987): 39–44.

*Chapter Two*

# The Roman Stoics on Habit

William O. Stephens

The ancient Stoics believed that the cultivation of proper habits is indispensable for making progress toward virtue. They maintained that the goal of life is to live in agreement with nature.[1] For human beings, they insisted, this entails living in agreement with reason. The perfection of reason they understood to be virtue. Consequently, according to Stoic theory, rehearsing rational judgments about what is good, what is bad, and what is neither good nor bad, and consistently applying these judgments in our daily circumstances to decide what to do and how to live, enables us to become virtuous and thereby live happily. But these rational judgments and the appropriate actions that flow from them require vigilant practice and discipline to maintain in the face of life's challenges, which non-Stoics mistakenly believe are debilitating hardships. Such so-called hardships are conceived by Stoics as opportunities to exercise one's virtue(s) by applying the proper judgments to each event that occurs and making the correct decisions in each situation of public and private life. Consequently, the virtues result from disciplining oneself *consistently* to make sound judgments about (a) the actions performed by accountable human agents, (b) the behaviors of children and nonhuman animals, (c) events uncaused by human beings, and (d) one's personal and professional roles and social relationships. This consistency is manifested in habitually acting in accord with those judgments. For virtually everyone, achieving this takes a lifetime of training, or longer. The Stoics called this rigorous, deliberate, and painstaking training *askēsis* in Greek and *meditatio*[2] in Latin. They compared it to the grueling program of exercises adopted by athletes preparing to compete in the Olympic Games, medical treatment of disease, and the boot camp drills and active duty service of soldiers. In this chapter I will outline the views on habit of three of the four[3] great Roman Imperial period Stoic philosophers, Seneca the Younger, Musonius Rufus, and Musonius's student Epictetus.

## 1. SENECA

The corpus of Lucius Annaeus Seneca,[4] more commonly known as Seneca the Younger, is by far both the most diverse in types of writings, and easily double that of the philosophical writings derived from the other Roman Stoics combined. In addition to some epigrams, nine tragedies are attributed to him, a satire on the apotheosis of the emperor Claudius, a kind of scientific treatise, *Natural Questions* (in seven books), nine shorter essays on assorted ethical topics, three essays each written to console a loved one who had suffered a loss, *On Mercy* (in three books), a work Seneca composed to advise his student the young emperor Nero, and seven books on how to give and receive benefactions, or what we could call "favors." Seneca also composed 124 letters of varying length, addressed to a friend named Lucilius, which conduct an interpersonal philosophical exchange centering on the moral improvement of both the addressee and the author.[5] While the philosophical remains of Musonius Rufus, the four surviving books of the *Discourses* and the *Handbook* of Epictetus, and the *Memoranda* of Marcus Aurelius Antoninus are in Greek, Seneca's extant prose and poetry is in Latin.[6]

The semantic field of the English word *habit* is not tidily circumscribed by one or two words in classical Latin. Instead, there are a cluster of Latin terms, each of which conveys shades of meaning that intersect, to a greater or lesser extent, with the concept examined in this volume. *Habitus* can mean a habit or state of mind, but Seneca rarely uses the term, and in only a few of these texts of his does it carry this sense. The verb *habitō* can mean to wear habitually, to live in, inhabit, to dwell (in a place), to be housed, to lodge, and to spend all one's time. In its intransitive form, the verb *suēscō* means to be accustomed. In its transitive form, *consuēscō* means to accustom, inure, habituate, while in its intransitive form it means to accustom oneself, to become accustomed. These verbs are related[7] to the noun *consuētūdō*, whose range of meanings includes habit, custom, convention, etiquette, (linguistic) usage, or a chronic condition or illness. Seneca uses this family of terms often. *Dispositiō* can have the sense of *habit*, but its use in Seneca is very rare and has the sense of *orderly arrangement*. The Latin noun *mōs*, *mōris* can mean custom, usage, fashion, established practice, rule, law, or ordinance in the singular. The meaning of the plural form of the word, *mōres*, is immediately recognizable to English speakers, and the Latin term means conduct, behavior, manners, morals, or character. Seneca generally uses the term in these senses, and not so much in the sense of *habits*. Last, Seneca deploys *soleō* (*solitus*) to mean variously to be accustomed to, to be in the habit of, to be used to, to be wont to, to be prone to, to be apt to, to be likely to, often, general, usual, characteristic.[8]

In what follows in this section of the chapter, I do not offer a canvas of all instances of these terms. Instead, I select those texts which display Seneca's remarks about habit that I find characteristic of his thought, insightful, and most philosophically interesting. I have grouped them in a sequence designed to provide a particular narrative that illustrates a sensible analysis and progression of ideas on habit, its relation to virtues and vices, and the work it does for wisdom's guidance in the good life. Alternative groupings of these texts, as well as the inclusion of additional ones, would each yield alternative philosophical analyses, which would be not only possible, but probably also legitimate. My route through these texts, however, proceeds as follows.

(§A) To begin, certain features of human beings are implanted in us by nature, are intransigent, and thus limit those of our behaviors that are subject to change through rehabituation. Dimensions of our physicality cannot be amended by the intervention of reason. (§B) Within these limits, however, habit has the power to alleviate what we initially experience as disasters, as some people adapt better than others to the constraints imposed by fortune. What fortune inflicts as necessity, habit can transform into contentment. (§C) Poverty, grief, and ambition are experienced differently by different people, because our minds are colored by the habits and beliefs we adopt. False beliefs spawn bad habits. True beliefs about that which is unconditionally good (virtue), that which is really bad (vice), and that which is neither (e.g., wealth, poverty, prestige, infamy, health, illness, prolongation of life, death) free us from jealousy, resentment, anxiety, fear, panic, anger, intemperance, and mental disorder. (§D) Consequently, we imperil ourselves by neglecting to banish false beliefs about what is good, what is bad, and what is neither good nor bad. Rehearsing false beliefs about such things ingrains the beliefs in our thinking, thereby corrupting our minds, and inculcating the mental disorders known as vices. (§E) Several types of bad habits and the vices they entrench are discussed. The evil habits and mental illnesses of some people are incorrigible. Those of others can be remedied. (§F) Physical illness, sleeplessness, love pangs, and liquor can provoke the passion of anger. We cannot overcome our physical frailties related to these conditions, but the right kind of stern upbringing and the formative power of good habits can ameliorate them to some degree. In contrast, the soul is weakened by coddling and softened by luxury, spoiling the temperament and inflaming irascibility. Imbibing immoderately causes irritability that can trigger wildness, which can boil up into insanity. Moderate use of alcohol is not an evil habit. Illness hampers performance of physically active tasks, but a well-habituated mind remains unhampered though the body is bed-ridden. (§G) Habit returns us to nature and natural pleasures. Attention to utility allows us to measure our true needs, but habitually indulging in unnecessary pleasures risks deforming them into what people (wrongly) feel are indispensable needs. This explains the birth of perverse gratifications like cruelty and criminality. Dear attachment to our family, home, and the like is benign and arises partly from old habit and long familiarity. (§H) Perseverant philosophizing provides the wisdom needed to distinguish good habits from bad, and to become good persons. (§I) We must learn how to live reasonably on only what we genuinely need, instead of succumbing to the pressure to conform to custom and live as our consumptive, unreflective neighbors do. Seneca's own intellectual habits include appropriating items of wisdom found in other authors. (§J) I conclude with his discussion of the human habit of dividing the self in order to engage in self-evaluation.

## A. Intransigent Nature and the Limits of Reform via Rehabituation

Seneca reports having had a conversation with one of Lucilius's friends and notes the man's ability, intelligence, and the self-improvement he had already made. Speaking without forethought, at one point the man was caught off guard and blushed out of modesty. Seneca tells Lucilius that this hue of modesty is a good sign in a young man, as the blush seemed to well up from deep inside. Seneca expresses his confidence that the man's propensity to blush will stick with him after he has fully strengthened his character, stripped off all his faults, and grown wise.

> For by no wisdom can natural weakness of the body be removed. That which is implanted and inborn can be toned down by training (*arte*), but not overcome. The steadiest speaker, when before the public, often (*solet*) sweats profusely, as if he had exhausted or over-heated himself. The knees of some shake when they rise to speak. I know of some whose teeth chatter, whose tongues falter, whose lips quiver. Training and experience can never shake off this habit; nature exerts her own power and through such a weakness makes her presence known even to the strongest. I know that the blush, too, is a habit of this sort, spreading suddenly over the faces of the most dignified men.[9]

Seneca adds that blushing is more prevalent in the young, due to their warmer blood and more sensitive faces, yet seasoned and elderly men blush as well. Seneca instances Sulla, Pompey, and Fabianus, who reddened when he appeared as a witness before the senate. Seneca finds this embarrassment entirely apt given the gravity of the setting, and thus quite becoming to Fabianus. This kind of habit is due not to mental weakness, but to the novelty of the situation. An inexperienced person is not necessarily confused by the novelty, but is nonetheless affected by it, because he slips into his habit of blushing as a natural tendency of his body. Seneca observes that certain people are full-blooded, and others have quick, mobile blood that swiftly rushes to the face.[10] He insists that

> wisdom can never remove this habit, for if she could rub out all our faults, she would be mistress of the universe. Whatever is assigned to us by the terms of our birth and the blend in our constitutions, will stick with us, no matter how hard or how long the soul may have tried to master itself. And we cannot forbid these feelings any more than we can summon them.[11]

Consequently, no amount of habituation can erase our indelible genetic makeup. What nature implants in us at birth and knits into the very fabric of our physicality is permanent. The mind can neither summon nor vanquish the blush response that inheres in our flesh. "It comes and goes unbidden as a law unto itself."[12]

Passions, on the other hand, are a different, more complex matter. Seneca explains that the passion of anger, as it begins, grows, and gets carried away, unfolds in three stages or movements. The first movement is an involuntary preparation for the passion, like a kind of threat. The second movement is voluntary, but is not insistent. The third stage is out of control and has completely overcome the power of reason.[13] He writes:

> The first movement is a mental jolt which we cannot escape through reason, just as we cannot escape those physical reactions which I mentioned—the urge to yawn when someone else yawns, or blinking when fingers are flicked at the eye. These cannot be overcome by reason, though habituation and constant attentiveness may perhaps lessen them. The other sort of movement, generated by decision, can be eliminated by decision.[14]

Seneca allows for the possibility that concerted attempts to train ourselves not to yawn when others do or not to blink when someone suddenly thrusts his fingers toward our eyes may lessen the first stage reaction in the birth of anger. But it is the second stage that is generated by decision. This is the decision to assent to the judgments that (a) I have suffered an undeserved injury by another, (b) *and for that reason* it is right for me to (or I should) retaliate. To reject judgment (b), even if we assent to (a), is to issue a new decision "I will not retaliate" which eliminates and replaces (a) + (b). Seneca believes that the power of reason enables us to train ourselves to decouple (b) from (a), and for more advanced Stoics, perhaps even reject (a) at the outset. Strategies for how to cultivate the habit of not conjoining (b) with (a), and how to rethink and discard (a) whenever (a) suggests itself to us, occupy much of *On Anger*. The violent horrors that all too often result from anger[15] make it abundantly obvious that anger is a plague on the human mind that must be totally eradicated. Fortunately, we can decide to commit ourselves to the sturdy, vigilant practices needed to achieve this eradication.

## B. Habit Has the Power to Alleviate Disasters

Habitually training oneself to arrest the second stage of the three stage cognitive mechanism that produces anger requires repeating the same decision over and over again daily, monthly, or perhaps for years. But Seneca believes that even habits which we had no part in choosing to live with can alleviate our suffering. Indeed, conditions imposed upon us against our will that are initially onerous can gradually become lighter thanks to the effects of habit.

> Bear in mind that it is only at first that prisoners are worried by the burdens and shackles upon their legs. Later, when they have resolved not to chafe against them, but to endure them, necessity teaches prisoners to bear their shackles bravely, habit to bear them easily. In any sort of life you will find that there are amusements and relaxations and pleasures if you are willing to consider your evils lightly rather than to make them hateful. On no score has Nature more deserved our thanks, who, since she knew to what sorrows we were born, invented habit as an alleviation (*mollimentum*) for disasters, and thus quickly accustoms us to the most serious ills. No one could endure adversity if, while it continued, it kept the same violence that its first blows had. All of us are chained to Fortune.[16]

Young men with rapid blood are chained to Fortune in that they have no control over their blush response. We are all chained to Fortune when an object hurtles toward our eyes and we cannot help but blink. Fortune chains us to our skin's pigmentation, our sex, a host of allergies, astigmatism, macular degeneration, deformities of the teeth, skeleton, vital organs, limbs, and face, all the peculiarities of our phenotypes, and all the frailties of our biology.[17] Seneca reflects that our daily routines deceive us into believing that we can always postpone hard work another week or longer and just relax. There always seems to be more time, so why rush? What is it which makes us so lazy and sluggish? None of us thinks that some day we must depart from this house of life. Just so, Seneca notes, tenants are kept from moving by fondness for a particular place and by habit, despite bad treatment by their landlord and neglect of the properties they rent. Tenants such as these, like the shackled prisoners, are stuck in a rut they can no longer feel. The more familiar the rut, the cozier it feels.

Seneca offers the insight that necessity, despite how unpleasant it feels at first, can, given enough time, gradually become pleasant. "There is no unhappiness for those whom habit has brought back to nature. For what they begin from necessity becomes gradually a pleasure."[18] Nature is relentless. Yet those who struggle and strain against Her, striving to escape the gravitational pull of Nature's norms, are relieved of their misery by simply letting go and returning home to Her. Those habits in accord with the best parts of our human nature deliver us to this happy reunion.

## C. Different Strokes for Different Folks: How False Beliefs Lead to Bad Habits

Some prisoners feel the weight of their chains more heavily than others, just as some tenants are more tightly moored to their old, familiar, shoddy apartments than others. Different people are attached more or less strongly to different kinds of things. Some have sensitivities and vulnerabilities that others either largely or entirely lack. Thus, Seneca remarks that "poverty, grief, and ambition are felt differently by different people as determined by how their minds are colored by the habits they happen to have, and a false presumption. This false presumption arouses in them a fear of things that are not to be feared and makes them weak and unresisting."[19] For example, Stoics deny that poverty is an evil. Stoics reject grief as a mental disorder that results from the false belief that a truly bad thing has occurred that robs one of a good life. Stoics also discredit ambition aimed at fame, glory, or accumulating riches, since these things are fleeting, the pomp of empty names, and ultimately worthless. Non-Stoics, in contrast, are weak in the face of popular opinion and cannot resist the false opinions that poverty is bad, grief over the death of a loved one is proper and "natural," and fame, status, glory, wealth, and health make a life good or even contribute to happy living.[20] These false opinions are the false presumptions Seneca has in mind.

Take wealth. Suppose you consider wealth to be a good. If so, Seneca explains, then poverty will distress you. This is because, though you may be rich, since your neighbor is richer, you will suppose that you are poor by the exact amount in which you have less wealth than him. Take social position. If you judge that an elite job position is a good, you will be troubled at someone else's appointment to an office higher than yours. You will be jealous when another receives the renown or material blessings you don't. Take death. You may rate death as the worst of evils, despite the fact that only the fear that precedes death's approach is evil. If so, Seneca argues, you will be terrified out of your mind, not only by real dangers, but also by merely imagined ones.[21]

> For peace itself will supply more fears. Even in the midst of safety you will have no confidence if your mind has been shocked once. Once it has acquired the habit of blind panic, it is incapable of providing even for its own safety. For it does not avoid danger, but flees. Yet we are more exposed to danger when we turn our backs.[22]

Consequently, the repetition of false beliefs about poverty and wealth, good repute and ill repute, high and low social rank, death and life, and generally what is bad and what is good, harms a person's mind. The habit of blind panic induced by the fear arising from not knowing any better cripples our ability to make ourselves safe. And we are endlessly exposed to the dangerously false beliefs of the ignoramuses, the non-Stoics, who vastly outnumber and surround us.

Given how false beliefs lead to bad habits, and how bad habits, namely, those contrary to nature, guarantee misery, Seneca advises his friend Lucilius to act, in all their plans and conduct, just as they are in the habit of acting whenever they approach a huckster who offers to sell them certain wares. Seneca cautions: let's see how much we have to pay for what we want. All too often the commodities that cost nothing (i.e., no money), cost us the most heavily, that is, in the only currency that purchases happiness, that is, a free, virtuous mind supplied with true beliefs. Seneca promises that he can show his friend many baubles the quest for which, and the acquisition of which, have ripped freedom from our hands.[23] *Caveat emptor* is a time-tested, prudent policy. Seneca shrewdly applies it to the beliefs we cart home from the marketplace of opinions. The peddler's false opinions about what is good, bad, and neither, are too pricey. Freedom and peace of mind are worth far too much to barter over.

## D. Bad Habits That Ossify Cannot Be Broken and Ruin the Soul

In *Letter* 112 Seneca enacts a conversation with Lucilius by anticipating his friend's responses. The topic at hand is Lucilius's eagerness for a friend of his to be shaped and trained by the methods of self-improvement Seneca rehearses throughout the *Letters*. Seneca doubts that this can be achieved. Lucilius's friend has degenerated into a very hardened state, or rather what is worse, a very soft state, due to having been broken down by bad and inveterate habits.[24] To illustrate how this can happen both to human beings and to other living things, Seneca describes from his own experience how the technique of grafting vines varies according to the age and strength of the vines involved.[25] By analogy, the man in question has no strength to draw upon in order to receive the graft of a healthy, new habit. The problem is that he has pampered his vices. He has simultaneously become flabby and ossified. He can neither receive reason nor nourish it. "But," Lucilius protests, "the man desires reason of his own free will." "Don't believe him," Seneca replies. The flab-hardened fellow doubtless really *believes* that he desires the reason required to purge his bad, unhealthy habits. But this belief will be short-lived because gorging on luxury has merely upset his stomach for the moment. He will soon become reconciled to luxury again, Seneca assures Lucilius.[26] "But he says that he is annoyed by his former way of living," Lucilius replies. Seneca grants that this is quite likely. "People love and hate their vices at the same time. It will be the proper season to pass judgment on him when he has guaranteed us that he really hates luxury. As it is now, luxury and he are merely not on speaking terms."[27] The sick pleasures that vicious conduct gives to those who develop a taste for them are strongly seductive. That is why people love their vices. But the damage vicious behavior inflicts on their souls is severe. Healing these injuries requires reform of character, and this takes effort and time. Some cannot muster what it takes to reverse the degeneration. They hate their vices, but have become addicted to them.

In contrast, there are also certain men possessed of unusual qualities who reach without prolonged tutoring that which is ordinarily gained only by means of extensive teaching. These gifted individuals welcome honorable things as soon as they meet them. Their superior minds seize quickly upon virtue, or else they manufacture it from within themselves. But Lucilius's dull, sluggish friend who is hobbled by his evil habits, Seneca explains, must have the rust on his soul incessantly scraped off. As the former sort of people, who are inclined toward the good, can be raised to the heights of virtue more quickly, so the weaker spirits will be assisted and could be freed from their wicked opinions if Seneca and Lucilius entrust to them the accepted principles of philosophy.[28] The philosophical principles of Stoicism can elevate both those with a natural talent for virtue and the slow learners wallowing in bad habits of mind. A Stoic has ideals to strive for. Seneca remarks that life without ideals is erratic, and as soon as an ideal is to be set up, doctrines become necessary. Adherence to these doctrines, habitual application of them to one's daily life, demands attention, commitment, and perseverance. Progress in approaching Stoic ideals also requires courage. Seneca writes to Lucilius: "I am sure you will admit that there is nothing more shameful than uncertain and wavering conduct, than the habit of frightened retreat."[29] This is why Seneca is so pessimistic about the moral improvement of Lucilius's sluggish pal. He complains about his vicious habits and thinks he wants to shed them one day, but then wavers and fearfully retreats from an effort to put those bad habits to rout. The crud that accretes to his soul nourished by his diet of disgusting habits must be scoured again and again, so the likelihood he can burnish his soul into a condition of gleaming virtue is nil.

Yet assistance in breaking a bad habit can come from someone else too. Seneca suggests that if one person can help another put a halt to a fault—can get him to check his piece of bad behavior for a time—and he gets into the habit of stopping it on his own, then it's possible to make the fault cease altogether.[30] Perhaps this is the help Lucilius had hoped to give his sluggish friend. Seneca thinks that the sluggish fellow's "habit of frightened retreat" back into his vices undercuts the man's desire for self-help. If a person doesn't genuinely want to dispel his fault, the prompting of a friend who wants to help will fail.

## E. Two Harmful Habits

Two specific bad habits mentioned by Seneca are noteworthy. One is the harmful tendency to hear nothing that we don't like.[31] This habit is dangerous because when it is pierced it invites the false judgment that someone has wronged us, which we will recall is the judgment complicit in the first stage of the origin of anger. If we habituate ourselves to be happy only when what we hear pleases us, we will crave the company of toadies. Toadies cannot promote our self-improvement. Instead, we must teach ourselves to handle the truth about everything, not least of all ourselves.

Credulity is another risky habit of mind. Seneca thinks credulity is a source of great mischief. "We should believe only what is thrust under our eyes and becomes unmistakable, and every time our suspicion proves to be groundless we should chide our credulity. For this self-reproof will develop the habit of being slow to believe."[32] Diligence in examining evidence for a belief before adopting it increases the chances that the belief is true.[33] I will return to the importance of self-reproof for Seneca in §J below. Insofar as credulity and hearing nothing we dislike make us prone to judge that we've been wronged by another, they are clearly perilous. For Seneca sees anger as "the most hideous and frenzied of all the passions."[34] Human beings in the grips of rage are insane.[35]

## F. Sickness, Sleeplessness, Love, Liquor, and Anger

While some people have an angry disposition by nature, Seneca believes that many circumstances can have the same effect as nature. Some grow angry due to disease or physical injury. Others are led to ire by exertion or prolonged sleep deprivation. Still others are inclined to get angry as a result of attacks of anxiety during the night, yearnings, or pangs of love. But Seneca regards all these circumstances as just the initial causes of anger. He writes that the most powerful factor in the genesis of wrath is habit. If habit is oppressive, it fosters the fault.[36] Seneca opines that the best way to keep people from developing an angry temperament is to give children a sound upbringing from the cradle.[37] What a child needs is to learn how to compete without losing his cool. In contests with others of his age, we should urge him to do his best neither to be defeated nor to grow angry. We should encourage him to become a close friend of his regular opponents, so as to give him the habit, in sporting contests, of wanting not to hurt those whom he respects, but to win fair and square.[38] Exposure to luxury, a soft, coddling education, and material prosperity make people ill-tempered.[39] Seneca advises against ever flattering children. They should be told the truth, respect everyone, and rise for their elders. Children must never be allowed to get their way through tantrums or tears.[40] But the more prosperous one gets, according to Seneca, the more subject to anger one gets. Ill-temper is especially prevalent in the affluent, the privileged, and those in high positions in society.[41] Seneca is deeply suspicious of the supreme regard most people have for acquiring showy furnishings and mansions, accumulating expensive toys, and the race to keep up with the latest fashions, as I will discuss below in §I.

Excessive consumption of alcohol warrants caution as well. Seneca believes that just as a lingering illness makes people whiny and irritable and drives them wild at the least crossing of their desires, so too frequent, continued bouts of drunkenness bestialize the mind. For when people are often beside themselves in a fit of pique, the habit of insanity endures. Consequently, Seneca thinks that the vices which liquor generated retain their power even when the alcohol is gone.[42] Yet he does not prescribe teetotalism.

> As in freedom, so in wine there is a wholesome moderation. It is believed that Solon and Arcesilaus were fond of wine, and Cato has been reproached for drunkenness. But whoever reproaches that man will more easily make reproach honorable than Cato base. Yet we ought not to do this often, for fear that the mind may contract an evil habit, nevertheless there are times when it must be drawn into rejoicing and freedom, and gloomy sobriety must be banished for a while.[43]

Thus, Seneca believes that wholesome moderation in consuming liquor saves it from degenerating into an evil habit. Both gloomy sobriety without respite on the one hand, and alcoholism on the other, must be avoided.

Comments about illness and sick people are scattered throughout Seneca's *Letters*.[44] He talks about his asthma[45] and on two occasions being ill.[46] But when Lucilius complains that an illness prevents him from performing any of his duties, Seneca replies that illness hampers one's body, but not one's soul. "If your soul be habitually in practice, you will plead and teach, listen and learn, investigate and meditate."[47] Consequently, Seneca assures his friend that he has the ability to condition his soul to overcome the illness of his body. Even when laid up in bed, a Stoic can converse with others and thereby teach and learn from them. When alone in his sickbed,[48] a Stoic can read, remember, study, and contemplate on his own.[49] Indeed, Seneca thinks that illness is no excuse to stop caring about one's personal concerns and to forget one's professional affairs. Rather, one should try to recover as soon as possible.[50]

## G. The Needs of Nature: Pleasure, Pain, and Perversion

In *On Providence*, Seneca argues that frequent struggles with adversity toughen us up. Familiar exposure to danger will train us to have contempt for danger. Sailors' bodies are hardy from rough sea voyages. Farmers' hands are callused from working their fields. Soldiers' brawny arms can hurl heavy spears. Runners' legs are nimble. Regular exercise of a body part or faculty makes it strong and sturdy. Seneca reflects that the Germanic tribes along the Danube, oppressed by gloomy skies and eternal winter, eke out their sustenance scratching up meager crops from barren soil and ranging over icy marshes hunting wild beasts, and shelter in thatch-roofed hovels. Yet he imagines them happy, because their austere habits have returned them to nature. "For what they begin from necessity becomes gradually a pleasure."[51] His idea is this: what we get used to, we come to like. If what we get used to conforms to what our human nature really needs, then our way of life will be healthy, fit, and excellent. But if we indulge in superfluity so often that we develop a taste for it, our luxurious habit will make us sickly, reduce our bodies to flab, and infect our minds with disease.

Seneca argues that utility, not superfluity, measures our needs. But once people immerse themselves in unhealthy pleasures habitually and become so accustomed to them that they depend on those pleasures as crutches they cannot manage without, they have sunk into a most wretched condition.[52] In this way what once provided pleasure becomes an obsessive affliction. Withdrawal from what one has grown addicted to is torture.

Pretense is another kind of torture, according to Seneca. There are those who are bent on striking a pose. They never reveal themselves to anyone frankly. If you are candid with no one, your anxieties have no outlet. Many live a false life that is staged only for show, and it is torturous to be constantly watching oneself and to fear being caught out of one's usual role.[53] If you live your life constantly acting the part of a dramatis persona who is not you, worries about your theatrical mask slipping and revealing the real person underneath it will consume you. The habit of pretense takes you hostage and subjects you to agony.

Seneca thinks that everyone enjoys his own crimes. One person delights in an intrigue, because the very difficulty of pulling it off was an attractive challenge. Another enjoys forgery and theft and is only displeased with his sin when it fails to hit its target. All such vicious gratification is the result of perverted habits, according to Seneca.[54] Yet the consequences of this corrupt gratification are inevitably painful. So, people love and hate their vices at the same time.[55]

How do we measure our needs when it comes to what and how we eat? Food must be our most familiar source of pleasure. What does Seneca say about choice of diet? We read in the *Letters* that his teacher Sotion explained to him that Pythagoras and Sextius had different reasons for the same regimen of abstaining from animal food. Sextius believed that we have enough sustenance without resorting to blood, and that a habit of cruelty is formed whenever butchery is practiced for pleasure. Seneca recounts that after a year of abstaining from meat, his vegetarian habit was as pleasant as it was easy and that he was beginning to feel that his mind was more active. Unfortunately, during this time certain foreign rites were being inaugurated, and abstinence from certain kinds of animal food was adduced as evidence of interest in the strange foreign cult. Seneca explains that his father detested philosophy, and so presumably also the philosophical reasons that Seneca presented in defense of his vegetarianism. He confides to Lucilius that, at the request of his father, he abandoned his meatless diet.[56]

Seneca realized he could live well, perhaps even better, without meat. But some things we cannot live without. He divides necessary, as opposed to useful, favors (*beneficia*) into three groups: (1) those without which we are unable to live, (2) those without which we are able to live but ought not to live, and prefer to die than to lack them, and (3) those without which we are unwilling to live. Things in this third group are "dear to us through kinship and blood, through old habit and long familiarity, such as children, wives, home, and anything else that the mind becomes so attached to as to make it harder to be robbed of it than to be robbed of life itself."[57] Clearly Seneca regards these sorts of things as healthy attachments rather than unhealthy addictions. Seneca's remarks arguably conform to Stoic orthodoxy in grouping life itself and the human beings we marry or parent within the class of things that are neither good nor bad. How we *treat* our family members is very much either good or bad. Therefore, to be unwilling to lose your family or home, and to accept your own death more lightly than their deaths or the loss of your home, in no way betrays your virtue. Virtue alone counts as a Stoic's only true good.

## H. Love of Wisdom, Its Benefits, and the Happy Life

Seneca asserts that (1) no one can live an endurable life without studying wisdom and beginning to achieve it, and that (2) a happy life is reached only when one's wisdom is brought to completion. These commitments must be strengthened and implanted by daily reflection. Seneca urges Lucilius to persevere and develop new strength by continuous study until that which is only a good intention (*bona voluntas*) becomes a good, settled purpose (*bona mens*).[58] Whether fate chains us with inexorable law, or God as arbiter of the universe ordains everything, or chance impels and tosses about human affairs without method, Seneca argues that philosophy ought to be our defense. Philosophy will encourage us to obey God cheerfully, but Fortune defiantly. Philosophy will teach us to follow God and endure chance. Seneca cautions Lucilius against allowing his spirit to weaken and chill, and instead to hold fast to it and establish it securely, in order that what is now impulse may become a habit of the mind.[59]

To love and seek wisdom is to be a philosopher. To attain wisdom is to become a sage.[60] The Stoics taught that virtue is a single state of mind of the sage, and that what we may think are many different, separate virtues—justice, courage, temperance, generosity, equanimity, beneficence, cheerfulness, honesty, patience, diligence, and so on—are actually only different names of this single, unified, right state of mind, wisdom. Thus, the Stoics defended the view that only the sage has this right state of mind. Seneca wonders,

> What is more gentle than a human being when he is in a right state of mind? But what is more cruel than anger? What is more loving to others than a human being? What more hostile than anger? Human beings are born for mutual help; anger for mutual destruction.[61]

Anger is a kind of insanity. Ordinary people get angry. Hence, ordinary people suffer from a kind of insanity. A human being in the right state of mind is calm, gentle, and completely free of the insanity that is anger. His habits of mind over years of practice have extirpated all mental disorder and replaced it with abiding wisdom and philanthropy. The wise person is sane, loving, helpful to others, a mensch—the perfected human being.

## I. Conforming to What Reason Says We Need Rather Than to Custom

Seneca tells Lucilius that no one can have whatever he wants, but one can have this truth: that it's possible not to want what one doesn't have and to make cheerful use of what is on offer.[62] In order to experience this cheerful use, however, the philosopher must discipline himself with frequent tests. Seneca explains his practice of austerity to Lucilius in the following text worth quoting at length.

> You see, I have undertaken a kind of impromptu trial of my mind; this kind of test is more candid and revealing. For when the mind has prepared itself and commanded itself to endure, then it is not so obvious how much real firmness it has. The most reliable proofs are those which the mind gives without warning, if it contemplates troubles not just with equanimity but with contentment; if it does not flare up in anger, does not quarrel; if it makes up for the lack of something which it ought to have been given by not wanting it and if it reflects that although there might be something missing from what it is accustomed to, the mind itself lacks nothing. With many things we don't realize how superfluous they are until we begin to lack them. We made use of them not because we needed them but because we had them. And how many things do we acquire just because others have done so, because most people own them! One cause of our troubles is that we live by the example of others; we do not arrange our lives by reason but get swept away by custom. If just a few people did something we wouldn't want to imitate it, but when many start to do it, then we conform and do it too, as though it were more honorable because it is more popular. Once a mistake becomes widespread we treat it as being right.[63]

Seneca is no fan of fads, vogues, trends, or novelties. He encourages Lucilius, and himself, to guard against being bewitched by the ubiquitous refrain that everyone needs things that they don't already have. But Seneca doubts that satisfaction can be reached by grasping for what our neighbors tire themselves out trying to obtain. Rather, contentment comes from eschewing the practices of consumerism, materialism, ownership, and money-grubbing, which were as customary in the upper class Roman society of Seneca's day as they are in much of American society today. Seneca and the Stoics believed that wisdom is rare and ignorance is common, so the fact that many people value and pursue certain things is no good reason for thinking that those things are actually good and worth pursuing. That would be to commit the informal fallacy of appeal to popular belief.

Seneca shares with Lucilius the idea that "contented poverty is an honorable estate" and explains that he discovered this pearl of wisdom when reading Epicurus. Though he is an avowed Stoic, Seneca says that he is accustomed to cross over even into the enemy's camp, the camp of the Epicureans, not as a deserter, but as a scout.[64] Elsewhere Seneca mentions his habit of trying to extract and make useful some element from every field of thought he encounters, no matter how far removed it may be from philosophy.[65] Wisdom must be recognized and embraced no matter where we read or hear it.

## J. The Habit of "Dividing" the Self and Putting Oneself on Trial

An orthodox doctrine in Stoic philosophy of mind is that a person's mind is unitary, not divided into parts that can function separately or conflict with one another, as Plato[66] and Aristotle seem to have believed. While not rejecting this psychological monism, Seneca notes that "the instances in which habit leads us to divide ourselves into two persons are countless; we are accustomed to say: 'Let me converse with myself,' and 'I will give my ear a twitch.'" By the latter he means "I will jog my memory." He contends that just as it makes sense for us sometimes to get angry with ourselves, blame ourselves, cause ourselves loss, and injure ourselves, it makes equal sense for us sometimes to thank ourselves, praise ourselves, bring ourselves gain, and benefit ourselves.[67] Seneca sees this routine self-evaluation, self-critique, self-congratulation, self-recrimination, and self-help as integral to the quest of self-improvement. Thus, Seneca does not think that the human mind splits itself into two parts, but that it can, and regularly ought to, inspect and assess its own cognitive activities recursively.

Seneca elaborates on this practice of self-scrutiny in a final text in the third book of *On Anger* in which he admires this daily habit of a Roman philosopher in the reign of Augustus named Sextius.

> All our senses must be trained to endure. They are naturally capable of endurance, once the mind stops corrupting them. It should be summoned each day to give an account of itself. Sextius used to do this. At the end of the day, when he had retired for the night, he would interrogate his mind: "What ailment of yours have you cured today? What failing have you resisted? In what way are you better?" Anger will cease or moderate itself, if it knows that each day it must appear before a judge. Could anything be finer than this habit of sifting through the whole day? Think of the sleep that follows the self-examination! How tranquil, deep, and untroubled it must be, when the mind has been praised or admonished, and this secret sentinel and self-critic has taken stock of its own habits. I make use of this opportunity, daily pleading my case at my own court. When the light has been taken away and my wife has fallen silent, aware as she is of my habit, I scrutinize my entire day and review what I have done and said. I conceal nothing from myself. I omit nothing. For why should I fear any of my errors when I can say: "See that you never do that again. I pardon you this time. In that dispute, you spoke too pugnaciously. In the future don't have anything to do with ignorant people—those who have never learned don't want to learn. You were franker than you should have been in admonishing that person, and as a consequence you didn't mend him, you offended him. In the future, don't just consider the truth of what you're saying, but whether the person to whom you're saying it can handle the truth. While a good man is glad to be admonished, the worse a man is, the more bitterly he resents anyone correcting him."[68]

Seneca's self-examination continues with more examples in this vein for several paragraphs. Much could be said about this fascinating homily to himself which space does not permit. A brief point to make is to emphasize the importance for Seneca of this introspective method of being his own sentinel, his own prosecutor, defendant, and judge rolled into one. The habit of thoroughly inspecting his own words and deeds, and his reactions to the words and deeds of the people he encounters, at the end of each day when he and his wife go to bed and his wife drifts off to sleep, and conscientiously tracking his moral progress, is an ingredient in not only calming his mind and achieving sound sleep, but gaining wisdom and living well.

## 2. MUSONIUS RUFUS

Gaius Musonius Rufus was born before 30 CE in Volsinii, an Etruscan city of Italy. A member of the Roman equestrian order, he belonged to the class of aristocracy ranked second only to senators. He was highly respected, a teacher famous in Rome by the time of Nero, and had a considerable following of students during his life, including Epictetus. Musonius conceived of philosophy as nothing but the practice of noble behavior. He called for austere personal habits in order to achieve a virtuous, sturdy life in accord with the principles of Stoicism. He taught that philosophy must be studied not to cultivate brilliance in arguments or an excessive cleverness, but to develop good character, a sound mind, and a tough, robust body. Either Musonius wrote nothing himself or what he wrote was lost because none of his own writings survive. His philosophical teachings survive as thirty-two apothegms and twenty-one longer discourses, all evidently preserved by others.[69]

In a lecture titled "Whether habituation or reasoning is more effective" Musonius contends that habituation is more effective in the acquisition of virtue. He presents this argument. Suppose there are two doctors. One can speak about medicine as though he was experienced in it, yet he has no practical experience treating the sick. The other doctor is unable to speak about medicine, but is experienced in providing treatment in accordance with medical theory. Clearly, we'd choose the latter physician to provide us care. Further, suppose there are two men. One has sailed on many voyages and captained many ships, and the other has sailed a few times and never captained a ship. Suppose the latter can speak eloquently about captaining a ship, but the experienced captain gives a terrible speech on the topic. Plainly, we would hire the experienced captain when we sail. Finally, suppose there were two musicians. One knows music theory and speaks fluently about it but cannot sing or play the kithara or the lyre. The other is ignorant of music theory, but is a virtuoso on the kithara and the lyre and sings beautifully. Clearly, the one we'd want as a music teacher for a child who doesn't know music is the one good at the practice of music. Given our preferences in examples like these, Musonius reasons, when it comes to self-control and temperance it's much better to *become* self-controlled and temperate in all one's actions than it is to be able to *talk about* self-control and temperance and *say* how one should act. Therefore, he concludes, practice and habituation give us the ability to act, whereas knowing the reasoning and theory behind the action give us the ability to speak. Reasoning contributes to action by teaching us how one should act, and it precedes habituation in time. One cannot be habituated to anything good and honorable unless one is habituated in accordance with reason. But habituation remains prior to reasoning in its impact, Musonius observes, because it is more effective in getting people to act than reasoning is.[70]

Since Musonius understands philosophy to be nothing but the practice of noble behavior,[71] he asserts that anyone who claims to study philosophy must practice it even more diligently than someone studying the art of medicine or some similar skill, inasmuch as philosophy is more important and more difficult to master than any other pursuit. Since a human being is a composite of soul and body, Musonius holds that both must be trained.

The body must be trained for work and properly nourished. The proper diet, according to Musonius, is lacto-vegetarian.[72] These foods are least expensive and most readily available: raw fruits in season, certain raw vegetables, milk, cheese, and honeycombs. Cooked grains and some cooked vegetables are also suitable for humans, whereas a meat-based diet is too crude for human beings and is more suitable for wild beasts. Those who eat lots of meat seem slow-witted to Musonius. We are worse than brute animals when it comes to food, he thinks, because we obsessively embellish the presentation of our food and fuss about what we eat and how we prepare it, merely to amuse our palates. Moreover, too much rich food harms the body. For these reasons, Musonius thinks that gastronomic pleasure is undoubtedly the most difficult pleasure to combat. Consequently, he rejects gourmet cuisine and delicacies as a dangerous habit. He judges gluttony and craving fancy food to be most shameful and a lack of moderation. Indeed, Musonius opines that those who eat the least expensive food can work harder, tire less when working, get sick less often, tolerate cold, heat, and lack of sleep better, and are stronger than those who eat expensive food.[73]

Musonius also insists on the simplest, least expensive footwear, clothing, and houses built to keep out cold, excessive heat, and the elements. Couriers do not wear sandals on the roads and competitive runners would be slowed if they wore sandals. So, if possible, better to go shoeless and let one's feet breathe. Money should be spent on people, not on colonnades, gilded ceilings, or fancy architecture. The protection afforded by our dwelling should be what we would expect from a cave.[74]

A different type of training is appropriate for the soul, but we train both soul and body when we accustom ourselves to cold, heat, thirst, hunger, scarcity of food, hardness of bed, thin clothing, cave-like houses, abstention from pleasures, and endurance of pains. Through these methods of habituation, Musonius contends, the body grows strong, fit for every task, and inured to suffering. At the same time, this training in toughness (*askēsis*) strengthens the soul, trains it for courage by enduring hardships which frighten the soft, and trains it for self-control by abstaining from pleasures. Musonius defends the central ethical doctrine of Stoicism that pain, death, poverty, ill repute, sickness, and other things devoid of wickedness are in no way bad, and that pleasure, life, wealth, fame, health, and other things that have no share in virtue are not good. Virtue and the things pertaining to virtue are the only good, whereas vice and the things pertaining to vice are the only evil, according to the Stoics. Pain, death, poverty, and the like, as well as pleasure, life, wealth, and the like, are indifferent. It is how all such things are *used* that is good or bad. Yet, Musonius explains, because of the corruption ingrained in us from the cradle by non-Stoics, and because of the wicked behavior caused by this corruption, we have been brainwashed into thinking it is a bad thing when pain happens and it is a good thing when pleasure happens. We cringe at death as the worst misfortune and we cling to life as the greatest good. When we lose or give away money, we are distressed as if we are injured. When we receive money, we rejoice as if we are benefited. In too many circumstances, Musonius thinks, we fail to deal with our affairs with correct assumptions and instead we follow thoughtless habit. The person practicing to become a Stoic must overcome these thoughtless habits ingrained in his mind, heal their corrupting effect on his character, and thereby free himself from false, widely popular beliefs about pleasure, pain, life, death, money, honor, and happiness.[75] Stoic philosophy is thus the remedy for anti-Stoic propaganda about what is good, what is bad, and what is indifferent. But the Stoic remedy requires daily doses, as it were, to restore soundness of mind. New habits in accord with sound Stoic understanding must replace the noxious habits deeply ingrained in us over many years and repeatedly reinforced by the non-Stoics who surround us.

Naturally, Musonius believes that kings should also study philosophy. Philosophy—that is, *Stoic* philosophy—he conceives of as the knowledge which diagnoses what is good and evil, useful and useless, helpful and harmful. Philosophy teaches us what justice is. It is philosophy which draws us to self-control and teaches us to be above pleasure and greed. Philosophy teaches us to love frugality and avoid extravagance, Musonius argues. It accustoms us to be modest and tactful. Philosophy brings about discipline, order, decorum, and fitting conduct in action and in habit. These qualities make a person dignified and self-controlled. Any king who has these qualities is most like a god and worthy of reverence, according to Musonius.[76] The discipline of Stoic philosophy trains us to develop the virtues that result from good habits of living. These good habits have the power to transform an ordinary ruler into a kingly person of virtue. Such a kingly paragon is godlike.

## 3. EPICTETUS

Epictetus was born into slavery as the son of a slave woman in the city of Hierapolis in the province of Phrygia between 50 and 60 CE. At some point he traveled to Rome, where he was owned by Nero's freedman and administrative secretary Epaphroditus, who allowed him to be a pupil of Musonius. After he was manumitted, Epictetus set up his own school in the city of Nicopolis in northwest Greece to teach Stoicism to adolescent Romans preparing for public service. The influence of the master on the pupil is evident on many topics, including habit and its vital importance in making progress in living well.[77]

Epictetus explains to his students that each professional expertise is augmented and preserved by the corresponding actions. The carpenter is made by his carpentry. The grammarian is made by his grammatical exercises.

> But if someone falls into the habit of writing ungrammatically, his expertise must be undermined and demolished. In the same way the respectful person is preserved by respectful actions, and undone by disrespectful ones.[78]

Epictetus generalizes this point about the habituation of activities producing skills and establishing the quality of a person's mind and character.

> Every habit (*hexis*)[79] and capacity (*dunamis*) is preserved and strengthened by the corresponding actions, that of walking, by walking, that of running, by running. If you want to be a reader, read; if a writer, write. But if you fail to read for thirty days in succession and turn to something else, you will see the consequence. So also if you lie down for ten days, get up and try to go on a fairly long walk, you will see how wobbly your legs are. In general, then, if you want to do something, make it a habit. And if you want not to do something, abstain from doing it, and accustom yourself to something else in its place. This is also the case when it comes to things of the mind. Whenever you are angry, be assured that this is not only a present evil, but that you have strengthened the habit, and added fuel to the fire. When you yield to someone in sexual intercourse, do not count it a single defeat, but know that you have fed, that you have strengthened, your incontinence. For habits and capacities must necessarily be affected by the corresponding actions, and become implanted if they were not present previously, or be intensified and strengthened if they were.[80]

The Stoics regarded anger as one of the very worst of all passions.[81] Each instance of anger is a present evil for the angry person, but each instance of ire disposes us to get angry that much more easily in the future, the next time we judge we've been provoked by another. Outbursts of wrath add fuel to the fire, compounding the mental disorder and exacerbating the vice of irascibility. Similarly, each time we succumb to lust, Epictetus explains, we ought to regard it not as an isolated failure, but as a bad decision that will bring with it in the future more bad decisions in the face of sexual temptation.

If we recognize that anger is bad and we don't want to be hot-tempered, Epictetus offers this advice: Don't feed the habit. Give the habit of irascibility nothing to promote its growth.

> Keep quiet to begin with, and count the days on which you have not been angry. I used to be angry every day; now every other day; then every third and fourth day: and, if you avoid it as many as thirty days, offer a sacrifice of thanksgiving to god. For the habit is first weakened, and then entirely destroyed.[82]

Anger results from the double judgment that we have been wronged by another and that we ought to retaliate against this wrongdoer.[83] Epictetus advises us to banish this base and sordid double judgment and introduce a fair and noble judgment to replace it. What might such a judgment be?

Perhaps that all human beings err and that, as our kinfolk, we ought to foster fellowship with them instead of discord.[84] If we become habituated to this exercise of replacing base judgments with noble ones, we will in effect be starving the monster that is rage inside us, and it will weaken, wither, and die. Meanwhile, we will become true athletes and watch our shoulders, sinews, and vigor grow mighty.[85] What he means is that we will develop brawny virtues. We will become athletes of character who have eliminated their ravenous vices.

The method of countering bad old habits with good new ones is also effective in battling other anti-Stoic beliefs. Consider the hugely popular belief that death is bad. People are in the habit of regarding death as evil. Epictetus urges his students to discover as an aid against that habit the contrary habit.

> You hear ignorant laymen say, "That poor man! He is dead; his father died, his mother died, he was cut off before his time and in a foreign land." Listen to the contrary arguments, draw away from these expressions. Oppose to one habit the contrary; to sophistic arguments, the art of reasoning, and the frequent use and exercise of it. Against specious appearances we must have clear preconceptions, polished and ready for use. When death appears an evil, we ought immediately to remember that evils may be avoided, but death is a necessity.[86]

Epictetus cautions his students about hanging around with ignorant laymen because their false beliefs might rub off onto them and impede their progress as Stoics. Associating with non-Stoics who talk about death being terrible can thus be dangerous.

Like his master Musonius, Epictetus is sensitive to the corrupting influence of anti-Stoics on impressionable Stoics in training. The environment in which one strives to adopt the healthy habits of Stoic thinking matters. Non-Stoics disbelieve the truths of Stoicism. Some non-Stoics are Epicureans, Skeptics, or Peripatetics who are familiar with the arguments for Stoicism, but reject them nonetheless. Other non-Stoics are "laymen" who just haven't thought things through. Both types of non-Stoics suffer from the mental illness of their false beliefs. What is worse, their noxious non-Stoic beliefs can infect those whose newborn Stoic beliefs are not yet firmly fixed. Until those new judgments of the Stoic student have become so strongly fastened inside him that they become part of him, and he has developed the ability to guarantee the security of his convictions, which will be routinely ridiculed by laymen who far outnumber him, Epictetus urges caution about disputing with such antagonists. Otherwise, he explains, whatever lecture notes his student writes down on his wax tablet,[87] intent upon assimilating them, will instead melt away like wax left out in the boiling sun. To avoid this, Epictetus recommends that his student withdraw to a sheltered, shady spot as long as his new Stoic conceptions are as squishy as fresh wax. Epictetus says that it is for this reason that the philosophers even advise us to leave our country, because old habits distract us, and prevent us from beginning to develop new ones.[88]

> Thus physicians send patients with chronic disorders to a different place and a different climate, and rightly so. And you too should adopt different habits. Fix your opinions, and exercise yourself in them. No, but from here you go to the theater, to a gladiatorial combat, to a gymnasium colonnade, to the circus, and then back here again, and then back there, remaining just the same persons all the time. No sign of any good habit, no regard or attention to yourself. You do not watch yourself closely.[89]

The goal Epictetus upholds before his students is to be mindful about every event and deal with it appropriately, in accordance with Nature as a whole, and one's special nature as a rational being. The target is to regard everything that lies outside our volition (*prohairesis*)[90] as of no concern to us. Only our judgments, beliefs, and acting as we should ought to concern us. This is a lofty goal, but it secures for us freedom of mind, peace of mind, and invulnerability to the vicissitudes of events and to coercion by others. For Epictetus, it is the *only* goal worthy of a human being. If you are not yet in this state of mind, he says, flee from your former habits, flee from all laymen, if you ever want to make a start on becoming somebody.[91]

Our former, non-Stoic habits are a plague from which we must flee if we want our minds to heal. To acquire Stoic habits, one must train oneself to have the right desires and the right aversions. Since we have countless desires and aversions daily, the *askēsis* of the Stoic is unrelenting. In a discourse titled "On Training" (*Peri askēseōs*) Epictetus explains:

> For, without severe and constant training, it is impossible to ensure that our desire should not fail or our aversion should not fall into what it would avoid. So you should know that if you allow your training to be directed towards external things that lie outside volition, your desire will neither gain its object, nor your aversion avoid it. And because habit has a powerful influence, when we have become habituated to apply our desire and aversion to externals only, we must oppose one habit to another, and where impressions are most liable to make us slip, there resort to training to counter the risk. I am inclined to pleasure. I will move to the opposite side of the deck to a greater extent than usual for the sake of training. I have an aversion to suffering. I will train and exercise my impressions to ensure that my aversion is withdrawn from everything of this kind. For who is the man under training? The man who practices not exercising his desire, and directing his aversion only to things that lie within volition, and who practices the hardest in the things most difficult to achieve. So, different people will have to practice harder in different respects.[92]

Each Stoic-in-training has his own peculiar susceptibilities to non-Stoic behaviors. To use the medical analogy: each self-doctoring patient must know what maladies he is susceptible to in order to tailor his remedies accordingly.[93] This course of treatment, Epictetus insists, must be administered aggressively and continually. To use the gymnastic analogy: each athlete must know which of his muscles are underdeveloped and call for targeted weight lifting exercises. Is he a poor runner? Then he must practice harder to run longer and faster. Is he a weak swimmer? Then he needs harder workouts doing laps in the pool. For the Stoic athlete of character, it is his desires, aversions, beliefs, judgments, and decisions—the bones, muscles, and sinews of his mind—that must be closely examined, tested for firmness, and ceaselessly trained.

Concentration is indispensable for successful Stoic habituation. Epictetus argues that the Stoic may never relax or take even a short break from his practice of vigilant mental focus.

> When you relax your attention for a while, do not expect you will recover it whenever you please. But remember this: that because of your fault of today your affairs must necessarily be in a worse condition on future occasions. First, and this is the gravest matter of all, a habit arises in you of not paying attention, and next a habit of deferring attention, and so you get into the habit of putting off from one time to another the happy and befitting life that would enable you to live, and continue to live, in accord with nature.[94]

Epictetus grants that it is impracticable to be altogether faultless, but holds that it is possible to *strive* never to commit faults. Constant perseverance in paying attention is the only safeguard against slipping into a habit of not paying attention. Postponing our dedication to attentiveness is deadly, because it ushers in the habit of delaying living a happy life agreeable to nature. Attention to the cognitive fitness of consistent Stoic thinking, desiring, and averting, is urgent for Epictetus. It cannot be put off, or we will never live happily.

Stoic training is certainly not for the faint of heart. Epictetus describes it as the greatest of contests, and those engaged in it must not shrink back from the many blows they can expect to receive. It is not an Olympic contest like wrestling or the *pankration* but rather a contest for good fortune and joyfulness. Those who compete and lose in the Olympic Games must wait four years for their next chance to compete. But he who falters in the contest of character that is Stoic *askēsis* is not prevented from picking himself up, renewing his zeal, and rejoining the contest. Epictetus teaches his students not to make light of each of their stumbles. When someone indulges a bad desire, like feeling lust when one sees a pretty girl, or the desire to disparage somebody, the bad desire itself is a kind of punishment. He likens the bad desire to disobeying one's physician's orders and as a consequence contracting a fever or suffering a headache.[95]

> So, when you disparaged somebody the other day, did you not act like an ill-natured person? Was it not foolish nonsense that you spoke? And did you not feed this habit of yours by setting before it the example of other actions akin to it? And when you were overcome by the pretty girl, did you get off unpunished? Why, then, do you talk of what you were doing just recently? You ought to remember it, I think, as slaves do their whippings, so as to refrain from the same faults again. But the case is not the same, for with slaves it is the pain that brings back the memory, but what pain, what punishment, follows on your offenses? And when did you ever acquire the habit of shunning evil actions?[96]

The athlete of character needs to cultivate feeling pain when he succumbs to a bad desire or un-Stoic aversion. In this way he punishes himself for each of his offenses, for each mistaken desire. If the misstep along the journey to virtue is not attended by a self-punishment, then Epictetus thinks there will be no impetus for the person to self-correct. The habit of feeling shame[97] when one acts badly is essential for a Stoic's progress.

Following their intellectual forebears, the Cynics, the Stoics emphasized the virtue of self-sufficiency. This is particularly true of Epictetus, who scolds one of his students for falling into the habit of looking to others and lamenting, groaning, and eating in fear of not having food tomorrow, and hoping for nothing from himself.[98] Moreover, proper habits also create proper relationships with others.

> Appropriate actions are generally measured by our social relationships. He is a father. This implies, taking care of him, giving way to him in everything, putting up with him if he abuses you, or hits you. . . . Do not examine what he is doing, but what you must do to keep your volition consistent with nature. No one will hurt you, unless you want that. You will be hurt when you think you are hurt. In this way, then, you will discover the appropriate action to expect from a neighbor, a citizen, a general, if you acquire the habit of observing relationships.[99]

Epictetus believes that by focusing on fulfilling *our* familial roles as child, parent, and sibling, *our* social role as neighbor, and *our* civic roles as citizen, leader, and so on, and the activities flowing from those roles which are up to us, we won't make the mistake of worrying about how other people in our lives are behaving toward us. How *they* behave is ultimately not up to us. If we perform the tasks we are responsible for, do our duties, and fulfill our social roles, and thereby observe *our* relationships habitually, then we will discover the appropriate actions to expect from others. Making a habit of playing our social roles well and being content with that protects us from ignorantly believing that we are harmed when others play their social roles poorly.[100] Our concern must be on making our own judgments rational, making our own decisions wise, and keeping our own volition in harmony with nature, every single day.

## CONCLUSION

Stoic habits—the habits of mind required to make progress in the lifelong project of becoming a fully realized, free human being free of distress—are incompatible with ambivalence, laziness, lapses in attention, procrastination, dependence on others, excuses, forgiving one's own faults, and tolerating one's own mistakes. The Roman Stoics were convinced, however, that striving to adopt Stoic habits can earn oneself a happier life.

## NOTES

1. See G. Striker, "Following Nature: A Study in Stoic Ethics," *Oxford Studies in Ancient Philosophy* 9 (1991): 1–73.

2. For a magisterial study of the *meditatio* in the Roman Stoics, see R. J. Newman, "*Cotidie meditare*. Theory and Practice of the *meditatio* in Imperial Stoicism," *ANRW* II. 36.3: 1473–1517.

3. In his *Memoranda* Marcus Aurelius Antoninus has little to add to his predecessors' comments on habit. My reasons for departing from the popular custom of labeling Marcus's collection of philosophical writings *Meditations* are explained in *Marcus Aurelius: A Guide for the Perplexed* (Continuum, 2012), 2. Seneca's contemporary Lucius Annaeus Cornutus could be counted as a lesser Roman Stoic. He wrote on rhetoric in Greek and Latin and authored a treatise on Greek mythology as interpreted using etymologies and the lens of Stoic physics.

4. For his life and career, see M. T. Griffin, *Seneca: A Philosopher in Politics* (Oxford University Press, 1976). For an overview of his philosophy, see K. Vogt, "Seneca," *The Stanford Encyclopedia of Philosophy* (Winter 2012 edition), ed. E. N. Zalta. http://plato.stanford.edu/archives/win2012/entries/seneca/.

5. See Brad Inwood, *Seneca: Selected Philosophical Letters* (Oxford: Oxford University Press, 2007), xii–xxi.

6. The extant letters of correspondence of the rhetorician Marcus Cornelius Fronto with his student Marcus Aurelius Antoninus are also in Latin.

7. *Mānsuēsco* means to tame, literally "to accustom to the hand" (of mastery, discipline), and *mansuētus* means gentle, mild, or tame. *Adsuēsco* = accustom to, train; *adsuētus* = customary, accustomed.

8. I thank Gregory S. Bucher for his comments on this paragraph.

9. *Epistulae morales* 11.1–3. For translations of Seneca's letters I have consulted, and freely modify, R. M. Gummere, *Seneca. Ad Lucilium epistulae morales* (Harvard: Harvard University Press, 1917).

10. *Ep.* 11.4–5.

11. *Ep.* 11.6.

12. *Ep.* 11.7.

13. *De ira* II.4.1.

14. *De ira* II.4.2. Translations of *De ira* are by J. M. Cooper and J. F. Procopé in *Seneca: Moral and Political Essays* (Cambridge: Cambridge University Press, 1995), rarely modified.

15. For a discussion of Seneca on anger in public life, see M. C. Nussbaum, *The Therapy of Desire* (Princeton: Princeton University Press, 1994), chapter 11.

16. *De tranquillitate animi* 10.1–3. For translations of Seneca's *Moral Essays* I have consulted J. W. Basore (Cambridge, MA: Harvard University Press, 1985) and Peter Anderson's new translations are in press at Hackett Publishing.

17. At *Ep*. 53.5–6, after very slowly recovering from a case of seasickness Seneca reflects on how we forget or ignore the frailties of our body and describes a slight ague growing into a fever, pain in the foot, tingling in the joints, swollen ankles, and gout.

18. *De providentia* IV.15.

19. *Consolatio ad Marciam* 7.4.

20. Thus the Stoics reject Aristotle's more nuanced position (*Nicomachean Ethics* Bk I. Chs. 8–10) that external goods and goods of the body make a virtuous life *better* or more blessed.

21. *Ep*. 104.9–10.

22. *Ep*. 104.10.

23. *Ep*. 42.8.

24. *Ep*. 112.1.

25. *Ep*. 112.2.

26. *Ep*. CXII.3.

27. *Ep*. 112.4.

28. *Ep*. 95.36–37.

29. *Ep*. 95.46.

30. *Ep*. 29.8.

31. *De ira* III.8.7.

32. *De ira* II.24.2.

33. See W. K. Clifford, "The Ethics of Belief," *Contemporary Review* (1877) and in print in *The Ethics of Belief and Other Essays* (Amherst, MA: Prometheus Books, 1999).

34. *De ira* I.1.1.

35. *De ira* I.1.3.

36. *De ira* II.20.1–2.

37. *De ira* II.21.1.

38. *De ira* II.21.5.

39. *De ira* II.21.6.

40. *De ira* II.21.8.

41. *De ira* II.21.7.

42. *Ep*. 83.26. At *Ep*. 59.15 he notes that a single hour of hilarious, crazy bingeing can leave a hangover that lasts for many days.

43. *De tranquillitate animi* 17.9.

44. See 6, 7, 17, 25, 28, 52, 56, and 64.

45. *Ep*. 54.

46. *Ep*. 65 and 104.

47. *Ep*. 78.20. See Newman, 1483–1496.

48. In *Ep*. 9 Seneca states that even the wise man, when in his sickbed, prefers to have someone sit by him.

49. Seneca shares his views on mind and body in more detail in *Ep*. 15. In *Ep*. 14 he says that we have an inborn affection for our body and are its guardian. For this reason Seneca doesn't believe that the body is never to be indulged at all, but only that we must not be slaves to it. Elsewhere, however, in *Ep*. 24 he speaks of the "clogging burden of a body to which nature has fettered" him. According to the Stoic theory of *oikeiōsis*, love of self begins in infancy as the love of one's body and what benefits it, but matures into love of one's mind upon development of rationality in adolescence, and later expands to love of all rational beings, philanthropy, in (virtuous) adulthood. See T. Engberg-Pedersen, *The Stoic Theory of* Oikeiosis (Aarhus: Aarhus Universitetsforlag, 1990) and R. Blondell, "Parental Nature and Stoic *Oikeiosis*," *Ancient Philosophy* 10 (1990): 221–42.

50. *Ep*. 53.9.

51. *De prov*. IV.12–15.

52. *Ep*. 39.6.

53. *De tranquillitate animi* 17.1.

54. *Ep*. 97.12.

55. *Ep*. 112.4.
56. *Ep*. 108.17–22.
57. *De beneficiis* I.11.4 (Cooper and Procopé's translation modified).
58. *Ep*. 16.1.
59. *Ep*. 16.6.
60. See Julia Annas, "The Sage in Ancient Philosophy," in *Anthropine Sophia*, ed. F. Alesse et al. (Naples: Bibliopolis, 2008), 11–27, esp. 17–27 on the Stoic sage.
61. *De ira* I.5.2.
62. *Ep*. 123.3.
63. *Ep*. 123. 5–6. For this translation I consulted and freely modified Brad Inwood, *Seneca: Selected Philosophical Letters* (Oxford: Oxford University Press, 2007), 95–96; his comments on this text are on 356–57.
64. *Ep*. 2.5. On Seneca's appropriation of Epicurus, see *Ep*. 21.3–10.
65. *Ep*. 58.26.
66. Or rather, some of the characters in some of his dialogues.
67. *De beneficiis* V.7.6.
68. *De ira* III.36.1–4 (translation by Cooper and Procopé modified).
69. See C. King, trans., *Musonius Rufus: Lectures and Sayings* (Lulu, 2010), 13–19, and C. E. Lutz, "Musonius Rufus," *Yale Classical Studies* 10 (1947): 32–147.
70. Stobaeus 2.15.46. Chapter 15: about seeming and being and that one must judge a person not by word but by character, for without action all words are useless. King & Irvine, Lecture no. 5, 34–35.
71. Stobaeus 2.31.123. Chapter 31: on training and education. King and Irvine, Lecture #4, 33.
72. Compare Seneca's vegetarian experience discussed above in the penultimate paragraph of §G above.
73. Stoabaeus 3.17.42. Chapter 17: on self-mastery. King and Irvine, Lecture no. 18, 71–75.
74. Stobaeus 3.1.209. Chapter 1: about virtue. King and Irvine, Lecture no. 19, 76–77.
75. Stobaeus 3.29.78. Chapter 29: about love of hard work. King and Irvine, Lecture no. 6, 36–37.
76. Stobaeus 4.7.67. Chapter 7: advice about kingship. King and Irvine, Lecture no. 8, 40–41.
77. For a study of Epictetus's conception of happiness as mental freedom, see W. O. Stephens, *Stoic Ethics: Epictetus and Happiness as Freedom* (London: Continuum, 2007).
78. *Discourses* 2.9.10–11 (Long's translation, modified). See A. A. Long, *Epictetus: A Stoic and Socratic Guide to Life* (Oxford: Oxford University Press, 2002), 225–26 on lack of integrity as self-inflicted.
79. For discussion of the Stoics' account of traits of character and their concepts of *hexis* (which she translates "condition"), *diathesis*, *epitēdeumata* ("habitudes"), "proclivities," "sicknesses," and "infirmities," see M. R. Graver, *Stoicism and Emotion* (Chicago: The University of Chicago Press, 2007), chapter 6.
80. *Disc.* 2.18.1–7 (Hard's translation, modified), 119–20.
81. Seneca's *De ira* is a tour de force analysis of the pathological passion of anger, the psychological mechanism that produces it, the harms that it brings to the angry person, the horrors it inflicts on those around the angry person, and therapies for eradicating it.
82. *Disc.* 2.18.12. Hard and Gill, 120.
83. This is Seneca's analysis of the cognitive mechanism of anger in *De Ira*, but there is no evidence in the *Discourses* that Epictetus would object to it.
84. For a discussion of Epictetus and Marcus Aurelius on the virtue of tolerance, see Andrew Fiala, "Stoic Tolerance," *Res Publica* 9 (2003): 149–68.
85. *Disc.* 2.18.25–26. Hard and Gill, 121. On this discourse compare A. A. Long 2002, 214–15.
86. *Disc.* 1.27.5–7. Hard and Gill, 60. Cf. *Disc.* 4. 1. 137.
87. In Epictetus' time, pupils inscribed lecture notes on wax tablets.
88. *Disc.* 3.16.9–11.

89. *Disc.* 3.16.12–15 (Hard's translation modified), 182. The self-attention Epictetus urges here is suggestive of Seneca's nightly self-scrutiny in *De ira* III.36.

90. See R. Dobbin, "Προαίρεσις in Epictetus," *Ancient Philosophy* 11 (1991): 111–135.

91. *Disc.* 3.16.16.

92. *Disc.* 3.12.5–8. Hard and Gill, 174. See Long 2002, 241.

93. For the importance of the medical analogy in the Stoics, see M. C. Nussbaum, *The Therapy of Desire*, chapter 9.

94. *Disc.* 4.12.1–2. Hard and Gill, 281 (modified).

95. *Disc.* 3.25.7.

96. *Disc.* 3. 25. 8–10; Hard and Gill, 218–19. This text is also discussed by Long 2002, 195–96.

97. The Greek word is *aidōs*. See Rachana Kamtekar, "ΑΙΔΩΣ in Epictetus," *Classical Philology* 93, no. 2 (April 1998): 136–60.

98. *Disc.* 3.26.11–12.

99. *Encheiridion* 30. Hard and Gill, 296.

100. For a discussion of the concepts of station (*taxis*) and role (*prosōpon*) in Epictetus, see B. E. Johnson, "Socrates, Heracles and the Deflation of Roles in Epictetus," *Ancient Philosophy* 32 (2012): 125–45.

## BIBLIOGRAPHY

Annas, Julia. "The Sage in Ancient Philosophy." In *Anthropine Sophia*, edited by F. Alesse et al., 11–27. Naples: Bibliopolis, 2008.

Blondell, Ruby. "Parental Nature and Stoic *Oikeiosis*." *Ancient Philosophy* 10 (1990): 221–42.

Clifford, William K. "The Ethics of Belief." In *The Ethics of Belief and Other Essays*. Amherst, NY: Prometheus Books, 1999.

Dobbin, Robert. "Προαίρεσις in Epictetus." *Ancient Philosophy* 11 (1991): 111–135.

Engberg-Pedersen, Troels. *The Stoic Theory of* Oikeiosis: *Moral Development and Social Interaction in Early Stoic Philosophy*. Aarhus: Aarhus Universitetsforlag, 1990.

Epictetus. *The Discourses, The Handbook, Fragments*. Translated by R. Hard. Edited by C. Gill. London: J. M. Dent, 1995.

Fiala, Andrew. "Stoic Tolerance." *Res Publica* (2003): 149–68.

Graver, Margaret R. *Stoicism and Emotion*. Chicago: University of Chicago Press, 2007.

Griffin, M. T. *Seneca: A Philosopher in Politics*. Oxford: Oxford University Press, 1976.

Inwood, Brad. *Seneca: Selected Philosophical Letters*. Oxford: Oxford University Press, 2007.

Johnson, Brian Earl. "Socrates, Heracles and the Deflation of Roles in Epictetus." *Ancient Philosophy* 32 (2012): 125–45.

Kamtekar, Rachana. "ΑΙΔΩΣ in Epictetus." *Classical Philology* 93, no. 2 (April 1998) 136–60.

Long, A. A. *Epictetus: A Stoic and Socratic Guide to Life*. Oxford: Oxford University Press, 2002.

Lutz, Cora E. "Musonius Rufus: 'The Roman Socrates.'" *Yale Classical Studies* 10 (1947): 32–147.

Musonius Rufus. *Lectures and Sayings*. Translated by C. King. Edited by W. B. Irvine. Lulu, 2010.

Newman, Robert J. "*Cotidie meditare*. Theory and Practice of the *meditatio* in Imperial Stoicism." *Aufstieg und Niedergang der römischen Welt*, Band II. 36.3: 1473–1517.

Nussbaum, Martha C. *The Therapy of Desire: Theory and Practice in Hellenistic Ethics*. Princeton: Princeton University Press, 1994.

Seneca. *Ad Lucilium epistulae morales*. 3 vols. Translated by R. M. Gummere. Cambridge, MA: Harvard University Press, 1917.

Seneca. *Moral Essays*. 3 vols. Translated by J. W. Basore. Cambridge, MA: Harvard University Press, 1985.

Seneca. *Moral and Political Essays*. Edited and translated by J. M. Cooper and J. F. Procopé. Cambridge: Cambridge University Press, 1995.

Stephens, William O. *Stoic Ethics: Epictetus and Happiness as Freedom*. London: Continuum, 2007.

———. *Marcus Aurelius: A Guide for the Perplexed*. London: Continuum, 2012.

Striker, Gisela. "Following Nature: A Study in Stoic Ethics." *Oxford Studies in Ancient Philosophy* 9 (1991): 1–73.

Vogt, Katja. "Seneca." *The Stanford Encyclopedia of Philosophy*. Winter 2012 edition. Edited by Edward N. Zalta. http://plato.stanford.edu/archives/win2012/entries/seneca/

## *Chapter Three*

# Aquinas on *Habitus*

Robert C. Miner

The aim of the whole *Secunda Pars* of the *Summa Theologiae* of Thomas Aquinas is to illuminate the rational creature's motion toward God. Its first part, the *Prima Secundae*, considers morals in general; the *Secunda Secundae* undertakes a more particular examination of virtues and vices. Beginning with an interrogation of the human end (Questions 1–5), the *Prima Secundae* moves backward, as it were, to consider acts directed to the end (Questions 6–48) and the principles from which these acts spring (Questions 49–114). Thomas distinguishes two kinds of principles: "intrinsic" (Questions 49–89) and "extrinsic" (Questions 90–114). The consideration of *habitus* in general, occurring at Questions 49–54, stands at the beginning of the treatment of intrinsic principles, followed by questions on specific habits—that is, the virtues (Questions 55–69) and vices (Questions 70–89).

The *Prima Secundae*'s treatment of habit seems to feature Aquinas at his most "scholastic." My aim is to penetrate beneath the intensely technical character of Questions 49–54, in order to grasp what is distinctive about Aquinas's conception of habit. The exposition proceeds in four steps. First, I show what Aquinas means by habits as "intrinsic principles" of human action, examining Question 49's consideration of the "substance" (*substantia*) of habits. Here I consider his reasons for distinguishing between dispositions in general, which are easily changeable, and habits, which by nature are enduring. Second, I will turn to Question 50's consideration of the "subject" (*subiectum*) of habits, probing Aquinas's view that the full range of human powers—sensitive, intellectual, and volitional—can receive habits. Third, I examine the "cause" (*causa*) of the generation, augmentation, and corruption of habits, the topic of Questions 51–53. Here we see Aquinas's concern to reconcile Aristotle's claim that habits are caused by repeated human acts with the quite different view that habits can be generated by no human agency at all. In a final section, I turn to the question of the relation between habits and freedom, showing that for Aquinas *habitus* do not preclude freedom, but are required to attain freedom in its most desirable form. To place Aquinas's view in sharper relief, I will compare it with Nietzsche's claim that "brief habits" are more desirable than enduring habits. Beginning a dialogue between Aquinas and Nietzsche on this point is valuable, not least because it shows more clearly what is at stake in the apparently technical treatment of habit.

## 1. HABITS VERSUS DISPOSITIONS

Any particular thing can have a relation to itself (*se habere in seipsa*) or to some other thing (*se habere ad aliud*).[1] But how? By what "mode of having" (*modus se habendi*) do such relations exist? The mode of having, Aquinas claims, occurs "according to some quality." Any quality that underlies such relations is a "habit" (*habitus*). Efficient digestion, easy breathing, responsive nerves—if we have these things, we do so by the quality of health. Aquinas quotes Aristotle: "habit is called a disposition, according as the thing so disposed is disposed well or badly, and regarding either itself or another, as health is a certain habit" (49.1.co).[2] It seems that habit is a particular kind of quality—a disposition. A paradigm case of habit, as the above quotation suggests, is health (*sanitas*).

But Aquinas proceeds to undermine, or at least seriously qualify, this appearance. To identify habit with disposition, he argues in the next Article, is unsound. First, "disposition" seems to be a generic term. "Habit" is not the same as "disposition"; it is a species of the genus "disposition." This alone would undermine any proposed identity between "disposition" and "habit." But Aquinas prefers another strategy. Rather than make "habit" a species of the genus "disposition," he argues that properly speaking, dispositions and habits are opposed to one another as two species within the same genus, that is, "quality." But how to construe this opposition? One way would be to take dispositions as easily changeable qualities which later become habits when they reside "in their subject perfectly, so as not to be lost easily." On this view, "disposition becomes a habit, just as a boy becomes a man" (49.2 ad 3).

Aquinas does not exactly reject the claim that habits are grown-up dispositions. But he is not satisfied with it, since he proposes a third way of construing the habit/disposition distinction, one that he takes to conform more closely to the *intentio Aristotelis*.[3] Habits and dispositions are two "diverse species of one subaltern genus" (49.2 ad 3). One does not change into the other while preserving its species. (A boy who grows into a man changes, while remaining human.) Dispositions are qualities easily lost, because their causes are changeable. Aquinas gives sickness and health as examples, thus undermining the previous Article's suggestion that health is a paradigm case of habit. Katharine Breen observes that in Question 49 "Aquinas offers three different accounts of the relation between *dispositio* and *habitus*."[4] This is true, though Aquinas is not simply inconsistent. His strategy is dialectical; it moves from an initial appearance (habits = dispositions) through a qualification (habits = dispositions grown up) to his ultimate position (habits ≠ dispositions). Breen perceptively notes that the *Summa* itself is "an attempt to inculcate virtue through repetition and variation."[5] Question 49's unfolding of the habit/disposition contrast is itself an instance of the *Summa*'s dialectical pedagogy.

Owing to the strong contrast between *habitus* and *dispositio*, Brian Davies's advice to render *habitus* in Aquinas by "disposition" cannot be followed.[6] Yet Davies and others are right to warn that Aquinas's *habitus* is far removed from the dominant sense taken by "habit" in modern languages.[7] As Breen writes:

> While *habit* suggests a pattern of mindless or unconscious repetition . . . *habitus* supplements natural capacities through deliberate and diligent practice. If the paradigmatic example of *habit* is drug use, especially in American vocabularies, the equivalent examples of *habitus*—for figures as chronologically disparate as Aristotle, Boethius, Isidore of Seville, and Thomas Aquinas—are knowledge and virtue, *scientia* and *virtus*.[8]

What makes "sciences and virtues" exemplary habits (49.2 ad 3)? Aquinas argues that unlike dispositions, sciences and virtues have unchangeable causes, and are therefore changed themselves only with difficulty. A person can be "disposed" to a particular way of knowing, but this implies nothing more than a shaky grip on the science, one that can easily be lost. Displaying a casual interest in a science, or even knowing some of its facts and theorems, is not to "have" the science in any profound sense. To acquire the science as *habitus*, one must grasp it from the inside, possessing it at the deepest level. The move from casual disposition to internal possession is not a small step, a difference of degree. It is more nearly a quantum leap, a difference in kind.

As Aquinas understands it, habits are neither identical to nor on the same plane as dispositions. Habits are hard to gain and hard to lose, unlike dispositions, which are essentially transient, for example, sickness and health. Habits have a "long duration" (*diuturnitas*: 49.2 ad 3) that no disposition has or can have. It is not that habits are altogether impossible to change. But they are, Aquinas insists, "difficult to change, according to their very notion (*ratio*)" (49.2 ad 3). One might think that health is not only a weak example of a habit, but not even a habit at all, since its essence is to come and go. Yet Aquinas refrains from concluding that health in no sense is a habit. It is, he says, "called" (*dicitur*) a habit or a "habitual disposition" (49.3 ad 3)—not in relation to operation, but in relation to nature, considered as a principle of operation. Enough of a connection between health and action exists for health to count as a habit in a wide sense, one that blurs the distinction between habit and disposition, as the phrase *habitualis dispositio* does.[9]

But just what makes some qualities deeply rooted and others so transitory? To answer this question, we must probe Aquinas's thinking about the soil in which habits are deeply rooted. The clearest examples of habit, he says, are "sciences and virtues." For a science to exist in a person as a *habitus*, it does so as an improvement of the intellect. When the intellect succeeds in grasping truth in a particular domain, it accomplishes what is suitable to its nature, since its natural end is to know truth. This accomplishment does not merely alter its condition temporarily, in a way that can easily be lost. ("Learning changes us; it does what all nourishment does which also does not merely 'preserve'—as physiologists know.")[10] It actualizes its potential; it brings it closer to being the kind of thing that it naturally is. It does so by completing its form, achieving the good at which it aims. Such progress, once made, is not easily lost. In fact, the challenge for Aquinas will be to account for the way in which a quality so deeply rooted in a thing's nature can be lost at all. (Aquinas takes up this challenge in Question 53.)

Habit is the actualization of potential. But this does not, Aquinas emphasizes, prevent it from *also* being a type of potentiality, though in a different sense. To acquire a command of Latin means to have the capacity for reading and writing Latin. But "to have Latin," as we still say, does not mean that one is actually reading or writing Latin at every moment. It means that with respect to any particular act of using Latin, its possessor stands in a relation of potency. *Habitus* in this sense is Aristotle's "first actuality," standing midway between pure power and act.[11] It is ready potential, able to be actualized in an operation (Aristotle's "second actuality") whenever the possessor of the habit wishes. For any quality to be a habit, it must be the enabling condition of some operation.

If habits are qualities that actualize a thing's potential, enabling it to achieve what suits its nature, then it appears that habits are essentially good qualities. But if this is true, how can there be evil habits? That Aquinas thinks there are evil habits (*habitus malus*) is clear. These are habits which dispose a person to acts that are "discordant with human nature, since they are against reason" (54.3 co). Evil habits, though "not suitable" (*non conveniens*) to human nature, are nonetheless capable of taking root in the soul when they are connected with acts that the agent perceives as suitable in some respect. Like virtuous habits, vicious habits are intrinsically connected to the agent's apprehension of what he or she desires *sub ratione boni*.

But to say that habits are intrinsically connected to some perception of what is good or suitable for that agent does not imply their necessity. What, then, makes habits necessary? Asking what kind of being requires habit, Aquinas isolates three requirements. First, the being must be imperfect, in a state of potency. "If something of its nature is not composed of potency and act, and whose substance just is its operation, and is itself on account of itself, then there is no place for habit or disposition, as is clear in God" (49.4 co). Second, the being must be in potency toward many things. A stone by nature moves downward and only downward; its natural potency is to only one thing. For a thing to admit of habituation, it must be capable of "being determined by means of multiple modes, and toward diverse things" (49.4 co). Both God and the stone (even when thrown up 10,000 times, as Aristotle says) fail this test. The third requirement is that "many factors concur to disposing the subject toward one of the things to which it is in potency, factors which can be made to correspond in diverse ways, so that the subject is disposed well or badly toward its form or its operation" (49.4 co). In this sense, Aquinas suggests, health and beauty are useful illustrations, because many things must come together in some equilibrium to produce these qualities. Is there anything common to all three requirements? Composition of act and potency, multiplicity of determination toward diverse things, the necessity for many things in proportion—each of these is a mode of complexity. For Aquinas, a certain complexity seems to be the basic precondition of *habitus*.

## 2. SITES OF HABITUATION: BODY, SENSITIVE APPETITE, INTELLECT, WILL

The overt topic of Question 50 is "What is the subject of habits?" This is to ask in what the habits are seated, or which aspects of the human person are susceptible to habituation. The body cannot be directly habituated, since the natural qualities of the body are determined to a single mode of operation, rather than in potency *ad multa*. Nevertheless, bodily qualities like health and beauty which have some connection to the soul can be called "habitual dispositions," without being habits in the full sense. "A habitual disposition can be in the body, since it is related to the soul as a subject is to a form. And in this way health, beauty and the like are called 'habitual dispositions'" (50.1 co). But if *habitus* is taken more strictly, then it seems difficult to see how health can be a habit, since only "qualities of the soul are called habits *simpliciter*" (50.1 ad 1).[12] Though Aquinas likes to quote Aristotle's teaching that health is a habit, he recognizes the difficulty of reconciling the claim that health is a habit in the strict sense with the distinction between transient dispositions and enduring habits. Thus he ultimately rejects the view that health is an exemplary case of habit. Yet he seems reluctant to understand himself as departing from Aristotle, even appealing to his Greek. Aristotle does not say that enduring health is a habit, but that it is "*like* a habit (*ut habitus*), as is attested in the Greek" (50.1 ad 2).

If habits are seated principally in the soul, Aquinas asks in Article 2 of Question 50, are they to be found in the entire soul, its very essence? Or ought we to look to its particular powers? Aquinas addresses this question by recalling that habit can be related either to nature or to action (*operatio*). If habits are enabling conditions of action, as they principally are, then they are necessarily seated in the particular powers of the soul, since "the soul is the principle of action through its powers" (50.2.co). But what if habits are related to nature, as in the case of habitual dispositions? The same result holds, because "habitual dispositions" like health and beauty are easily changeable and thus not to be confused with the soul, "since the soul itself is the completive form of human nature" (50.2 co). Transient dispositions would not be sufficiently noble, Aquinas implies, to belong to the soul's essence. In fact, they are not even located in the soul's powers, but in the body "through an ordering to the soul" (50.2 co). Yet there is an exception. If we are speaking of habitual dispositions that are ordered not to human nature, but to a superior nature of which "man can be a participator," then we can acknowledge a habit that permeates the entire soul. This is the habit of grace, which belongs to the soul according to its essence (see also 110.4). The exception of grace is important to note. It marks the precise point at which Aquinas breaks from the Aristotelian teaching (quoted at 50.2.sc) that diverse habits necessarily belong to diverse parts of the soul.

If, however, we are speaking of acquired rather than infused habits, then Aristotle points us in the right direction. To determine what in the human person can be habituated, we must look to the soul's particular powers. The remainder of Question 50 considers three: the powers of the sensitive part (Article 3), the intellect (Article 4), and the will (Article 5). To the extent that the senses are moved by natural instinct as opposed to reason, they are not susceptible to habituation, since natural instinct is ordered *ad unum* rather than *ad multa*. It would seem to follow that brute animals moved only by natural instinct can have no habits at all. Regarding *habitus* in the strict sense, this does follow. But Aquinas does not deny some analogue of habit in brute animals. "Since brute animals are by human reason disposed through a kind of custom (*per quandam consuetudinem*) to some action or another, in this way there can be in brute animals a certain mode of habit" (50.3 ad 2). Brute animals can be subjects of conditioning; while not possessing *habitus*, properly speaking, they do have "custom" (*consuetudo*).

Breen argues that a strong contrast between *habitus* and *consuetudo* pervades medieval thought—beginning with Augustine, for whom "the evil customs associated with *consuetudo* are regularly contrasted with a holier way of life."[13] Those who aspire to this holier way of life wear not a costume (etymologically linked to "custom") but a *habitus*.[14] Medieval authors, Breen claims, "tend to use *consuetudo* to designate the second natures of pagans, heretics, and layfolk, while *habitus* refers to Christians, orthodox believers, and vowed religious—in some cases regardless of the actual practices involved."[15] However apt a description of a general medieval tendency, does it apply to Aquinas specifically? In the treatment of sin, Aquinas notes that sin becomes "in a way connatural, according as *consuetudo* and *habitus* alter nature" (78.2 co).[16] Any power held by custom to degrade nature seems to be shared by *habitus*. If Aquinas privileges *habitus* over *consuetudo*, he does so not because he thinks habits are necessarily less corruptive than customs. In fact, the worst *habitus* are *more* corruptive than bad customs, since their closer relation to reason and will gives them the power to corrupt what is higher. The closer relation to reason is *both* what makes habits potentially more corrupting than and yet superior to custom. For Aquinas, this relation is attested by *habitus* good and bad. As Torrell writes:

> However, and this is also part of what it means to be human, there are also bad *habitus*, the vices or sins that, while developing the perfective ease that is implied in the notion of *habitus*, are exercised in a direction that turns away from the final end and so lead us astray (qq. 71–89). A substantial treatise is devoted to them, so we know what we are dealing with. But it must also be said that its place in the movement of the whole does not emphasize sin. Thomas's attention is positively oriented.[17]

Properly speaking, *habitus* is something more and other than *consuetudo*. The reason, Aquinas says, is that custom "lacks the notion (*ratio*) of habit with respect to use of the will, since it does not have the power (*dominium*) of using or not using, which seems to belong to the notion of habit" (50.3 ad 2). Aquinas's use of *dominium* suggests a deep connection between the capacity for *habitus*, in the proper sense, and the possession of *dominium* reserved for creatures made to the image of God (cf. Gen 1:26).[18]

Only creatures with reason and will can possess habits, as distinct from customs. But this does not imply that only reason and will are susceptible to habituation. Since the sensitive appetite in human beings is capable of obeying rational command, it can be habituated. How does this happen? Aquinas says little about the matter in the Questions on habit in general; he waits until considering the particular habits that perfect the concupiscible and irascible parts of the sensitive appetite. Here he emphasizes that what is chiefly capable of being habituated is sensitive appetite rather than sensitive apprehension. Within the latter, the exterior apprehensive powers (e.g., vision and hearing) are not susceptible to habituation at all, since they are by nature ordered to determinate acts. They lack the indeterminacy that habituation requires. But Aquinas does not bluntly conclude that none of the sensitive apprehensive powers can be habituated. On the contrary, the imagination, memory, and the cogitative power (also called the "particular reason") can receive habits.[19] That not only the sensitive appetite, but also the interior powers of sensitive apprehension, can be habituated is crucial. Were this not the case, there would be no possibility of educating the passions.[20]

Beyond the sensitive appetite, habits are seated in the intellect and will. This is true because both powers are in potency, capable of any number of operations that will move the rational creature nearer to or further from its telos. Article 4's consideration of intellectual habits gives little information about the virtues of wisdom, science, and understanding (this is postponed until Question 57). It does indicate Aquinas's resolute opposition to Averroes's reading of Aristotle on the "possible intellect" (*intellectus possibilis*).[21] On the Averroist reading, differences among human beings with respect to the intellectual virtues must be traced back not to the possible intellect, which is common to all, but to the interior sensitive powers, which vary from one person to the next. Aquinas combats the Averroist proposal both by a series of arguments about the proper reading of Aristotle and by the assertion that Averroes's proposal is "contrary the truth of the thing" (50.4 co). As for the will, it requires habits not in order to be inclined to good as such—this belongs to its nature as a power—but because the human approach to good is complex. "Since the good of reason is varied in multiple ways, it is necessary that the will be inclined to some determinate good of reason through some habit" (50.5 ad 3). But we approach what is simply good by desiring and willing particular goods. For this to happen, the power of *voluntas* must receive multiple habits that correspond to the multiform character of the *bonum rationis*.

In human beings, habits arise from and are shaped by complexity and multiplicity. Complexity and multiplicity do not, however, constitute the deepest grounding of habit. Aquinas shows this by Question 50's concluding treatment of habits in angels. As immaterial substances, angels do not seem to require habits, as the Article's third objector observes: "since angels are simple substances, it seems that there are not dispositions and habits in them" (50.6 obj. 3). Yet angels are not to be confused with pure act. Despite their intellectual superiority to human beings, they too are in potency. "Since no angel attains to the perfection of God, but stands apart from him by an infinite distance (*in infinitum distat*)—on account of this, in order to attain to God himself through intellect and will, the angels need some habits, existing in potency as it were with respect to that pure act" (50.6 co). What ensures that even angels need habits are two things. First, the simple fact of not being identical to God—and therefore infinitely distant from Him. Second, the capacity for participating in divine wisdom and goodness. If angels met only the first condition, they would not necessarily require habits, since there are other beings that are not God and yet cannot receive habits, because their natural potency is to only one thing. Angels, however, participate in God through the exercise of intellect and will, by means of multiple species and things (50.6 ad 2). For these powers to be perfected, for their potential to become more fully actual, habits are necessary.

The closing article of Question 50 might strike the reader as a classic case of "scholasticism" (in the pejorative sense). It seems as though Aquinas were asking whether habits are required for angels (however many) to dance on the head of a pin. But attending to the angelic case is valuable, because it shows that the deepest grounding of *habitus* is not material complexity but potency itself. What most radically ensures the need for habits is the combination of infinite distance from God with the capacity for participation in divine wisdom and goodness.

## 3. BIRTH, GROWTH, DIMINUTION, AND CORRUPTION OF HABITS

After saying what habits are, where they are seated, and why they are necessary, Aquinas turns to their generation (Question 51), their augmentation (Question 52), and their diminution and corruption (Question 53). The task of Question 51 is to harmonize Aristotle's teaching that habits are naturally caused by repeated human acts with a strikingly different teaching about the divine origin of habits. To what extent is nature the cause of habits? The question is complex, since both terms in the expression "from nature" are ambiguous. "Nature" can mean either "specific nature" (e.g., humanity) or "individual nature" (e.g., Socrates or Plato). "From" can mean either "entirely from nature" or "partly from nature, partly from an outside source." A *habitus*, then, can be "from nature" in the following ways[22]:

1. Entirely from a thing's specific nature
2. Entirely from its individual nature or temperament
3. Partly from its specific nature, and partly from an outside source
4. Partly from its individual nature, and partly from an outside source

Habitual dispositions, as opposed to habits in the strict sense, may be (1) or (2). Health can derive entirely from a person's nature (whether specific or individual), with no extrinsic principle intervening. But since a person can be healed by means of medicine, cooperating with nature, health can also fit (3) or (4). By contrast, a habit in the strict sense—one that is seated in a power of the soul and ordered to action—can never fit (1) or (2). No *habitus* in the strict sense arises entirely by nature. While we may call some habits "natural," *habitus naturales* always arise partly from nature and partly from an exterior principle; they conform only to (3) or (4). This holds for both apprehensive and appetitive habits, he adds, but in different ways. Natural habits exist in apprehensive powers "according to beginnings" (*secundum inchoa-*

*tionem*). This is true of some natural apprehensive habits that fit (3). Aquinas's example: the habit of understanding principles, for example, "every whole is larger than its part." This capacity is present naturally, but only *secundum inchoationem*. For the habit to be fully formed, its possessor must have recourse to intelligible species received through external phantasms, so that she knows what a whole is and what a part is. Other natural apprehensive habits are also present *secundum inchoationem*, but according to (4). Aquinas's example: one person understands better than another, because his sensible organs are more developed than another's, and "we need the sensitive powers for the operation of intellect" (51.1 co).

Natural appetitive habits, by contrast, are not necessarily present *secundum inchoationem*. What, then, makes them natural, if nothing of their substance is given by nature? Here Aquinas distinguishes an appetitive habit's "substance" (*substantia*) from its "origins" (*principia*). His example is the *principia iuris communis*. The "principles of common law," while not the same as the virtues, are nonetheless rightly called the "seeds of the virtues" (*seminalia virtutum*), since they are planted in the human soul by nature. If these seeds are to grow into habits, an exterior principle must cooperate. This is the rule for virtues whose *principia* are implanted in human nature, according to (c). There are, however, some appetitive habits that do seem to arise from individual bodily temperament. Such habits, and not just their beginnings, are present in particular persons *secundum inchoationem*, conforming to (d). "There are certain people who are disposed by their own bodily temperament to chastity or meekness, or to other such things" (51.1 co). While the substance and not merely the seeds of such habits are authentically present, their presence is still inchoate. Full formation requires the work of an exterior principle. Aquinas does not go back on his claim that in human beings, natural habits are never present entirely from nature.

If habits are never simply given by nature, how are they caused? In Articles 2 and 3 of Question 51, Aquinas develops an Aristotelian response to this question. Habits are intrinsic principles or causes of acts. But before any habit can perform this function, it must itself be caused by a series of acts. These habit-causing acts cannot be traced back to the habit in question, since *ex hypothesi* the habit has not yet been generated. From what, then, do habit-causing acts arise? Aquinas answers: "Acts of the appetitive power proceed from the appetitive power according as it is moved by the apprehensive power representing the object" (51.2 co). Such acts, whether passions or volitions, will occur repeatedly in accordance with the apprehensive power, which in humans is directed or misdirected by reason (*ratio*). These repeated acts will produce habits. "For everything which is acted upon and moved by another, is disposed by the act of the agent, whence from multiple acts is generated a certain quality in the power that is acted upon and moved, a quality which is termed 'habit'" (51.2 co). The active power, the mover which produces the original habit-causing passions and volitions, is apprehension. This holds, Aquinas says, for both appetitive and apprehensive habits. "Just as habits of moral virtue are caused in the appetitive powers, according as they are moved by reason (*ratio*), so habits of the sciences are caused in the understanding (*intellectus*), according as it is moved by the first propositions (*primae propositiones*)" (51.2 co). In both cases, habits are passive principles caused by an active principle.[23] For the appetitive power, the mover is some version of *ratio*. For the apprehensive power, the mover is the "understanding of first principles" (*intellectus principiorum*: 51.2 ad 3).

Rarely is a single act sufficient to cause a habit. But why are multiple acts required? Aquinas compares the appetitive power to recalcitrant material, unable to be conquered by a single act, even if the conqueror is reason.[24] The appetitive power comports itself diversely toward many things, indeed as many as are perceived as either suitable or repugnant. But any particular act of reason is a judgment about here and now, concerning what "is to be desired according to determinate reasons and circumstances" (51.3 co). Owing to the mismatch between the indeterminacy of appetite and the determinacy of reason, it follows that "appetitive power is not entirely conquered by a single act, so as to be inclined in a natural manner to the same thing in the majority of cases, which belongs to the habit of virtue. And thus a habit of virtue cannot be caused by one act, but by many" (51.3 co). Is this true of the apprehensive power as well? Yes, Aquinas says, if the habit to be caused is opinion. Many particular acts are needed to produce an abiding opinion. But if the habit is one of genuine knowledge (*scientia*), only a single act is required. "Just one proposition known through itself convinces the understanding to assent firmly to the conclusion." This does not, however, hold with respect to the lower apprehensive powers, such as memory. In this case, "it is necessary for the same acts to be reiterated, so that something is firmly impressed on the memory" (51.3 co). Yet even regarding lower habits, Aquinas does not univocally hold that multiple acts are necessary. Some bodily habits, he says, can be caused by a single act if the active principle is sufficiently strong, "as sometimes a dose of strong medicine immediately brings about health" (51.3 co).

Question 51 moves from the usual case, in which the causation of habit requires multiple acts, to an acknowledgment of atypical cases, for which a single act suffices. What about the most extreme case? This would be the possibility of a habit that is caused neither by nature nor by a single human act. Aquinas concludes Question 51 by arguing that such habits are not only possible, but even necessary. The premise is the one stated at the very beginning of the *Summa*, that humans have a supernatural end that surpasses the power of human nature. To be disposed to this end, there must be habits that also surpass the power of human nature, "since habits must be proportioned to whatever humans are disposed to according to those habits" (51.4 co). The argument seems unlikely to convince anyone who does not already take human beings to have a supernatural end. But this would not trouble Aquinas, for whom *sacra doctrina* derives its very necessity from the assumption that humans are directed to God, as to an end that surpasses reason's grasp. If the end is above nature, and if habits must be proportioned to their end, then it follows that such habits cannot be of human origin. "Whence such habits cannot be present in man except from divine infusion, just as with all the gratuitous virtues" (51.4 co). Aquinas gives a second reason for divinely infused virtues. God can directly produce the effects of secondary causes without the mediation of these causes. Sometimes to manifest his power, God infuses into man "even those habits which can be caused by natural power. Thus he gave the Apostles knowledge of the Scriptures and all the tongues, which men can acquire by study or custom, though not so perfectly" (51.4 co).[25] Both of the response's arguments are frankly theological. This fact is difficult to explain by readings which construe the relation between the *prima secundae* and *secunda secundae* as a distinction between philosophy and theology.

In Question 52, Aquinas turns to the growth or "increase" (*augmentum*) of habits. Can habits increase, and if so, how is this possible? The issue is surprisingly controversial. Aquinas notes four different opinions on the topic, before concluding Article 1's exceptionally lengthy response with a brief statement of his own position. "Intensity and lessening may be considered in habits and dispositions in two ways" (52.1 co). The first occurs according to the habit itself: "just as health is called greater or lesser, or greater or lesser knowledge (*scientia*), which extends itself to more or fewer things." The second occurs according to the subject's participation, "just as equal science or health is received more in one than in another, according to diverse aptitude, either from nature or from custom" (52.1 co). Given that habits can increase, Article 2 asks, do they increase by addition? The question seems bizarre: how else would they increase? By subtraction? But Aquinas has nothing so outré in mind. He means to draw a contrast between "addition," in the sense of adding one form to another, and an increase in the subject's intensity of participation in the form, without anything being added to the form. Habits do not generally increase by addition, he argues, because adding a form tends to change the species, as adding one to the number three changes the species of number to four. The typical mode of increase is not addition, but an intensifying of a subject's participation in a form which remains constant. Even so, Aquinas concludes, some habits do increase by addition. If a person has geometry as a habit, and proceeds to add to the number of geometrical conclusions she knows, she has increased her habit of geometry by addition.

Question 52 closes by asking whether every act increases its corresponding habit. It would seem that it does. But Aquinas rejects this claim: "not every bit of food consumed actually increases an animal's size, nor does every drop of water hollow a stone, but the multiplication of food results at last in growth" (52.3 co). The example is not fully persuasive, since every drop of water, no matter how tiny, works to hollow out a stone. (Cf. Lucretius, *De rerum natura* 1.313: "stilicidi casus lapidem cavat.") More insightful is Aquinas's suggestion that some acts actually weaken their habits. This does not happen generally. It occurs in the special case in which a rational agent has genuinely established a *habitus*, but comes to perform its acts feebly or apathetically, in a manner that "proportionally falls short of the intensity of the habit" (52.3 co). Torrell gives the example of a craftsman who stops using his *habitus* to the maximum capacity, so that his skill "degenerates into a repetitive routine and, instead of the artist in potentiality that he was, the artisan remains an honest tinkerer. Only creative work in search of perfection and new ways of expression could boost him to a higher level."[26]

Habits may be gradually weakened by languid performance of their acts. Such weakening or "diminution" (*diminutio*) leads to their corruption: "the diminution of a habit is a road to its corruption" (53.2 co). Aquinas argues that corruption occurs in two ways: *per se* and *per accidens*. *Per se* corruption occurs when the habit itself has a contrary that can replace it, for example, when a vice supplants a moral virtue through acts caused by an erroneous judgment of reason. Intellectual virtues also admit of *per se* corruption, though less clearly. The habit of *scientia*, Aquinas says, can be corrupted, since either the true premises from which *scientia* derives may be replaced by false premises, or the demonstrative syllogism which constitutes *scientia* can be replaced by a sophistical syllogism. Unlike *scientia*, the habit of *intellectus* (insight into first principles) cannot be corrupted, since the mind cannot actually think the contraries of the first principles that are a condition of any thinking at all. *Per accidens* corruption involves not the replacement of a habit by its contrary, but the corruption of the subject in which the habits are seated. If the subject is immaterial and incorruptible, such as the intellect, the habit seated there is not vulnerable to *per accidens* corruption. Nonetheless, even intellectual habits are not purely seated in the intellect. The habit of *scientia*, Aquinas says, is "indeed principally in the possible intellect, but secondarily in the apprehensive sensitive powers." The dependence on sense is sufficient to render it vulnerable to corruption *per accidens*, since "the intellect in its act has need of the sensitive powers, which are impeded by a bodily change" (53.1 ad 3).

The final Article of Question 53 asks whether a habit can be corrupted or diminished simply by ceasing to act. That this is not just one mode of corruption, but more nearly *the* way in which habits are lost, is strongly suggested by Question 53's proemium, which characterizes Article 3 as an article "de modo corruptionis et diminutionis" (53 pr). Though deeply rooted in our nature, habits are not so entrenched as to be invulnerable. Breen's claim that for Aristotle "established habits are unchangeable" is overstated, since Aristotle argues that virtuous friendships can end precisely because one party to the friendship can lose virtue.[27] According to Aquinas, any number of causes threaten to destroy or weaken established habits. If continual action is not undertaken to overcome such causes, they will reassert themselves and destroy the habit. Aquinas writes:

> For any habit whose contraries grow up over time, contraries that must be taken away by an act proceeding from the habit—habits of this kind are diminished or even wholly destroyed by long cessation from act, as is clear in both science and virtue. (53.3 co)

Habits are difficult but not impossible to lose. On this point Aristotle and Aquinas agree. But in giving a fuller explanation of *how* habits are lost, Aquinas seems to go beyond Aristotle.

## 4. *HABITUS* AND FREEDOM

When a person with the *habitus* of generosity encounters someone in need, she will give as she is able. Does she have a choice in the matter? In some sense, she does not. Often she engages in no decision procedure; she performs no cost-benefit analysis. She simply gives what she can, because "that's the kind of person she is" (as her admirers rightly say). Her action appears determined by her character. It may seem not to proceed from free choice, as it might for a different kind of person who, lacking the *habitus* of generosity, will need to *decide* whether it makes sense for him to do what a generous person would do, or else to act in some other way. Some commentators take these Aristotelian considerations to imply that for those whose characters are formed, free will has no place. Since Aquinas believes in free will, these commentators think, he seems obliged to break with Aristotle. Thus Katharine Breen: "*Habitus* [for Aquinas] works by whittling down an array of possible actions to the most likely, though unlike Aristotelian *hexis* it never entirely precludes free will."[28] This judgment is valuable. What makes it so valuable? Not because it is correct—it is in fact deeply questionable—but because it brings to light a way of thinking that we are likely to take for granted, while being alien to both Aristotle and Aquinas.

Let us begin with Aristotle. What could lead an interpreter to believe that for Aristotle, action that proceeds from a *hexis* or *habitus* is unfree? The answer cannot be Aristotle's text, which forcefully points in the opposite direction. Someone with a good *hexis* (a virtue) engages in actions that deserve praise; someone with a bad *hexis* (a vice) engages in actions that deserve blame. Which actions deserve praise and blame? Aristotle's answer:

those which are "voluntary" (*hekon*). But is not the generous person constrained by her character to act in a certain way? Aristotle does not think so. Though actions done under constraint are unfree, "an act is done under constraint when the initiative or source of motion comes from without" (*Nicomachean Ethics* 1110a1–2). Since actions that proceed from generosity (or any other *hexis*) originate from within, they are not in Aristotle's sense "done under constraint." Human actions done from a *hexis* are voluntary. They are also—and more strongly—the result of what Aristotle calls "choice" (*proairesis*).[29] "For choice seems to be very closely related to virtue and to be a more reliable criterion for judging character than actions are" (1111b7).

Since Aristotle expressly argues that virtuous actions are voluntary and chosen, it seems difficult to sustain the verdict that he takes acting from *hexis* to preclude freedom. But why do Breen and others suppose the contrary? Not from any textual evidence, but from a tendency to identify a very specific notion of freedom with freedom itself. To see what generates the appearance of a conflict between freedom and acting from habit, recall the example of generosity. Many options that are open to the calculating non-virtuous agent are closed to the person with the *habitus* of generosity. Actions that are live options for others are not possibilities for her; they are "ruled out" by her character. If freedom consists in having the largest possible number of options, along with the ability to decide between them, then indeed the generous person is unfree. But whose idea of freedom is this? Certainly not Aristotle's, since an act is voluntary as long as it proceeds from within, regardless of whether there are other options from which to choose. It is not the medieval idea of free will as stated by Peter Lombard: "free will is that faculty of reason and will whereby one chooses the good with the help of grace, or evil without this help."[30] So which idea of freedom is it? One may be tempted to say "the modern idea." But this would not be quite correct, since (beyond the fact that one finds different and conflicting ideas of freedom within modernity), it too has medieval origins. It is, Servais Pinckaers argues, the idea of freedom as theorized by William of Ockham. For Ockham, freedom does not proceed from intelligence and will. It is radically prior to both. "For I can freely choose to know or not to know, to will or not to will," he said.[31] After Ockham, Descartes and others call this the "freedom of indifference." In Pinckaers's summary:

> It was the power to opt for the *yes* or the *no*, to choose between what reason dictated and its contrary, between willing and not willing, acting and not acting, between what the law prescribed and its contrary. Thus freedom consisted in an indetermination or a radical indifference in the will regarding contraries, in such a way that actions were produced in a wholly contingent way.[32]

If one simply identifies “free will” with “freedom of indifference,” as described above, then it does seem that *habitus* eliminates or minimizes free will. When Breen says that Aristotelian *hexis* “entirely precludes free will,” she clearly (if not consciously) has in mind the freedom of indifference. But if we identify freedom with what Pinckaers terms “freedom for excellence”—a move far more in keeping with Aristotle’s text—then the tension between *habitus* and freedom vanishes. Virtue is not only compatible with maximum freedom, but also its necessary condition, since only the virtuous person can consistently and voluntarily choose to perform acts that manifest human excellence.

We are now in a position to return to Aquinas. As for Aristotle, so for Thomas: if one has in mind the freedom of indifference, then habits will necessarily appear as restrictions of freedom. But the freedom conferred by good *habitus* has little to do with the freedom of choosing among a wide range of options. When Aquinas describes a good *habitus* (that is, a virtue) as the “perfection of a power” (55.1 co), he does not mean an expansion of the capacity to decide between alternatives. The description of virtue as *perfectio potentiae* implies a very different type of expansion: the freedom to perform acts that are possible only for those in whom the power is perfected, or is growing to perfection. I have already mentioned the example of someone who possesses the command of a language. A person who “has Latin” has the power or freedom to express herself in Latin, quite unlike the person who has no Latin or is merely “disposed” to Latin. Pinckaers provides an even more powerful example. Consider a child with musical aptitude who is enrolled in piano lessons. At first she will likely experience the demand to practice daily as an abridgement of her freedom, since it prevents her from doing other things that she finds more pleasurable. But if she continues her lessons, she will learn to play her assigned pieces accurately, rhythmically, and sensitively—that is, musically. Eventually, she will learn to go beyond the set pieces and improvise, or begin to compose works of her own. Pinckaers comments:

> In this very example, we can clearly see a new kind of freedom. Of course anyone is free to bang out notes haphazardly on the piano, as the fancy strikes him. But this is a rudimentary, savage sort of freedom. It cloaks an incapacity to play even the simplest pieces accurately and well. On the other hand, the person who really possesses the art of playing the piano has acquired a new freedom. He can play whatever he chooses, and also compose new pieces. His musical freedom could be described as the gradually acquired ability to execute works of his choice with perfection. It is based on natural dispositions and stabilized by means of regular, progressive exercises, or properly speaking, a *habitus*.[33]

For Aquinas this is precisely the kind of freedom conferred by a *habitus*. Such freedom for excellence, as Pinckaers argues, is “not to be confused with the freedom to make mistakes, which is implied by the choice of contraries, but lies rather in the ability to avoid them, without conscious effort."[34] Having little to do with the freedom of indifference, it more nearly resembles the kind of freedom that Spinoza calls "power of acting."

Good *habitus*, in Aquinas's sense, have the power to confer freedom on their possessor. But this will not be clear to a person whose primary sense of freedom is freedom of indifference. From a different perspective, my argument may fail to persuade someone who suspects that abiding habits, even if "good" in some sense, necessarily oppose free play and experimentation. Nietzsche voices something like this suspicion:

> *Enduring habits* I hate. I feel as if a tyrant had come near me and as if the air I breathe had thickened when events take such a turn that it appears that they will inevitably give rise to enduring habits; for example, owing to an official position, constant association with the same people, a permanent domicile, or unique good health. Yes, at the very bottom of my soul I feel grateful to all my misery and bouts of sickness and everything about me that is imperfect, because this sort of thing leaves me with a hundred backdoors through which I can escape from enduring habits.[35]

It appears that Nietzsche's perspective could not be more opposed to Aquinas. While he professes to love "brief habits" (*kurze Gewohnheiten*), his nature rebels against "enduring habits" (*dauernden Gewohnheiten*). For Aquinas, as we have seen, the only habits in the strict sense of the term are enduring habits, as distinct from transient states or habitual dispositions. Aquinas's insistence that every habit, in the true sense of the term, is an enduring habit, suggests that we are left with an impasse.

Nonetheless, I do not think we are stuck with an intractable opposition between Aquinas and Nietzsche on the point. What are the "enduring habits" whose tyranny Nietzsche fears? They are not so much qualities of character as customs contracted through relations with others. The fear of holding an official position (to take his first example) is perfectly valid. As another aphorist whom Nietzsche admired writes: "we say that a person occupies an official position, whereas it is the official position that occupies him."[36] A person who identifies himself with a position, and thereby loses the power to detach himself from it, will likely be dominated by the customs proper to the position. Nietzsche is right to suspect that such customs are to be resisted. They close the person to new ways of seeing; they stifle the spirit and prevent its flourishing. Similarly, living in the same place or always associating with the same people can reinforce the ego's need to remain attached to particular customs, long after they have outlived their usefulness.

These considerations suggest that Nietzsche's attack on "enduring habits" is not as opposed to Aquinas as it first appears. Aquinas can agree that "enduring habits" in Nietzsche's sense should be resisted, particularly if the habits in question are not innocuous routines, but stubbornly held customs that prevent the self from acquiring genuine *habitus* which confer the freedom to act in ways that are noble and excellent. Moreover, despite his "immoralism," Nietzsche himself recognizes that some dispositions are worth cultivating, even going so far as to call them "virtues" (*Tugenden*). His attack on enduring habits does not make him hostile to the very idea of *habitus* in Aquinas's sense. We can go further, noticing that Nietzsche recognizes both the discipline needed to acquire good *habitus* and the freedom conferred by these *habitus*. He invokes the example of language: "one should recall the compulsion under which every language so far has achieved strength and freedom—the metrical compulsion of rhyme and rhythm." Anarchists who throw around such terms as "free" and "free-spirited," contrasting them with an alleged "tyranny of capricious laws," fail to perceive, Nietzsche says, a "curious fact."[37] What is this curious fact? He writes:

> All there is or has been on earth of freedom, subtlety, boldness, dance, and masterly sureness, whether in thought itself or in government, or in rhetoric and persuasion, in the arts just as in ethics, has developed only owing to the "tyranny of capricious laws"; and in all seriousness, the probability is by no means small that precisely this is "nature" and "natural"—and *not* that *laisser aller*.[38]

Nietzsche neither provides nor intends to provide grounds for contesting the core idea of Aquinas's *habitus*. Nonetheless, we should conclude by noting two important differences. First, the particular virtues that Nietzsche would recognize as good *habitus* differ strikingly from Aquinas's catalog of virtues. He has no room for the infused virtues, let alone the gifts. And when he does name four virtues, as he occasionally likes to do, they are not the cardinal virtues of prudence, justice, courage, and justice. *Daybreak* commends honesty, magnanimity, courage, politeness, claiming that these are "what the four cardinal virtues want us to be."[39] Second, although Nietzsche substantially rejects the freedom of indifference and may even articulate his own version of the "freedom for excellence," he nonetheless remains suspicious of the idea that good *habitus* pose no threat at all to human freedom. He exhorts his reader "to remain master of one's four virtues: of courage, insight, sympathy, and solitude." Not only one's passions and vices, but even one's virtues can compromise one's freedom, unless one remains their master. For Aquinas, this is not coherent. If good *habitus* inform the deepest, most ruling part of the human person, it is difficult (if not impossible) to see how anything else in the person would be capable of "mastering" them. This is a genuine and significant difference.

Yet even here, the comparison to Nietzsche is instructive. Aquinas does not regard *habitus* seated in the powers of the soul as supreme rulers. They must be guided, if not exactly "mastered" in Nietzsche's sense, by something else. This "something else" cannot be another habit seated in the soul's powers. It must come from outside the soul. For Aquinas, this is the extrinsic principle of human actions with which the *Prima Secundae* concludes. *Habitus* seated in the soul's powers must finally yield to what is above and beyond them—to grace.

## NOTES

1. It is customary to note the derivation of *habitus* from the Latin *habere*, "to have" (see, e.g., Jean-Pierre Torrell, O.P., *Saint Thomas Aquinas*, vol. 2, *Spiritual Master*, trans. Robert Royal [Washington, DC: Catholic University of America Press, 2003], 264). But as Katharine Breen observes, "Aquinas derives the philosophical branch of *habitus* not from *habere* but from the reflexive verb *se habere*, to have or hold oneself" (*Imagining an English Reading Public*, 1150–1400 [Cambridge: Cambridge University Press, 2010], 71).

2. All references to the texts of Aquinas are given parenthetically. Citations of the *Prima Secundae* indicate the question, article, and portion of article (e.g. 49.1 co). References to other parts of the *Summa theologiae* are the same, except that an initial part number is prefixed (e.g., 1.78.4 co). I have worked from the Latin texts of Aquinas as established by Enrique Alarcón, whose electronic version of Aquinas's *opera omnia*, published at http://www.corpusthomisticum.org, is the most complete, accurate, and up-to-date edition that currently exists. All translations of Aquinas's texts are my own. Latin nouns that appear in the text have generally been converted to their nominative forms, unless they appear within a clause with their grammatically correct cases.

3. Breen's reading misses this nuance, attributing without qualification to Aquinas the view that dispositions become habits *sicut puer fit vir* (*Imagining an English Reading Public*, 72).

4. Breen, *Imagining an English Reading Public*, 240n48.

5. Breen, *Imagining an English Reading Public*, 77.

6. Brian Davies, *Aquinas* (London and New York: Continuum, 2002), 124.

7. The warnings have by now become commonplace. For a small sample, compare Torrell, *Saint Thomas Aquinas,* vol. 2, *Spiritual Master*, 264; Bonnie Kent, "Habits and Virtues (IaIIae, qq. 49–70)," 116, in *The Ethics of Aquinas*, ed. Stephen J. Pope (Washington, DC: Georgetown University Press, 2002), 513–38; Servais Pinckaers, *The Sources of Christian Ethics*, trans. Sr. Mary Thomas Noble, O.P. (Washington, DC: Catholic University of America Press, 1995), 225.

8. Breen, *Imagining an English Reading Public*, 43.

9. The appearance of *habitualis dispositio*, as well as the appearance of *dispositio* in the definition of *habitus* at 54.1, qualifies Breen's claim that Aquinas "consistently contrasts *dispositio* as a mutable position or location with the quasi-permanent internal state of *habitus*" (240n48). Breen correctly sees that the dominant usage in Questions 49–53 reflects this contrast. But 54.1's summarizing claim that "habitus sunt dispositiones quaedam alicuius in potentia existentis ad aliquid, sive ad natura, sive ad operationem vel finem naturae" leads the reader to wonder about the depth of Aquinas's commitment to a consistent *habitus/dispositio* contrast.

10. Friedrich Nietzsche, *Beyond Good and Evil* §231, trans. Walter Kaufmann (New York: Vintage, 1966), 162.

11. See 1.87.2 and discussions in Mark Jordan, *Ordering Wisdom* (Notre Dame: University of Notre Dame Press, 1986), 130–32; Stanley Hauerwas, *Character and the Christian Life: A Study in Theological Ethics* (Notre Dame: University of Notre Dame Press, 1975), 73.

12. Here one may notice a contrast between Aquinas and Bourdieu, for whom *habitus* are necessarily in the body.

13. Breen, *Imagining an English Reading Public*, 47.

14. On *habitus* as monastic garment, see Breen, *Imagining an English Reading Public*, 50–62.

15. Breen, *Imagining an English Reading Public*, 47.

16. Breen herself quotes this passage (*Imagining an English Reading Public*, 75), without noticing its power to suggest that Aquinas is an exception to her proposed rule that for medieval thinkers "while *habitus* is formally bivalent . . . its actual usage is stubbornly asymmetrical" (49).

17. Jean-Pierre Torrell, O.P., *Aquinas' Summa: Background, Structure and Reception*, trans. Benedict M. Guevin, O.S.B. (Washington, DC: Catholic University of America Press, 2005), 33.

18. Not everyone finds Aquinas persuasive on the point. Bonnie Kent, for example, writes that "Thomas's distinction between habit and custom seems rather strained—and, from the perspective of ancient philosophy, hopelessly misguided" ("Habits and Virtues," 120; quoted in Breen, 238n13).

19. For a discussion of Aquinas's "particular reason" and its role in the origin and persistence of passions, see my *Thomas Aquinas on the Passions* (Cambridge: Cambridge University Press, 2010), 76–82.

20. Kent claims that Aquinas "sees more room for habits in the sensory *appetite*, the seat of emotions, than in powers of sensory *apprehension* such as memory and imagination" ("Habits and Virtues," 119; her emphasis). This formulation obscures Aquinas's distinction between interior and exterior powers of sensitive apprehension. Regarding the latter, Kent is correct, since for Aquinas the exterior powers (vision, hearing, etc.) cannot be habituated. The interior powers, however, *are* susceptible to habituation. At 50.3 ad 3 Aquinas cites memory as an example, appealing (perhaps questionably) to *On Memory and Reminiscence* 452a.

21. On Aquinas's opposition to Averroist "monopsychism," see Torrell, *Thomas Aquinas: Spiritual Master*, 258 and Fernand Van Steenberghen, *Thomas Aquinas and Radical Aristotelianism* (Washington, DC: Catholic University of America Press, 1980), 29–74.

22. This is not to deny that other combinations are possible. For example, something might derive partly from its specific nature, partly from its individual nature, and partly from an outside source. But in 51.1, Aquinas seems most interested in the four combinations noted.

23. Hauerwas writes that for Aquinas habit "is not a passive and inert modification of a man's being, for to have acquired a habit in this sense is to have acquired a real actuality" (*Character and the Christian Life*, 73). This is not wrong, since as we have seen from 49.3, every *habitus* is somehow ordered to act. But this should not obscure the sense in which habits in their origin are passive principles, produced before they can be producing.

24. Breen insightfully suggests that Aquinas understands good *habitus* as "a counterbalance to original sin, itself a habit-like disorganization of the soul" (49).

25. Who can receive the infused virtues? Breen suggests that according to Aquinas, "God bestows on Christians" infused virtues (*Imagining an English Reading Public*, 76). I cannot find a passage where Aquinas says this. As far as I can tell, he leaves open two possibilities: (1) not all who self-identify as Christians have infused virtues; (2) God is capable of infusing virtues into anyone he likes, including those who do not self-identify as Christians. Alasdair MacIntyre claims that "the acknowledgment by oneself of radical defect is a necessary condition for one's reception of the virtues of faith, hope, and charity" (*Three Rival Versions of Moral Enquiry* [Notre Dame: University of Notre Dame Press, 1990]). This seems closer to Aquinas, though it should not be taken to imply that a person must first act without divine help in order to receive infused virtue, particularly if the infused virtue of humility is a necessary condition of receiving faith, hope, and charity.

26. Torrell, O.P., *Thomas Aquinas: Spiritual Master*, 354.

27. Breen, *Imagining an English Reading Public*, 49. Aristotle, *Nicomachean Ethics*, 7.10 (1152a30). I owe this point to conversation with Margaret Watkins.

28. Breen, *Imagining an English Reading Public*, 49.

29. Choice is even more proper to rational agents than the voluntary, according to Aristotle, since "even children and animals have a share in the voluntary" (*Nicomachean Ethics*, 1111b8).

30. "Liberum vero arbitrarium est facultas rationis et voluntatis, qua bonum eligitur gratia assistente, vel malum eadem desistente" (II. *Sentences*, dist. 24 c. 3, quoted in Pinckaers, *The Sources of Christian Ethics*, 331).

31. Quoted in Pinckaers, *The Sources of Christian Ethics*, 331.

32. Pinckaers, *The Sources of Christian Ethics*, 332. For the *libertas indifferentiae* in Descartes, see *Principia Philosophiae*, 1.41. Descartes's view of the matter is too complicated to be addressed here.

33. Pinckaers, *The Sources of Christian Ethics*, 355.

34. Pinckaers, *The Sources of Christian Ethics*, 356.

35. Nietzsche, *Gay Science* §295, trans. Walter Kaufmann (New York: Vintage, 1974), 236.

36. Georg Christoph Lichtenberg, *The Waste Books*, Notebook F, aphorism 47, trans. R. J. Hollingdale (New York: New York Review of Books, 1990).

37. Nietzsche, *Beyond Good and Evil* §188, 100.

38. Nietzsche, *Beyond Good and Evil* §188, 100. Pinckaers notices the significance of this passage (*Sources of Christian Ethics*, 361). Freedom in Nietzschean terms involves discerning the relations between four levels of the self, as well as attending to the "order of rank" that obtains among the drives. For a fuller reading of Nietzsche on these points, see my "Nietzsche's Fourfold Conception of Selfhood," *Inquiry* 54 (2011): 337–60.

39. Nietzsche, *Daybreak* §556, trans. R. J. Hollingdale (Cambridge: Cambridge University Press, 1982), 224.

## BIBLIOGRAPHY

Aquinas, Thomas. *Summa Theologiae*. Edited by E. Alarcón. Electronically published at http://www.corpusthomisticum.org.

Breen, Katharine. *Imagining an English Reading Public, 1150–1400*. Cambridge: Cambridge University Press, 2010.

Hauerwas, Stanley. *Character and the Christian Life: A Study in Theological Ethics*. Notre Dame: University of Notre Dame Press, 1975.

Jordan, Mark. *Ordering Wisdom*. Notre Dame: University of Notre Dame Press, 1986.

Kent, Bonnie. "Habits and Virtues (IaIIae, qq. 49–70)." In *The Ethics of Aquinas*, edited by Stephen J. Pope, 513–38. Washington, DC: Georgetown University Press, 2002.

Lichtenberg, Georg Christoph. *The Waste Books*, Notebook F, aphorism 47. Translated by R. J. Hollingdale. New York: New York Review of Books, 1990.

MacIntyre, Alasdair. *Three Rival Versions of Moral Enquiry*. Notre Dame: University of Notre Dame Press, 1990.

Miner, Robert. "Nietzsche's Fourfold Conception of Selfhood." *Inquiry* 54 (2011): 337–60.

———. *Thomas Aquinas on the Passions: A Study of Summa Theologiae 1a2ae qq. 22–48*. Cambridge: Cambridge University Press, 2010.

Nietzsche, Friedrich. *Beyond Good and Evil*. Translated by Walter Kaufmann. New York: Vintage, 1966.

———. *Gay Science*. Translated by Walter Kaufmann. Vintage: New York, 1974.

———. *Daybreak*. Translated by R.J. Hollingdale. Cambridge: Cambridge University, Press, 1982.

Pinckaers, Servais. *The Sources of Christian Ethics*. Translated by Sr. Mary Thomas Noble, O.P. Washington, DC: Catholic University of America Press, 1995.

Steenberghen, Fernand Van. *Thomas Aquinas and Radical Aristotelianism*. Washington, D.C.: The Catholic University of America Press, 1980.

Torrell, Jean-Pierre, O.P., *Saint Thomas Aquinas*, vol. 2, *Spiritual Master*. Translated by Robert Royal. Washington, DC: Catholic University of America Press, 2003.

, *Aquinas' Summa: Background, Structure & Reception*. Translated by Benedict M. Guevin, O.S.B. Washington, DC: Catholic University of America Press, 2005.

## *Chapter Four*

# Negotiating with a New Sovereign

## *Montaigne's Transformation of Habit into Custom*

Margaret Watkins

> This book was written in good faith, reader. It warns you from the outset that in it I have set myself no goal but a domestic and private one. . . . I have dedicated it to the private convenience of my relatives and friends, so that when they have lost me (as soon they must), they may recover here some features of my character [conditions] and temperament, and by this means keep the knowledge they had of me more complete and alive.
>
> If I had written to seek the world's favor, I should have bedecked myself better, and should present myself in a studied posture. I want to be seen here in my simple, natural, ordinary fashion, without straining or artifice; for it is myself that I portray. My defects will here be read to the life, and also my natural form, as far as respect for the public has allowed. Had I been placed among those nations which are said to live still in the sweet freedom of nature's first laws, I assure you I should very gladly have portrayed myself here entire and wholly naked.
>
> —From "To the Reader," Preface to Montaigne's *Essays*, 2[1]

To whom does Montaigne address the *Essays*? His repeated publication of his "attempts" (*essais*) belies his insistence that he writes only for his "relatives and friends." Nor does the prevalence of untranslated Latin suggest that he wrote for common people. Yet Montaigne has nothing but contempt for the scholars of his day, making fun of them in ways that would surely amuse the general public: "I know a man who, when I ask him what he knows, asks me for a book in order to point it out to me, and wouldn't dare tell me that he has an itchy backside unless he goes immediately and studies in his lexicon what is itchy and what is a backside" (I.25, 101).

Such jabs do suggest that Montaigne writes for his friends—or perhaps that he is searching for friends who can appreciate both his Latin and his jokes. This supposition illuminates his profession that he wants to be seen in his "simple, natural, ordinary" mode, "without straining or artifice." Those tired of false friends want nothing more than company who allow them to be simply who they are. But this claim, along with the provocative assertion that he would have just as soon offered himself "wholly naked," contributes to the sense that the *Essays* represent a fundamental break with the traditions that come before him, out of which he nonetheless grows. Such a tradition, rather than glorifying the "sweet freedom of nature's first laws," extols a *second* nature—formed not by the quirks of one's "character and temperament" ("*conditions et humeurs*") but by the *habitus* of the virtues.

Montaigne recognizes a second nature as well—but it is the nature of *custom*—that which his critical reader, Pascal, calls a "second nature that destroys the first."[2] Montaigne is not the first to use the word for custom, as opposed to habit, to refer to second nature. But I will argue that the dominance of this choice in the *Essays* raises challenging questions and has significant implications. First, I will show that custom plays several roles associated with habit in the Aristotelian tradition dominating late-medieval philosophy: custom is a second nature; it makes some actions easier than they would otherwise be, and it can determine our perceptions of goods and evils. Second, I will examine the tensions between the older understanding of habit and Montaigne's custom, showing that one such tension intensifies the possibility that one might experience this second nature as a constraint to freedom and threat to identity. In the final two sections, I discuss the ways that one can liberate oneself from this constraint, according to Montaigne. Surprisingly, we will see that he accepts, in concert with his predecessors, that some escape may come from having a steadfast, virtuous character. Because this remedy is available to few, however, Montaigne offers another route to liberation—the escape of the essays themselves.

## 1. "AND NO LESS POWERFUL": MONTAIGNE'S ELEVATION OF CUSTOM OVER HABIT

Famously, the *Essays* themselves possess little constancy: they are often cited as a wondrous marriage of form and content. If Montaigne means to argue that the self is a fragmented, ever variable, ever revisable thing, then what better form than a series of discussions with no obvious ordering principle, revised multiple times, but without the intention to "correct my first imaginings by my second" (II.37, 574)?[3] Given the association of habit with settled dispositions and continuity of action, do we find any such concept in the *Essays* at all?

Habit itself, of course, is not a univocal concept. By the mid-sixteenth century, all of its varied senses were established in both Latin and French.[4] These senses of habit include clothing or costume, dispositions to act mechanically or automatically (from "force of habit"), and any settled character trait, understood as involving both reason and the passions, as in Aristotle's and Aquinas's theories of virtue and vice. Montaigne does occasionally use "*habitude,*" which in modern French corresponds to English's common senses of "habit." Far more often, however, does he use words more literally related to "custom," such as "*coustume,*" which appears in the title of I.23 ("Of custom, and not easily changing an accepted law"). English translations often obscure the prevalence of these words, and the rarity of the words for "habit," by translating *coustume* and its variants by "habit" or "habituation." I have used more literal translations to overcome this problem, and have identified the French original of any related words in brackets beside the English translation.

Putting aside, for the moment, the question about whether or not Montaigne's anthropology has room for genuine constancy or integrity, it is still clear that custom plays, in the *Essays*, many roles traditionally assigned to habit. First, custom is, for Montaigne, our second nature; it is something that we add to our naked dispositions, as we add clothing to our naked bodies. (Interestingly, "habit" and "custom" share an association with words for clothing or dress.) Second, like habits, it makes certain kinds of actions *easier* than they would otherwise be. And finally, customs can determine our perceptions of goods and evils.

At the beginning of Book II of the *Nicomachean Ethics*, Aristotle argues that virtue of character, unlike virtue of thought, results from habituation. It follows, he says, that virtue is not in us "by nature," because if it were, then training could not produce it in someone who failed to possess it from birth. "For example, it is impossible for a stone, which has a natural downward movement, to become habituated to moving upward, even if one should try ten thousand times to inculcate the habit by throwing it in the air."[5] It does *not* follow, however, that virtuous habit must be *against* nature. It is rather the completion of nature; indeed, it forms a kind of "second nature." Later in the *Ethics*, in the discussion of weakness of will, Aristotle considers the depth and permanence of characteristics acquired by habit: ". . . it is easier to change habit than to change nature. Even habit is hard to change, precisely because it resembles nature, as Euenus says: 'A habit, friend, is of long practice born, and practice ends in fashioning man's nature.'"[6] Habit, then, can effect change to such a degree that its results have the character of natural dispositions, but these dispositions are not quite as deeply rooted and immalleable as truly natural dispositions.

Montaigne explicitly embraces the notion of a second nature, but formed by *coustume*, not *habitude*. We find this remarkable passage in "Of husbanding your will":

> If what Nature flatly and originally demands of us for the preservation of our being is too little . . . then let us grant ourselves something further: let us also call the usage [*usage*] and condition of each of us *nature*. . . . For in going thus far we certainly seem to me to have some justification. Custom [*accoustumance*] is a second nature, and no less powerful. What my custom [*coustume*] lacks, I hold that I lack. (772)

This is far from the first instance of calling custom, rather than habit, second nature. Katharine Breen, in her study of medieval senses of habit, notes that the medievals call both *habitus* and *consuetudo* (custom) second nature. But she argues that there was nonetheless a significant distinction between the two. *Habitus* was associated with "spiritual elites" and virtue. *Consuetudo,* on the other hand, was often linked with laypeople, "practices that gain their authority from simple iteration" without being formed in "knowledge and consciousness," and even sin.[7] Against this background, Montaigne's privileging of *coustume* over *habitude* seems not only unusual, but revolutionary.

At times, it seems that Montaigne gives custom even more power than Aristotle gives habit. In "That the taste of good and evil depends in large part on the opinion we have of them," he reports stories of the Iberian Jews' resistance to forced conversion at the hands of Portuguese kings. Despite the intense suffering that followed the choice to continue practicing their religion, he tells us, only a few converted. These stories may read as tales of the power of devotion to resist the influence of custom, and to some degree they are. Yet Montaigne does not rest there. In a wry reflection on the paranoid suspicion of some of his Christian contemporaries, he notes: "Some of [the persecuted Jews] turned Christians; of their faith, or of that of their descendants, even today, a hundred years later, few Portuguese are sure, though *custom* [coustume] *and length of time are far stronger counselors than any other compulsion*" (36, my emphasis). What began as a story of strong and constant human spirit ends with the reflection that custom has more power than any king, no matter how creative he is in devising torments. The king has only limited power to change the nature of his subjects; custom's sovereignty, on the other hand, is absolute.

We will consider this complex essay in more detail below. For now, it is only important to see that this ascription of immense strength to custom is not an isolated note in the *Essays*, nor is there any reason to interpret this line as a backhanded suggestion that the Portuguese are in fact justified in their suspicion of these Jews' descendants (among whom Montaigne is one!).[8] To the contrary, we have every reason to believe that he finds the contemporary suspicion irrational and possibly amusing: what a desperate and angry king cannot accomplish with all the power at his disposal, time and custom effects with no effort whatsoever. To see this, let us turn to two essays that include extended and focused discussions of custom and its power: "Of custom" and "Of experience."

Montaigne embeds his perception of the power of custom into the full title of the twenty-third essay of the first volume: "Of custom [*coustume*], and not easily changing an accepted law." The essay brings to mind his comparison, at the beginning of "Of friendship," between the *Essays* and a wall of grotesques: it is full of fantastical stories of customs strange and shocking (135). The mask of custom, at the beginning, is dark and frightening:

> For in truth custom [*coustume*] is a violent and treacherous schoolmistress. She establishes in us, little by little, stealthily, the foothold of her authority; but having by this mild and humble beginning settled and planted it with the help of time, she soon uncovers to us a furious and tyrannical face against which we no longer have the liberty of even raising our eyes. We see her at every turn forcing the rules of nature. *Usage is the most effective teacher of all things* [Pliny, "*Usus efficacissimus rerum omnium magister*"]. (77)

Let us not pass over the power of this image. Montaigne's dim view of schoolmasters, expressed three essays later in "Of the education of children," surely lies behind his selection of the metaphor. He does not want a pupil "given up to the surly humors of a choleric schoolmaster," his mind spoiled "by keeping him in torture and at hard labor, as others do, fourteen or fifteen hours a day, like a porter" (121). But the clothing of this image in the feminine, of course required by the gender of *coustume*, adds another dimension. *This* tutor at first beguiles with warmth and nurturing; she pretends to be kind while luring us into the circle of her influence; and only once we are her loyal and devoted children does she reveal her true face. Centuries of tales of cruel nannies and stepmothers—however unjust—would have ensured this metaphor's resonance.[9] Custom at first lulls our nature; it is easy to drift off to her dictates. Only this is a sleep from which it is all too difficult to awake.

Throughout this essay, Montaigne relentlessly maintains the view of custom as the source of much of what we consider natural. As I discuss in more detail below, his "custom" encompasses both behaviors of an individual (corresponding to one sense of our "habit") and the general practices of a community. Wearing the same perfume three days in a row accustoms our nose to it so thoroughly that we no longer notice its pleasant smell (78). He has seen a man "born without arms, who has so well adapted his feet for the service his hands owed him that in truth they have half forgotten their natural function" (79). And there is no practice so apparently revolting or absurd that some culture has not embraced it: brides proving their honor by having sex with as many men as possible before the groom, people using their genitals as napkins, nephews inheriting property rather than sons, dogs revered as the "most desirable sepulture," women being circumcised as well as men, children nursing to the age of twelve, people killing lice with their teeth "like monkeys" (80–82).

This tour of "grotesques," however, is mere prelude to the truly shocking claims of the essay. Careless sixteenth-century readers, overwhelmed by a litany culminating in what may have struck them as the most horrifying examples of all—paternal abuse and male homosexuality—might fail to notice the revolutionary sentence that follows: "The laws of conscience, which we say are born of nature, are born of custom [*coustume*]" (83). One suspects, indeed, that Montaigne meant his structure to encourage certain readers not to notice. It is one thing to point out that individual people, particular families, or even whole communities adopt—and adapt themselves to—practices that seem disgusting or immoral. It is quite another—and more subversive—thing to suggest that the laws of conscience themselves, by many considered the imprint of the natural law, are not written on our hearts by God but carved there after birth by the workings of a tyrannical and cruel schoolmistress. In a striking anticipation of Freud, Montaigne even offers a naturalistic explanation of how this engraving works: "Each man, holding in inward veneration the opinions and the behavior approved and accepted around him, cannot break loose from them without remorse, or apply himself to them without self-satisfaction" (83).

Of course, not all of Montaigne's contemporaries would have thought that we have immediate access to the natural law through our individual consciences. Perhaps the individual must be tutored through the work of the community. And perhaps the form of political community best suited to such tutelage is itself determined by the demands of common human nature. Such a theory is central to Aristotle's own view of second nature: no one generates his or her own virtue in isolation. Neither are individual families sufficient to the task of teaching virtue by themselves. (The worthless progeny of excellent fathers would have been, of course, a theme familiar to readers of Plato.) What is needed, in addition to virtuous parents and stable domestic settings, is a *polis* structured by just law:

> Accordingly, if, as we have said, a man must receive a good upbringing and discipline in order to be good, and must subsequently lead the same kind of life, pursuing what is good and never involuntarily or voluntarily doing anything base, this can be effected by living under the guidance of a kind of intelligence and right order which can be enforced. Now, a father's command does not have the power to enforce or to compel, nor does, in general, the command of a single man, unless he is a king or someone in a similar position. But law does have the power or capacity to compel, being the rule of reason derived from some sort of practical wisdom and intelligence. While people

> hate any men who oppose, however rightly, their impulses, the law is not invidious when it enjoins what is right.[10]

Such reasoning explains why Aristotle subsumes the study of ethics under politics.[11] The work of moral education and transformation *requires* the study of what political order best suits the human animal.

Montaigne, however, offers no refuge for the natural law in the sanctuary of the state. Whether we find any particular form of government suitable or natural itself depends on the "sovereignty of custom": "Nations brought up to liberty and to ruling themselves consider any other form of government monstrous and contrary to nature. Those who are accustomed [*Ceux qui sont duits*] to monarchy do the same" (83).

The proper response to *this* sovereign, according to the end of "Of custom," is by no means revolution—not *political* revolution, at least. Nonetheless, this essay leaves the reader seeing custom with the face of a tyrant, whose "principal effect . . . is to seize and ensnare us in such a way that it is hardly within our power to get ourselves back out of its grip and return into ourselves to reflect and reason about its ordinances" (83). If this were Montaigne's last word on the subject, then custom would play only half the role of an Aristotelian habit, if that. On Aristotle's view, vice is ensnaring, but not virtue. Indeed, Aristotle explains why one does not experience virtue as a tyrant in terms that may sound familiar to readers of Montaigne: vice makes us at war with our *nature*, whereas virtue is the completion of it. "In most men," he says—meaning men without virtue—"pleasant acts conflict with one another because they are not pleasant *by nature*, but men who love what is noble derive pleasure from what is *naturally pleasant*."[12] If custom only dominates and cruelly subjects human nature to its will, then it cannot play the role of habit as virtuous second nature at all.

Even in "Of custom," Montaigne complicates the view of custom as tyrant by arguing that we usually should submit to custom for the sake of the community. His view of custom is even more nuanced, however. To show this, I will now turn to the last-written essay, which closes volume three: "Of experience." This is a long and sometimes rambling essay, beginning with a theme familiar from "Of custom": the origin and modification of laws. Here, too, he does not shy away from sinister descriptions of the power of custom. "It is for custom [*coustume*]" he says, "to give form to our life, just as it pleases; it is all-powerful in that; it is Circe's drink, which varies our nature as it sees fit" (827). Despite the ominous association of custom with a goddess who transforms her enemies into beasts, his judgment of custom is not nearly so harsh here as we have seen it before. The larger point in this passage is that guarding one's health generally requires continuing to do what one has always done, accepting the dominance of one's individual and cultural customs, and not attempting to fight them through dubiously interventionist medical techniques. The previous sentence tells us: "I believe nothing with more certainty than this: that I cannot be hurt by the use of things that I have been so long accustomed [*accoustumées*] to."

There follows an extended discussion of the ways in which customary practice determines what we find healthy—which is to say, what is indeed healthy for us. "You make a German sick if you put him to bed on a mattress, like an Italian on a feather bed, and a Frenchman without curtains and a fire" (827). But there is an important shift here, as Montaigne suggests that we are not wholly at the mercy of such determinations. The healthiest course may be to use the insight that we *can* become accustomed to various ways of living to help make us more "supple," adaptable creatures. Consider the surprising ending to this repetition of the point that custom can change our form:

> These are the results of custom [*accoustumance*]. It can shape us not only into whatever form it pleases (therefore, say the sages, we must choose the best form, which custom [*elle*, referring back to *accoustumance*] will promptly make easy for us), but also shape us for change and variation, which is the noblest and most useful of its teachings. The best of my bodily qualities is that I am flexible and not very stubborn. I have inclinations that are more personal and customary [*ordinaires*], and more agreeable to me, than others; but with very little effort I turn away from them, and easily slip into the opposite way [*la façon contraire*]. A young man should violate his own rules to arouse his vigor and keep it from growing moldy and lax. And there is no way of life so stupid and feeble as that which is conducted by rules and discipline. (830)

In other words, once we realize that custom has the power to make any number of practices healthy and feel natural for us, we may be able to keep ourselves from becoming set in our ways. This contemporary idiom, however, may lead us to overlook the seriousness and difficulty of Montaigne's point. Why *is* it so important to be "pliable and supple" in this way? What justifies his claim that this is not only a quite *useful* teaching of custom, but indeed its *noblest*? Again, he encourages lightheartedness himself—trash-talking about manliness in a way reminiscent of his claims in "Of the education of children" that a pupil ought to learn to drink heavily—even with the Germans! (He uses *souple* here as well: while "the body is still supple, it should for that reason be bent to all fashions and customs [*coustumes*]" (123).) "It is shameful for a man to keep from doing what he sees his companions do, because he cannot or dare not. Let such men stick to their kitchens" (830). But it would be a mistake to let this playful spirit distract us from the solemnity of the preceding language. "Noble" is not a word that Montaigne uses lightly.

I will return below to why Montaigne might think that being shaped for change and variation deserves association with nobility. For now, simply note that the association suggests that "suppleness" itself might be a kind of virtue or excellence, according to Montaigne. It is not the only excellence that he thinks custom can prepare us for. And thus we come to the second point about the way in which custom, in Montaigne, plays roles formerly associated with habit: it makes some actions *easier* than unadorned nature makes them.

Montaigne alludes to this point in the long passage quoted above, when he notes that the sages say "we must choose the best form, which custom will promptly make easy for us." Also in "Of experience," he says that his father's methods of child-rearing made use of this insight, affirming his father's having sent him to live among the poor as a child. Young boys will benefit, he claims, if we let "them be formed by fortune under the laws of the common people and of nature; leave it to custom [*coustume*] to train them to frugality and austerity, so that they may have rather to come down from rigorousness than climb toward it" (844). The immediate context here concerns avoiding fastidiousness with respect to eating habits. One can hear echoes of Socrates in the *Republic*, warning his interlocutors that those trained on luxury will find the removal of pleasures far more painful than those who have never gotten used to them in the first place.[13] And again, there is an emphasis on manliness: this is a recommendation for male children only, whose early rearing wise fathers will never take on themselves, and "still less give to [their] wives" (844). Parents are simply too soft on their own children. It is worth noting, however, that Montaigne also discusses at length another goal of his father's practice—one which he commends highly: "to ally me with the people and that class of men that needs our help . . ." (844). Regardless, the point is that even a child of relative nobility can come to find a simple, vigorous way of life pleasant, through early customary practice.

Interestingly, Montaigne suggests twice in this passage that custom may need the help of nature. First, and somewhat ambiguously, there is the recommendation that we let boys be formed "under the laws of the common people and *of nature*." The French reads, "*des loix populaires et naturelles*," leaving unclear whether we should understand the common laws to be natural, or whether he means to refer to two sets of laws—the laws of the common people and the natural laws.[14] Regardless, the close juxtaposition of this appeal to the importance of natural laws—in whatever sense—with the recommendation to leave the training to custom, shows that Montaigne cannot believe custom and nature to be necessarily opposing forces. Second, he goes on to suggest that the project of binding his sympathy to the common people has been successful through the workings of his *own* nature. His father's plan, he says, "has succeeded not at all badly. I am prone to devote myself to the little people, whether because there is more vainglory in it, or through *natural* compassion, which has infinite power over me" (844, emphasis added). This, too, is puzzling, particularly if we assume that nature and custom are opposed to one another. If Montaigne's compassion is natural, in what sense is it a result of his father's plan? Again, we find something of a partnership, rather than a battle, between custom and nature. It is not implausible to read Montaigne as saying that his father's imposition of a *custom*—living with common people and eating common foods—has made a way of life that would otherwise be difficult for someone born into the upper classes much easier, so that is *feels natural*. Custom takes the edge off difficult practices, smoothing the way for a human nature at peace with itself.

One of the most interesting examples of this "smoothing" function of custom comes in an unlikely place—in Montaigne's extended discussion of his struggle with kidney stones. Among a list of reasons why this particular affliction, which he seems to have experienced as often as once a month, is not the worst disease to have, we find:

> I am obliged to Fortune for assailing me so often with the same kind of weapons. She fashions and trains me against them by use [*usage*], hardens and accustoms [*habitue*] me. Henceforth I know just about at what cost I shall be quit of them. . . . Custom [*accoustumance*] also serves to give me better hopes for the future. For now that this process of evacuation has continued so long, it is probable that nature will not change this course and that no worse will come of it than what I already feel. (837–38)

The interest of this passage may not be readily apparent. It may seem to be a fairly quotidian observation: people are able to endure familiar illnesses better than unfamiliar ones. But it is not at all clear that this is true: many people are broken down by prolonged and recurring illnesses, particularly those involving chronic or recurring pain.[15] Past experience creates a cycle of anxiety, fear, and pain that can be difficult to escape. Note also, however, that Montaigne is not suggesting that familiarity or "usage" will have the same effect on everyone. And he is far from passive in response to this onslaught of fortune.

This part of the essay is less about the physicality of kidney stones (though we should by no means underestimate the importance of physicality for Montaigne) than the use and misuse of the *imagination*. His experience with "the stone" illustrates the following boast:

> I treat my imagination as gently as I can, and would relieve it, if I could, of all trouble and conflict. We must help it and flatter it, and fool it if we can. My mind is suited to this service; it has no lack of plausible reasons for all things. If it could persuade as well as it preaches, it would help me out very happily. (836)

The role of the imagination in Montaigne is enormously important and complex, and space prevents an exploration of it here. What is important for us to see is that the imagination serves an important function in his quest to make of his experience something tranquil, reflective, and reasonable. Despite his reference to "fooling" his imagination, the various reasons that he offers it, to help take the edge off of the extraordinary pain that was such a large part of his later years, are often perfectly plausible: his illness is common, and his particular version of it is relatively mild. The fortitude that he shows in enduring bouts of it wins him admiration, compassion, and kindness from his friends. There is no clear evidence that it is a fatal disease. And perhaps most importantly for Montaigne, it prepares one for death; it "weans you from life and detaches you from the world," not with unremitting enfeeblement, but with occasional attacks that can be seen as "warning and instructions repeated at intervals, intermingled with long pauses for rest, as if to give you a chance to meditate and repeat its lesson at your leisure" (837). The imagination, as it does for later philosophers in the seventeenth and eighteenth centuries, mediates between reason and the passions. This mediation enables Montaigne to consider the real and available insights offered by his illness, and the calmer passions of hope and resignation then have some power against misery and despair.

The passage about fortune accustoming him to his illness is among these reasons, offered to the imagination with the aim of greater peace of mind. Custom, then, with the cooperation of an active, well-trained imagination, contributes to an extremely important kind of fortitude—that required to endure the inevitable decline and pain that go along with aging. Our tendency to de-emphasize this kind of fortitude, focusing instead on the martial virtue with which Aristotle was primarily concerned, is itself an interesting phenomenon.[16] Perhaps we irrationally underestimate the likelihood that we will need such a virtue, or perhaps the very commonness of its need means that it cannot carry the glory associated with courage needed in, for example, military settings. The ubiquity of need, however, does not correspond to ubiquity of the virtue itself: many succumb to greater or lesser versions of the despair that tempts those with prolonged illness. It would be stupid and callous to suggest that these people are to blame for such despair, but recognizing a practice of mind that might enable them to overcome or at least fight against it need not imply blame at all. Montaigne's description of his prolonged struggle with kidney stones is a monumental event in the history of western medicine and psychology—and, I submit, a beautiful example of the way in which the mind, taking advantage of the "useful and noble" properties of custom, can make certain activities easier for us. No one can argue that living with monthly attacks of kidney stones is an *easy* way of life, full stop. But Montaigne's commitment to "dealing gently with his imagination" enables him to continue conversing with his friends, participating in the activities of daily life, and possessing a lively and healthy self-respect in ways that would not only be difficult, but even impossible, for someone without such a commitment.

I have argued that, in Montaigne's *Essays*, custom plays two roles long associated with habit in Aristotelian ethics and its heirs. It acts as a powerful "second nature," and it makes difficult actions easier than they may otherwise be. It is worth noting, again, that the latter point is true of vicious as well as virtuous actions, and we find this point in Montaigne as well. A dark corollary to this point is that custom can make some practices so easy that we find the opposite practice near impossible in ways that we experience as restricting or even tormenting. It "is custom that makes impossible for us what is not impossible in itself," which we might experience as a severe restriction of freedom. I will return to this point (I.36, 167). But now we must consider the third and final role shared by Montaigne's custom and Aristotelian habit: it colors and sometimes even determines our perceptions of goods and evils.

It is deeply embedded in the theories of virtue that grow out of Plato and Aristotle that those with the virtues count as goods things that those without full virtue find indifferent or even undesirable. Likewise, the goods that direct the pursuits of the vicious or base person will have fewer charms for the virtuous person, who knows another order of goods altogether. We find this view over and over again in Plato's dialogues. It lies behind Callicles's insistence in the *Gorgias* that a man living the moderate or temperate life recommended by Socrates, in which one seeks to satisfy a small number of desires fully, is "living like a stone."[17] For Callicles, such a man misses all of the joys of life—its excitement, its opportunity for manly self-testing, the pleasures of "having as much as possible flow in."[18] He cannot comprehend why someone would forgo such goods for the pleasures of moderation and reflection. Likewise, it is behind Socrates's argument in the ninth book of the *Republic* that the philosopher is the only competent judge of what form of life is truly most pleasant. He, unlike lovers of profit and honor, has experienced the full range of pleasures, including those of "learning the nature of the things that are. . . ."[19] Again, his excellent habits enable him to appreciate goods that are closed off from those whose lives are directed by the search for profit.

Aristotle offers a performative verification of this hypothesis in his own discussion of the contemplative life in the final book of the *Ethics*: many an undergraduate has been stunned and puzzled by his claim that "everyone agrees that of all the activities that conform with virtue activity in conformity with theoretical wisdom is the most pleasant."[20] Only someone with a highly developed capacity for theoretical reflection—and a habit of exercising that capacity—could make such a claim. Despite the apparent exaggeration about what *everyone* agrees on here, however, Aristotle clearly recognizes that people with different habits desire and pursue different kinds of goods. Indeed, this recognition supports the claim that those with virtuous habits cannot share the highest kind of friendship with those without such habits. This kind of friendship requires joint pursuit of excellent goods, but how, he asks, can a virtuous person remain close to someone who has become so much worse that "they neither like nor feel joy and pain at the same things?"[21] Our habits shape what we find worth pursuing, what gives us joy, what forms of pain we seek most strenuously to avoid, and which activities we believe worth our efforts and the precious resource of the time in our daily lives.

We have already seen, in Montaigne, one way in which custom can transform our perceptions of goods and evils. The joint working of imagination and custom that allows him to endure and even appreciate the trials of his recurring illness works in part through custom's ability to effect such a change in our perceptions. For instance, conceptualizing physical pain as a useful reminder of our ephemeral existence, along with repeated experience of that pain and the effects of enduring it, allows him to lower its importance on the scale of evils. To explore the relationship between custom and the estimation of goods and evils more thoroughly, however, let us return to I.14, "That the taste of good and evil depends in large part on the opinion we have of them."

This is a fascinating and in many ways unusual essay. It is rich with caustic irony and ripe for misunderstanding. Among its uncharacteristic features is its clear plan of organization—a trait that Montaigne generally seems to disdain. The rambling, tangential form of many of the essays mirrors, as many have noticed, his conception of the mind and self as variable and "undulating." (See below.) In I.14, however, he proposes a clear question for consideration, a hypothetical for testing an answer to the question, and then proceeds to an ordered consideration of the disjuncts that constitute the antecedent of the hypothetical. The question is whether or not we can maintain the claim, reflected in an "old Greek maxim," that "what we call evil is not evil in itself—or at least, whatever it is, that it depends on us to give it a different savor and a different complexion; for all this comes to the same thing" (33). In other words, are certain things evil in themselves, or does our denomination of them as evil depend only on our opinion of them?

This, of course, is a profound metaphysical question about the nature of goods and evils, but, true to his general stance, Montaigne's interest in it is relentlessly practical. Were it always true that evil is merely a matter of opinion, there "would be a great point gained for the relief of our wretched human lot. . . . For if evils have no entry into us but by our judgment, it seems to be in our power to disdain them or turn them to good use" (33). Here we find Montaigne wrestling with a thesis shared, in some version, by the Stoics, certain skeptics, and even some representatives of medieval Christianity. He is fascinated by the liberation offered by such a view; if true, we might be able, through strength of mind or will, to overcome the suffering occasioned by violent war, loneliness, extreme physical pain, or even the loss of a dear friend. Montaigne himself knew each of these forms of suffering intimately, and it would be plausible to claim that the search to overcome them motivates the writing of the essays as a whole.[22]

If the question, then, is whether or not we determine what evils truly are by our "opinion," how might we seek an answer? Montaigne suggests a hypothetical to test: "If the original essence of the things we fear had power to lodge in us of its own authority; it would lodge alike in everyone; for men are all of a kind, and are furnished, though some more and some less, with similar tools and instruments for thought and judgment" (33).[23] In other words, were evils determined as evils by their nature, then we would all (more or less) fear them and avoid them to the same degree. In general, it seems that we do not, so we have a neat *modus tollens*. Montaigne is not content, however, to rest here. To see if there are any essential evils, we must consider the three most plausible candidates: death, pain, and poverty. In the rest of the essay, he considers each of these in turn.

For each of these apparent evils, Montaigne finds that "opinion" has great power over how we endure them and even whether we see them as evils at all. With respect to poverty and death, he seems to believe that opinion can have perfect sovereignty: it can prevent our seeing them as evils at all. Perhaps ironically, he is not so sure about pain, although there is of course a long history of seeing pain as potentially *good* and certainly not as bad as death. This is the subversive Montaigne, undermining forms of Christianity, for example, that consider pain potentially good and even sacred—that which can bring us closer to Christ or fulfill divine justice, as in the pain of childbirth ordered by God as punishment for Eve's sin. Those who have claimed that pain is *not* an evil "have admitted it in practice" by crying out and writhing despite their denials and best efforts (37). It is, he says, "the worst accident of our being," and continues the subversion by inverting the traditional elevation of the mind over the senses: "Here all does not consist in imagination. We have opinions about the rest; here it is certain knowledge that plays its parts. Even our senses are judges of it. 'And if these be not true, all reason then is false'" (37).[24]

And yet: even with pain, even with the "worst accident of our nature," there is much that we can do to temper its evil. The general thrust of the essay encourages us to believe that no one need be completely at the mercy of even these worst forms of suffering. And the kinds of things that enable us to achieve some tranquility in the face of such suffering are precisely those that he has called customs of various sorts in different essays. Some are cultural, as with the wives of Narsinga, who, he says, "endure being buried alive, not only with fortitude but gaily, at their husbands' funerals" (34). Others belong in the category of personal practice, such as the happy tendencies that twenty years of relative poverty effected in Montaigne's own early adulthood (43–44). He laments the damage that a period of increased wealth, along with the practice of saving his money, did to this early carefree attitude: “once you are accustomed [*accoustumé*] to a certain pile and set your fancy on it, it is no longer at your service: you wouldn’t dare to make a dent in it” (45). All of these various forms of custom have the potential to radically alter our appreciation of various goods and our horror of various evils: “just as study is a torment to a lazy man, abstinence from wine to a drunkard, frugality to the luxurious man, and exercise to a delicate idler, so it is with the rest” (46).

As the last sentence reveals, however, we cannot understand the full force of Montaigne’s thought if we insist on taking custom to mean something mechanical (like a tick of nature) or imposed by an external culture. Custom works through the modification of the subject faced with a prospective good or evil. A certain kind of reader will find little in this essay beyond confirmation that Montaigne is a “moral skeptic.” After all, is he not arguing against the idea that there is goodness or evil in the “essence of things”? Does he not claim, “Each man is as well or as badly off as he thinks he is” (46)? If goodness and evil are relative to our nature, how can we truthfully speak of moral goodness at all?

But this is a wooden reading, which fails to take into account the overwhelming presumption in this essay that what we are in search of is *virtue*—excellence that will allow us to endure what those with weaker souls cannot take. Despite the title, Montaigne is almost exclusively concerned with evils rather than goods; and he repeatedly appeals to various goods of the soul as if their status were beyond question. The passage about the torments of study to the lazy, et cetera, continues: “Things are not that painful or difficult of themselves; it is our weakness and cowardice that make them so. *To judge of great and lofty things we need a soul of the same caliber*; otherwise we attribute to them the vice that is our own” (emphasis added). After offering the example of a prelate who has given up the management of his finances to a servant, Montaigne offers the beautiful reflection: “Confidence in the goodness of others is no slight testimony to one’s own goodness; and so God gladly favors it” (46). And in his discussion of the most threatening evil—pain—he offers the following diagnosis and prescription:

> What makes us endure pain so poorly is that we are not accustomed [*accoustumez*] to find our principal contentment in the soul, and that we do not concentrate enough on it; for the soul is the one and sovereign mistress of our condition and conduct. The body has, except for differences of degree, only one gait and one posture. The soul may be shaped into all varieties of forms, and molds to itself and to its every condition the feelings of the body and all other accidents. Therefore we must study the soul and look into it, and awaken in it its all-powerful springs. (39)

Again, we find Montaigne claiming that a concurrence between our inner lives and custom may be the answer to the difficulties posed by the human condition. The precise form of this concurrence raises many difficult questions, which will take us to the next step in our inquiry. What is clear by now, however, is that Montaigne relies heavily on custom to play the three different roles of traditional habit which I have identified: custom becomes our second nature, eases the difficulty of certain actions, and transforms our assessments of the goods and evils that we encounter in both the momentous and everyday events of our lives.

## 2. CUSTOM COMMUNAL AND IDIOSYNCRATIC: THE CONSTRAINING EFFECT OF CUSTOM ON A PATCHWORK SELF

Montaigne's reliance on custom rather than habit raises a number of interpretive and philosophical difficulties. First, as we have seen repeatedly above, "custom," unlike "habit," encompasses both cultural and individual practice. Contemporary English preserves some of this ambiguity. Although we are more likely to use "custom" to mean something cultural—particularly in reference to foreign practices, it still makes sense to speak of one's personal "customs." Asked to explain why we take a walk after dinner every evening, for example, we might say "It has always been my custom," though we would sound a bit stilted in doing so. For Montaigne, however, custom seems as likely—or more likely—to refer to individual as to cultural behavior.

The same does not seem to be true of habit. The *Oxford English Dictionary* reports that the English term "habit" evolves "in Latin and the modern languages taken together," progressing through "holding" or "having," through an external sense referring to mode of presentation and dress, to the use most familiar to us in English—"in mind, character, or life; hence, mental constitution, character, disposition, way of acting, comporting oneself, or dealing with things . . . personal custom, accustomedness."[25] None of these more developed concepts primarily refer to attributes of cultures or communities as well as individual persons, although we might use the term in some relevant analogical or metaphorical sense.

This blurring of the line between individual and cultural custom is not just a quirk of language. I am not suggesting that Montaigne is *inventing* a flexible use of "*coustume*"; on the contrary, he seems to be using it in a way that would have been perfectly familiar to his readers. Also available to him, however, was "*habitude*," with its more individual connotations, but he rarely chooses this term. Whether intentional or not, the effect is to obscure the distinction between what is simply given to one as a member of a particular community and what can be an identifying or distinguishing personality trait. This, in turn, suggests the possibility of a certain distance between a person and even her individual "customs," so that they can be experienced as external and even threatening to her identity. Of course, one might experience one's own habits as a threat to integrity, and one might so closely identify with one's surrounding culture that its customs seem constitutive elements of oneself. But the former possibility is a reflective thought, arrived at through the philosophical stance; my point is simply that the *language* of custom immediately brings to mind this kind of distance in a way that the language of habit does not. And the latter possibility—where one identifies so intimately with one's culture that its ways just are one's own—was certainly not available in Montaigne's own setting, if it ever really was. This was a time of violent, divisive religious wars, continual political disintegration and reunification, and economic transition. In such a time, which customs help form one's identity is, to some degree, necessarily a matter of choice.

By using the same language for personal and cultural customs, Montaigne brings into relief the necessity of this choice, thereby suggesting a conception of personal identity that is partially self-constructed. I do not mean to suggest here any great emphasis on the *freedom* of such a choice, if we construe such freedom as a metaphysical ability to escape determination. But, as I have discussed above, he certainly does suggest that we might experience custom as constraining or even tyrannical—the sort of thing from which it may seem imperative to escape. So there is some kind of freedom that is relevant here. It is the freedom to affirm the various parts of oneself, to cease experiencing the world as in tension with one's nature. Part of Montaigne's point, I would suggest, is that such freedom requires affirmation not only of customs that one inherits from the outside, but ones that are idiosyncratic. It may also require pruning some of these customs from oneself to whatever degree that proves possible. The language of custom, unlike the language of habit, opens a continuity between the ways in which we relate to our individual traits and the ways in which we relate to the attributes of our culture. For Montaigne, our response to both can be active affirmation or denial, rather than passive acceptance of the given.

Custom's implied reference to the norms of a culture as well as the practices of an individual suggests another difference with the habit traditions: different customs serve different cultures equally well, but on the Aristotelian and Thomist conception, there is one set of habits *uniquely* suited to human nature—the habits of the virtues. There was never complete unanimity on which particular virtues make up this catalogue, but Montaigne would have been familiar with a schema including the four cardinal virtues (prudence, courage, temperance, and justice) and the three Christian theological virtues (faith, hope, and love). But if *custom*, rather than *habit*, forms second nature, we seem without any grounding for the claim that one set of traits suits human nature particularly well. And this is an aspect of custom that Montaigne not only recognizes but exploits: again, several of the essays contain long lists of strange and shocking customs that work perfectly well for the cultures that practice them.

A related but distinct issue concerns the relationship between customs and personal integrity or constancy. We have plenty of direct statements from Montaigne questioning the possibility of human constancy—not to mention the form of the essays, which sometimes revel in their own internal contradictions as a reflection of the contradictory nature of the self. Very early in his book, he tells us, "Truly man is a marvelously vain, diverse, and undulating object. It is hard to found any constant and uniform judgment on him" (I.1, 5). And the second book of the *Essays* begins with "Of the inconsistency [*inconstance*] of our actions"—a fast-paced and almost didactic reflection on the variability of human nature even within each person. "We are all patchwork, and so shapeless and diverse in composition that each bit, each moment, plays its own game. And there is as much difference between us and ourselves as between us and others" (244).[26]

The emphasis on custom, rather than habit, reinforces this patchwork view of the self: habits are that which one *has*, that shape one's nature so that one's actions are predictable. Virtues in particular, as opposed to vices, possess this power. Again in his discussion of friendship, Aristotle claims that "a good man remains consistent in his judgment, and he desires the same objects with every part of the soul."[27] For such a man, the "same thing is at all times pleasant to him, and not different at different times."[28] Base people, on the other hand, "are at variance with themselves and have appetite for one thing and wish for another," meaning that their behavior is unpredictable, and they possess neither true self-love nor the ability to be good friends.[29] Montaigne himself seems to recognize this connection between habit and constancy: in "Of the inconsistency of our actions," we find one of his rare uses of *habitude*: "If valor were a habit [*habitude*] of virtue, and not a sally, it would make a man equally resolute in any contingency, the same alone as in company, the same in single combat as in battle" (242). He associates custom, on the other hand, with images of changeability: it is the cup of Circe, whose "noblest use" is its ability to "shape us for change and variation."

For Plato, Aristotle, and much of the medieval tradition so profoundly influenced by them, the relationship between the idea that there was *one* set of virtues uniquely suited to human nature and the possibility of genuine human constancy was no accident. If humans are essentially, for example, animals differentiated from others by the function of reason, then one set of excellences or virtues constitutes their perfection. (We need not accept the somewhat naïve view that all of these philosophers—or even the "Aristotelians"—agreed about the precise nature of humanity.) Those excellences keep the animal in good working order, at least until its somewhat weaker physical nature fails in its support of that function. The Jewish, and later Christian, doctrine of the Fall of course complicates this understanding quite a bit, and Montaigne is clearly the heir of this more complex tradition. But a fallen human nature is still *a* human nature—fragmented by its failure to live up to its potential, but still having a potential constituted by and accessible through an identifiable group of virtues, though we might now see some of those virtues as only achievable with the help of divine grace.

It is not at all clear that Montaigne believes that there is any such thing as a single "human nature"—still less a single form of life that will uniquely suit that nature.[30] And he delights in making fun of people who judge those with alien customs on the basis of some such idea. At the end of "Of cannibals," for instance, he concludes a long discussion on the virtues of various "barbarians" with biting sarcasm: "All this is not too bad—but what's the use? They don't wear breeches" (159). He employs a different kind of irony in "Of custom" when he says, "Everyone acts the same way inasmuch as usage [*usage*] robs us of the true appearance of things" (84). The relationship between humanity, nature, and custom in Montaigne, again, is vexed and complex. I would like to move beyond, however, the metaphysical question of whether or not humans have a single, essential nature—the sort of question for which Montaigne generally has little patience. Rather, let us consider the practical implications of his lack of confidence in our ability to identify and achieve a set of excellences that would complete such a nature.

We have seen that, for Aristotle, the virtues ensure a degree of personal integrity and help prevent the regret that follows when one acts against one's own desires or commitments. Such integrity has long been associated with a particular kind of freedom—not the freedom to choose any particular course of action, regardless of past or present desires and commitments—but rather the freedom to choose in accordance with the highest part of our nature, or the freedom to choose the genuine good. We see this not only in Aristotle, but in Plato, Aquinas, and Augustine, among others. If Montaigne doubts our ability to have such virtues, does he likewise suspect that we will often feel a certain lack of freedom with respect to our own behavior?

Indeed he does, as we have already seen. Custom can play the role of bitch-goddess dominating us with "violence" and "treachery." Montaigne himself expresses feeling the dictates of custom as constraints in matters both great and small. In "Our feelings reach out beyond us," he reports on his own scrupulousness, except "under great stress of necessity or voluptuousness," about revealing "to the sight of anyone the members and acts that our custom [*coustume*] orders us to cover up" (11). "I suffer from more constraint in this," he says, "than I consider becoming to a man, and especially to a man of my profession."[31] Yes, this example amuses and appears insignificant. But it is not only the case, for Montaigne, that custom might constrain us by "ensnaring" us into practices that we cannot escape, or by making it difficult for us to perform great actions that challenge the status quo. Its constraint consists also in its everyday, insidious, ever-present whispering, preventing us from daily joy in the “freedom of nature’s first laws,” as Montaigne says in his preface. Anyone who has rebelled against the boundaries of a society in which tightly controlled manners stand in place for genuine human expression or intimacy can identify with this delicately intense form of suffering.

## 3. A VIVID DYE: THE LIBERATION OF VIRTUE

Given the power of custom, however, is there any hope for escape? We have seen Montaigne suggest that we can turn this power to our good, but we have yet to explore how exactly one might do so. Before we return to this recommendation, however, we must countenance one surprising possibility: in spite of his insistence on the patchwork, inconstant form of human beings, Montaigne clearly thinks that some people can find the relevant freedom in virtue.

Even in “Of the inconsistency of our actions,” there is evidence that Montaigne accepts the possibility of steadfast virtue. He does not simply identify inconstancy as a neutral fact about human beings; our inability to stand fast to resolutions is rather “the most common and apparent *defect* of our nature” (239, emphasis added). And he has strong words about virtue, which, he says, “is a strong and vivid dye, once the soul is steeped in it, and will not go without taking the fabric with it” (243). There are also several references to the universality of inconstancy, but taking these literally renders incoherent examples like that of “the younger Cato: he who has touched one chord of him has touched all; he is a harmony of perfectly concordant sounds, which cannot conflict” (241).

These references are not isolated anomalies. The *Essays* are full of condemnations of vice, praise of virtue, and examples of strong and constant characters. We have seen his allusion in “That the taste of good and evil . . .” to “great and lofty souls.” Also striking is his praise of Epaminondas in “Of the most outstanding men.” This leader of Thebes, whom Montaigne admires for his intelligence and magnanimous justice as well as his statesmanship, holds pride of place even above Homer and Alexander the Great. Montaigne’s description of him is both striking and relevant that I will quote at length:

> But as for his character and conscience, he very far surpassed all those who have ever undertaken to manage affairs. For in this respect, which must principally be considered, which alone truly marks what we are, and which I weigh alone against all the others together, he yields to no philosopher, not even to Socrates.
>
> In this man innocence is a key quality, sovereign, constant, uniform, incorruptible. (573)

Clearly, Montaigne believes that some souls escape the shackles of inconstant custom through extraordinary virtue. It is telling that among the examples of Epaminondas's virtue are several behaviors that would have been suspect to those steeped in his culture's customs, such as his refusals to let patriotism override friendship or humanity.

One might think that such examples show only that Montaigne is willing to admit, among a sea of general inconstancy and variability, the possibility of some rare freaks of nature, superhuman in their virtue. And I would agree that he believes virtue to be quite rare. He cannot believe it to be as rare as this proposal suggests, however. It is a premise of the essay on education, for instance, that rearing can effect genuine cultivation of character, even against prevailing customs. The goal of such education is to help the student trade the too-prevalent "vulgar qualities, most often seen in the meanest souls" for "rare, strong, and philosophical qualities" (114). Of course, education will not always achieve its goal, but Montaigne is hopeful that it can at least make some difference when done charitably and thoughtfully. And he is clear that there is no foretelling its effects in advance: the notion that one can divine a child's potential through "trivial conjectures and prognostications" is best replaced with the general aim to "guide [children] always to the best and most profitable things" (109).

As with Aristotle, however, some of the most compelling evidence of Montaigne's commitment to the possibility of genuine virtue and constancy comes in his discussion of friendship. His essay on the topic is both a description and defense of his friendship with Etienne de La Boëtie, who had died in 1563, and whose work was being co-opted by rebels in the religious wars. In explaining his assurance that La Boëtie would never act seditiously, he offers the story of Caius Blossius insisting to Roman consuls that he would have done anything his friend wanted him to do, as he knew that his friend would never want him to do something vicious. Here Montaigne echoes Aristotle's claim that genuine friendship requires virtue, although Frame's translation obscures the point: "if you assume that this team was guided by the strength and leadership of reason [*par la vertu et conduitte de la raison*], as indeed it is quite impossible to harness it without that, Blossius' answer is as it should have been. If their actions went astray, there were by my measure neither friends to each other, nor friends to themselves" (140). Screech has, more helpfully, "guided by virtue and led by reason."[32] Virtue and reason ensure the reliability of one friend to the other, meaning that in true friendship one can avoid following the suggestion of Chilo (which Montaigne finds otherwise prudent): "Love him . . . as if you are to hate him some day . . ." (140). Again, although Montaigne insists on the absolute uniqueness of his friendship with La Boëtie, his offering of other examples of the form show that he believes that this kind of mutual trustworthiness, while rare, is not unprecedented.

It is also significant that Montaigne explicitly yokes this kind of constancy and trust to freedom. Both fathers, brothers, and wives, he says, are poor candidates for this highest kind of friend, in part because one's relationship to them is *not* characterized by freedom. The problem is that "the more they are friendships which law and natural obligation impose on us, the less of our choice and free will there is in them. And our free will has no product more properly its own than affection and friendship" (137). (Again, the translation is not perfectly helpful; the words that Frame translates as "free will" are "*liberté volontaire*," which bring to light a play on words. The work in question by Boëtie was called "*De la Servitude volontaire*." Screech has "willing freedom.") Those of us in happy marriages, who lament Montaigne's claim that marriage "is a bargain to which only the entrance is free" may take some comfort in his suggestion that "if such a relationship, *free and voluntary*, could be built up, in which not only would the souls have this complete enjoyment, but the bodies would also share in the alliance, so that the entire man would be engaged, it is certain that the resulting friendship would be fuller and more complete" (138, emphasis added).

These examples are instructive because they offer insight into the relationship between freedom, integrity, and constancy that I believe is at the heart of Montaigne's ideas about how we might escape the tyranny of schoolmistressly custom. This is a freedom of harmony, where one does not feel one's friend as a burden, because one's desires and aims are perfectly consonant with those of the friend. Likewise, the more of one's being is bound up in such a relationship, the more complete the harmony—so that, were women of stronger stuff!—marriages might constitute an even higher form of friendship, inasmuch as the harmony brings in the physical nature as well. We do not, in other words, necessarily become free by protecting the boundaries between the self and what appears to be external. We might become free by effacing those boundaries, so that one's soul expands and becomes more powerful. Montaigne's description of his own friendship suggests an extreme but compelling case: "our souls mingle and blend with each other so completely that they efface the seam that joined them, and cannot find it again" (139). Genuine friendship is a liberation.

## 4. A WHIPLASH TO THE ORDINARY STUPIDITY OF JUDGMENT: ESSAYING AS LIBERATION AND INTEGRATION

I have argued that Montaigne, contrary to first appearances, accepts the possibility of a constancy that can avoid the sense of being burdened or tyrannized by custom. The liberating effects of such virtue work whether the custom refers to individual or societal practices. Such people have the strength to resist pressure from the community, should the demands of the community conflict with the demands of their character. And the unity of that character prevents the experience of feeling tyrannized by one aspect of it, when that aspect conflicts with other significant parts of the person's individual nature.

Nonetheless, we cannot and should not ignore the relative rarity of such characters, for Montaigne. He does think they are possible—and he does not think they are only to be found in the work of doxographers. But they are nonetheless the exceptions rather than the rule. With respect to most people, it will be more reasonable to presume that they are conflicted, inconstant, and somewhat unpredictable even to themselves. "Nothing is harder for me," he says, "than to believe in men's consistency, nothing easier than to believe in their inconsistency" (II.1, 239).

If we are not blessed with such characters, Montaigne has little hope for our developing them through our own devices. We have seen his claim that, with respect to "his character and conscience," Epaminondas "yields to no philosopher, not even to Socrates." This is high praise indeed, given Montaigne's overwhelming admiration for Socrates, as he understands that character.[33] In "Of physiognomy," Montaigne tells us that Socrates "was a perfect model in all great qualities" and repeats the famous story according to which "Socrates said of his ugliness that it betrayed what would have been just as much ugliness in his soul, if he had not corrected it by training." But then he adds: "But in saying this I hold that he was jesting according to his wont. So excellent a soul was never self-made" (810). This comment, added in the last revision of his essays, suggests that Montaigne has come to the view that extraordinary greatness and constancy must be—at least in significant part—a gift of one's nature.[34]

So what are those of us, not blessed by nature with the greatness of Epaminondas or Socrates, supposed to do? Are we doomed to flounder in the net of custom, prisoners of our own prior actions or the practices of whatever community we find ourselves in? Fortunately, for those of us of a more ordinary admixture, there does seem to be a method within our grasp: it is the method of the essays themselves.

In a particularly poignant moment in "Of custom," Montaigne notes that "what is off the hinges of custom, people believe to be off the hinges of reason: God knows how unreasonably, most of the time" (83). Following, however, is a recipe for avoiding such unreasonableness: "If, as we who study ourselves have learned to do, each man who hears a true statement immediately considered how it properly pertains to him, each man would find that it is not so much a good saying as a good whiplash to the ordinary stupidity of his judgment" (83). The suggestion is that self-study—the kind of study of which the essays themselves are an extraordinary example—might help one overcome stupidity of judgment. And the precise form of stupid judgment preceding this remark is the assumption that mere custom reflects sound reasoning about the nature of things. Even more significantly, he suggests later in the same essay: "Whoever wants to get rid of this violent prejudice of custom [*coustume*] will find many things accepted with undoubting resolution, which have no support but in the hoary beard and the wrinkles of the usage [*usage*] that goes with them; but when this mask is torn off, and he refers things to truth and reason, he will feel his judgment as it were all upset, and nevertheless restored to a much surer status" (84–85).[35] Here, a search into the history of customs will reveal them as the "masks" that they are, thus liberating us and our judgment to some degree. And in all but the last edition of the *Essays*, this passage began, "And whoever wants to *essay* himself in the same way, and get rid of . . ." (84, emphasis added). This "essay" reflects the original meaning of the title of the *Essays*: they are "attempts." In combination with the earlier passage about self-study, it is not a big leap to presume that Montaigne is claiming that his own "attempts"—the *Essays* themselves—are models for how one might effect some liberation from the tyranny of custom.

At times, Montaigne characterizes the *Essays* as direct defiance of custom. For example, in "Of practice," he laments that the general remedy against weakness—that of "exercising and forming" our souls through practice—cannot help us with the "greatest task we have to perform"—dying (267). Fortunately, we are not lost; "we can approach it, we can reconnoiter it" by certain experiences that resemble death (268). He then recounts one of his own experiences having such an effect, when he lost consciousness after being thrown from a horse. This powerful experience, he reports, relieved him of some of his own anxiety about dying. But the experience alone is not enough. "This account of so trivial an event would be rather pointless," he says, "were it not for the instruction that I have derived from it for myself. . . . Now as Pliny says, each man is a good education to himself, provided he has the capacity to spy on himself from close up. What I write here is not my teaching, but my study; it is not a lesson for others, but for me" (272). In the following, he offers an extended defense against the custom [*coustume*] that "has made speaking of oneself a vice," comparing it to a custom that prohibits wine because of some people's propensity to drunkenness (273). While recognizing that some people who speak of themselves do so from conceit, and thereby only add to that conceit, he insists that "this excess arises only in those who touch themselves no more than superficially . . ." (274). But this playing with self-imagining is not Montaigne's project. He aims instead to, like Socrates, try himself against the wheel of self-exploration, for the aim of self-knowledge, wisdom, and freedom.

This theme, of course, is one that Montaigne returns to in "Of experience." We hear its echo in the following famous passage:

> Then whatever may be the fruit we can reap from experience, what we derive from foreign examples will hardly be much use for our education, if we make such little profit from the experience we have of ourselves, which is more familiar to us, and certainly sufficient to inform us of what we need.
>
> I study myself more than any other subject. That is my metaphysics, that is my physics. (821)

It is this self-study that enables him to use his imagination, together with custom, to help endure his suffering from "the stone." As I argued above, custom alone could not produce such a result; it is as likely to increase suffering as assuage it. It is, after all, custom that makes us set in our ways so that we see any new change in our routine—let alone a change that involves monthly pain—as more evil than it would otherwise be. Montaigne suggests, however, that the intervention of an active mind might turn custom toward our good. It can help us become more supple, more flexible, and more able to identify the edifying features of even painful experience. But it is now important to see how significant the *Essays* themselves are in forwarding this goal. It is one thing to attempt, in the face of pain, to remind oneself that it has salutary effects; it is quite another, more powerful, thing to compose a list of them, collate supporting examples, and laugh in writing at one's own failings to appreciate their lessons. Here, in the midst of an essay written at the end of his life, as he offers whatever wisdom he has achieved to his family, friends, and posterity, he does not abandon his genial self-deprecation. In the passage quoted above about the powers of his mind in soothing his imagination, we find his common juxtaposition of self-praise and self-abasement: "My mind is suited to this service; it has no lack of plausible reasons for all things. If it could persuade as well as it preaches, it would help me out very happily."

Such irony, I submit, is not merely for the sake of comic relief. Those committed to *essaying* themselves must face their own faults with open, brave eyes. Montaigne's biting wit would not be honest were it not often turned against himself. He has no hope that we might escape the power of custom altogether, and he has only qualified hope that we can use our imaginative powers to use custom's shaping influences to mold us into a pleasing form. He acknowledges that his best efforts have not kept him, as he ages, from becoming more dependent on the practices that he has always known. It does not follow, however, that the only remaining option is being buffeted about by the customs we happen to fall into or inherit. Through acquiring a new custom—the custom of writing the essays themselves—Montaigne finds some degree of liberation. They liberate through reinforcing customs that are helpful, unmasking those that are not, and through giving their author some control over what he sees as his own. They are both self-revelation and self-creation. In "Of experience," he seems to denounce his work: "To compose our character is our duty, not to compose books, and to win, not battles and provinces, but order and tranquility in our conduct. Our great and glorious masterpiece is to live properly" (851). But the contrast here is not between those who compose books, like Montaigne, and those who do not. It is between those who put off the work of improving themselves for the sake of glory, and those who "have done the greatest task of all," which is "to think out and manage" their own lives (850). For Montaigne, writing a book became inseparable from that task. When he says in "Of practice," "It is not my deeds that I write down; it is myself, it is my essence," a careful reader will realize that the seam between book and author, like that between the author and his friend, is being effaced, so that it will be difficult to find again (274).

## 5. CONCLUSION: CUSTOM, ESSAYING, AND THE EXPANSION OF THE SOUL

I have argued that in Montaigne's *Essays*, custom usurps many of the roles traditionally played by habit, and that this usurpation has several significant implications. In particular, it suggests the possibility of feeling enslaved to one's everyday practices to a dangerous and significant degree. It is part of the work of the *Essays* themselves to effect some liberation from such enslavement. This is not wholly unlike Aristotle's idea that habits worthy of the name of virtue must be reflective in a certain way. It is not enough, on this view, to be disposed to some kind of action as a result of natural propensity or as a mechanical reflex. These dispositions must be "guided by right reason."[36] Montaigne offers no necessary and sufficient conditions for when one's individual "customs" are sufficiently reflective to be conceived of as virtues. He does, however, offer a sustained example of the kind of reflection that will make us more active, and therefore more free, with respect to our customs.

This reflection is neither reasoning in a void, but neither is it, as with Aristotle, reasoning together with a stable community of relatively like-minded companions. We may worry that it seems to be a profoundly individualistic pursuit, like Descartes's only liberating reflections. From the beginning, Montaigne seems to intentionally distance himself from his readers, and we can picture him, alone in his library, deliberately withdrawing from a world that appears to him to be going mad. It often seems to me that a mood of melancholy solitude hangs over the essays, so that every few pages I am reminded that this is the work of a man of extraordinary, probably isolating abilities, who has lost his dearest friend. Do the essays, after all, elevate individual practice over the outside world of custom?

Ultimately, it is useless to deny that a certain individualism calls from the pages of the *Essays*. And since I find this individualism powerful and often compelling, I have no desire to do so. But if we conceive of individualism as necessarily narrowing and constricting, ascribing it to Montaigne is profoundly unfair.

We have seen him argue that reflection on the variety of customs and their suitability in different contexts can itself be an act of liberation: it can unmask practices for what they are, and free us from the burden of feeling ourselves bound in reason by what binds us only in repetition. The extensive, relentless list of such customs is not a narrowing: it is an expansion. With each example, Montaigne enlarges the scope of his experience and, by extension, our own. The act of *essaying* is expanding as well: it has the effect of deepening one's inner life, both in its particulars, and in its doubling and sometimes tripling of one's perspectives on oneself. Montaigne is no longer just the man who falls off the horse. He is the man who uses that experience to reflect on the nearness of death. And *then* he is the man who reflects on the usefulness of such reflections. And finally, he is the man laughing at all of the below.

But this is not all: Montaigne makes it clear in several of his essays that genuine *essaying* requires not only self-examination, but the testing of and by others as well. Despite the alleged blending of the will in perfect friendship, he identifies "admonitions and corrections" as "one of the chief duties of friendship" (136). The tragic "disadvantage of greatness" identified in the essay of that name is that others will not genuinely challenge the great. Kings thus lose one of the great pleasures of life—the "trials of strength we have with one another, in rivalry of honor and worth, whether in exercise of the body or of the mind" (701). The word translated "trials of strength" here is: "Essays." And in "Of the art of discussion," he celebrates the kind of companion who is not afraid to offer contradiction, and therefore instruction. "I like a strong, manly fellowship and familiarity, a friendship that delights in the sharpness and vigor of its intercourse, as does love in bites and scratches that draw blood" (750).

The overcoming of tyrannical custom and its transformation into something that can be more reflective, more integrated into a tranquil life, requires expansion of experience, expansion of thought, and expansion of one's circle of friends. To return to the question with which we began, I suspect that Montaigne writes the essays not only for his present friends, but also in search of kindred spirits who might aid him in this project of self-expansion. It is no accident, I submit, that at the very end, he identifies his hero in the quest for self-knowledge, Socrates, as the best exemplar of true "*grandeur de l'ame*" (852ff). The search for self-knowledge, for Montaigne, is indeed a quest requiring—and adding to—the greatness of one's soul. We have here a form of magnanimity that shares in common with Aristotle's the capacity for truthful self-assessment.[37] But the self to be assessed is much messier, much more "patchwork," than anything Aristotle envisioned as a candidate for such greatness. It will not necessarily reveal its greatness in the stunning honorability of its actions; it may, instead, do so in its active assimilation and adaptation of that which is given for its use, including custom.[38]

## NOTES

1. Michel de Montaigne, *The Complete Essays of Montaigne*, trans. Donald M. Frame (Stanford: Stanford University Press, 1965). Unless otherwise indicated, page references to Montaigne are from this edition. Although I rely heavily on Frame's translation, I have literalized references to *coustume* and related terms, as I explain below. The original French appears in brackets beside these changes. In cases where I have indicated the specific essay in the body of the paper, I will give only the page number in parentheses. In other cases, I will identify the essay by a Roman volume number and Arabic essay number, followed by a page number. French quotations from the *Essais* come from the extremely helpful Montaigne Project website, at http://www.lib.uchicago.edu/efts/ARTFL/projects/montaigne/.

2. Blaise Pascal, *Pensées*, trans. A. J. Krailsheimer (London: Penguin, 1966), fragment 126/93. Krailsheimer translates *coustume* as "habit" in this passage. See Blaise Pascal, *Pensées*, ed. Dominique Descotes (Paris: Garnier-Flammarion, 1976), 77.

3. In the last revisions, Montaigne cheekily adds, "well, yes, perhaps a word or so, but only to vary, not to delete." Even this qualified claim is not quite true.

4. See the *Oxford English Dictionary* online (Oxford: Oxford University Press, March 2011), etymology of "habit." http://www.oed.com/view/Entry/82978?rskey=uKNGC6&result=1 (accessed June 2, 2011).

5. Aristotle, *Nicomachean Ethics*, trans. Martin Ostwald (Englewood Cliffs: Prentice Hall, 1962), 33, line 1103a21–22. I will cite future references to this edition of the *Ethics* by line number only.

6. Aristotle, *Nicomachean Ethics*, 1152a30–34.

7. Katharine Breen, *Imagining an English Reading Public: 1150–1400* (Cambridge: Cambridge University Press, 2010), 45–46.

8. See Michel de Montaigne, *The Complete Essays*, trans. M. A. Screech (London: Penguin, 2003), 56n.

9. For an interesting study of the history and continued resonance of such stories, see Wednesday Martin, *Stepmonster: A New Look at Why Real Stepmothers Think, Feel, and Act the Way We Do* (New York: Houghton Mifflin Harcourt), 2009, chapter 2, "'She's Such a Witch!'" Fairy Tale History and the Stepmothering Script."

10. Aristotle, *Nicomachean Ethics*, 1180a14–24.

11. See, for example, Aristotle, *Nicomachean Ethics*, 1094a27ff.

12. Aristotle, *Nicomachean Ethics*, 1099a11–13, emphasis added.

13. See, for example, Plato, *Republic*, in *Plato: Complete Works*, eds. John M. Cooper and D. S. Hutchinson (Indianapolis: Hackett, 1997), IX, 573aff.

14. Frame's translation seems to suggest the latter, but not all translators do so. Screech has "the natural laws of the common people" (Montaigne, *The Complete Essays*, 1249).

15. For an interesting study of the effects of prolonged or chronic pain, which takes into account the history of pain and its mental effects, see Melanie Thernstrom, *The Pain Chronicles: Cures, Myths, Mysteries, Prayers, Diaries, Brain Scans, Healing, and the Science of Suffering* (New York: Farrar, Straus and Giroux, 2010).

16. For a helpful discussion of the tendency to overlook virtues that we need because of our biological vulnerability and dependency, which both draws on and is critical of Aristotle, see Alasdair MacIntyre, *Dependent Rational Animals* (Chicago: Open Court, 1999).

17. Plato, *Gorgias*, in *Plato: Complete Works*, 837.

18. Plato, *Gorgias*.

19. Plato, *Republic*, 1190.

20. Plato, *Republic*, 1177a23–24.

21. Plato, *Republic*, 1165b27–28.

22. Montaigne reports that, hoping for peace of mind and tranquility, he retired to his estate and to his library. Retirement, however, gave rise to new troubles of mind. See, for example, the beginning of "Of the affection of fathers for their children" (278ff) and the end of "Of Idleness" (21).

23. Cf. the beginning of Descartes's *Discourse on the Method of Rightly Conducting One's Reason and Seeking the Truth in the Sciences*: ". . . the power of judging well and of distinguishing the true from the false—which is what we properly call 'good sense' or 'reason'—is naturally equal in all men . . ." (*The Philosophical Writings of Descartes*, vol. 1, trans. John Cottingham, Robert Stoothoff, and Dugald Murdoch [Cambridge: Cambridge University Press, 1985], 111). The first lines of Part One seem taken almost directly from a passage in Montaigne's "Of presumption," but it may be that Descartes and Montaigne had simply both heard a common joke. See *Essays*, 499.

24. The quotation is from Lucretius: *"Qui nisi sunt veri, ratio quoque falsa sit omnis*" (*De Rerum Natura*, 4.486). In his handwritten notes on the 1588 edition, Montaigne adds a comma between his sentence and the quotation, making clear that he means the quotation to refer back to the senses being true judges.

25. *Oxford English Dictionary*, online version, March 2011, etymology of "habit, *n*."

26. See also the end of "Apology for Raymond Sebond," in *The Complete Essays of Montaigne*, 454–55.

27. Aristotle, *Nicomachean Ethics*, 1166a13–15.

28. Aristotle, *Nicomachean Ethics*, 1166a27–28.

29. Aristotle, *Nicomachean Ethics*, 1166b7–9. Interestingly, both Aristotle and Montaigne identify regret or repentance as indications of inconstant character. See Aristotle, *Nicomachean Ethics*, 1166a28–29 and 1166b24, and *Essays*, 243, in Montaigne's discussion of Alexander's inconstancy.

30. For an argument that Montaigne replaces the idea of human nature with the "human condition," which appeals to his ideas about custom, see Ann Hartle, *Michel de Montaigne: Accidental Philosopher* (Cambridge: Cambridge University Press, 2003), 54.

31. Montaigne means his profession as a soldier. Many of his contemporaries considered his claim to be a member of the military nobility to be ridiculous pretension. See Hugo Friedrich, *Montaigne*, ed. Philippe Desan, trans. Dawn Eng (Berkeley: University of California Press, 1991), 9–11.

32. Michel de Montaigne, *The Complete Essays*, 213.

33. For a helpful discussion of the way that Montaigne uses varying sources about Socrates's life, and the way that he transforms the character for his own purposes, see Friedrich, *Montaigne*, 52–55.

34. Cf. "That to philosophize is to learn to die": "In truth, in all things, unless nature lends a hand, it is hard for art and industry to get very far" (60).

35. Cf. Lucretius, *De Rerum Natura,* 3.55–58.

36. Aristotle, *Nicomachean Ethics*, 1144b23.

37. For Aristotle's discussion of the virtue of magnanimity, see *Nicomachean Ethics*, 4.3.

38. I am very grateful to Ann Hartle and the Institute for the History of Philosophy, whose 2010 summer seminar enabled me to think more deeply about Montaigne in an extraordinarily hospitable setting with wonderful conversation partners. I am also grateful to Robert Miner, from whose thoughtful conversation and comments I benefited greatly, and to Tom Sparrow and Adam Hutchinson, for their vision and patience in putting together this volume.

## BIBLIOGRAPHY

Aristotle. *Nicomachean Ethics*. Translated by Martin Ostwald. Englewood Cliffs: Prentice Hall, 1962.

Breen, Katharine. *Imagining an English Reading Public: 1150–1400*. Cambridge: Cambridge University Press, 2010.

Descartes, René. *Discourse on the Method of Rightly Conducting One's Reason and Seeking the Truth in the Sciences*. In *The Philosophical Writings of Descartes*. Vol. 1. Translated by

John Cottingham, Robert Stoothoff, and Dugald Murdoch. Cambridge: Cambridge University Press, 1985.

Friedrich, Hugo. *Montaigne*. Edited by Philippe Desan. Translated by Dawn Eng. Berkeley: University of California Press, 1991.

Hartle, Ann. *Michel de Montaigne: Accidental Philosopher*. Cambridge: Cambridge University Press, 2003.

MacIntyre, Alasdair. *Dependent Rational Animals*. Chicago: Open Court, 1999.

Martin, Wednesday. *Stepmonster: A New Look at Why Real Stepmothers Think, Feel, and Act the Way We Do*. New York: Houghton Mifflin Harcourt, 2009.

Montaigne, Michel de. *The Complete Essays of Montaigne*. Translated by Donald M. Frame. Stanford: Stanford University Press, 1965.

Montaigne, Michel de. "Apology for Raymond Sebond." In *The Complete Essays of Montaigne*, 318–457.

———. *The Complete Essays*. Translated by M. A. Screech. London: Penguin, 2003.

———. *Essais*. Montaigne Project. Accessed January 10, 2013. http://www.lib.uchicago.edu/efts/ARTFL/projects/montaigne/.

Pascal, Blaise. *Pensées*. Translated by A. J. Krailsheimer. London: Penguin, 1966.

———. *Pensées*. Edited by Dominique Descotes. Paris: Garnier-Flammarion, 1976.

Plato. *Gorgias*. In *Plato: Complete Works*. Edited by John M. Cooper and D. S. Hutchinson. Indianapolis: Hackett, 1997.

———. *Republic*. In *Plato: Complete Works*. Edited by John M. Cooper and D. S. Hutchinson. Indianapolis: Hackett, 1997.

Thernstrom, Melanie. *The Pain Chronicles: Cures, Myths, Mysteries, Prayers, Diaries, Brain Scans, Healing, and the Science of Suffering*, New York: Farrar, Straus, and Giroux, 2010.

# *II*

# Habits of Thought, Action, and Memory in Modernity

*Chapter Five*

# From Habits to Traces

Dennis Des Chene

Experience makes its mark on us in many ways. It leaves traces; it instills habits. A trace, as I define it here, is a quality of the soul or mind which is distinguished by its content. Aristotelian species and Cartesian ideas are traces. A habit I take, following Suárez, to be a quality of the soul which assists in the acts of a power of the soul, enabling them to be performed more easily and promptly. I will use the Latin word *habitus* for habits so understood.

This chapter examines the fate of *habitus* in early modern philosophy. In comparing just two authors, Suárez and Descartes, it can only suggest, schematically, how that fate is to be understood. My suggestion is that the role of *habitus* in Suárez's psychology is occupied in Descartes's by association, understood mechanistically, and by resolution—the mind's act of binding itself to be guided by certain judgments. These, being acts of will directed toward ideas, are traces rather than habits.

No doubt the history is not so simple as this contrast makes it appear. Already in Suárez and Descartes, we must complicate the scheme: in Suárez's case, by the fact that some *habitus* seem to be expressible as rules, and in Descartes's by phenomena resembling the Suárezian *habitus*, in particular the readiness and ease with which certain judgments are said to be made or recalled. Nevertheless, I think the scheme offers a useful first approximation to the early modern history of habit.[1]

For philosophers now, the interest in the discussion is twofold. The first is that the problems to which the concept of *habitus* was a response are still with us: learning includes the acquisition not only of knowledge but of skill, and skill includes not only the bare *how-to* but also readiness and ease in use. Suárez's discussion, like those of his Scholastic predecessors and contemporaries, offers a subtle analysis of habit in relation to the acts and powers of the mind; even after the Aristotelian framework itself has been discarded, it remains the case that the ambit of psychology includes if not *habitus* itself then at least the phenomena that *habitus* was intended to account for. Moreover, the treatment of habit in contemporary philosophy of mind tends to ignore the phenomenology that habit was meant to explain or to subsume it, insofar as it concerns intensity, under something like degrees of belief. In my view treatments of action and belief would benefit from the study of the work of Suárez and his contemporaries on habit.

## 1. SUÁREZ ON *HABITUS*

In the *Disputationes metaphysicæ*, Suárez devotes a number of disputations to the Aristotelian categories, one of which is quality. Following Aristotle he divides quality into four kinds, the first of which consists of *habitus* and *dispositio*. *Dispositio*, which will become a key term for Descartes, is the "order of a thing having parts," either actual, as in the case of something beautiful, or virtual, as in the order of virtues in the soul.[2] *Habitus* is first defined briefly as "a form which confers ease and promptness of operation," and later more precisely as "a species of quality proximately ordered to assisting a power in its operation." He takes note of but sets aside a broader sense of the term, found in Thomas for example, according to which *habitus* denotes any quality which disposes a thing well or ill in its *esse* (42§3no4, 26:611).[3] In this sense, but not in the stricter sense, health is a *habitus*.

*Habitus* in the stricter sense is of two sorts. Those of the first sort are required by a power in order that it should be conjoined with its objects. Intentional species are "like the seeds or instruments of objects by whose means they conjoin their virtue with the cognitive powers" of the soul; by their means alone are acts of sensing, remembering, and so forth possible. Suárez mentions these only to set them aside; they have been discussed in his *De Anima*.

*Habitus* of the second sort, though not required for the operation of a power, determine the manner of that operation. They are invoked to explain how it is that certain acts become easier and quicker to perform through repetition. We learn not only by acquiring species representing the things we know; and not only by combining representations in various ways so as to make judgments and demonstrations; we learn also by practice, we acquire skills. In what follows *habitus* denotes only the second sort of learning.

The essence of *habitus* is to assist in the operations of a power. Suárez argues that to do so a *habitus* must be stable (and thus distinct from the operations themselves, which exist only so long as they receive the "actual influx of the soul": 44§1no6, 26:665), and it must inhere in the power itself, from which it is nevertheless distinct (since a soul can have the power without the habit).

*Habitus* need be invoked only to explain only the operations of those powers which exhibit some latitude in their operations, some indifference or indetermination. The acts of inanimate things are determined entirely by their powers and the objects they act on; nothing additional is required to explain either the act or its manner (no10, 666). It follows that the only powers of the soul in which *habitus* occur are the will and the intellect, and with them the sensitive appetite and the imagination or *phantasia* in those creatures that have will and intellect. The will is evidently free; the intellect is indifferent in its operation when evident cognition is lacking or when the relation between premises and conclusion is hard to follow, as in mathematics. Appetite, insofar as it can be governed by will and reason, must also be supposed to exhibit indifference. When, for example, the human good runs contrary to what the senses delight in, *habitus* may intervene so as to decide in favor of one or the other. For similar reasons, the imagination is said to be capable of acquiring habits.

Higher animals, or *bruta*, share with humans the faculties of appetite and imagination. It might be thought that they too can acquire *habitus*. After all, "sometimes an animal by performing several acts [of the same sort] acquires a facility or virtue for judging an object, concerning which it has no innate virtue or natural instinct" (44§3no1, 26:669). Augustine speaks of "custom" (*consuetudo*) among the beasts (83 *Quæst*., no. 36); Thomas says of animals that some sort of *habitus* can be attributed to them (*Summa theologiæ* 1pt2q50art3). Suárez argues that because in animals appetite and imagination are always entirely determined by their objects, there is no need to suppose that those faculties can take on habits. They no more need habits than a stone does in order to fall. What seems like *habitus* is merely a "firmer adherence" of the *phantasma* or species in the imagination. That, together with the object, determines the action of the animal (44§3no4, 26:670).

*Habitus*, then, are qualities of those powers of the soul which, because their operations are not entirely determined by their objects or by extrinsic causes, require something additional to explain certain aspects of those operations. That I am capable of judging whether two plus two is four follows from my having an intellect; but that I can do so quickly and easily follows from my having acquired the science of mathematics, and requires a new principle of explanation. That new principle is required, however, only in humans.

## Causes of Habitus

Practice makes perfect: habits seem to be caused, and Suárez holds that they are caused, by acts of the sort they assist in causing. Not only that but they are strengthened by repetition of those acts, and weakened if we cease to perform them. The role of repetition in forming habits, and the role of idleness in weakening them, both require explanation.

*The cause of* habitus *is its corresponding act*. That much was common ground. The precise nature of the effects of *habitus*, and likewise of their causes, was disputed. I will take as given Suárez's conclusion that the effect of a *habitus* is the act it assists in, and not merely a mode of that act. The cause he also takes to be the act. The act functions as an efficient cause, and not, as Durandus thought, as a disposing cause, nor as Buridan thought, as the *via* by which the power in which the *habitus* inheres produces it (44§8no4, 5; 26:682).[4] In response to certain difficulties about the causation of the qualities of a thing by that thing's own acts, Suárez draws on arguments made elsewhere in the *Disputations*, according to which an immanent act (which is the only sort at issue) is at once an *actio* (in the categorical sense) of its power and a *qualitas*. Acts by which *habitus* are produced do so by virtue of being qualities (44§8no13; 26:684).

It would seem that we have *mutual* causation of act and *habitus*. We might see here a positive feedback loop, especially since repeated acts can strengthen a *habitus*, and thereby incline the corresponding power more strongly to perform them. The eventual result would be that the power would always be inclined by *habitus* to the highest degree. To remove that difficulty Suárez notes that the *habitus* alone is never the *sufficient* cause of acts; it only assists the power in producing it.

*The role of repetition*. Experience seems to tell us that habits are acquired only by repeated acts (by *consuetudo*, custom). Aristotle in the *Ethics* says that virtues are acquired through teaching and experience, and that it takes time to acquire them. Yet that does not seem possible. If one act won't do, then neither will many. The force of one could be multiplied only if several occurred together. But they do not. Even a virtuoso cannot perform the same piece twice at the same time. Thus it would seem that habits cannot be acquired at all.

Suárez, following Henry of Ghent, effectively turns that argument on its head. If a first act does nothing to alter the power that produces it, then a second act, confronted with a power still equally "indisposed" to being affected by it, will likewise accomplish nothing. But since acts do induce habits, we must conclude that by just one act a habit may be effected (44§9no6, 26:687).

Nevertheless practice does make perfect. We know from experience that habits can increase both in intensity and in breadth. A habit is more intense insofar as it inclines its power more strongly and to more intense acts; it is broader insofar as it assists in acts toward a greater range of objects. Charity properly nurtured not only becomes more intense, but also extends from the love of God to joy in the goodness that proceeds from him.

In general the intensity of a *habitus* corresponds to the intensity of the acts that cause it. Like Thomas, Suárez holds that the intensity of a *habitus* can be increased only by more intense acts. If sometimes we observe that acts of equal intensity make a habit more intense, that is because an act does not always bring about a habit whose intensity corresponds to its own. There may be, for example, in the power a tendency contrary to the habit—a relish for food, for example, which is contrary to temperance. Or else the power itself may resist alteration by an act by virtue of its indifference and "the inclinations it has toward other acts or objects" (§10no13, 693). Indifference, in other words, gives rise to inertia in the taking of habits.

The increase of breadth of habits becomes for Suárez the occasion for examining the "celebrated question" of the unity of habits (§11no9, 26:696). First of all, even if increase of breadth can sometimes be explained by supposing that some habits are complexes of qualities, to which more can be adjoined, still we must eventually arrive at qualities which are simple. Suárez holds that those simple qualities must themselves be habits (no23, 701).

How, then, is it possible for a simple habit to be extended to several objects? It can be if those objects all share the same "formal reason," or if they are all connected by necessity so that "one is virtually contained in another" (no27, 702). If justice applies to a great many objects, and if it is simple, Suárez's account directs us to look for a single formal reason under which all objects of justice can be subsumed; this turns out to be "saving the equality of each person in his possessions." Or again since from love there follows, if the thing loved is absent, desire, and if it is possessed, joy, all those qualities of the soul, insofar as they are *habitus*, are "rooted" in the single *habitus* of love (no31, 703).

## Decay of Habits

Just as habits grow through use, they decay through disuse. Because Suárez, in agreement here with Thomas, holds that everything, *quantum est ex se*, "postulates its own conservation," and because *habits*, unlike acts, do not depend on the actual influx of their cause to exist, the cessation of acts cannot by itself be the cause of their decay. It is at most the occasion (44§12no4–11, 26:716–17). In general qualities are corrupted by their contraries; here *habitus* are corrupted by acts inconsistent with them, or (in the case of imagination and appetite) by the deterioration of the organs their powers require in order to operate. The cessation of the acts that brought about the *habitus* originally merely leaves the way open for corruption to occur; left to itself, the *habitus* will remain, in its final intensity.

## Summary

Habits for Suárez are qualities of powers. They perfect those powers both by virtue of completing the determination of acts, and—when they are good habits—by virtue of inclining those powers, which may otherwise be indifferent, toward the ends for which those powers exist. Our appetite is, sadly, often indifferent as between the healthy and the harmful; its end, all the same, is to operate so as to promote health and other things beneficial to us. Temperance in appetite leads us to perform more easily and promptly those acts which are in fact beneficial.

Nevertheless habits do not represent the objects of the acts they assist in causing, nor the ends promoted by those acts. Considered in itself, a habit is merely the readiness to perform acts of a specific sort, and the acquisition of a habit, though integral to *scientia* (in the case of intellectual habits) or to acting morally (in the case of moral habits) is not the acquisition of any sort of intentional state. It is an instrument by which intentional states are translated into acts.

# 2. DESCARTES

If in matters of explanation your instincts are Cartesian, you will be dissatisfied with the preceding. Explanations deal, you will say, in mechanisms and laws. Suárez has given us at best a description of the phenomena to be explained, and conceptual arguments showing how it is possible, for example, given what *habitus* and acts are supposed to be, for a *habitus* to be intensified by repeated acts. The only glimmer of an explanation is in Suárez's treatment of animals, when the "firmer adherence" of the species in memory is said to explain the greater ease of action acquired through practice. It is not my purpose here to adjudicate between styles of reasoning in natural philosophy, but only to consider how Descartes, with *his* conception of explanation, treats some of the phenomena adduced by Suárez.[5]

## Mechanization of Habit

The first steps toward the mechanization of habit are taken in the *Treatise on Man*. In its treatment of memory, phenomena which are also characteristic of habit are explained in terms of the motions of the animal spirits in sensation and their lasting effects on the brain. The animal spirits that issue from the pineal gland enter the nerves through pores in the interior surface of the brain, which is composed of fibers with intervals between them. By virtue of their motion, the spirits have sufficient force to "enlarge these intervals a bit, and to fold and dispose in various ways the small fibers they encounter in their paths." They trace figures "which are related to those of the objects" of sensation, and as time goes by they do so better and better, "accordingly as their action is stronger, and lasts longer, or is more often repeated" (11:178). By that means the figures thus created in the brain are "in some manner conserved", and can continue to direct the animal spirits so as to leave impressions on the gland even when the action of the object on the senses has ceased. The fibers acted on by the spirits acquire a disposition "by means of which they can be more easily opened" than before. Descartes compares the surface of the brain to a piece of cloth pierced by needles; even if the holes made by the needles close up, still they leave "traces" in the cloth which make the holes easier to open (179).

*Association.* By this means also the association of images can be explained. If two holes have been opened together several times, and if they "do not have the custom" of being opened separately, then they will both open even if only one of them is acted on by the animal spirits. This "shows how the recollection of one thing can be excited by that of another which was previously impressed on the memory at the same time." Descartes later explains what we would call involuntary recollection in the presence of those movements of the spirits that account for the passions: the "humors" whose varied movements cause in us various passions point the pineal gland in various directions. If in the part of the brain toward which the gland is directed, "the figure of some particular object is impressed much more distinctly than any other," the gland cannot but receive the impression made on it by the spirits when they encounter that figure (184). If several figures are impressed in that place, the gland will receive the impressions of all of them, in part or in whole; by this means the "creativity" of the imagination is explained. Thus the indeterminacy or indifference of imagination, on the basis of which Suárez holds that imagination can take on *habitus*, is merely apparent. It is an artifact of ignorance. Imagination, considered as a corporeal power, has no *habitus*.

What applies to memory applies more broadly to the acquisition of habits in animals—that is, to learned regularities of behavior. In a letter of 1646 to the Marquis of Newcastle, Descartes, responding it would seem to the citation of Montaigne and others according to whom animals have thought and understanding, briefly explains how animals can be taught to utter words "even though those words or signs need not be related to any passion" (21 November 1646). A magpie that has learned to say hello to its mistress when she arrives, has been made to connect the utterance (*prolation*) of the word to one of its passions, namely the "movement of hoping to eat"; this association will have been produced by giving it some morsel whenever it says hello in the right circumstances. When Descartes speaks here of *hope*, he means not a mode of thought or a passion properly speaking, but rather the movements of the animal spirits that in both humans and animals characteristically accompany the passion (Alquié 3:695).

Setting aside the question of whether these are fully mechanistic explanations—Descartes was content with them—what we seem to have is a transposition into more or less mechanistic terms of the doctrine by which Suárez explains the acquisition of traits of behavior in animals. The difference is that *force* by which memories are made to adhere, as Suárez puts it, more or less firmly in the brain is just what Descartes in his physics calls the quantity of motion. And though the figures created in the brain by sensation and passion have no intentional objects, and cannot be said to "intend" anything, we may attribute objects to them on the basis of their causal role in producing or being produced by thoughts in the mind.

## Use and Mastery of the Passions

Suárez and Descartes agree, though for different reasons, that animals have no *habitus*.[6] Suárez holds that in humans imagination and appetite, though corporeal, differ specifically from their analogues in animals, and admit of indifference; *habitus* is then invoked for them as for will and intellect to complete the determination of their acts. Descartes effectively denies that there is a difference; in humans too, imagination and appetite are corporeal, and exhibit no indifference.

Humans certainly acquire habits in the broad sense. The question is whether in Descartes's psychology there is any need to suppose that *habitus* in Suárez's restricted sense are required to explain the phenomena, and in particular to explain regularities in behavior.

*Association again*. It is clear, first of all, that some acquired traits can be explained by an extension of association. In animals, association occurs between impressions in the brain. In humans, some "corporeal actions" are joined with thoughts in such a way that to each action there is a corresponding thought which will occur on the occasion of that action. The *Meditations* argue that God has instituted certain relations of this sort so that from the thoughts produced by certain movements, actions will follow that help preserve the union. These relations are innate.

But we also have the capacity to acquire such relations, whether involuntarily through experience or voluntarily through practice. In the *Passions*, by way of explaining why love is joined with a "gentle heat in the chest" and with improved digestion, Descartes notes that certain experiences can give rise to enduring relations between corporeal actions and thoughts, and indirectly between one thought and another. Those who have "taken with great aversion some beverage when they were sick cannot eat or drink anything afterward which has a similar taste without having the same aversion; nor can they think of the aversion one has to medicines without having that taste return to their thoughts" (*PA* art107, 11:408; see also art136, 11:428–29). So too when the soul was joined with the body, the first passion it experienced occurred when it encountered "a foodstuff more suited than usual" to maintain the heat of the body, and thus preserve it. The soul thereupon loved that stuff; at the same time the spirits flowed from the brain toward the muscles, which in turn caused the stomach and the intestines to send more of the same stuff toward the heart. The relation that occurred on this occasion between bodily movements and love, and so also those movements, has since then "always accompanied the passion of love."

*Intensity*. We can also control the *intensity* of our passions in various ways. New objects, or those that seem to us new, give rise to movements of the spirits in proportion to their novelty. To the force of those movements there corresponds a greater or lesser intensity of wonder. Sometimes wonder is excessive, and leads us to esteem objects more than they deserve. In general wonder decreases with repeated exposure. But if it leads us "to fix our attention only on the first image of the objects presented" to the mind (art78, 11:386), then it "leaves behind a habit (*habitude*) which dispose the soul to fix itself in the same way on all the other objects presented to it, provided that they appear even a little bit new to it." An excess of wonder, and the stronger fixation of attention that follows from it, can lead to a habit of seeking novelties, an addiction one might say to wonder.

Wonder normally gives rise to a desire for knowledge of its object, and knowledge brings about a decrease in wonder. The habit of excessive admiration would amount to nothing other than the abnormal absence or weakness of that desire. But we might then ask whether combatting excessive wonder requires the formation of a *habitus* toward that desire—a thirst for knowledge, a greater readiness for inquiry. Descartes suggests that those people are given to excessive admiration who, though they have a sufficiently good common sense, nevertheless do not "have a great opinion of their sufficiency" (*suffisance*), or in other words who are diffident about their ability to acquire knowledge (art77). The natural condition is to have the desire to knowledge, with an intensity proportionate to the perceived novelty of the object. The habit of excessive admiration arises from a judgment that inhibits that desire. Given that judgment and the other qualities of mind required for wonder, we have all we need to explain the susceptibility of such people to wonder. It would seem that there is no need to invoke *habitus*.

*The role of judgment*. Judgments, then, can control the occurrence and the intensity of passions. In his "general remedy for the passions," Descartes summarizes the means we have to attain mastery over the passions. The "easiest and most general remedy" for excess of passion is "to remind oneself that everything which is presented to the imagination tends to deceive the soul and to make appear to it reasons that serve to persuade it [to act on the object of the passion in accordance with that passion] stronger than they are, and those that serve to dissuade it weaker." On that basis we should will ourselves to "consider and follow the reasons contrary to those that the passion represents," even if they seem weaker (art211, 11:487). To moderate excessive desire, for example, we should consider that only our own thoughts are truly within our control; that judgment will tend to diminish the intensity of desire by putting its objects beyond our certain grasp (art144–46, and already in the *Discours*).

Judgments of this sort, which I will call resolutions, are clearly not *habitus*. They have intentional objects; they are traces rather than habits in Suárez's sense. As in the case of excessive admiration, to explain the facility of the mind to have various passions, and the intensity of those passions, we need only invoke the circumstances of their production and the judgments by which they are controlled.

## Conclusion

In Cartesian natural philosophy, intensities, if not reducible to force—that is, to quantity of motion—present a problem. Even in his psychology I think Descartes would have preferred to avoid reference to them. *Habitus*, whose task in Aristotelian psychology is to explain certain intensities—promptness, facility—attributable to the operations of certain powers of the human mind, is therefore to be avoided also. I have suggested that it is to be supplanted in two ways: first, by reference to physical structures like pores, and flows, whose perfectly respectable modes (figure and size in one case, speed and volume in the other) can be recruited to the task of explaining the phenomena previously explained by invoking *habitus*; second, by reference to resolutions, that is, to certain sorts of judgment.

Nevertheless there remain in the Cartesian setup certain ineliminable intensities—that of desire, for example—which cannot be entirely reduced to flows or to cognitive acts. In particular the dimension of *weakness or strength* of minds, in the face, say, of the tendency of wonder to bring about its own repetition, must be regarded as a feature of the mind not yet amenable to science.

## NOTES

1. An earlier version of this paper was given at the conference "Transformations of the Soul," Humboldt University, Berlin, November 2006, organized by Dominik Perler.
2. On *dispositio*, see Dennis Des Chene, *Physiologia* (Ithaca, NY: Cornell University Press, 1996).
3. All references to Suárez are to the *Opera omnia* (Paris: Ludovico Vivès, 1856). The *Metaphysical Disputations*, first published in 1597, are included in volumes 25 and 26 of the *Opera*. References will be to disputation, section, and numbered paragraph; and to volume and page.
4. See Durandus, *In Sent.* 3dist33q2, and Jean Buridan *Comm. in Ethicam* 2q3.
5. On memory and traces in Descartes, see especially John Sutton, *Philosophy and Memory Traces: Descartes to Connectionism* (Cambridge: Cambridge University Press, 1998), and

"Porous Memory and the Cognitive Life of Things," in Darren Tofts, Annemarie Jonson, and Alessio Cavallaro, eds. *Prefiguring Cyberculture: An Intellectual History* (Cambridge, MA: MIT Press, 2002).

6. On Descartes's physiology and its relation to the passions, see Dennis Des Chene, *Spirits and Clocks* (Ithaca, NY: Cornell Universiry Press, 2001); Lisa Shapiro, "What Do the Expressions of the Passions Tell Us?" *Oxford Studies in Early Modern Philosophy* 1 (2003): 45–66.

## BIBLIOGRAPHY

Des Chene, Dennis. *Physiologia*. Ithaca, NY: Cornell University Press, 1996.

———. *Spirits and Clocks*. Ithaca, NY: Cornell University Press, 2001.

Shapiro, Lisa. "What Do the Expressions of the Passions Tell Us?" *Oxford Studies in Early Modern Philosophy* 1 (2003): 45–66.

Suárez, Francisco. *Opera omnia*. 28 vols. Paris: Ludovico Vivès, 1856.

Sutton, John. *Philosophy and Memory Traces: Descartes to Connectionism*. Cambridge: Cambridge University Press, 1998.

———. "Porous Memory and the Cognitive Life of Things." In *Prefiguring Cyberculture: An Intellectual History*, edited by Darren Tofts, Annemarie Jonson, and Alessio Cavallaro, 130–41. Cambridge, MA: MIT Press, 2002.

# *Chapter Six*

# Habit, Custom, History, and Hume's Critical Philosophy

Peter S. Fosl

While articulating his distinctive "solution" to the doubts of skepticism, a solution better understood as an embrace, Hume famously writes in Section 5 of the *Enquiry concerning Human Understanding* (1748) that "Custom, then, is the great guide of life."[1] In the paragraph just preceding this remark, describing the great guide and how it leads us to think, feel, and judge in spite of the corrosive force of skeptical reasoning, Hume finds it suits his purposes to alternate "custom" with "habit":

> This principle is CUSTOM or HABIT. For wherever the repetition of any particular act or operation produces a propensity to renew the same act or operation, without being impelled by any reasoning or process of the understanding; we always say that this propensity is the effect of *Custom*. (EHU 5.1, p. 37)

This essay undertakes to explore the meaning of habit and custom in Hume's thought and do so with special attention to the way this central feature of his work informs what might be called Hume's critical philosophy. By "critical" philosophy, I mean both the sense in which Kant later used the term "critical," to explore the limits of reason and the conditions of possibility for thought and action per se, but also something of the way "critical" has gained currency in political projects like "critical" race theory, as well as moral and aesthetic criticism and "critical theory" addressing the reading of texts. In other words, I wish to explore the load ideas of "custom" and "habit" bear in undertaking Humean forms of criticism. Consider first a number of salient qualities of habits and customs.

## 1. INHABITING THE WORLD

If nothing else, habit and custom are temporal. They require repetition across time, and they require those repetitions to count. Habit and custom become what Hans-Georg Gadamer (1900–2002) calls "effective" in the sense of making it possible to appropriate historical meaning in new acts of meaning and understanding. Indeed, Gadamer calls the way historical meaning makes possible new ways of thinking and acting, "effective history" (*Wirkungsgeschichte*).[2]

Customs and habits in this sense largely constitute what Hume calls "common life," and customs of this sort are necessary conditions of conceptual thought. As Hume tells us in *A Treatise of Human Nature* (1739–1740), that repetitions can be made effective through the mind's capacity for finding resemblance underwrites the very possibility of thinking through general concepts and, in our language, using general, abstract terms.[3] In repeatedly applying a general, abstract term (for example, "book") to a number of resembling particular experiences, we come to apply the term to new ones, as well as to the proper recollections.

In Hume's account, when we encounter a word functioning as a general term, the mind recalls one of the particular instances named by the term, but also something else. In addition, the mind recalls or, more precisely, "revives that custom" of relating the initial perception to a specific group of other perceptions (*Treatise* 1.1.7, 19). In other words, the use of abstract, general terms is made possible through (1) an idea associated with that term plus (2) a habit or custom of relating that idea to others. It is not too much to say, in this Humean sense, that general concepts and general terms as they are effective in language themselves are species of custom.

As Donald W. Livingston has rightly argued, ideas per se, for Hume, are also themselves historical.[4] In Hume's well-known formulation, ideas are "copies" of impressions that temporally precede them; and to understand an idea by rooting it or comparing it with the impressions from which it derives is an historical process, a kind of Humean conceptual archeology.[5] General concepts, as well as the ideas of individuals, then, are not only temporally composed of habits; they are also themselves historical artifacts, and apprehending the meaning of ideas is an historical project.

In this way, of course, Hume's idea of custom labors in service of the early modern nominalistic project of displacing Platonic and Aristotelian theories of "form" (*eidos*) that had dominated much of the ancient and medieval worlds as the ground of thought in general and general terms in particular. The reorientation had preceded Hume, and his work caps in many ways nominalist, empiricist, and naturalist streams that stretch back to the ancient world.

For Plato, the meaning of general terms (e.g. "dog" or "good") is grounded not in the many individual, particular objects of perceptual experience to which such terms refer but to transcendent "forms" that exist independently and in important ways beyond the world we perceive. For Aristotle, forms do not exist in a transcendent way, beyond the phenomenal world, but certainly remain independent of thought and language.

Ancient "atomism" and "skepticism," however, develop alternatives to metaphysics and semantics grounded in forms, alternatives that resurface in modernity in the work of thinkers such as Pierre Gassendi, Galileo Galilei, and René Descartes. What philosophers have come to call "nominalism" during the Middle Ages advances the critical work of the ancients by exploring theories of cognition and meaning not dependent upon the independent existence of forms. Modern naturalists and empiricists—including Francis Bacon, Thomas Hobbes, John Locke, George Berkley, Joseph Butler, and Francis Hutcheson (all influences on Hume)—labor to articulate philosophical theories using terms defined more or less strictly by just the observed natural order, minimizing the explanatory role of things divine, transcendent, or otherwise unobservable.[6] Hume takes up and radicalizes the naturalistic, empiricist, and nominalist streams that preceded him, reconceiving, diminishing, and in some cases thoroughly excising not only "form" but also time-honored theoretical posits such as "substance," causation, and "God," as well as the realist pretensions of natural science. Hume, however, more radically and more systematically than those from whom he draws, situates thinking, acting, and meaning in a temporal and historical way.

While Hume follows other nominalists, empiricists, and naturalists in arguing that the "many" phenomena of each of the various kinds we encounter are not so because they are metaphysically rooted in "one" distinct metaphysical form (transcendent or immanent), he exceeds them by recognizing that it is our customs and habits, and not simply experience and our natural cognitive faculties, that do the job of collecting and cementing individuals into types. In other words, for Hume the many individuals of any specific kind are gathered under a general concept or term through the temporally and logically prior existence of a custom—that is, through the prior existence of repetitions of cognition, thinking, speaking, writing, and otherwise doing that renew themselves. These habits are themselves certainly underwritten and modulated by what Hume calls natural "principles of association."[7] But without the linking work habit achieves over time those associations could not come to build and structure our effective historicity.

One might say then, anticipating the historical philosophies of the century that would follow him, as well as recent phenomenological and deconstructive critiques of "presence," that Hume replaces the presence of both eternal Platonic and Aristotelian forms, as well as the presence of positivist sense data, with effective customary history across a temporal horizon that is *not* fully present—in other words, with habit. The universal is grounded in the particular for Hume through habit.

Hume observes, in fact, that "the far greatest part of our reasonings, with all our actions and passions, can be deriv'd from nothing but custom and habit" (*Treatise* 1.3.10, 81). But perhaps the best known among the habits of reasoning Hume describes is the habit of causal inference. After repetitions of experiencing one set of impressions that are both spatially contiguous and temporally successive in a regular way—in Hume's terms as a "constant conjunction"—we come to feel a sense of "necessity" to their contiguity and succession such that the appearance of the one we call a "cause" brings to mind the expectation that the other, which we call the "effect," is sure to follow, and to follow necessarily (*Treatise* 1.3.2). "Our idea, therefore, of necessity and causation," writes Hume in the first *Enquiry*, "arises entirely from the uniformity, observable in the operations of nature; where similar objects are constantly conjoined together, and the mind is determined by custom to infer the one from the appearance of the other" (EHU 8.1, 63). Reason may be, in Hume's famous phrase, "the slave of the passions" (*Treatise* 2.3.3, 266), but the passions are articulated and shaped by custom and habit.

Discursive reasoning of all kinds, then, depends upon habit, and habit leads us beyond ourselves, to the belief in a world that extends past our field of perception, to a past that extends beyond our memory, to others and to a self that we fictitiously think endures (*Treatise* 1.4.6, 170; EHU 5, 43). "All inferences from experience, therefore, are effects of custom, not of reasoning" (EHU 5.1, p. 37). In the *Treatise* Hume affirms: "Now as we call every thing custom, which proceeds from a past repetition, without any new reasoning or conclusion, we may establish it as a certain truth, that all the belief, which follows upon any present impression, is deriv'd soley from that origin" (*Treatise* 1.3.8, 72).

Søren Kierkegaard's character Constantin Constantius, so compelling in his meditations on "repetition," is from a Humean point of view, then, only in part right when he argues that it is through repetition that the self is maintained and that the universal can be reconciled to the particular.[8] Repetition does so, says Hume, not when it is resolute, the result of existential choice, but when it becomes habitual, customary, and historical.[9] And repetition becomes habitual, customary, and historical for Hume only through the possibilities of our humanness we find ourselves bound to—the natalities and fatalities of our human nature. That is to say, habits are a kind of human mimesis; or, rather, habits mimetically repeat human existence. Ideas for Hume are "copies" of "impressions," but each new iteration or repetition of a habit in a sense also copies prior manifestations of that habit. So, habits are in a sense not only mimetic copies of the world as we experience it but also mimetic repetitions of ourselves as composites of prior and continuing habits.

Along just these lines, Kierkegaard's Constantius argued that unlike Platonic "recollection," repetition is forward looking: "repetition and recollection are the same movement, except in opposite directions, for what is recollected has been repeated backwards."[10] And for Hume repetition that achieves the standing of habit and custom, or anyway emerges as habit and custom, is always and already forward looking, turning us toward a future that we expect will resemble our present as well as our past, grounding a belief in the uniformity of nature now, beforehand, and henceforth, leading us, for example, to believe, with characteristically Humean optimism, that the sun will rise tomorrow (*Treatise* 1.3.8, 73; EHU 4, 24).

In this sense of the always already forward-looking repetition of the past and our selves, habit functions as something like the Humean a priori—or what philosophers have come to call the *toujours déjà,* the *immer schon da.* It is not resolute choice or the temporal, projective *existentialia* of *Dasein,* according to Hume, that carry us from the present into a meaningful future on the basis of the historical past. It is, rather habit and custom that do so, the same sorts of habit and custom that in part compose what Hume calls common life.[11] Hume writes in the *Treatise*:

> The supposition, *that the future resembles the past*, is not founded on arguments of any kind, but is deriv'd entirely from habit, by which we are determin'd to expect for the future the same train of objects, to which we have become accustom'd. (*Treatise* 1.3.12, 92)[12]

In this sense, human reasoning depends upon the prior historical ground of habit and custom. So, in a sense prior to all judgment, for Hume, lies the prejudice (or pre-judgment) of habit. Joel Weinsheimer finds a similar implication in Gadamer: "The startling consequence Gadamer draws is this: prejudices, which from the viewpoint of Enlightenment rationalism appear as obstacles to understanding, are historical reality itself and the condition of understanding it."[13] In their function of underwriting standards of judgment, habits also approximate what Alasdair McIntyre means by "practices."[14]

Moral judgments, unsurprisingly, depend for Hume upon custom and habit. Moral judgments apply to people's character, but character is manifest in habits of conduct. So, moral judgments not only depend upon habit and custom but are about them. Moral judgments exhibit remarkable variation across time, space, and culture, too. Hume's short essay, "A Dialogue," appended to the second *Enquiry*, the *Enquiry concerning the Principles of Morals* (1751), outlines how, among other things, what passed for morally proper conduct among the ancients would to moderns seem incestuous and murderous.[15] Variations, in fact, according to Hume, "are the *natural* effects of customs" (EPM, 121). Aesthetic pleasures are, for Hume, variable and shaped by custom, too.[16] Accordingly, writes Hume in his essay, "The Sceptic": "You will never convince a man, who is not accustomed to Italian music, and has not an ear to follow its intricacies, that a Scotch tune is not preferable."[17]

While, however, the habits of moral judgment exhibit substantial variation, the habits of sociability and discourse that expose us to the thoughts and feelings of others generate a countervailing effect and even bring us, according to Hume, to relatively impartial standards of moral judgment. As John P. Wright articulates Hume's theory: "it is by constantly exposing our feelings to the feelings of others, and by hearing their judgments even in those cases which directly concern us, that we reach an impartial moral point of view."[18]

Hume announces in a section of the *Treatise* entitled "Of the Effects of Custom," that "nothing has a greater effect both to encrease and diminish our passions, to convert pleasure into pain, and pain into pleasure, than custom and repetition" (*Treatise* 2.3.5, 271). Custom and habit render various ways of thinking and feeling easy, agreeable, strong, and durable—constitutive of what Hume calls "calm passions" (*Treatise* 2.3.5, 271). The calm habit of mind characteristic of philosophy in particular (unlike the enthusiasm-generating habit of religion and "false" metaphysics) "insensibly refines the temper, and it [philosophy] points out to us those dispositions which we should endeavour to attain, by a constant *bent* of mind, and by repeated *habit*."[19]

Habit, however, for Hume not only shapes the character traits of emotion, passion, and sentiment. Habit and custom also sculpt the dispositions and inclinations of will and conduct: "Custom has two *original* effects upon the mind, in bestowing a *facility* in the performance of any action or the conception of any object; and afterwards a *tendency* or *inclination* towards it, and from this we may account for all its other effects, however extraordinary" (*Treatise* 2.3.5, 271). But while custom renders feeling and acting easy and familiar, it can also intensify them. Custom can diminish the force of those feelings, beliefs, and practices to which people have little adherence (what Hume calls "*passive* habits"), but it can also reinforce beliefs and practices strongly embraced ("*active* habits").[20]

Indeed, in an important sense, habit and custom exist only insofar as they exist in act and in conduct. It would be simply incoherent to say, "I am in the habit of X, but I no longer do that." In fact, the very meaning of breaking or letting go of a habit (habit literally means "to hold") is that the act is no longer performed. The intelligibility of the world, therefore, for Hume depends not only upon the propositional states we occupy but also upon our conduct in the world, our continuing historical actions in both word and deed.

As deed habit is more than a mental condition, state, or disposition. Habits are embodied. But as the loci of habit, bodies are also more than physical states, more than biochemical composites, and more than the particular causal sequences of any given moment. Our bodies are the sites where the historical sediment and accretions of many streams of culture, society, and civilization intersect and transect. Our bodies enact and are enacted by the intersections of the habits composing—among other lines of custom—race, class, gender, religion, taste, and the complex transactional bundle of habits composing identities. In this sense, too, our bodies are for Hume ideological.[21]

Habits, of course, can be broken; but to recognize this is also to acknowledge that habits are variable and contingent, fragile, and uncertified by anything beyond themselves. The contingencies that pervade Humean philosophy are what Gilles Deleuze recognizes as connecting Hume's thought with his own. They are what, in Deleuze's view, make both him and Hume "empiricists."[22] Along similar lines, habits are what Stanley Cavell would call "unsponsored" dimensions of ordinary life.[23]

The variability and contingency of custom and habit does not mark, for Hume, however, a distinct boundary between judgments of natural science and those in morals and aesthetics. Through habit and custom as a prior condition of their possibility, judgments in morals, aesthetics, and the sciences share a common ground. Judgments in natural science vary over time, too, and what counted as scientifically uncontroversial among medievals became no longer so among moderns. Galen's (129–c. 217 CE) theories of bodily humors and animal spirits endured in the habits of medicine for well over a thousand years—but they are now almost universally rejected. Indeed, as Hume writes in "The Standard of Taste":

> Though in speculation, we may readily avow a certain criterion in science and deny it in sentiment, the matter is found in practice to be much more hard to ascertain in the former case than in the latter. Theories of abstract philosophy, systems of profound theology, have prevailed during one age: In a successive period, these have been universally exploded: Their absurdity has been detected: Other theories and systems have supplied their place, which again gave place to their successors: And nothing has been experienced more liable to the revolutions of chance and fashion than these pretended decisions of science. (*Essays*, 242)

Among the characteristics of habits and customs Hume acknowledges, we also find that they may be either individual or collective.[24] When habits do become social, they produce conventions that, like sympathy, make it possible for people literally to come together ("convene," literally meaning to come together) and overcome the separateness of persons that underwrites skepticism with regard to other minds. Hume's parable of two rowers (*Treatise* 3.2.2, 315) exemplifies people who take up forms of conduct without verbal consent or argument but nonetheless are able to convene and achieve coordinated action. Without any scientific analysis of space and time, agency, transportation, water, and without the need of any formal agreements, contracts, or promises, the background conditions composed of habits of thought and action make it possible for people to sit down next to one another and pull against oars in coordinated ways, to in-habit forms of life that are aligned and in agreement.[25]

Tying this all together, then, we find that custom and habit comprise for Hume not only repetitive, social as well as individual, temporal-historical-embodied acts that compose character, shape pleasure as well as judgment, and ground the practices of rationality. We also find that habits and customs are variable and contingent.

The contingency of habits and customs lies at the heart of Hume's philosophical program, and it underwrites especially his skeptical criticism in a way that precedes both analytic and continental critiques of rationalistic attempts to ground science, morality, aesthetics, and politics in the necessities and certainties of reason.[26] In every context, Hume's critical agenda repeats itself along this formulation: "when we pass from the impression of one to the idea or belief of another, we are not determin'd by reason, but by custom" (*Treatise* 1.3.7, 97). Not belief in the causal connection, not the discursive connections of deduction or induction, not our conviction in the external world or the continuing existence of objects beyond our perception, not our moral judgment or our regard for the feeling and position of others, not our standards of taste, not our inclinations to believe in things supernatural, not the agreements that ground society and social conventions—none of these for Hume are ultimately grounded in reason. Indeed, for Hume, without custom reason is unable to establish even its own warrant.[27] Contrary to Samuel Clarke and the deists, contrary to the Cartesians and Spinozists, contrary even to the Newtownians and Lockeans, for Hume it is not reason but habit, custom, and history that ground our lives and their intelligibility. It is through habit and custom that we in-habit a meaningful and intelligible world, populated by people like ourselves. In this sense, habits and customs compose what Heraclitus called the *ethos* of our lives, the *topoi* or places of our thinking, speaking, acting, and meaning.[28]

## 2. PROGRESSIVE HABITS AND CRITICAL CUSTOMS

That Hume holds our lives to be grounded in habit, custom, and history has led a number of commentators to misunderstand him as a deeply conservative traditionalist thinker of the same stream of thinking that produces Edmund Burke (1729–1797) and Michael Oakeshott (1901–1990).[29] In Laurence Bongie's phrase, for example, Hume is the "prophet of the counter-revolution."[30] Donald W. Livingston's *Philosophical Melancholy and Delir-*

*ium* (1998) and *Hume's Philosophy of Common Life* (1984) pursue a similar reading. This interpretation in my view, however, misunderstands the normative power of Hume's thought and rests on a fallacy of false alternatives.

Sir Leslie Stephen accused Hume of a "cynical conservatism."[31] But the reading of Hume as a conservative traditionalist is earnest, and turns upon the way Hume refuses what Donald W. Livingston calls "political Cartesianism," a view of philosophical activity as operating from a commanding, detached position that has transcended the "gross earthy mixture" (*Treatise* 1.4.7, 177), as Hume calls it, of "common life," in particular human custom.[32] According to Hume in Livingston's reading, "false" and pathological species of philosophy pretend to have completely transcended the customs of common life, acquiring what Nagel has called a "view from nowhere," absolute autonomy and independence from history, culture, and opinion as well as its own overriding authority to pronounce judgments upon common life.[33] False philosophy and religion, in fact authorize in their mad "philosophical melancholy and delirium" (*Treatise* 1.4.7, 175) totalized judgments, judgments legitimating the wholesale overturning of the beliefs and practices of custom and history in favor of the ideal "plans of imaginary republics" purportedly spun from free-floating philosophical reason. In precisely the same way, Descartes announced that he was "razing" the whole of his past beliefs in favor of what his detached and solitary *cogito*—with its self-generated, self-verifying method—would establish.[34] Criticizing the political culture that put Charles I to death, Hume complains that theology and metaphysics of this pathological variety had corrupted and rendered dangerously malignant the ordinary worlds of politics and even commerce: "inquiries and debates concerning tonnage and poundage went hand in hand with . . . theological or metaphysical controversies" (*History,* 334).[35]

Although they are wrong in describing its implications, Livingston, Bongie et al. are right in their description of Hume's critique of false philosophy, religion, and metaphysics. Humean skepticism does refuse the pretense of metaphysical claims about the causal connection, the external world, God, morality, and the self. In his trenchant claim that consent to agreement already presupposes the prior existence of society, Hume attacks social contract theory, the darling of political liberals and Whigs, in its attempt to establish rationally the basis of state and social authority (*Treatise* 3.2.1–11).[36]

Hume does argue that long possession and even conquest can be sufficient to establish sovereign authority over territory (*Treatise* 3.2.8–9). Hume refuses the existence of Lockean natural rights, grounding social relations instead in sympathetic and sentimental concord and secondarily on instrumental and deliberative rationality. Moreover, although Thomas Jefferson misunderstood Hume as a Tory, he properly understood that Hume's *History of England* does not portray Charles I as a simple tyrant or follow a Whiggish historiography that posits an ancient constitution and charts the unfolding of liberty from the *Magna Carta*, or even prior to it in Anglo-Saxon social practices, through the English Civil War. Instead, Hume works to understand historical figures in their own context, in terms of the values, ideas, and rationality available to them at their time and not by timeless and placeless standards of judgment.[37]

The traditionalist and conservative reading of Humean philosophy, however, runs aground on the insistence with which Hume's work advances reformist and even progressive ideas. Hume's own political positions seem inclined in progressive directions, and the implications that may be drawn from his theory are in many ways even radical. Hume's *Natural History of Religion,* his *Dialogues Concerning Natural Religion*, and various among his essays launch devastating criticisms of the false philosophies of both modern rationalistic religion and traditionalist religious enthusiasm, offering a naturalistic account of the development of religious belief and devastating criticisms of theistic teleology, intelligent design, immortality, providence,[38] and prohibitions against suicide.

Unlike the views of then-contemporary religious conservatives, Hume's moral theory is naturalistic and Ciceronian. In a letter to Adam Ferguson he explicitly rejects popular Christian virtue, explaining that: "Upon the whole, I desire to take my catalogue of Virtues from *Cicero's Offices*, not from the *Whole Duty of Man*. I had, indeed, the former Book in my Eye in all my Reasonings."[39] Hume's *Treatise* and *Enquiries* reject Christian values and character traits like humility, poverty, and meekness.[40] Hume articulates cutting-edge naturalistic accounts of mind, political theory, and epistemology. He generates critical norms militating against traditional beliefs and prescribes evidentiary practices like proportioning belief to the evidence, disciplining our causal judgments (*Treatise* 1.3.15), guiding the "general point of view" in our moral and aesthetic judgments (EPM 4, 407; 2.2.5, 362), as well as progressively configuring the architecture of the state to diminish faction (e.g., "On the Idea of a Perfect Commonwealth"). A supporter of American independence and the aspirations of the Glorious Revolution, Hume in his essays condemns slavery (e.g., "Of the Populousness of Ancient Nations"); and he praises emerging liberties of thought and publication ("Of the Liberty of the Press," "Of Civil Liberty," and "Of the Independence of Parliament"). More generally, Hume also supported the development of new economic relations and the newly developing natural and social sciences (e.g., "Of Commerce"). It should be unsurprising then that Hume's essays were frequently consulted by revolutionaries and progressives in the newly established United States.[41]

Hume's general philosophical prescription crystallizes in his skeptical injunction to eschew metaphysics and purported claims to transcendence. Instead, he argues, philosophers and other theorists should limit their work, as Voltaire might put it, to cultivating the garden of common life. Hume, along these lines, writes famously in the first *Enquiry* that, properly undertaken, "philosophical decisions are nothing but the reflections of common life, methodized and corrected" (EHU 12.3, 121). It is, however, in misunderstanding this methodizing and correcting project that those who have interpreted Hume as a traditionalist have erred. To infer from Hume's rejection of false philosophical transcendence a normative embrace of traditionalist conservatism depends upon the erroneous position that traditionalist conservatism is the *only* alternative to false transcendence for a philosopher who roots so much of the human world in custom. It is not. Hume the skeptical, philosophical critic articulates another alternative.

The proper contrasting alternatives for Hume are not those of transcendence vs. custom and tradition but rather methodized custom vs. unreflective custom. In this, Hume seems to prefigure the contemporary progressive political philosopher Chantal Mouffe, who argues against both liberalism and traditionalism (as well as against Carl Schmitt and post-political anti-democratic politics in general) in favor of an alternative form of contested democracy.[42] Like Mouffe, Hume does not pretend to overcome otherness and faction through instrumental reason—either in the proprietary and instrumental rationality of Lockean liberalism, with the idealized forms of communication of which Habermas fantasizes, or even through simple but comforting conservative appeals to tradition.[43] Rather Hume accepts and acknowledges the often unpleasant persistence of difference and faction; and he works to manage them just skeptically, through provisional agreements and rules of reflection that emerge in a critical engagement with custom among the participants of a political contest.

When Humean "reflection" casts its gaze upon custom, it can, when properly disciplined, generate what Hume calls "general rules" of a "second influence" (*Treatise* 1.3.13, 102) rooted in custom itself.[44] These rules can subsequently turn back upon custom to methodize and correct it, but not forever or with the presumption of final closure. Although in common life we act by habit and custom in generally unreflective ways, as if by a "secret operation" (*Treatise* 1.3.8, 73), through our capacity for reflection we can nevertheless, like the Owl of Minerva, later look back upon and regulate habit and custom (*Treatise* 1.3.13, 99ff.). Custom, in short, can itself for Hume become the ground for revising and reforming custom, even in a progressive manner.

Consider as an analogy to politics the practices of language. The practices of vernacular English, for example, in common life are not grounded in an autonomous and sovereign act of philosophical transcendence or, for that matter, in divine revelation. The traditions and customs composing the ordinary languages of common life instead develop gradually, even naturally, over time in an unreflective way. By reflection only upon the customary practices of ordinary language, however, people can generate grammatical rules which then, in turn, can be deployed to discipline, correct, and methodize the linguistic practices of common life. People can do this, moreover, without the pretense of revelation or transcendence beyond the phenomena of common linguistic life, or the pretense of finishing language and bringing it to peaceful, final completion for all time. The process of reflectively methodizing general rules used to correct other general rules is for Hume an open-ended, zetetic process.

While criteria of criticism and judgment are initially generated through a reflective engagement with experience, through custom criteria of this sort become durable. They thereby compose what might be regarded, in contrast to mere "prejudice," second-order customs of criticism. Hume describes this process in his influential essay on aesthetics, "Of the Standard of Taste";[45] but the process of generating second-order critical customs is not restricted to aesthetic judgment. Criticism is underwritten by a similar process in scientific, moral, and also political judgment. Habits and customs related to gender and marriage, for example, might be revised—certainly not by metaphysical appeals to the divine or through self-evident principles of reasoning, but rather by appeal to second-order principles self-consciously generated from within common life itself. Conversations, dialogues, and contests about these topics situated in common life might in a Humean way enlist principles concerned with the usefulness, durability, and pleasures of the contingent habits we call, for example, "marriage," "family," "love," "parent," "liberty," and "fairness," that people currently inhabit, as well as alternatives to them. Think about how through critical Humean second-order reflections grounded in common life people might inhabit differently or cease to inhabit the habits of race.

Self-understanding critical theories and practices of this sort themselves even offer, for Hume, distinctive pleasures, at least for those who acknowledge skeptically the ultimately unsponsored status of reflective second-order criticism. Criticizing and correcting existing habits through second-order reflections rooted in the habitual matrix of common life itself yields a special ironic (and revealing) pleasure Hume describes in this way:

> The vulgar are commonly guided by the first [kind of general rule, prejudice], and wise men by the second [kind of reflective general rules]. Mean while the sceptics may here have the pleasure of observing a new and signal contradiction in our reason, and of seeing all philosophy ready to be subverted by a principle of human nature, and again sav'd by a new direction of that principle. The following of general rules is a very unphilosophical species of probability; and yet 'tis only by following them that we correct this, and all other unphilosophical probabilities. (*Treatise* 1.3.13, 102)

Reflectively generated second-order general rules subvert the metaphysical and epistemological realisms and enthusiasms dogmatists had recognized as philosophy. But this same kind of second-order reflection subsequently "saves" philosophy by offering a new, unsponsored direction to philosophical theory and criticism. This new direction resolves the puzzle facing traditionalist readers of explaining how Hume's rooting so much of our lives in habit, custom, and history can be made consistent with his normative, reformist, and progressive criticism. It may seem to a dogmatist a "contradiction" that the habits constitutive of critical general rules subvert rationalism but also underwrite critical judgment.[46] But Hume's progressive theory of habit exhibits how customs may be used critically to correct and to modify one another without the requirement of ultimate grounds beyond the practices of human life itself, or what Hume calls "common life." In short, the reflective and progressive use of habit and custom as it functions in second-order general rules saves Hume from being understood in the figure of a Burkean conservative traditionalist, offering instead a "progress of sentiments" (*Treatise* 3.2.2, 321) in Humean thinking that is both critical and progressive.

## NOTES

1. David Hume, *An Enquiry concerning Human Understanding*, ed. by Tom L. Beauchamp (Oxford: Clarendon Press, 2000), 5.1, p. 38. Hereafter, EHU.

2. Hans-Georg Gadamer, *Truth and Method*, 2nd rev. ed., trans. J. Weinsheimer and D. G. Marshall (London: Continuum, 2004).

3. David Hume, *A Treatise of Human Nature*, eds. David Fate Norton and Mary J. Norton (Oxford: Clarendon Press, 2007), 20. Hereafter, *Treatise*.

4. Donald W. Livingston and James T. King, eds., *Hume: A Re-Evaluation* (New York: Fordham University Press, 1976), 213–18.

5. It would be interesting to compare Hume's method and purpose, beyond just its empiricist epistemology, to French philosopher-sociologist Michel Foucault's "archeological" investigations. See Foucault, *L'archéologie du savoir* (Paris: Éditions Gallimard, 1969).

6. Alexander Broadie and others have explored the extent to which Scottish philosophy and therefore the cultural tradition in which Hume was weaned exhibits especially strong anti-transcendent tendencies toward nominalism, naturalism, empiricism, and common life generally. Even the scholastic fourteenth-century Duns Scotus, born in Berwickshire near Hume's family home, is often read as driving a more naturalistic epistemology against those of the high Gothic thinkers who had preceded him to the south. See A. Broadie, *The Tradition of Scottish Philosophy* (Edinburgh: Polygon, 1990).

7. Hume's three "natural relations" among ideas are "resemblance, contiguity in time or place, and causation" (*Treatise*, 1.1.4, 12).

8. Søren Kierkegaard, *Repetition*, trans. and eds. H. V. Hong and E. H. Hong (Princeton: Princeton University Press, 1983).

9. Augustine, immersed as he was in the discourse of ancient virtue, had some intimation of the importance of habit in recommending to unbelievers that they go through the motions of attending church because through the establishment of that habit real faith might emerge.

10. Kierkegaard, *Repetition*, 131. Kierkegaard criticizes Socrates's ahistorical consciousness in *Concluding Unscientific Postscript to the Philosophical Fragments*. Plato is well known for arguing in the *Meno* that knowledge manifests a special kind of remembering or

recollection, an idea that underwrites philosophical claims to having grasped the *a priori*—or what is prior.

11. Heidegger would, on the other hand, argue that it is the ontologically prior projective structure of *Dasein*'s temporality that makes custom and habit possible, that gives ontological grounding to what we ontically call custom and habit. But what is really added to the idea of custom by saying this? Why should temporality (*Zeitlichkeit*) be more ontologically basic than custom? Or, rather, perhaps we might say that the implication of Hume's "science of man" is that nothing can be more basic than custom (an idea with which, as a pun, anyway, Heidegger might actually agree). See Martin Heidegger, *Being and Time*, trans. John Macquarrie and Edward Robinson (New York: Harper & Row, 1962).

12. That "like objects, place'd in like circumstances, will always produce like effects; and as this principle has establish'd itself by a sufficient custom, it bestows an evidence and firmness on any opinion, to which it can be apply'd" (*Treatise*, 1.3.8, 73).

13. Joel C. Weinsheimer, *Gadamer's Hermeneutics: A Reading of Truth and Method* (New Haven: Yale University Press, 1985), 170. I am grateful to Joseph A. Edelheit for many of these thoughts about Gadamer and references to Gadamer's texts. See his "'I don't roll on shabbas!' Jewish Identity and the Meaning of History in *The Big Lebowski*," in *The Big Lebowski and Philosophy*, ed. Peter S. Fosl (Hoboken, NJ: John Wiley & Sons, 2012): 262–73.

14. For McIntyre, practices are "any coherent and complex form of socially established cooperative human activity through which goods internal to that form of activity are realized in the course of trying to achieve those standards of excellence which are appropriate to, and partially definitive of, that form of activity, with the result that human powers to achieve excellence, and human conceptions of the ends and goods involved, are systematically extended." Alasdair McIntyre, *After Virtue* (Notre Dame, IN: University of Notre Dame Press, 1982), 188.

15. David Hume, *Enquiry concerning the Principles of Morals*, ed. Tom L. Beauchamp (Oxford: Oxford University Press, 1998), 111–23. Hereafter, EPM.

16. "If we consider all the hypotheses, which have been forme'd either by philosophy or common reason, to explain the difference betwixt beauty and deformity, we shall find that all of them resolve into this, that beauty is such an order and construction of parts, as either by the *primary* constitution *of our nature, by custom*, or by *caprice,* is fitted to give a pleasure and satisfaction to the soul" (*Treatise*, 299). Eva M. Dadlez, "The Vicious Habits of Entirely Fictitious People: Hume on the Moral Evaluation of Art," *Philosophy and Literature* 26 (2002): 143–56. In "Of the Standard of Taste," Hume writes: there are "two sources of variation" in aesthetic judgment, the "one is the different humours of particular men; the other is the particular manners and opinions" (*Essays*, 243).

17. David Hume, *Essays Moral, Political, and Literary* (with an apparatus of variant readings from the 1889 edition by T. H. Green and T. H. Grose), ed. Eugene F. Miller (Indianapolis: Liberty Fund, 1985), 217. Hereafter, *Essays*. This is not to say that custom can actually change human nature, those dimensions of humanness we find through experience to be resistant to change, fixed and enduring. Hume accordingly—in the short essay "A Dialogue," appended to the *Enquiry concerning the Principles of Morals*—offers a counterpoint to the many instances of cultural and customary variability he had chronicled, that: "I shall conclude this long discourse with observing, that different customs and situations vary not the original ideas of merit (however they may, some consequences) in any very essential point, and prevail chiefly with regard to young men, who can aspire to the agreeable qualities, and may attempt to please. The manner, the ornaments, the graces, which succeed in this shape, are more arbitrary and casual: But the merit of riper years is almost every where the same; and consists chiefly in integrity, humanity, ability, knowledge, and the other more solid and useful qualities of the human mind" (EPM, 121).

18. John P. Wright, "Butler and Hume on Habit and Moral Character," in M. A. Stewart and John P. Wright, *Hume and Hume's Connexions* (State College: Pennsylvania State University Press, 1994), 116.

19. "The Sceptic," *Essays*, 171. As Wright indicates, James Moore and M. A. Stewart argue that Hume may have advanced his view of the refining and tempering effects of the habits of philosophy in opposition to the Christian Stoicism of Francis Hutcheson, which instead empha-

sizes self-control through will rather than habit. M. A. Stewart, "The Stoic Legacy in the early Scottish Enlightenment," in M. J. Osler, ed., *Atoms, Pneuma, and Tranquility* (Cambridge: Cambridge University Press, 1991), 273–96. James Moore, "Hume and Hutcheson," in *Hume and Hume's Connexions*, 23–57. See Wright, "Butler and Hume on Habit and Moral Character," 111.

20. Hume, *Treatise*, 2.3.6, p. 272; in this Hume seems to have followed naturalistic moralist Joseph Butler. See Wright, "Butler and Hume on Habit and Moral Character," 105–18.

21. In this sense, contemporary philosophers of the body and ideology such as Judith Butler and Slavoj Žižek are just catching up to Hume. See Žižek, *The Sublime Object of Ideology*, 2nd ed. (New York: Verso, 2009); and Butler, *Bodies That Matter: On the Discursive Limits of Sex* (New York: Routledge, 1993).

22. Gilles Deleuze, *Empiricism and Subjectivity,* trans. Constantin Boundas (New York: Columbia University Press, 2001).

23. Stanley Cavell, *The Claim of Reason: Wittgenstein, Skepticism, Morality, and Tragedy* (Oxford: Clarendon Press, 1980). See Part I, Chapter 5, "The Natural and the Conventional" (86–128) and its subsection, "The Normal and the Natural" (111–28). See also Cavell's essay, "Founding as Finding," in *This New Yet Unapproachable America* (Albuquerque: Living Batch Press, 1989), 77–118.

24. If for some purposes "custom" and "habit" can be substituted for one another, Hume's usage does suggest that "custom" is social or collective while "habit" is more properly individual. Hume does write in §9 of the first *Enquiry* of a "general habit" that "we" acquire, explaining that, "When we have lived any time, and have been accustomed to the uniformity of nature, we acquire a general habit, by which we transfer the known to the unknown" (EHU 81). But this usage seems to be actually about individuals, in the sense in which we each develop this habit.

25. Wittgenstein seems to refer to something like this kind of "agreement" at PI #355: "the point here is not that our sense-impressions can lie, but that we understand their language. (And this language like any other is founded on convention [*Übereinkunft*])." Wittgenstein also writes, in a way reminiscent of Hume, that in following rules we ultimately do so "*blindly*" (PI #219) and "act, without reasons" (PI #211). Ludwig Wittgenstein, *Philosophical Investigations*, trans. G. E. M. Anscombe, 3rd ed. (Oxford: Basil Blackwell, 1953). Cited as PI above.

26. For example, W. V. O. Quine, "Two Dogmas of Empiricism," in *From a Logical Point of View: Nine Logico-Philosophical Essays* (Cambridge, MA: Harvard University Press, 1980), 20–46. Edmund Husserl, *The Crisis of European Sciences and Transcendental Phenomenology: An Introduction to Phenomenological Inquiry*, trans. David Carr (Evanston: Northwestern University Press, 1970).

27. Hume's skepticism characteristically does not argue that reason is incapable of determining truth, but that reason cannot establish its own warrant for its claim to do so. This interpretation, which I share, is argued effectively by David Owen in *Hume's Reason* (Oxford: Oxford University Press, 1999). See Henry Allison, *Custom and Reason in Hume: A Kantian Reading of the First Book of the Treatise* (Oxford: Oxford University Press, 2008), for a critical reading of Hume on custom and reason that defends a Kantian position but is sensitive to Hume's views on custom.

28. "Man's *ethos* [habit/character] is his *daimon* [fate, spirit, divinity, fortune]" (CXIV, D.19). Charles H. Kahn, *The Art and Thought of Heraclitus: An Edition of the Fragments and Commentary* (Cambridge: Cambridge University Press, 1979).

29. Edmund Burke, *Reflections on the Revolution in France* (Oxford: Oxford University Press, 2009). Michael Oakeshott, *Rationalism in Politics and Other Essays*, expanded edition (Indianapolis: Liberty Fund, 2010). Oakeshott's article, "Rationalism in Politics," first appeared in *Cambridge Journal* 1 (1947): 65–74. See also Sheldon S. Wolin, "Hume and Conservatism," *American Political Science Review* 48, no. 4 (December 1954): 999–1016.

30. Laurence L. Bongie, *David Hume: Prophet of the Counter-Revolution*, foreword by Donald W. Livingston (Indianapolis: Liberty Fund, 2002); originally published by Oxford University Press, 1965. See also: David Resnick, "David Hume: A Modern Conservative," *European Legacy* 1.1 (1996): 397–402.

31. Leslie Stephen, *History of English Thought in the Eighteenth Century*, 3rd ed., vol. 2 (New York: Peter Smith,1949), 181. See Wolin, "Hume and Conservatism," 999.

32. See chapter 12, "Conservatism," of Donald W. Livingston, *Hume's Philosophy of Common Life* (Chicago: University of Chicago Press, 1984); and see "Cartesianism in Politics" (275–78).

33. Thomas Nagel, *A View from Nowhere* (Oxford: Oxford University Press, 1986). Nagel plays off Spinoza's recommendation to regard the world "*sub specie aeternitatis,*" under the aspect of eternity (*Ethics* II, prop. 44).

34. David Hume, *The History of England, From the Invasion of Julius Caesar to the Abdication of James the Second, 1688*, 6 vols. (Boston: Phillips Sampson, 1854), Book V, Chapter lix, 334); hereafter, *History*. Descartes opens the first of his well-known *Meditations on First Philosophy* with this (in Livingston's view ominous) announcement that: "Several years have now passed since I realized how numerous were the false opinions that in my youth I had taken to be true, and thus how doubtful were all those that I had subsequently built upon them. And thus I realized that once in my life I had to raze everything to the ground and begin again from the original foundations, if I wanted to establish anything firm and lasting in the sciences."

35. For Livingston's use of these quotes see, *Hume's Philosophy of Common Life*, 317ff.

36. See also Hume's essay "Of the Origin of Government" (*Essays*, 37–41).

37. Thomas Jefferson is well known for reading Hume as an illiberal Tory. In a 14 June 1807 letter to John Norvell Washington, Jefferson wrote that "as we have employed some of the best materials of the British constitution in the construction of our own government, a knowledge of British history becomes useful to the American politician. There is, however, no general history of that country which can be recommended. The elegant one of Hume seems intended to disguise & discredit the good principles of the government, and is so plausible & pleasing in it's style & manner, as to instil its errors & heresies insensibly into the minds of unwary readers." To William Duane on 12 August 1810, Jefferson wrote that Hume's *History* "has spread universal toryism over the land." On 25 November 1816, Jefferson wrote to John Adams that, "This single book has done more to sap the free principles of the English Constitution than the largest standing army."

38. Hume, EHU §11: "were an effect presented, which was entirely singular, and could not be comprehended under any known *species*, I do not see, that we could form *any conjecture or inference at all* concerning its cause" (110–11, emphasis mine). He also writes in §11: "Are there any marks of a distributive justice in this world? If you answer in the affirmative, I conclude that, since justice here exerts itself, it is satisfied. If you reply in the negative, I conclude, that you have then no reason to ascribe justice, in our sense of it, to the gods. If you hold a medium between affirmation and negation, by saying, that the justice of the gods, at present, exerts itself in part but not to its full extent; I answer, that you have no reason to give it any particular extent, but only so far as you see it, at present, exert itself" (106).

39. Letter #13, in David Hume, *The Letters of David Hume,* ed. J. Y. T. Greig, 2 vols. (Oxford: Clarendon Press, 1932), I:34. A passage in his essay "Of Eloquence" shows that Hume regarded Cicero (106–43 BCE) as one of the ancient world's two greatest orators (Demosthenes being the other): "It is observable, that the ancient critics could scarcely find two orators in any age, who deserved to be placed precisely in the same rank, and possessed the same degree of merit. CALBUS, CÆLIUS, CURIO, HORTENSIUS, CÆSAR rose one above another: But the greatest of that age was inferior to CICERO, the most eloquent speaker, that had ever appeared in Rome" (*Essays*, 98). "The Whole Duty of Man" was a popular and influential book of Christian didactics published anonymously by, it seems, Richard Allestree.

40. Nicholas Phillipson, *Hume* (London: Penguin, 2011).

41. Samuel Adams, Benjamin Franklin, John Dickinson, Charles Lee, George Washington, John Randolph of Roanoke, Benjamin Rush, and Robert Carter of Nomini Hall are all thought to have been influenced by Hume. The 1780 Committee on Finance in the Continental Congress, for example, studied Hume's economic essays, and in the 1787 Philadelphia Congress Alexander Hamilton appealed to Hume in arguing against legally penalizing corrupt office-holders. Hume also apparently taught Hamilton that an expanding commercial order is consistent, even complementary, with a stable republic. See Gerald Stourzh, *Alexander Hamilton and*

*the Idea of Republican Government* (Stanford: Stanford University Press, 1970). Garry Wills, *Explaining America: The Federalists* (New York: Doubleday, 1981). See Mark G. Spencer, *Hume and Eighteenth-Century America* (Rochester: University of Rochester Press, 2010); John M. Werner, "David Hume and America," *Journal of Philosophy* 33, no. 3 (September, 1972): 439–56; and Donald W. Livingston, "Hume, English Barbarism, and the American Crisis," in Richard B. Sher and Jeffrey R. Smitten, *Scotland and America in the Age of Enlightenment* (Princeton: Princeton University Press, 1990), 133–47.

42. Mouffe argues in favor of a kind of agonistic democracy that refuses the liberal-rationalist objective of overcoming conflict through reason and communication (in, e.g., Locke, Kant, and Habermas) in favor of a democratic theory that reconfigures conflict in a manageable way. In *On the Political* (New York: Routledge, 2005) she echoes both Hume's rejection of political rationalism and also his progressive sympathies when she writes: "the belief in the possibility of a universal, rational consensus has put democratic thinking on the wrong track. Instead of trying to design the institutions which, through supposedly 'impartial' procedures, would reconcile all conflicting interests and values, the task for democratic theorists and politicians should be to envisage the creation of a vibrant 'agonistic' public sphere of contestation where different hegemonic political projects can be confronted. This is, in my view, the *sine qua non* for an effective exercise of democracy"; Chantal Mouffe, *The Democratic Paradox* (New York: Verso, 2000), 3. Similarly, while Hume's essay "On an Ideal Commonwealth," thought by some to have influenced *Federalist* 10, presents technical means for managing faction, it does not pretend to eliminate faction. Sympathy, too, while mediating agreements among people, for Hume also has its limits. It may underwrite contingent alignments but not likely what Kant called a "perpetual peace." See also *The Return of the Political* (New York: Verso, 1993).

43. Jürgen Habermas, *The Theory of Communicative Action*, 2 vols., trans. Thomas McCarthy (Boston: Beacon Press, 1985).

44. See Deleuze, *Empiricism and Subjectivity*, chapter 2, "Cultural World and General Rules."

45. David Hume, "Of the Standard of Taste," *Essays*, 226–52.

46. It is just this replacement of reason with habit and association that leads Henry Allison to judge in favor of Kant over Hume. See Allison, *Custom and Reason in Hume*.

## BIBLIOGRAPHY


Allison, Henry E. *Custom and Reason in Hume*. Oxford: Oxford University Press, 2008.

Bongie, Laurence L. *David Hume: Prophet of the Counter-Revolution*. Foreword by Donald W. Livingston. Indianapolis: Liberty Fund, 2002.

Broadie, Alexander. *The Tradition of Scottish Philosophy*. Edinburgh: Polygon, 1990.

Burke, Edmund. *Reflections on the Revolution in France*. Oxford: Oxford University Press, 2009.

Butler, Judith. *Bodies That Matter: On the Discursive Limits of Sex*. New York: Routledge, 1993.

Cavell, Stanley. "Founding as Finding." In *This New Yet Unapproachable America*. Albuquerque: Living Batch Press, 1989, 77–118.

Cavell, Stanley. *The Claim of Reason: Wittgenstein, Skepticism, Morality, and Tragedy*. Oxford: Clarendon Press, 1980.

Dadlez, Eva M. "The Vicious Habits of Entirely Fictitious People: Hume on the Moral Evaluation of Art." *Philosophy and Literature* 26 (2002): 143–156.

Deleuze, Gilles. *Empiricism and Subjectivity*. Translated by Constantin Boundas. New York: Columbia University Press, 2001.

Edelheit, Joseph A. "'I don't roll on shabbas!' Jewish Identity and the Meaning of History in *The Big Lebowski*." In *The Big Lebowski and Philosophy*, edited by Peter S. Fosl, 262–73. Hoboken, NJ: John Wiley & Sons, 2012.

Foucault, Michel. *The Archaeology of Knowledge*. Translated by A. M. Sheridan Smith. London: Routledge Classics, 2002.

Gadamer, Hans-Georg. *Truth and Method*, 2nd rev. ed. Translated by Joel Weinsheimer and D. G. Marshall. London: Continuum, 2004.

Habermas, Jürgen. *The Theory of Communicative Action.* 2 vols. Translated by Thomas McCarthy. Boston: Beacon Press, 1985.

Heidegger, *Being and Time*. Translated by John Macquarrie and Edward Robinson. New York: Harper & Row, 1962.

Hume, David. *A Treatise of Human Nature*. Edited by David Fate Norton and Mary J. Norton. Oxford: Clarendon Press, 2007.

———. *An Enquiry concerning Human Understanding*. Edited by Tom L. Beauchamp. Oxford: Clarendon Press, 2000.

———. *Enquiry Concerning the Principles of Morals*. Edited by Tom L. Beauchamp. Oxford: Oxford University Press, 1998.

———. *Essays Moral, Political, and Literary* (with an apparatus of variant readings from the 1889 edition by T. H. Green and T. H. Grose). Edited by Eugene F. Miller. Indianapolis: Liberty Fund, 1985.

———. *The Letters of David Hume*. 2 vols. Edited by J. Y. T. Greig. Oxford: Clarendon Press, 1932.

———. *The History of England, From the Invasion of Julius Caesar to the Abdication of James the Second, 1688*. 6 vols. Boston: Phillips Sampson, 1854.

Husserl, Edmund. *The Crisis of European Sciences and Transcendental Phenomenology: An Introduction to Phenomenological Inquiry*. Translated by David Carr. Evanston: Northwestern University Press, 1970.

Kahn, Charles H. *The Art and Thought of Heraclitus: An Edition of the Fragments and Commentary*. Cambridge: Cambridge University Press, 1979.

Kierkegaard, Søren. *Repetition*. Translated by Howard V. and Edna H. Hong. Princeton: Princeton University Press, 1983.

Livingston, Donald W. "Hume, English Barbarism, and the American Crisis." In *Scotland and America in the Age of Enlightenment*, edited by Richard B. Sher and Jeffrey R. Smitten, 133–147. Princeton: Princeton University Press, 1990.

Livingston, Donald W. *Hume's Philosophy of Common Life*. Chicago: University of Chicago Press, 1984.

Livingston, Donald W. and James T. King, eds. *Hume: A Re-Evaluation*. New York: Fordham University Press, 1976.

McIntyre, Alasdair. *After Virtue*. Notre Dame, IN: University of Notre Dame Press, 1982.

Moore, James. "Hume and Hutcheson." In *Hume and Hume's Connexions*, edited by M. A. Stewart and John P. Wright, 23–57. State College: Pennsylvania State University Press, 1994.

Nagel, Thomas. *A View from Nowhere*. Oxford: Oxford University Press, 1986.

Mouffe, Chantal. *The Return of the Political*. New York: Verso, 1993.

———. *The Democratic Paradox*. New York: Verso, 2000.

———. *On the Political*. New York: Routledge, 2005.

Oakeshott, Michael. "Rationalism in Politics." Originally published in *Cambridge Journal* 1 (1947): 65–74.

———. *Rationalism in Politics and Other Essays*, expanded ed. Indianapolis: Liberty Fund, 2010.

Quine, W. V. O. "Two Dogmas of Empiricism." In *From a Logical Point of View: Nine Logico-Philosophical Essays*, 20–46. Cambridge: Harvard University Press, 1980.

Phillipson, Nicholas. *Hume*. London: Penguin, 2011.

Resnick, David. "David Hume: A Modern Conservative." *European Legacy* 1, no. 1 (1996): 397–402.

Spencer, Mark G. *Hume and Eighteenth-Century America.* Rochester: University of Rochester Press, 2010.

Stephen, Leslie. *History of English Thought in the Eighteenth Century*, 3rd ed., vol. 2. New York: Peter Smith, 1949.

Stewart, M. A. "The Stoic Legacy in the Early Scottish Enlightenment." In *Atoms, Pneuma, and Tranquility*, edited by Margaret J. Osler, 273–96. Cambridge: Cambridge University Press, 1991.

Stourzh, Gerald. *Alexander Hamilton and the Idea of Republican Government*. Stanford: Stanford University Press, 1970.

Weinsheimer, Joel C. *Gadamer's Hermeneutics: A Reading of Truth and Method.* New Haven: Yale University Press, 1985.

Werner, John M. "David Hume and America." *The Journal of Philosophy* 33, no. 3 (September 1972): 439–56.

Wills, Garry. *Explaining America: The Federalists*. New York: Doubleday, 1981.

Wittgenstein, Ludwig. *Philosophical Investigations*, 3rd ed. Translated by G. E. M. Anscombe. Oxford: Basil Blackwell, 1953.

Wolin, Sheldon S. "Hume and Conservatism." *American Political Science Review* 48, no. 4 (December 1954): 999–1016.

Wright, John P. "Butler and Hume on Habit and Moral Character." In *Hume and Hume's Connexions*, 105–118.

Žižek, Slavoj. *The Sublime Object of Ideology*, 2nd ed. New York: Verso, 2009.

## *Chapter Seven*

# Between Freedom and Necessity

## *Ravaisson on Habit and the Moral Life*

Clare Carlisle

> That a bare and naked *liberum arbitrium* is a chimera is best seen by the difficulty, the long, long continuous effort, which is necessary merely to get rid of a habit, even if one ever so earnestly has made a resolution.
>
> — Kierkegaard, *Journals and Papers* II, 1260 (1849)

Two of the most important moral philosophers in the European tradition have presented very different views of the role of habit in moral life.[1] In the *Nicomachean Ethics* Aristotle states that "moral goodness is the child of habit, for we acquire the moral virtues by first exercising them."[2] Kant, on the other hand, insists that habits must be excluded from the moral sphere; indeed, he suggests that "as a rule, all habits are objectionable." In his *Anthropology from a Pragmatic Point of View*, Kant describes habit as "a physical inner necessitation to continue behaving in the same way we have behaved thus far," which as such "deprives even good actions of their moral value because it detracts from our freedom of mind; moreover, it leads to thoughtless repetition of the same action (mechanical uniformity) and so becomes ridiculous."[3] And in *The Metaphysics of Morals* he argues that "moral maxims . . . cannot be based upon habit (since this belongs to the natural constitution of the will's determination); on the contrary, if the practice of virtue were to become a habit the subject would suffer loss of that freedom in adopting his maxims which distinguishes an action done from duty."[4] As these passages indicate, Kant's dismissal of habit is due to the dichotomy between necessity and freedom that separates his theoretical and practical philosophies, according to which the world of our experience and knowledge, conditioned by causal laws, cannot coincide with the domain of moral action, for the latter presupposes an absolutely free will. Insofar as a person acts out of habit, her actions are shaped by past actions and experiences, and seem removed from deliberation and rational choice; habit thus becomes a mere mechanism, an automatism that deprives the moral subject of her autonomy.

This sketch of the Aristotelian and Kantian accounts of habit is simplistic, but it provides a useful starting point for the present discussion of the role of habit in the moral life. Even more broadly speaking, we may attribute the negative evaluations of habit that we find in many modern philosophers—from Kant to Kierkegaard, and from Maine de Biran, through Bergson, to Sartre—to dualisms that are frequently identified as fundamental to philosophy since Descartes: between freedom and necessity; will and inclination; reason or spirit and the body; subject and world. Twentieth-century phenomenology set itself the task of finding a new philosophical perspective from which to challenge these dualisms, and in texts such as Merleau-Ponty's *Phenomenology of Perception* (1945) and Ricoeur's *Freedom and Nature* (1950) we find an appeal to the phenomenon of habit in the service of this project—for habit, as Merleau-Ponty writes, "presents great difficulties to traditional philosophies."[5]

However, over a century before these French phenomenologists directed their attention to habit, the philosopher Félix Ravaisson had argued that habit cannot be understood in mechanistic terms; that it overcomes the dichotomy between freedom and necessity; and that it forces us to think beyond the traditional alternatives of idealism and empiricism. Ravaisson was an Aristotelian, and was also strongly influenced by Leibniz—but his seminal essay *De l'habitude* (1838) reveals a preoccupation with these basic questions of modern European thought. In this chapter I will draw on Ravaisson's essay, recently published in English as *Of Habit*, in order to reflect on the role of habit in moral life. If habit does play an important role in morality and ethics, then we must try to understand what it is, how it operates, and its relationship to human freedom. We cannot merely return to Aristotle, or espouse a more recent version of virtue ethics, without first inquiring further into the nature of habit, nor without considering its significance within the context of the history of modern philosophy.

Ravaisson's *Of Habit* includes a section, toward the end of the text, that is devoted to the moral significance of habit. The author here refers to the English moralist Joseph Butler, who like Ravaisson situates his ethical thinking clearly within the Aristotelian tradition. Bishop Butler seems to have been the first thinker to remark on a double effect of habit that features in several subsequent discussions of the topic: in *The Analogy of Religion, Natural and Revealed, To the Constitution and Course of Nature* (1736), he notes that habit strengthens action and weakens feeling—that, in other words, it has apparently opposing effects on the active and passive aspects of moral conduct. This "double law," as Ravaisson describes it, is central to the analysis presented in *Of Habit*.

In Section 3 of this chapter, where I discuss Ravaisson's views about habit and morality, I will return to the connection with Butler. Before this, though, we will see that the two thinkers are linked not only by the influence of Aristotle and by their conviction of the importance of habit in moral life, but also, historically, by an intervening century of scientific and philosophical discourse on the nature and operation of habit in general. Section 1 of my chapter examines this discourse, showing how it constitutes the philosophical background to Ravaisson's discussion of habit. I will then examine, in the second section, Ravaisson's own account of habit in general, and elucidate his view that habit cannot be adequately understood on the basis of dualisms between freedom and necessity, mind and body, will and instinct, et cetera—and that, more positively, this means that reflection on habit provides a basis for a philosophical challenge to these dualisms. The third section focuses on how this analysis applies to morality: I will show how Ravaisson, echoing Butler, develops Aristotle's insights into the importance of habit in the moral life, and also responds to some questions that trouble Kantian ethics. In the fourth and final section I will draw out some further implications of Ravaisson's analysis by considering an important practical issue that he does not address—namely, how to deal with bad habits. Here I suggest that when one has to counter the force of undesirable or unhelpful habits, this effort should be conceived, after Ravaisson, not as the struggle of a pure will against inclination, nor as a rational mastery of irrational impulses, but instead as the persistent endeavor to become aware of and attentive to the habits in question.

## 1. BACKGROUND TO RAVAISSON'S *OF HABIT*

Ravaisson's analysis of habit responds, though not explicitly, to certain philosophical issues that are raised by Aristotle's account of the moral life.[6] In particular, we can identify in the *Nicomachean Ethics* two distinct concepts: *ethos*, which we may translate as "habit" or perhaps "practice," and *hexis*, which comes from the verb *ekhein*, "to have," and which may be translated as "disposition." Aristotle states that "moral goodness is the child of habit (*ethos*)," and he defines the virtues as *hexeis*, or dispositions. Elsewhere he discusses the concept of *hexis* in terms of the distinction between potentiality and actuality: a *hexis* is a potentiality or capacity (*dunamis*) to act in a certain way, but this is itself acquired—that is to say, actualized— through a process of acting. For example, a *hexis* of mathematical knowledge is the actualization of a human being's potential, qua human being, to have this knowledge, to grasp mathematics; on the other hand, the *hexis* is itself a potentiality or capacity that is actualized only when the agent is in the process of exercising his knowledge.[7] *Hexis* can thus be understood as a determinate, formed capability to execute a certain range of action—a capability that mediates between pure potentiality and activity itself, and which is a form of power distinct from both of these. This conception of *hexis*, actual in one sense and potential in another, remains rather ambiguous in Aristotle's work, but in Ravaisson's essay we find an attempt to think through the concepts of habit and disposition, and the relationship between them. We find, in fact, a Leibnizian interpretation of *hexis* in terms of a dynamic tendency to act in a particular way, and an explanation of how such a tendency is produced, over time and gradually, by habit—that is to say, by repetition.[8]

But Ravaisson's analysis of habit also draws on, and responds to, a more modern philosophical discourse.[9] In Book II of the *Treatise of Human Nature*, David Hume acknowledges Joseph Butler in remarking that "custom encreases [*sic*] all *active* habits, but diminishes *passive*, according to the observation of a late eminent philosopher."[10] Hume here generalizes Butler's insight from the moral context in which it was articulated: both Hume and Thomas Reid invoke a principle of habit as the foundation of the intelligible order of experience, and thus of human judgment, although their commitment to empiricism prevents them from offering a positive account of habit itself.[11] By the end of the eighteenth century, this question of habit was taken up in France, particularly by Xavier Bichat, whose influential *Physiological Researches on Life and Death* included a more detailed examination of the double effects of habit.[12] In 1800 the Institut de France—no doubt prompted by Bichat's work—announced an essay competition on the topic of the influence of habit on the faculty of thinking. This competition was won by Pierre Maine de Biran, whose lengthy essay exhibits the influence of both Bichat and the Scottish empiricists, but also ventures further in presenting an explanation of the effects of habit, and in combining physiological research with an emphasis on the will. Ravaisson takes up Maine de Biran's account of habit, and makes many references to it in his own essay—but he gives to habit a very different, and wholly original, philosophical interpretation.[13]

At the heart of Ravaisson's account of habit is what he calls its "double law." This double law of habit is based on the distinction between activity and passivity, or between voluntary movement and sensation. Ravaisson formulates the double law of habit as follows: "The continuity or the repetition of passion weakens it; the continuity or repetition of action exalts and strengthens it." More specifically, "prolonged or repeated sensation diminishes gradually and eventually fades away. Prolonged or repeated movement becomes gradually easier, quicker and more assured. Perception, which is linked to movement, similarly becomes clearer, swifter and more certain."[14] This law gives expression to our everyday experience of habit and habituation: we find that repeating a certain action leads to this action becoming more dexterous, precise and efficient; we find that sense-data that are repeatedly or continuously present to us decline in intensity after some time. We say that we have become used or accustomed to something—to the color of my front door, for example, or to the way a pen feels when I hold it—to the point that we no longer notice it, are no longer aware of the sensations caused by the familiar object. Ravaisson remarks in *Of Habit* that "most of the authors who have examined habit have apprehended this law,"[15] but the most sophisticated discussion of it is provided by Maine de Biran, who makes the distinction between activity and passivity central to his analysis of habit.

We may turn briefly to Maine de Biran's essay *The Influence of Habit on the Faculty of Thinking* (1802) in order to set out the key points of the analysis that were to be taken up by Ravaisson, while at the same time providing some background to the latter's 1838 essay that will help to clarify the particularity and originality of its contribution to the philosophy of habit. Maine de Biran, himself drawing on earlier discussions of the double influence of habit, describes how "sensation, continued or repeated, fades, is gradually obscured and ends by disappearing without leaving any trace. Repeated movement gradually becomes more precise, more prompt, and easier."[16] For Biran, this double influence serves to confirm his dualistic psychology, which identifies distinct systems of perception and sensation, belonging to distinct spheres of the voluntary and the involuntary. He argues that we cannot ascribe the two contrary effects of repetition to the same faculty of the mind, since to do so would be to make the seemingly absurd supposition "that this unique faculty can become at once more inert and more active by the same process of habituation."[17] However, in the course of his discussion Biran struggles to maintain the distinction between activity and passivity, between a faculty of moving and a faculty of feeling: he argues, against any mechanistic interpretation of sensation, that even the most apparently passive experience involves a "*sensitive* activity," that is to say "a real action peculiar to the sensitive organ which . . . gives the tone rather than receives it," and he admits that activity and passivity are so intimately connected that "there is hardly any impression that does not result from their mutual co-operation."[18] Nevertheless, he distinguishes sense-impressions as passive, insofar as they escape the agency of the subject, from the *motor* activity that is classed as activity proper, insofar as it is voluntary.

Integral to Biran's analysis of habit is the claim that its influence can only be accounted for by a modification that "persists and more or less outlasts the impression." Biran calls this modification a "determination," which, he explains, "is effectuated when the organ or the central nervous system is returned to the same condition in which it was by virtue of the original action."[19] This can happen "spontaneously," in the absence of the original action, "by virtue of a lively force inherent in the organs." Corresponding to passive and active impressions are "sensory determinations" and "motor determinations." According to Biran, a motor determination is a "tendency of the organ or of the motor centre" to repeat an action. It is on this issue that his analysis moves beyond physiology, for he can only account for the being of such tendencies by invoking the metaphysical concept of potentiality or virtuality: determinations exist as *powers* that will be actualized under certain conditions, namely, "renewed external stimulation."[20] Maintaining that the processes of thought are as subject to habit as physical movements, Biran argues that the imagination, which retains and synthesizes impressions, is constituted by determinations of the brain.[21]

From a philosophical point of view, one of the most interesting aspects of Biran's philosophy is his account of self-consciousness, which, he claims, involves both activity and passivity. One's sense of oneself can be identified with an impression of effort that is felt when the will, in initiating movement, encounters the resistance of the motor organs, which in turn encounter resistance from external objects. Effort is thus a sort of meeting point of activity (the will) and passivity (resistance). This allows us to see how the contrary effects of habit on active and passive elements combine into a unitary phenomenon: the passive element of sensation diminishes with repetition, while the active, motor element becomes more precise and assured—but because we are conscious both of our movements and of ourselves as moving through a *feeling* of effort, this feeling and consequently the self-consciousness it produces decline at the same time as activity is perfected. Eventually, voluntary movements become lost to consciousness: "the perception may become more distinct and more precise on the one hand, while on the other the individual is more completely blinded to the active part which he takes in it." This means that habit "effaces the line of demarcation between voluntary and involuntary acts, between acquisitions of experience and instinctive operations, between the faculty of feeling and that of perceiving."[22] The influence of habit might be best understood in terms of a distinction between activity and passivity, but at the same time the influence of habit itself undermines this distinction. One of the key conclusions that Biran draws from his analysis of habit, then, is that the faculties of feeling and perception are "indivisibly united."

For Biran, reflection on the double law of habit leads to an ambivalent assessment of its influence: habit is the "general cause of our progress on the one hand, of our blindness on the other," for while we owe to habit the facility, precision, and rapidity of our movements and voluntary actions, "it is habit also which hides from us their nature and quantity."[23] Overall, however, his estimation of habit is more negative than positive, since he is most concerned with its influence on thinking, and as we have seen habit tends to blur the distinctions established by reason. At the end of his text Biran portrays habit as both a cause of erroneous belief and a force that binds people "servilely" to their routines, and his conclusion that "all that happens exclusively under the sway of habit should lose its authority before the eyes of reason"[24] could easily be attributed to Kant. Biran's whole account of habit is characterized by tensions and inconsistencies that testify to a kind of struggle between reason and habit: on the one hand, there is the insistence on a dualistic psychology, and on the other hand the acknowledged failure clearly to separate activity and passivity, perception and sensation, the voluntary and the involuntary.

## 2. RAVAISSON'S ANALYSIS OF HABIT

In *Of Habit*, Ravaisson retains the key elements of Maine de Biran's account of the double law of habit. These can be summarized as follows:

1. the claim that sensations are the result of differences between two physical states—that is to say, of felt changes from one state to another;[25]
2. the distinction between activity and passivity: recognition of the contrary effects of repetition on activity and passivity produces the double law of habit;
3. the idea of passivity-within-activity and activity-within-passivity: sensation involves a kind of activity, and motor activity involves passive impressions insofar as movement meets resistance, producing a feeling of effort;
4. the interconnection of passivity and activity in action in general, and in self-consciousness in particular, produces the unified effect of the double law of habit;
5. the claim that habit cannot be accounted for solely in physical or mechanistic terms: the idea of a "determination" (understood as a kind of potency, potentiality or virtuality) that manifests itself as a "tendency" to respond to stimulus in a certain way.

However, whereas Maine de Biran wants to resist the way in which habit undermines the distinction between the voluntary and the involuntary, regarding this as a pernicious effect of habit that threatens rational thought, Ravaisson argues that in undermining this distinction—which is also that between will and instinct, mind and nature, freedom and necessity—habit reveals a deeper unity that cannot be directly apprehended by the senses, nor grasped by the rational understanding. For Ravaisson, the progress of actions, through the development of habit, from the sphere of will and conscious reflection to spontaneous, quasi-instinctive bodily responses, can be possible only insofar as there is continuity between the mind and the body, between freedom and necessity. And unlike Maine de Biran, he does not believe that distinguishing between activity and passivity requires him to posit two separate faculties of the mind.

This willingness to look beyond the dualistic framework within which Maine de Biran confines his reflection on habit might be due in part to the influence of F. W. J. Schelling, whose Munich lectures Ravaisson is thought to have attended in the early 1830s, and whose ideas were at this time promoted in France by Victor Cousin. In 1835, Ravaisson published a translation of Schelling's preface to a volume of Cousin's work;[26] Schelling, for his part, expressed his regard for Ravaisson, describing him in the *Philosophy of Revelation* as "a Frenchman to whom we owe important work on Aristotle."[27] However, the extent of Ravaisson's contact with and debt to Schelling's philosophy is difficult to establish, and remains a point of disagreement among French commentators. Perhaps it was rather his intensive study of Aristotle in the years leading up to the publication of *De l'habitude* that allowed Ravaisson to gain some distance from the dualisms of modern thought, for Aristotle's view that intellectual, moral, and technical capacities alike are acquired *hexeis* constitutes, it may be argued, "the exact metaphysical antithesis of the Cartesian order of method."[28]

Having said this, Ravaisson's advance on Maine de Biran is articulated in unmistakably modern terms: he argues that it is impossible to provide either a materialist or a rationalist explanation for the double law of habit. In particular, it is the *tendency* produced by habit that eludes materialism, while the accompanying decline of will and consciousness renders a rationalist account inadequate:

> The gradual weakening of the sensations and the increasing ease of the movements could perhaps be explained hypothetically by some change (which anatomy has not discovered) in the physical constitution of the organs. But no organic modification can explain the *tendency*, the inclination whose progress coincides with the degradation of sensation and effort. The attempts made to explain the increasing ease and certainty of the movements, and the disappearance of sensation, by the progress of attention, of will, and of intelligence, might still be considered capable of a certain level of success. But if the sensation disappears in the long run because attention tires of it and turns elsewhere, how is it that sensibility increasingly demands this sensation that the will abandons? If movement becomes swifter and easier because intelligence knows better all its parts, and because the will synthesises the action with more precision and assurance, how is it that the increasing facility of movement coincides with the diminution of will and consciousness?[29]

Insisting that "both physical and rationalist theories are lacking on this point," Ravaisson claims that the double law of habit "can be explained only by the development of a Spontaneity that is at once active and passive, equally opposed to mechanical Fatality and to reflective Freedom." Here, in contrast to Biran, he positively affirms the way in which *reflection* on habit *overcomes* the distinction between activity and passivity, since the *principle* of habit *underlies* this distinction. While Ravaisson's vocabulary now appears dated, his philosophical critique of mechanistic theories is not only historically interesting, but accords with contemporary critiques of mechanism that draw on developments in the neurosciences. As Catherine Malabou argues, the plasticity of the brain—its ongoing formation through the individual's actions and interactions—that is central to current theories of neuronal functioning renders outmoded the analogy between brain and machine, and replaces rigid determinism with a new view of the brain as a "self-cultivating organ."[30] It is therefore important to recognize the distinction between materialism and mechanism, and Ravaisson's critique of the latter resonates with the most recent ways of conceptualizing the former.

Ravaisson describes the simultaneously active and passive "spontaneity" that develops through habit as an "obscure" or "secret" activity within sensibility. As we have seen, Biran had already posited a pre-reflective and involuntary "sensitive activity," but Ravaisson develops this idea and uses it to explain the double law of habit. He argues that an activity within the sense-organs responds to stimulation by bringing the organ "up to the tone of the sensation" (this is what Biran describes as a "sensory determination"), thus reducing the difference that a renewed sensation will make to the organ, and so lessening the sensation's impact and intensity. For Ravaisson, this "obscure" activity is nothing mystical or unfathomable, but rather the force of inertia: the "tendency to persist" in a particular way of being that the French philosopher, after Leibniz, identifies as "the universal law, the fundamental character" of all beings.[31] When sensations are continued or repeated, "there develops within sensibility . . . a tendency to persist in the same state to which the impression has brought it, or else to come back to this state," and this explains why the difference "between the state of the subject and the state to which the external impression has brought it increasingly disappears," causing the sensation to fade.[32] In the absence of the sensation to which the individual has become habituated, this activity will manifest itself as desire for the sensation. So, the same process that removes sensations from conscious awareness also creates an attachment to and a need for these sensations, which reveals itself only when the cause of the sensation is no longer present.

Since movements always involve a degree of passivity—that is, of resistance and a corresponding feeling of effort—the same "secret activity" (or desire) develops here, reducing resistance and effort and thus facilitating actions as well as making them less conscious. As Ravaisson explains, through habit

> The [repeated] action itself becomes more of a tendency, an inclination that no longer awaits the commandments of the will but rather anticipates them, and which even escapes entirely and irremediably both will and consciousness. . . . In this way, continuity or repetition brings about a sort of obscure activity that increasingly anticipates (*prévient*) both the impression of external objects in sensibility, and the will in activity. In activity, it reproduces the action itself; in sensibility it does not reproduce the sensation, the passion—for this requires an external cause—but calls for it, invokes it; in a certain sense it implores the sensation.[33]

Behind the double law of habit, then, lies a single force; continuity or repetition weakens sensibility and excites the power of movement "in the same way, by one and the same cause: the development of an unreflective spontaneity, which breaks into passivity and the organism, and increasingly establishes itself there, beyond, beneath the region of will, personality and consciousness."

Crucially, Ravaisson argues that this spontaneity is both intelligent and free even though it has left the sphere of will and reflection—even though it is "blind," as he puts it. It is for this reason that his estimation of habit is so much more positive than Biran's, who echoes Kant in identifying intelligence and freedom with reflection and the will. For Biran, the "blindness" of habit is an obstacle to knowledge, whereas for Ravaisson this same fact reveals an intelligence not confined to mental faculties, but dispersed throughout the body. He argues that although movements, as they become habitual, leave the sphere of will and reflection, they do not cease to be intelligent. A habit "does not become the mechanical effect of an external impulse, but rather the effect of an inclination that follows from the will." Such inclinations are formed gradually, and when a habitual action is traced back to its origin in consciousness, one "always finds that it inclines towards the end that the will had originally proposed. But every inclination towards a goal implies intelligence"[34]—and this means that habit cannot be regarded as a mechanism. According to Ravaisson, habit does have a kind of necessity, but this is not physical or mechanical necessity, "not an external necessity of constraint, but a necessity of attraction and desire. . . . It is the final cause that increasingly predominates over efficient causality and which absorbs the latter into itself."[35] The force of habit is not opposed to freedom, but rather *follows from* freedom: it is "a law of the limbs, which follows on from the freedom of the spirit"; "an inclination that follows from the will."

On this account, then, just as intelligence is not confined to reflective thought, freedom and purposiveness are not confined to the will, and are therefore not annulled by habit, but rather *made flesh*: as habit develops, freedom increasingly pervades the body, and increasingly animates it. The goals that the will originally proposes become the form of the body. This formed body, or "habit-body," as we might call it, is not a physical thing, but rather a dynamic unity of capacities and dispositions to move, to sense, to experience, and to understand in particular ways. What happens in habit is that freedom and intelligence become more immediate, in a sense more natural: "inclination, as it takes over from the will, comes closer and closer to the actuality that it aims to realise; it increasingly adopts its form. . . . The interval that the understanding represents between the movement and its goal gradually diminishes; the distinction is effaced; the end whose idea gave rise to the inclination . . . becomes fused with it."[36] In other words, the progression of habit arrives eventually at the "immediate intelligence" of instinct: this is why habit can be called a "second nature." Ravaisson puts this same point in different terms by stating that habit transforms ideas (i.e., goals, purposes) into actions, into concrete movements:

> In reflection and will, the end of movement is an idea, an ideal to be accomplished: something that should be, that can be, and which is not yet. It is a possibility to be realised. But as the end becomes fused with the movement, and the movement with the tendency, possibility, the ideal, is realised in it. The *idea* becomes *being,* the very being of the movement and of the tendency that it determines. . . .
>
> Ultimately, it is more and more outside the sphere of personality, beyond the influence of the central organ of the will—that is to say, *within* the immediate organs of movements—that the inclinations constituting the habit are formed, and the ideas are realised. Such inclinations, such ideas become more and more the form, the way of being, even the very being of these organs.[37]

Ravaisson here recognizes what Merleau-Ponty will later call embodied intelligence, a kind of "knowledge in the hands." Merleau-Ponty follows Ravaisson in arguing that habit challenges a dualistic view of the human being, according to which the body is merely a mechanism while the mind is of a wholly different order:

> [I]t is the body which "understands" in the acquisition of habit. This way of putting it will appear absurd, if understanding is subsuming a sense-datum under an idea, and if the body is an object. But the phenomenon of habit is just what prompts us to revise our notion of "understand" and our notion of the body. To understand is to experience the harmony between what we aim at and what is given, between the intention and the performance—and the body is our anchorage in a world.[38]

However, for Ravaisson reflection on habit not only challenges Cartesian and Kantian dualisms, and makes us look at the human being differently. He makes the further claim that insofar as habit is analogous to nature it reveals to us the inner reality of nature as a whole. Just as the progress of habit demonstrates the continuity between freedom and necessity, between mind and matter, *within* the human being, so it also shows us this continuity throughout nature—which is thus, like the human body, pervaded by a spontaneous unreflective intelligence that inclines toward, or rather desires, the good. In habit, we begin with the will and reflection and move down, as it were, to an unconscious immediacy of embodied inclinations. But Ravaisson argues that in fact this intelligent but unreflective spontaneity was there all along, as the very essence of nature, and that the reflective will is but the manifestation of this within the developed form of consciousness that distinguishes the human being from other creatures.

## 3. RAVAISSON ON HABIT IN THE MORAL SPHERE

Ravaisson devotes a section of his essay to habit in the moral sphere. Here he simply applies to this sphere his general analysis, which as we have seen focuses on the "double law" of habit, and on the notion of an active tendency that is produced by habit. From an historical point of view, the eighteenth- and nineteenth-century discourse on habit here comes full circle, or folds back upon itself: the double influence of habit was first discussed, by Butler, in a specifically moral context, and subsequently taken out of this context, or at least generalized from it, by Hume in the *Treatise*; the Scottish empiricist philosophy of habit was then taken up in France by Bichat and Maine de Biran, whose analysis of habit was at once echoed and transformed by Ravaisson. By the time the latter comes to reflect on habit, then, Butler's remarks on the double influence of repetition on moral conduct have been developed into a much fuller account that incorporates both physiological and metaphysical explanation. Only Ravaisson's work brings together a clear formulation of the "double law of habit"; a properly philosophical attempt to explain this law, which challenges the dualisms of modern thought; and a return to the ethical considerations that were first highlighted by Butler. As we shall see, Ravaisson's philosophy of habit also returns to the explicitly Christian context of the English bishop's moral psychology.

When he turns to reflect on the moral significance of the effects of habit, then, Ravaisson recalls the discussion presented in Butler's *The Analogy of Religion, Natural and Revealed, To the Constitution and Course of Nature*. Having made a distinction between active and passive habits—the former including perceptions and actions of both the body and the mind, the latter denoting "associations of ideas" as well as feelings—Butler describes how active habits are formed and strengthened through repeated exercise, while "passive impressions, by being repeated, grow weaker: thoughts, by often passing through the mind, are felt less sensibly." The examples he provides of the diminution of feeling clearly situate his discussion in the context of moral psychology: becoming accustomed to danger lessens fear; becoming accustomed to distress lessens pity. When we consider that actions are often motivated by feelings, we find that the dual effects of habit work in combination:

> From these two observations together, that practical habits are formed and strengthened by repeated acts; and that passive impressions, by being repeated upon us, grow weaker; it must follow, that active habits may be gradually forming and strengthening, by a course of acting on such and such motives and excitements, whilst these motives and excitements themselves are, by proportionate degrees, growing less sensible, i.e., are continually less and less sensibly felt, even as the active habits strengthen. And experience confirms this; for active principles, at the very time that they are less lively in perception than they were, are found to be, some how, wrought more thoroughly into the temper and character, and become more effectual in influencing our practice.[39]

Butler does not make his view of the implications of this double law of habit especially clear, but his comments on the examples of distress and pity indicate that he regards the double law of habit as an aid to the development of a good moral character. Through habit, he suggests, a person will become less upset by the suffering of others but better able to act to help to relieve this suffering. Making reference to Butler, Ravaisson states that repetition "gradually leads the pleasure of action to replace the more transient pleasure of passive sensibility. In this way, as habit destroys the passive emotions of pity, the helpful activity and the inner joys of charity develop more and more in the heart of the one who does good . . . . [L]ove is augmented by its own expressions."[40]

This argument raises questions about the role of feelings, or emotions, in the moral life—questions that neither Butler nor Ravaisson addresses. According to some theories of virtue—notably that of Aristotle—a virtuous person is one who has a settled disposition to *feel* in certain ways as well as to act in certain ways.[41] It would seem, therefore, that anyone wishing to develop such a moral theory has to consider the implications of the double law of habit. If habit causes feelings to decline, presumably to the point of expiration, then how is the role of emotional response—whether as a character trait; as the pleasure and pain accompanying virtuous and vicious acts; or as a motivational factor in action—to be accommodated? A preliminary answer to this question (which requires more extensive discussion than is possible here) must appeal to Ravaisson's insistence, after Maine de Biran, that activity always includes an element of passivity, and passivity always includes activity. Indeed, prior to his discussion of habit in the moral sphere, Ravaisson contrasts active and passive sensation, invoking the example of two drinkers: the first, who drinks merely to get intoxicated, loses his powers of taste with repetition; the second, who is a connoisseur, develops a more refined and discerning palate. This distinction may be applied to the moral domain, and in fact gains some credibility when we consider a phenomenon such as compassion fatigue, which is most often discussed in the particularly passive context of seeing images of distress on television. The sympathy felt in this situation would, then, be a passive feeling that declines with repetition, whereas in a more active context—say, when training to be a counselor or therapist—a person may well develop a refined sensitivity to the suffering of others. Although Ravaisson does not explicitly present this argument in relation to morality, his emphasis on love indicates that in this sphere, as elsewhere, the distinction between activity and passivity rests on a more profound coincidence or unity: love is at once passive and active; at once a feeling and a power.

Ravaisson goes on to show how his philosophical analysis of habit's progress from reflective will to spontaneous inclination applies to moral life. Just as motor habit develops to the point where it meets the immediacy of instinct, so moral habit can become a second nature:

> Ultimately, in the activity of the soul, as in that of movement, habit gradually transforms the will proper to action into an involuntary inclination. Mores, morality, are formed in this manner. Virtue is first of all an effort and wearisome; it becomes something attractive and a pleasure only through practice, as a desire that forgets itself or that is unaware of itself, and gradually it draws near to the holiness of innocence. Such is the very secret of education: its art consists in attracting someone towards the good by action, thus fixing the inclination for it. In this way a *second nature* is formed.[42]

In a sense this just takes us back to Aristotle's ethics—but, as I hope to have shown, in Ravaisson's essay these insights are accompanied by both a detailed account of the operation of habit, and an appreciation of its significance from the point of view of the history of modern philosophy. More than this, however, the philosophy of nature that Ravaisson develops on the basis of his interpretation of habit provides a wider context for his moral psychology, for he finds that "it is the natural spontaneity of desire that is the very substance of action, at the same time as being its source and primary origin." In other words, there is a natural orientation to the good that is prior to the exertion of the reflective will:

> just as in movement, if it is the will that poses the goal in space, and determines the direction, it is not the will—or at least it is not reflective will—that works out and devises in advance the very production of movement; for this can only arise from the depths of instinct and desire, where the idea of nature becomes being and substance. In the same way, in the moral world the understanding distinguishes the end and the will proposes it, but it is neither the will nor the abstract understanding that can initially stir the powers of the soul at their source so as to push them towards the good. It is the good itself, at least

> the idea of the good, which descends into these depths, engendering love in them and raising that love up to itself. Will constitutes only the form of the action; the unreflective freedom of Love constitutes all its substance. . . . Nature lies wholly in desire, and desire, in turn, lies in the good that attracts it.[43]

In identifying this natural orientation toward the good that underlies the will, Ravaisson implicitly offers a response to the problem of motivation that persists within Kantian moral philosophy: why should I be moral? why should I heed the call of duty? why should I follow reason rather than inclination? why should the feeling of respect for the moral law outweigh other feelings and desires? Ravaisson's solution involves the claim—which is based on his analysis of habit—that it is love rather than reason that grounds the moral life. This love constitutes, he suggests, a kind of "grace" insofar as the natural inclination to the good is something effortless, a gift given to the will to prepare it and guide it. "Nature is prevenient grace," he writes, quoting the seventeenth-century theologian Fénelon.[44] For Ravaisson, nature itself may be regarded by human beings as a gift that is given prior to action, to assist and facilitate it, because the principle of nature is love, which expresses itself within each individual as a spontaneous desire for and tendency toward the good that precedes the understanding and the will. In the end, this love and desire that is the "intimate source of ourselves" can be identified as "God within us." Just as he posits continuity between freedom and necessity, mind and body, will and instinct, so this "continuism"[45] encompasses the theological distinction between nature and grace. In *Of Habit* Ravaisson presents this conclusion as following from his philosophical analysis, rather than as a dogmatic basis for philosophical reflection. However, if, as I have suggested elsewhere,[46] the text has a circular structure and makes most sense read backward, so to speak, then the ontology of habit becomes more closely linked to a theology of grace.

It may well be that these conclusions of Ravaisson's account of habit in the moral sphere appear rather optimistic. How, on this view, are we to explain our apparently natural inclinations toward what reason can recognize as undesirable ends, and the bad habits to which these inclinations often lead? Although he acknowledges that habit can degenerate into tics and addictions, Ravaisson does not address this question: curiously, he writes of grace but not of sin; of desire for the good but not of perversity. However, the theological interpretation that he appends to his analysis of virtue may illuminate rather than obscure the issue of vice, for in the Christian tradition the doctrine of grace is accompanied by the idea than people close themselves to this grace, turn away from it. Even if we put the religious vocabulary to one side and regard the word "gift" as signifying a pre-reflective, involuntary, natural orientation toward the good, we can quite easily recognize that a gift may be offered but not accepted: it may be unnoticed, ignored, or rejected. So, it may be that we have a profound inclination toward the good, that we *are* motivated by love, and yet a certain degree of ignorance distorts or displaces this tendency. It may even be the case that love is so essential to human life, so great a need, that its absence, withdrawal, or contingency is deeply disruptive. This would mean that Ravaisson's optimism is at least compatible with the fact that people often have unhealthy inclinations—which, indeed, gain more force and thus become more problematic when they develop into habits. Furthermore, we may draw from his philosophical analysis of habit the terms in which to comprehend a person's failure to receive, to appropriate or to utilize the gift of habit, for he understands passivity in two ways: as receptivity and as resistance.[47] Of course, both of these forms of passivity involve an element of activity and can be understood dynamically, as opening and as contraction. Ravaisson does not develop this distinction between receptivity and resistance, but doing so would not only help to account for the possibility of refusing what is given—such as a prevenient *hexis* or capability for virtuous action: a capability that, insofar as it is also an inclination, may be conceived as love itself—but would also enrich our understanding of human affectivity in general.[48]

## 4. FROM BAD HABITS TO GOOD HABITS

Whereas Kant argues that habits are to be excluded from morality, Aristotle regards moral life as consisting in the avoidance or elimination of bad habits and the cultivation or preservation of good habits. While Kant opposes habit to freedom, moral virtue for the Greek philosopher is grounded in an acquired habit *of choosing* (*hexis prohairetike*), a gradual determination of desire, a shaping of freedom. Ravaisson, in showing that habit is not opposed to freedom and intelligence, gives us good reason to prefer Aristotle's view to Kant's, and also provides us with elements of the philosophical analysis of habit that is required in order to make progress with this kind of ethical theory. To conclude, I now wish to consider briefly how Ravaisson's account of habit might contribute to moral practice. Is there anything in his discussion of habit that will actually help us to live well? Given that we do often find ourselves struggling against the force of old, unwanted habits, how can we bring about the transition from bad habits to good habits?

Let us first clarify the nature of the problem. We are beings who change and develop through time. It may well be that our habits reflect consciously chosen purposes, and are thus not essentially opposed to freedom and intelligence, but it is quite possible that we might change our purposes and yet continue to carry—indeed, to *embody*—habits that developed according to out-of-date purposes. We then find that our old but persistent habits are in conflict with our new goals, and this conflict will be particularly acute when the will has undergone a profound reorientation. We find in Augustine's *Confessions* a description of precisely this predicament. Augustine, recalling his own struggle to live a pure life once he has converted to Christianity, comments on the famous passage in Romans 7, where Paul writes that "I can will what is right, but I cannot do it." Augustine depicts habit as the constraining force:

> the rule of sin is the force of habit, by which the mind is swept along and held fast even against its will . . . I was held fast, not in fetters clamped upon me by another, but by my own will, which had the strength of iron chains . . . [For desire had grown from my will] and when I gave in to desire habit was born, and when I did not resist the habit it became a necessity. . . . These two wills within me, one old, one new, one the servant of the flesh, the other of the spirit, were in conflict and between them they tore my soul apart.[49]

Here Augustine, like Ravaisson, finds that habit proceeds from "will" to "necessity," so that desires come to be embodied, made "flesh"; they become, as the French philosopher puts it, "laws of the limbs that follow on from the freedom of the spirit." But Augustine encounters a problem that Ravaisson does not consider: he finds himself with a habit-body that is in opposition to his "new will" to serve God and live a good life. In fact, what has happened in Augustine's case is that his conception of the good life has changed: his *telos* is no longer sensual enjoyment—sought in one instance by stealing pears from the orchard—but the spiritual fruits of renunciation and obedience. Whereas he once equated freedom with licentiousness, he now seeks liberation from the bondage of his appetites and passions.

Ravaisson, whose moral thinking is clearly Aristotelian rather than Platonic, does not discuss or even acknowledge this possibility. Nevertheless, his analysis of habit suggests that conceiving the moral life in terms of a struggle between two opposed factions of the human being—between mind and body, between will and inclination—cannot lead to an adequate understanding of habit, and indeed will only exacerbate the kind of conflict that Augustine describes. Ravaisson's account emphasizes the depth of habit, the way in which it reaches "all the way down" into the body: through habit certain purposes "become more and more the form, the way of being, even the very being of [the] organs," and this manner of being is not just a shape or pattern but a dynamic tendency that has its own momentum. This explains why seeing things differently, changing one's mind and even making a firm resolution are usually insufficient to counter the force of habit: will and reflection are powerful but, it seems, relatively superficial aspects of ourselves. Our very being is conditioned by habits whose rationales are long forgotten, or which may never have been grasped explicitly.

However, Ravaisson also indicates that habit is a reversible process. The fact that there is continuity from will to inclination implies that one can move by degrees in the other direction, too:

> it is by a succession of imperceptible degrees that inclinations take over from acts of will. It is also by an imperceptible degradation that these inclinations, born from custom, often decline if custom comes to be interrupted, and that the movements removed from the will return to its sphere after some time. . . . Consciousness feels itself expire along with the will, and then come back to life with it, by a gradation and degradation which are continuous; and consciousness is the first, immediate and unique measure of continuity.[50]

When habits are to be undone, there are three practical points to take into consideration—and each of these is supported and illuminated by the discussion presented in *Of Habit*. First, just as habits take time to develop, to establish themselves in the depth of the lived body, so they take time to retreat. Getting rid of a habit may be a slow process that requires patience and persistence, and recognizing this is likely to help the struggling person to remain patient when no change of behavior is apparent. Kierkegaard writes of "the long, long continuous effort, which is necessary merely to get rid of a habit, even if one ever so earnestly has made a resolution,"[51] suggesting that unwanted habits are not to be countered by brute force, or by a single moment of clear vision and decision, but by a "long, continuous effort" to retrace the progress of habit gradually, just as the habit first developed through continuity or repetition and by a series of imperceptible degrees.

Second, the elimination of a habit is likely to be painful even when the habit is unhealthy. Ravaisson makes this point with respect to habits at the organic level, but it applies to other kinds of habit, too: "one becomes accustomed over time to the most violent poisons . . . the most unhealthy air and food become the very conditions of health."[52] This means that giving up any habit, even an unhealthy one, will bring about a transitional period of instability and discomfort. On the other hand, the same point means that a new, healthier habit that is initially inconvenient and uncomfortable will eventually become natural and easy: "Movements or situations that initially are most difficult and tiring become over time the most convenient, and end up by making themselves into indispensable conditions of the functions to which they have always been associated"[53]—and it is for this reason, at least, that habit can be considered a form of grace. Ravaisson's reference here to particular environmental and situational conditions also accentuates the contextual nature of habit: habits can be traced only partially within the physical body, for they are constitutive of a lived body that is irreducibly worldly, relational, intentional, erotic, responsive. This is why a change of scene is sometimes sufficient to break a habit, although if the change is temporary then the break may well prove, on returning home, to be merely an interruption. In his book on Proust—who, aided by Ravaisson's legacy, is one of the great modern thinkers of habit—Samuel Beckett writes that "Habit is a compromise effected between the individual and his environment. . . . Habit is the generic term for the countless treaties concluded between the countless subjects that constitute the individual and their countless correlative objects."[54]

The third and last practical point to be drawn from *Of Habit* is perhaps the most important: one way to deal with a tenacious unwanted habit is to lead it back to the sphere of consciousness, for only here can it be influenced by reflection and the will. As Ravaisson argues, habits take root in passivity: in sensations and in feelings that have faded to obscurity; and their activity, their power, is that of desire, need, attachment, craving. We can follow Joseph Butler in including in this category of passivity "associations of ideas," those thoughts which pass through the mind unbidden, and perhaps unacknowledged. Several thinkers have observed that the power of habit lies to a great extent in the degree to which it remains concealed: Hume, for example, remarks that "custom, where it is strongest, not only covers our natural ignorance, but even conceals itself, and seems not to take place, merely because it is found in the highest degree";[55] Kierkegaard writes that "of all enemies, habit is perhaps the most cunning, and above all it is cunning enough never to let itself be seen, because the person who sees the habit is saved from the habit. Habit is not like other enemies that one sees and against which one aggressively defends oneself; the struggle is actually with oneself in getting to see it."[56] This "seeing" is not to be understood in intellectualist terms, for no act of cognition is going to change one's embodiment. And if habit resides in passivity, rather than in the activities that manifest it, then this is where it must be "seen": awareness of habit has to be cultivated at the level of sensations, feelings, and involuntary thoughts. This kind of awareness is deliberately cultivated in certain therapeutic and spiritual exercises—for example, in psychoanalysis or cognitive behavioral therapy, and in Buddhist meditation techniques, which reportedly provide accomplished practitioners with the ability to observe sensations, emotions, and thoughts as they arise, from moment to moment. This kind of awareness can itself become a capability and even a tendency—a *hexis*.

While the Kantian view of ethics would lead to the ignoring, dismissal, or suppression of involuntary affects, regarded as merely mechanical, a view that takes habit more seriously makes attentiveness to these affects, to the connections between them, and to the conditions under which they recur an important element of moral life. Developing the faculty of awareness of passive phenomena—which, after all, are available to attention at every moment—can gradually enable a person to discriminate between habits in order to choose which to maintain and which to let go of, which to yield to and which to resist. Moral practice, on this account, would consist not merely in the cultivation of good habits and the elimination of unwanted habits, but in preventing the latter from taking hold within the body through the development of a certain pattern of receptivity and resistance that is based on clear and experiential understanding. This might serve as a definition of practical wisdom.

Just as—to return once more to Aristotle—one swallow does not make a summer, and one brave act does not make a courageous person nor one drink an alcoholic, so a single moment of insight is unlikely to break a habit. This is why the techniques used to cultivate awareness of habits mimic the acquisition of habits themselves in the duration, frequency, and regularity of their repetition: the analysand sees her analyst four or five times a week; the Buddhist maintains a daily meditation practice; the patient undergoing cognitive behavioral therapy keeps a diary of her thoughts and feelings, and so on. Establishing these routines may be "first of all an effort, and wearisome," as Ravaisson describes the development of moral virtues. His philosophy of habit suggests that techniques designed to support human development and flourishing—whether they operate within an ancient or modern, religious or medical paradigm—can share a theoretical basis in common with virtue ethics, and may thus be incorporated within that moral tradition's understanding of the aims, criteria, and practices of a good life.

A final point that should be noted is that although Ravaisson's analysis of habit as mediating between freedom and necessity resonates with materialist critiques of determinism, and with the most recent developments in the neurosciences, this does not imply that the latter eclipse or can replace philosophical reflection. Both Ravaisson's vocabulary—of tendency, desire, intuition, virtue, love, and grace—and his method, which includes introspection and phenomenological description, exemplify the first-personal order of his thinking of habit, and this in turn is mirrored in its practical, ethical applications. Knowledge of cerebral functioning and neurogenesis, articulated always in the third person, is no doubt valuable, but such knowledge is not in itself psychically transformative, nor even morally significant, and will not by itself lead to human flourishing. A good human life *can* be lived in ignorance of scientific theory, but not in ignorance of habit.

## NOTES

1. This chapter originally appeared in *Inquiry* 53, no. 2 (2010): 123–45.
2. Aristotle, *Nicomachean Ethics*, Book 2, Ch. 1.
3. Immanuel Kant, *Anthropology from a Pragmatic Point of View*, trans. Mary Gregor (The Hague: Martinus Nijhoff, 1974), 148–49.
4. Immanuel Kant, *The Metaphysics of Morals*, trans. Mary Gregor (Cambridge: Cambridge University Press, 1996), ms. 6: 409. See also 6: 407: "An *aptitude* (*habitus*) is a facility in acting and a subjective perfection of *choice*. —But not every such *facility* is a *free* aptitude (*habitus libertatis*); for if it is a *habit* (*assuetudo*), that is, a uniformity in action that has become a *necessity* through frequent repetition, it is not one that proceeds from freedom, and therefore not a moral aptitude."

5. Maurice Merleau-Ponty, *Phenomenology of Perception*, trans. Colin Smith (London: Routledge, 1994), 142.

6. For discussion of the role of habit in Aristotle's ethics, see Myles Burnyeat, "Aristotle on Learning to Be Good," in Amélie Oksenberg Rorty, ed., *Essays on Aristotle's Ethics*, 69–92 (Berkeley and Los Angeles: University of California Press, 1980); Eugene Garver, "Aristotle's Metaphysics of Morals," *Journal of the History of Philosophy* 27 (January 1989): 7–28; and Joe Sachs's Preface and Introduction to his translation of Aristotle, *Nicomachean Ethics* (Newburyport, MA: Focus Publishing, 2002), vii–xvii.

7. See Aristotle, *On the Soul*, 417a23–b2. On Aristotle's concept of *hexis*, see Garver, "Aristotle's Metaphysics of Morals"; and Pierre Rodrigo, "La dynamique de *l'hexis* chez Aristote," *Alter* 12 (2004): 11–25.

8. The concept of repetition is not itself problematized in Ravaisson's text, and he often presents "continuity or repetition" as alternative—and, implicitly, equivalent—sources of habit. Like earlier philosophers of habit, he takes repetition for granted, ignoring the crucial question of the possibility of repetition: *What* is repeated? What counts as "the same"? This question was raised, albeit obscurely, by Søren Kierkegaard just four or five years after the publication of *De l'habitude*: in both *Johannes Climacus, or De omnibus dubitandum est* and *Repetition* (1843) the Danish philosopher notes the impossibility of repetition in both empirical reality (which is characterized by infinite variation) and in ideality (an atemporal realm of abstract identity). Kierkegaard argues that the possibility of repetition is "the most interior problem" and must be located "within the individual"—within subjective consciousness, conceived as the intersection or synthesis of ideality and empirical actuality—where "it is not a question of the repetition of something external but of the repetition of his freedom." See Søren Kierkegaard, *Repetition*, trans. Howard V. and Edna H. Hong (Princeton: Princeton University Press, 1983), 274–75; 304. Subsequently, philosophers such as Henri Bergson, Edmund Husserl and Gilles Deleuze have engaged extensively with this problem of repetition; for Ravaisson's influence on later French thought, see Dominique Janicaud, *Ravaisson et la métaphysique*, 2nd edition (Paris: Vrin, 1997); for a short overview, see Claire Marin, "L'être et l'habitude dans la philosophie française contemporaine," *Alter* 12 (2004): 149–72. The issue requires sustained discussion and cannot be explored adequately within the confines of the present chapter, where I follow Ravaisson in focusing on other aspects of the question of habit.

9. Ravaisson was responding to early modern scientific theories, as well as to philosophical discussions of habit; see Jean Cazeneuve, *La philosophie médicale de Ravaisson* (Paris: Presses Universitaires de France, 1958).

10. David Hume, *A Treatise on Human Nature* (Oxford: Oxford University Press, 1978), 424. For a discussion of Butler's account of habit and its influence on Hume, see John Wright, "Hume and Butler on Habit and Moral Character," in M. A. Stewart and J. P. Wright, eds., *Hume and Hume's Connexions* (State College: Pennsylvania State University Press, 1995), 105–18.

11. See, for example, David Hume, *Enquiries Concerning Human Understanding and Concerning the Principles of Morals* (Oxford: Oxford University Press, 1975), 43.

12. See Xavier Bichat, *Physiological Researches on Life and Death*, trans. Tobias Watkins (Philadelphia: Smith and Maxwell, 1809), 34–40.

13. Jacques Derrida comments that Ravaisson "derives his axioms from Maine de Biran," but does not appear to recognize the originality of Ravaisson's interpretation of his predecessor's analysis. See Jacques Derrida, *On Touching*, trans. Christine Irizarry (Stanford: Stanford University Press, 2005), 155.

14. Félix Ravaisson, *Of Habit*, trans. Clare Carlisle and Mark Sinclair (London: Continuum, 2008), 49.

15. See Ravaisson, *Of Habit*, 121.

16. Pierre Maine de Biran, *The Influence of Habit on the Faculty of Thinking*, trans. Margaret Donaldson Boehm (Westport, CT: Greenwood Press, 1970), 219.

17. Maine de Biran, *The Influence of Habit*, 87–88.

18. Maine de Biran, *The Influence of Habit*, 54–56.

19. Maine de Biran, *The Influence of Habit*, 68–69.

20. See Maine de Biran, *The Influence of Habit*, 70: "When this tendency passes from the *virtual* to the *actual*, as a result of renewed external stimulation, the individual wills and executes the same movement."

21. See Maine de Biran, *The Influence of Habit*, 108.

22. Maine de Biran, *The Influence of Habit*, 104.

23. Maine de Biran, *The Influence of Habit*, 49; 100–1.

24. Maine de Biran, *The Influence of Habit*, 226.

25. This claim can be traced back to Bichat, *Physiological Researches on Life and Death*, 35–37.

26. See Félix Ravaisson, "Jugement de Schelling sur la philosophie de M. Cousin, et sur l'état de la philosophie francaise et de la philosophie allemande en générale," *Révue germanique* 3, no. 10 (1835): 3–24.

27. F. W. J. Schelling, *Sämmtliche Werke* (Stuttgart: J. G. Cotta, 1856–1861), vol. 11, 328.

28. See Rodrigo, "La dynamique de l'*hexis* chez Aristote," 25. See also Jean-Luc Marion, *Sur l'ontologie grise de Descartes. Science cartésienne et savoir aristotélicien dans les Regulae* (Paris: Vrin, 1975), chapter 1.

29. Ravaisson, *Of Habit*, 53–55.

30. Catherine Malabou, *What Should We Do with Our Brain?*, trans. Sebastian Rand (New York: Fordham University Press, 2008), 30. In this text Malabou argues that the neuroscientific concept of plasticity takes us "between determination and freedom"—see especially chapter 1.

31. See Ravaisson, *Of Habit*, 27. This dynamic conception of inertia has more in common with Spinoza's *conatus* than with Newton's mechanistic theory. Leibniz argues, contra Newton, that a body has "in itself . . . a tendency to persevere in what sequences of changes it has begun": see "Nature Itself; or, the Inherent Force or Activity of Created Things," in *Philosophical Texts*, eds. R. S. Woolhouse and Richard Francks (Oxford: Oxford University Press, 1998), 217. For a discussion of Leibniz's influence on Ravaisson, see the Editors' Introduction and Commentary in *Of Habit*, 13–14; 79–81.

32. See Ravaisson, *Of Habit*, 51.

33. Ravaisson, *Of Habit*, 51.

34. Ravaisson, *Of Habit*, 55.

35. Ravaisson, *Of Habit*, 57.

36. Ravaisson, *Of Habit*, 55.

37. Ravaisson, *Of Habit*, 55–57.

38. Merleau-Ponty, *Phenomenology of Perception*, 44.

39. Joseph Butler, *Analogy of Religion, Natural and Revealed, to the Constitution and Course of Nature* (London: Bell and Daldy, 1857), 108.

40. Ravaisson, *Of Habit*, 69.

41. L. A. Kosman offers an excellent discussion of this aspect of Aristotle's ethics in "Being Properly Affected: Virtues and Feelings in Aristotle's Ethics," in Rorty, *Essays on Aristotle's Ethics*, 103–16.

42. Ravaisson, *Of Habit*, 69.

43. Ravaisson, *Of Habit*, 71.

44. The notion of prevenient grace can be traced back to Augustine, who distinguishes between the "prevenient grace" that brings a person to the point of conversion; the "operative grace" that accomplishes the liberation from sin that occurs at the moment of conversion; and the "co-operative grace" that, following conversion, assists the liberated will's pursuit of spiritual growth. Prevenient grace precedes the will and enables it, in spite of its sinful condition, to choose to seek salvation and to submit to God.

45. This term is used, disparagingly, by Derrida to describe Ravaisson's thought; see *On Touching*, 156.

46. See the Editors' Introduction to *Of Habit*, 15–17; and the Editors' Commentary, 112–14.

47. On receptivity, see *Of Habit*, 31, 35–37; on resistance, see 43–45, 61. Just as Ravaisson conceives passivity as both receptivity and resistance, so he conceives activity as both spontaneity and force.

48. The distinction between receptivity and resistance lies at the heart of the concept of plasticity, which is employed in current neuroscientific theory. See Malabou, *What Should We Do with Our Brain?*, 5. In clarifying the distinction between plasticity and flexibility, Malabou accentuates the political significance of the former, which denotes a capacity for resistance as well as for the reception of form. The scientific sources for her conception of plasticity include Joseph LeDoux, *Synaptic Self* (New York: Viking, 2002) and Jean-Claude Ameisen, *La sculpture du vivant: Le Suicide cellulaire ou la mort créatrice* (Paris: Seuil, 1999).

49. Augustine, *Confessions*, Book VIII, Section 5.

50. Ravaisson, *Of Habit*, 57.

51. Søren Kierkegaard, *Journals and Papers*, ed. and trans. Howard V. and Edna H. Hong (Bloomington and London: Indiana University Press, 1967–1978), vol. 2, 1260.

52. Ravaisson, *Of Habit*, 63.

53. Ravaisson, *Of Habit*, 63.

54. Samuel Beckett, *Proust* (London: John Calder, 1965), 18–19.

55. Hume, *Enquiries Concerning Human Understanding and Concerning the Principles of Morals*, 28–29.

56. Søren Kierkegaard, *Works of Love*, trans. Howard V. and Edna H. Hong (Princeton: Princeton University Press, 1995), 36.

# BIBLIOGRAPHY

Ameisen, Jean-Claude. *La sculpture du vivant: Le Suicide cellulaire ou la mort créatrice*. Paris: Seuil, 1999.

Aristotle, *Nicomachean Ethics*. Translated by Joe Sachs. Newburyport, MA: Focus Publishing, 2002.

Beckett, Samuel. *Proust*. London: John Calder, 1965.

Bichat, Xavier. *Physiological Researches on Life and Death*. Translated by Tobias Watkins. Philadelphia: Smith and Maxwell, 1809.

Burnyeat, Myles. "Aristotle on Learning to Be Good." In *Essays on Aristotle's Ethics*, edited by Amélie Oksenberg Rorty, 69–92. Berkeley and Los Angeles: University of California Press, 1980.

Butler, Joseph. *Analogy of Religion, Natural and Revealed, to the Constitution and Course of Nature*. London: Bell and Daldy, 1857.

Cazeneuve, Jean. *La philosophie médicale de Ravaisson*. Paris: Presses Universitaires de France, 1958.

Derrida, Jacques. *On Touching*. Translated by Christine Irizarry. Stanford: Stanford University Press, 2005.

Garver, Eugene. "Aristotle's Metaphysics of Morals." *Journal of the History of Philosophy* 27 (January 1989): 7–28.

Hume, David. *Enquiries Concerning Human Understanding and Concerning the Principles of Morals*. Oxford: Oxford University Press, 1975.

———. *A Treatise on Human Nature*. Oxford: Oxford University Press, 1978.

Janicaud, Dominique. *Ravaisson et la métaphysique*. 2nd ed. Paris: Vrin, 1997.

Kant, Immanuel. *Anthropology from a Pragmatic Point of View*. Translated by Mary Gregor. The Hague: Martinus Nijhoff, 1974.

———. *The Metaphysics of Morals*. Translated by Mary Gregor. Cambridge: Cambridge University Press, 1996.

Kierkegaard, Søren. *Journals and Papers*, vol. 2. Edited and translated by Howard V. and Edna H. Hong. Bloomington and London: Indiana University Press, 1967–1978.

———. *Repetition*. Translated by Howard V. and Edna H. Hong. Princeton: Princeton University Press, 1983.

———. *Works of Love*. Translated by Howard V. and Edna H. Hong. Princeton: Princeton University Press, 1995.

Kosman, L. A. "Being Properly Affected: Virtues and Feelings in Aristotle's Ethics." In Rorty, *Essays on Aristotle's Ethics*, 103–16.

LeDoux, Joseph. *Synaptic Self.* New York: Viking, 2002.

Leibniz, G. W. "Nature Itself; or, the Inherent Force or Activity of Created Things." In *Philosophical Texts*, edited by R. S. Woolhouse and Richard Francks. Oxford: Oxford University Press, 1998.

Maine de Biran, Pierre. *The Influence of Habit on the Faculty of Thinking*. Translated by Margaret Donaldson Boehm. Westport, CT: Greenwood Press, 1970.

Malabou, Catherine. *What Should We Do with Our Brain?* Translated by Sebastian Rand. New York: Fordham University Press, 2008.

Marin, Claire. "L'être et l'habitude dans la philosophie française contemporaine," *Alter* 12 (2004): 149–72.

Marion, Jean-Luc. *Sur l'ontologie grise de Descartes. Science cartésienne et savoir aristotélicien dans les Regulae*. Paris: Vrin, 1975.

Merleau-Ponty, Maurice. *Phenomenology of Perception.* Translated by Colin Smith. London: Routledge, 1994.

Ravaisson, Félix. "Jugement de Schelling sur la philosophie de M. Cousin, et sur l'état de la philosophie francaise et de la philosophie allemande en générale." *Révue germanique* 3, no. 10 (1835): 3–24.

———. *Of Habit*. Translated by Clare Carlisle and Mark Sinclair. London: Continuum, 2008.

Rodrigo, Pierre. "La dynamique de *l'hexis* chez Aristote." *Alter* 12 (2004): 11–25.

Schelling, F. W. J. *Sämmtliche Werke*. Vol. 11. Stuttgart: J. G. Cotta, 1856–1861.

Wright, John. "Hume and Butler on Habit and Moral Character." In *Hume and Hume's Connexions*, edited by M. A. Stewart and J. P. Wright, 105–18. State College: The Pennsylvania State University Press, 1995.

## *Chapter Eight*

# A Moralist in an Age of Scientific Analysis and Skepticism

## *Habit in the Life and Work of William James*

David E. Leary

In June 1874, a thirty-two-year-old sometime instructor of anatomy and physiology at Harvard College ruminated on the situation faced by the novelist George Eliot, especially as regarded her recent novel, *Middlemarch* (1871–1872), which he had previously described as "fuller of human stuff than any novel that was ever written."[1] "She seems to me to be primarily a moralist," he wrote, though "she writes in an age of scientific analysis and skepticism, and her own lot has been cast in a circle whose way of feeling and thinking is particularly adverse to anything like moral unction or enthusiasm." As a result, he continued, she "never gets her imagination fairly warmed and going without proceeding to reflect upon it herself and make a critical, often ironical, commentary as it runs." Thus, "the *mass* of her mental energy never pulls together," and the inner tension within her work leaves the reader "with an annoying uncertainty as to her purpose." Ah, but "what she might have done in an age of belief, when the best thought around her was constructive and enthusiastic and strengthened her native feelings instead of throwing cold water on them"! Had that been her lot, she would have been "twice as great as she is now."[2]

Thus wrote William James (1842–1910) in words he might have used to describe his own situation. For if Eliot was "married to [George] Lewes, hand in glove with [Thomas] Huxley, [Herbert] Spencer and a host of people" of that sort, as James said,[3] he himself was deeply engaged in reading the works of those same individuals and was thoroughly immersed in the same atmosphere, as represented and promulgated by his own older friend

Chauncey Wright, a similarly and in fact even more aggressively and reductively minded empiricist.

Just two years before he offered this assessment of George Eliot, James wrote a draft of what he hoped to be his first publication in psychology, a manuscript now labeled a "Draft on Brain Processes and Feelings" (1872). In that draft, as he told a colleague seventeen years later, he "excogitated" a "conscious automaton theory" that depicted human thought and action as produced automatically and entirely by brain processes that cause feelings of effort and decision along with thought and action. Though we might *feel* that our will had something to do with our thought or action, in fact (James had written) that feeling was determined mechanically, just as the thought and action were. James never published this draft, and soon ceased to advance its central argument, having come to realize "grounds to doubt it."[4] And seven years later, in an article entitled "Are We Automata?" (1879), he explained *why* he had become so adamantly opposed to that theory.

In this chapter I will review how James got from his earlier position, which so readily fit the scientific and skeptical tenor of his age, to his later position, and I will indicate how the views he began to articulate by the mid-1870s became central to the doctrines he presented in his magisterial *Principles of Psychology* (1890) and in his subsequent work in psychology and philosophy. Along the way I will make it clear that even before 1872, when he was attending lectures and doing physiological research in Harvard's Medical School, James was a deeply engaged advocate of philosophy, which he was determined to advance through a thorough yet critical understanding of the biological foundations of human thought, feeling, and action. He viewed this scientifically oriented yet analytical approach to philosophy as a means of clarifying not just what *is* the case in human life, but also what *should be* life's outcome. Morality, in short, was always interpolated in his thinking, teaching, researching, and writing. Although he took a biological view of cognition, and embedded it within a Darwinian selectionist framework (which he extended "all the way up" from the level of sensation through perception to cognition and beyond), his "naturalist approach" was not meant to eliminate consideration of "struggling with temptation" or the identification of the sources and targets of "true moral energy," as he put it in "Are We Automata?"[5] Quite the contrary!

## 1. YEARNING FOR ORDER, ACHIEVEMENT, AND SELF-ASSERTION

Habit, I plan to show, was the key to James's solution of the dilemma that he faced as he weighed the *intellectual* attractiveness of an entirely materialistic and causal explanation of human existence (a mode of explanation accepted by many in his scientific and skeptical age) against the equally compellingly *moral* imperative to believe that he could and should live a responsible and meaningful life (a life in which real decisions were made about actually possible alternative courses of action). James's interest in the nature and utility of habit reached back into the 1860s. It first appeared as a function of personal rather than professional concerns, initially revolving around his sensitivity to the possibly ameliorative effects that habits might bring into his life. For well before the beginning of his career, James sought greater direction and regularity in what he had come to experience as a somewhat random and purposeless life.

As already amply documented, James was the son of a wealthy and quirky father, whose whims assured that James spent much of his childhood and youth moving from place to place, from this to that side of the Atlantic, shifting tutors and schools, studying in one language and then another, while focusing now on science, now on art, now on something else, depending on whatever suited the present time, place, inclination, or available instruction.[6] And beyond the lack of sequential learning and personal stability that resulted from this fickle regimen, James was, by temperament, more than a little variable in his own inclinations. As his sister Alice famously put it, he was "just like a blob of mercury." It was impossible to "put a mental finger upon him."[7] Similarly, his brother Henry recalled that in their early years James "was always round the corner and out of sight."[8] And later in life, James exhibited "an extremely impatient temperament," as he himself admitted, adding that "I am a motor, need change, and get very quickly bored."[9]

Countering this tendency, James believed from early on—as early as 1858, at the tender age of sixteen—that it "ought to be everyone's object in life" to be "as much use as possible" in the grand scheme of things, not only because it is the "duty" of every person to be of "use," but also because no one, and certainly not himself, "would wish to go through life without leaving a trace." This personal concern about humans *leaving a trace*, not as passively mechanical objects but as actively choosing subjects who contribute "something which without us could not be," was so persistently important to James that he reported nine years later, in 1868, that the only thing keeping him from giving up and committing suicide during those "skeptical intervals" when "the waves of doubt are weltering" was the "feeling that by waiting and living by hook or crook long enough I might make my *nick*, however small a one" and thus "*assert my reality*." For James, only by asserting his personal reality, which he associated with "the thought of my having a will," could he alleviate the depressive effects of contemplating the kind of determinism typically associated with scientific understanding and analysis.[10]

Habit figured in two ways during and after these crucial years of James's personal development. In contrast to the "hundred side-tendencies, ambitions, interests" that pulled him this way and that, he came to realize that he had to choose "a few tolerable simple peaceable desires" and then pursue them with "simple patient monotonous" regularity. He felt that this alone—leading a life of more habitual behavior—would put him "on the path to accomplishing something some day." (His behavior had been so erratic, he said, that "I feel as if the greater part of the past 10 years had [been] worse than wasted.") And in addition to reforming his behavior, he determined that he had to cultivate "habits of attention and order in thinking," including attending to the thought of "my having a will," which alone could provide the "moral support" he so desperately needed.[11]

Such resolutions dot James's diary entries and letters from the 1860s into the 1870s, as do indications of the many starts and stops that characterized his tortured, by no means linear progress toward personal maturity, mental health, and professional achievement. Making matters more difficult, his resolve was complicated by his decision not only to commit himself to scientific endeavors but also to persevere in his ruminations upon the philosophical implications of those endeavors. Consistent with his strenuous approach to other issues, James chose not to take the easier route away from science, by which he could have escaped a key source of his anxiety and depression. Instead he took what he considered to be the more honest and manly approach,[12] embracing his attraction to science *as well as* his concern for morality, thus assuring continued conflict between the specter of scientific determinism and his yearning for moral efficacy. It all came to a head, though not a final conclusion, in an often cited crisis that began in early February and culminated in late April 1870.

On February 1, 1870, James recorded in his diary that he had "about touched bottom" and had to "face the choice with open eyes," whether to "throw the moral business overboard" or to "follow it, and it alone." Saying that he would "give the latter alternative a fair trial," he admitted that "hitherto I have tried to fire myself with the moral interest, as an aid in the accomplishing of certain utilitarian ends of attaining certain difficult but salutary habits," but "in all this I was cultivating the moral int [i.e., interest] only as a means, & more or less humbugging myself." Now, he wrote, "I must regard these useful ends only as occasions for my moral life to become active." Whatever the immediate result of this conviction, James's next diary entry is a drawing of a tombstone, commemorating the death of his beloved cousin Minny Temple on March 9. The entry after that, on March 22, is addressed to Minny and includes the comment: "Minny, your death makes me feel the nothingness of all our egotistic fury." One can only imagine what was going through James's mind at the time, but on April 30 he reported that

> I think yesterday was a crisis in my life. I finished the first part of [Charles] Renouvier's 2nd Essays and saw no reason why his definition of free will—the sustaining of a thought *because I choose to* when I might have other

> thoughts—need be the definition of an illusion. At any rate I will assume for the present—until next year—that it is no illusion. My first act of free will shall be to believe in free will.

James ended the paragraph noting that if he was better by the coming January, he might "perhaps return to metaphysic study & skepticism without danger to my powers of action." But in the meantime, he wrote, he needed to "recollect that only when habits of order are formed can we advance to really interesting fields of action" and that "one link dropped" from the interlocking chain of habit "undoes an indefinite number." And further on in the same diary entry, he remarked that

> Hitherto, when I have felt like taking a free initiative . . . suicide seemed the most manly form to put my daring into; now, I will go a step further with my will, [and] not only act with it, but believe as well; believe in my individual reality, and creative power.

Henceforth, he declared, he would put his faith in "the self governing *resistance* of the ego to the world."[13] Whatever he wrote next has been torn from his diary.

## 2. PREPARING FOR A CAREER IN PSYCHOLOGY AND PHILOSOPHY

The fact that James articulated a "conscious automaton theory" in his "Draft on Brain Processes and Feelings" (1872) written just two years after his famous declaration of free will, suggests the jagged path he still had to traverse, sometimes turning toward and sometimes away from a completely deterministic account of human behavior. In any case, James's next diary entry—the next one not ripped from his diary—is dated February 10, 1873, and it records his decision "to stick to biology for a profession in case I am not called to a chair of philosophy." Despite this prospect, James wrote that he would nevertheless continue to regard philosophy as his "vocation" and would "never let slip a chance to do a stroke at it."[14] Then, on April 10, James reported in his diary that he had told Charles Eliot, his former chemistry teacher and the current and subsequently long-serving president of Harvard, that he would "accept the anatomical instruction [i.e., instructorship] for next year, if well enough to perform it."[15] At the time, James was already engaged in teaching a semester-length course in comparative anatomy and physiology at Eliot's prior request. Thus James had begun to move from attending lectures, doing laboratory research, and engaging in a wide range of reading, to his first gainful employment, which led in turn to his appointment as acting director of Harvard's Museum of Comparative Anatomy (in 1874) and then as assistant professor of physiology (in 1876).

In the six years between his appointment to the Museum and 1880, in addition to teaching comparative anatomy and physiology, James offered the first course—a graduate course—in the new physiological psychology (in 1875), established and had his students use the first laboratory of experimental psychology in the United States (also in 1875), began teaching undergraduate and graduate courses in psychology under the auspices of the Philosophy Department (in 1877), delivered the Johns Hopkins University Lectures in Baltimore on "The Senses and the Brain and Their Relations to Thought" (1878), delivered the Lowell Institute Lectures in Boston on "The Brain and the Mind" (1878), directed the first Ph.D. in psychology—through the Department of Philosophy—at Harvard (in 1878), and finally received his coveted appointment as assistant professor of philosophy (in 1880). By then he had signed a contract (in 1878) to produce his *Principles of Psychology* and published his first substantive articles in psychology and philosophy (in 1878 and 1879). Thus he was well on his way to becoming the person who is now known as a founder of both scientific psychology and pragmatic philosophy.

To understand James's development and then rejection of "conscious automaton theory," and to situate his distinctive treatment of habit within its contemporary scientific context, we need to look back from his subsequent fame to the early 1860s, when he enrolled as a student at Harvard's Lawrence Scientific School. Having just given up his study of art in Newport, Rhode Island, James came to Cambridge to fulfill an earlier interest in natural history[16] under the guidance of such distinguished scientists as the zoologist and geologist Louis Agassiz, the botanist and taxonomist Asa Gray, and the anatomist Jeffries Wyman. All three, in varying ways, were intimately connected to significant ongoing scientific developments—the first two (Agassiz and Gray) having particularly close, though quite different relations to Charles Darwin, whose revolutionary *On the Origin of Species* (1859) was then just two years old. In addition, James came into contact with Charles Sanders Peirce, another student at the Scientific School, who would become one of his most treasured intellectual interlocutors.[17] Thus, when James turned toward the study of medicine in 1864, and returned to it after a year-long research trip to Brazil with Agassiz (in 1865–1866), he already had a solid grounding in science. And while in the Medical School, working towards his 1869 M.D. degree, he continued to explore anatomy with Wyman even as he studied medicine with Oliver Wendell Holmes Sr. In addition, during a break from his medical studies (in 1867), he spent time in Europe (in Berlin in particular), where he attended courses and lectures on physiology and was especially impressed by the eminent physiologist Emil Du Bois-Reymond's research on electrical charges accompanying muscle action, a topic that would be relevant to James's later understanding of habit. It was during this same stay in Europe that he became familiar with the experimental research of Hermann von Helmholtz and Wilhelm Wundt, and concluded that "perhaps the time has come for Psychology to begin to be a science."[18] From that time on, his interest in "mental science" solidified and became more prominent in his thinking.[19]

All in all, the 1860s were a heady time for James, even given his well-known bouts of ill health, and he absorbed all that he could from class, reading, laboratory, and conversation. Throughout the decade, as he pursued coursework in chemistry, natural history, anatomy and physiology, he also followed the most recent developments in the scientific study of force, energy, and matter, and he supplemented his scientific studies by reading broadly in psychiatry, philosophy, and literature. Besides Peirce, his friends toward the end of the decade included James Jackson Putnam, later a leading neurologist; Henry Bowditch, a future pioneering physiologist in whose laboratory he would continue his own research into the 1870s; and Chauncey Wright, a philosopher with broad and lively interests, whom Darwin would invite to address "when a thing may properly be said to be effected by the will of man."[20] The result of Darwin's invitation to Wright was an important article on the "Evolution of Self-Consciousness" (1873). At the same time, in the early 1870s, Wright was active in the Cambridge Metaphysical Club in which participants (including James and Peirce) addressed many of the pressing philosophical issues of the time, especially in relation to the import of scientific theory and practice.[21] And in the same period James initiated correspondence with Charles Renouvier and then, in mid-decade, participated in a second philosophical discussion group that focused primarily on Hegel.

Though James started his formal course of scientific and medical study from a less advanced position than students like Peirce, he quickly demonstrated sufficient ability and insight to capture the attention of his teachers. One of those teachers, Charles Eliot, remembered later in life that James had been "a very interesting and agreeable pupil," who supplemented his work in chemistry with "excursions into other sciences and realms of thought." "He liked experimenting," Eliot recalled, "particularly novel experimenting." And noting that James "possessed unusual mental powers," he added that James later came to be admired as a teacher and scholar for "his penetration, his mental alertness, and his free spirit."[22] In fact, Eliot told James himself in 1894 that, among his many stellar achievements as president of Harvard, "your coming to the University and your career as a teacher and writer" had offered some of "my most solid grounds of satisfaction."[23]

The main point I wish to make by reviewing this information is simple, but too rarely recognized: James made his initial mark and earned his later opportunities at Harvard by distinguishing himself in his early scientific studies and early teaching in scientific fields. He was not a dilettante who spied on science, psychiatry, or psychology from afar, much less from a proverbial armchair. He did his turn in the lab; he visited leading laboratories and attended lectures by leading scientists in Europe as well as in the United States; he became intimately familiar with the major scientific developments of his time; he reviewed significant works in anatomy, physiology, neurology, psychiatry, and natural history, including Darwin's work, for major periodicals; he visited asylums and clinics; he was seriously considered for an appointment at the new research-oriented Johns Hopkins University as well as at Harvard; and due to his unusual linguistic abilities, he enjoyed direct access, like few others, to multiple national literatures and to the preeminent scientific and clinical research of his time: the French and German, in particular, as well as the British and just-then-emerging American research.[24] So when James aimed his gaze toward psychological phenomena, he was not only prepared through reading, thinking, and conversations about philosophical authors and issues, he was also prepared through his training in science, which allowed him to make the best possible sense of these phenomena from the perspectives of evolutionary, physiological, neurological, and even physical science.[25]

## 3. FROM AUTOMATION TO HABIT

So what, then, about habit? And how did this topic—and James's distinctive take on it—relate to James's thoughts on "conscious automata"? We have seen that James turned to habit in the 1860s in the hope of bringing order and direction into his life, as he yearned not only for a sense of purpose but also to achieve something as the result of his own self-assertion. (The *possibility* of self-assertion, we saw, became for him a moral as well as scientific issue.) We have also noted that James spent the 1860s and '70s developing a first-hand understanding of major developments in the natural, biological, and medical sciences. Habits, he came to know, had been discussed by Darwin and others in relation to instinct; and the evolutionary approach—especially the question, what are habits good for?—was soon at the forefront of his consciousness. But beyond reflecting on this evolutionary question, James approached habit from a physiological and, more specifically, from a neurological perspective. And he subordinated these perspectives, in turn, to the emerging view of the universe as a theater of energy and force. Thus, when he focused on leading-edge research regarding the activity of the nervous system, he tended to conceptualize it in terms of the flow and transformations of measurable electrophysiological "currents" and "impulses."[26]

In this context, in 1870, James's former teacher Oliver Wendell Holmes Sr. delivered his notable Phi Beta Kappa address on *Mechanism in Thought and Morals* (1871). Although he explicitly stated that he was concerned only with "*that part* of mental and bodily life" that is "*independent* of our volition," thus indicating that (in his view) not all human thought and action was purely mechanical, Holmes nevertheless presented a strong case for the operation of "mechanistic principles" in human experience.[27] Just two years later, James extended Holmes's proposition, applying mechanistic analysis to *all* of human functioning in his "conscious automaton theory," as he called it seventeen years later, using terminology made famous by Thomas Huxley's celebrated address of 1874.[28] Interestingly, James admitted in his draft that he was offering only "a plausible hypothesis" and was doing so because he felt it necessary "to refute the charge that certain characteristics of thought cannot *possibly* depend on *mere* nerve action."[29] Thus, his proposing of conscious automata could be interpreted as simply doing what he would be doing throughout the rest of his career: giving the devil his due. But even if that was all that he intended, it is still relevant to ask how he justified his later rejection of what he had presented in this draft as an intellectually viable argument, one that incorporated contemporary notions of "habitual channels" for nervous impulses and that reduced "the Will" to a "quantum of force" resulting from "oscillations" of "current," which eventually overcomes "the mutual interferences and inhibitions of the conflicting waves" set up by these oscillations. What we typically regard as a voluntary "decision" at the end of this process, James conjectured, is simply a misconstrued sense of effort and achievement conveyed by prolonged tension followed by an abrupt resolution or action. The entire process is "determined mechanically" and "is not in essence a whit different from what we have all so often observed in flying a kite," during which "the play of the various forces" make the kite dart up and down, left and right, before it suddenly "sweeps headlong from the zenith to the ground."[30]

The soft spot in James's drafted argument, which led to his later rejection of conscious automaton theory, was his explicitly stated recognition that while "in ordinary thinking association by contiguity plays a dominant part," things are different in "rapt or passionate thought," in which "association by similarity is a marked peculiarity." In this latter case, James noted, "we are more intent" and "occult [distant and unexpected] analogies are apt to come to light." As a result, we not only "generalize," we also "make discoveries," seeing that "at bottom *this* . . . is really nothing but a case of *that*."[31]

In his draft, James swept the "peculiar" character of thought-by-similarity (thinking that is dependent upon the association of ideas, things, and properties that are similar) into the same explanatory scheme as thought-by-contiguity (thinking that is dependent upon ideas, things, and properties that have been experienced as proximate to one another in time or space), but the distinction between these two traditional ways of understanding human thought was the key to his subsequent liberation from—and critique of—a strictly mechanical account of human thought and action in lieu of an account that granted a consequential role to consciousness. The pivotal factors in this liberation were James's adoption of Darwinian *selection* as a crucial function in mental dynamics, combined with his attribution of a directive role in selection to *interest* and *attention*. Although there seems to have been no single moment of inspiration for this constellation of factors, a reconstruction of his thinking from available records reveals that a confluence of ideas—ideas taken from at least three individuals (William Wordsworth, Chauncey Wright, and Shadworth Hodgson) in addition to Darwin himself—provided the context within which he reached conclusions that remained central to his thought—and to his understanding of habit—from that time forward.[32]

The first clear hint of this context was given in March 1873, when James reported to his father that he felt much better than he had over the previous year (i.e., from around the time he had written his conscious automaton draft). The principal factor, he said, was that he had "given up the notion that all mental disorder required . . . a physical basis" and now "saw that the mind did act irrespective of material coercion, and could be dealt with therefore at first-hand."[33] This new conviction relieved his fear that he suffered, inescapably, from a physiologically based tendency toward neurasthenia, hypochondria, and melancholia—a fear that was far from assuaged by his articulation of conscious automaton theory.[34] Instrumental in his change of mind was not only his continued rumination upon Renouvier's philosophy, but also his reading of Wordsworth, on whom he had been "feeding" for "a good while."[35] More particularly, he had been reading and reflecting on Wordsworth's long poem "The Excursion," especially its fourth book ("Despondency Corrected"), which trumpets the healing effects associated with belief in "the mind's *excursive* power," which is to say, the mind's ability (figuratively speaking) to *walk about* nature, not passively "chained to its object[s] in brute slavery" but rather actively conferring "order and distinctness" upon them. In short, Wordsworth's theme was the productive *marriage* of mind and matter, in which mind contributes "interest" as well as "Will" to what otherwise would have been but "dull and inanimate" matter.[36] In offering a persuasive rendition of this theme, Wordsworth gave James "authentic tidings of invisible things."[37] And even before James had worked out the intellectual implications of these tidings, the "persuasion and belief" that Wordsworth helped bring about had "ripened," as Wordsworth himself put it, into a "passionate intuition" that would abide from then on at the heart of James's psychological and philosophical thought,[38] namely, that *each and every mind is characterized by the distinctive interests and willfulness that it brings to its activities*.

James encountered the concept of interest not only in Wordsworth's idealist poetry but also in Chauncey Wright's and Shadworth Hodgson's empiricist psychology and philosophy. Wright had no doubt expressed his views to James in personal conversations, but he also gave public voice to them in his "Evolution of Self-Consciousness," published just one month after James had spoken with his father about Wordsworth's beneficial impact. The crucial thing about interest, Wright claimed in this article, is that it directs one's attention.[39] As a result, as James put it in 1875, "*my* experience is only what I agree to attend to."[40] This individualizing of experience as a function of one's own interest and attention became a crucial "law" for James, separating his emerging psychology from that of Herbert Spencer and Alexander Bain. As he said, "Spencer shrinks from explicit recognition of this law" while "Mr. Bain," though "in principle" attuned to it, "does not work it out."[41] Only Chauncey Wright had done so, James asserted, even though he was already aware of Shadworth Hodgson's treatment of interest in *Time and Space* (1865). (In fact, he had begun a close study of this text in September 1873.) In later years it was Hodgson's, not Wright's, "law of interest" that James cited as crucially significant,[42] perhaps because of his greater sympathy with Hodgson's overall philosophy.

The upshot was that James approached his first substantive publications and his first major public addresses (all occurring in 1878) with a firm determination to articulate a physiologically based psychology that disavowed conscious automaton theory—and any related mechanistic form of associationism—in lieu of attributing active roles in mental dynamics to interest and attention, which he came to see as not only compatible with Darwinian selectionism, but as illustrative of its reach into the realm of consciousness. Among the happy fruits of this conjunction of ideas, for James, was the possibility it opened up for the moral life, as advanced and structured through the action of consciousness and the development of habits.[43]

The first step in articulating his emerging views, in print, took place in James's "Remarks on Spencer's Definition of Mind as Correspondence" (1878), in which he criticized Spencer's claim that the mind "adjusts" passively to its "outer relations" (i.e., its environment). To the contrary, James argued, the mind has "preferences and repugnances"—"subjective *interests*"—that guide its "selection," from among the dense array of environmental stimuli, of only those features that matter to it. The mind, in other words, has "a vote" in what it takes in; "it is in the game, and not a mere looker-on."[44]

James developed this theme further in his Hopkins Lectures on "The Senses and the Brain and Their Relation to Thought" (1878), which gave special emphasis to the role of selection in mental functioning. Then, in "Brute and Human Intellect" (1878), he returned to the issue of association-by-similarity, which he had treated in his conscious-automaton draft of 1872. But now, instead of reducing it to the same mechanistic explanatory scheme that seemed to work for association-by-contiguity, he noted that association-by-similarity depends upon active selection, that is, upon the mind's *dis*sociating of "interesting" features from the "originally vague syncretism [whole] of consciousness."[45] And in his Lowell Lectures on "The Brain and the Mind" (1878), he elaborated upon this point, arguing that features, once dissociated, are then *compared* by the mind in light of interests that are typically unique to the individual. Thus, the notion of an "impartial consciousness" that accompanies but plays no active role in mental dynamics does not fit the apparent facts. Beyond this, James laid out a systematic view of the mind as selective at each level of functioning, from bottom to top: i.e., from sensation to perception to reasoning to aesthetic activity and finally to ethical deliberation and choice. Notably, this systematic approach culminated in "the moral life" in which "choice reigns supreme,"[46] and it reflected the overall Darwinian framework of James's lectures and thought, a selectivist framework that James extended, through his knowledge of the nervous system as well as his observations of psychological processes, well beyond the boundaries set by Darwin himself.[47]

James spelled all of this out, in writing, in his article on "Are We Automata?" His explicit aim in this article was to show that the apparent functional utility of consciousness makes the existence of conscious automata unlikely. The crux of his argument revolved around the question, "Of what use to a nervous system is a superadded consciousness?"[48] Noting that consciousness has evolved across species and over time, he argued on both a priori and a posteriori grounds that the utility that prompted this evolution is almost certainly related to the fact that a selective consciousness, which can compare aspects of what is presented to it, can then focus its attention on the one that most closely accords with its vital interests. This would, in effect, "load the dice" so that the conscious individual could deal with the world in a way that is relevant to his concerns rather than suffer, without recourse, the utterly random impulses and responses to confront him.[49] As James put it in one of his most famous passages, repeated in his *Principles of Psychology*, "the mind is at every stage a theatre of simultaneous possibilities. Consciousness consists in the comparison of these with each other, the selection of some, and the suppression of the rest by the reinforcing and inhibiting agency of attention."[50]

After stating this conclusion, James returned in his article to "the ethical field" and discussed "the true moral energy" involved in striving for ends that have come to the fore through "selective attention."[51] Using the example of "an inebriate struggling against temptation," he underscored how "the selective pressure of consciousness," representing in this case the will to avoid alcohol, runs "counter" to "the strongest tendencies of automatic activity."[52] Thus, he showed how "the moral business" that had concerned him from a much earlier age could be preserved and pursued within the domain of scientific analysis. And in referring to the "tendencies of automatic activity," he introduced the topic (habit) that would become an essential part—both point and counterpoint—of his views on the active, even willful, activity of consciousness.[53]

## 4. HABIT AT THE FOUNDATION OF JAMES'S THOUGHT

Habit, as James had already noted in his Lowell Lectures on "The Brain and the Mind," is "the great thing" that allows the cerebral hemispheres to be free for "higher flights."[54] Lower levels of neurological functioning, he explained to his audience with a series of anatomical slides, are responsible for "fatal," that is, automatic or instinctual, responses, but the higher centers are clearly essential to intelligent behavior. And more than anything else, he said, habit provides "the best explanation" of how "acts of intelligence" come to characterize human behavior. On the one hand, habits represent what an individual has learned; on the other, because they occur with a minimum of consciousness and decision-making, habits free up the individual to attend to unexpected matters that warrant intelligent response.[55] So, functionally, habits bring order to the typical routines of life while allowing consciousness to focus on events that fall outside those routines. Thus, they make good sense within an evolutionary scheme.

Though we have only James's notes from his Lowell Lectures, it is clear that by October 1878, when the lectures took place, he had developed his basic ideas about the relation between brain functioning and mental processes, and between deterministic cerebral conditions and sometimes indeterminate cognitive and behavioral responses. And though he would go on to become famous for his descriptions of consciousness and his advocacy of the will, it becomes clear, as we review the development and structure of his thought, that it is habit, not consciousness or will, that holds his system together. Habit also provides a crucial means by which he was able to respond positively to the intellectual attraction of causal explanation while also accepting that there is a moral imperative—and an actual way—to live a responsible and meaningful life, one not absolutely predetermined by causal relations. Clearly, then, James's treatment of habit resolved his earlier personal dilemma and inspired his distinctive way of integrating physiology, psychology, philosophy, and ethics.[56]

One of the things that distinguished James's treatment of habit—the crucial element that he added to previous discussions of habit in the works of Spencer, Bain, and Carpenter—was his use of what he called "the Meynert scheme."[57] As early as his Lowell Lectures,[58] James had recognized that Theodor Meynert's neurological analysis of cerebral functioning provided the key to explaining "the education of the hemispheres," which is to say, the process by which human action becomes intelligent.[59] Through a lengthy review of neurological evidence, extending well beyond anything undertaken by earlier empirical psychologists, James arrived at a modified version of the sensory-motor theory of cortical functioning as proposed by Meynert and John Hughlings Jackson.[60] Although James readily admitted "how ignorant we really are" regarding "psychogenesis,"[61] he nonetheless felt confident, on both theoretical and empirical grounds, that something like Meynert's scheme, as modified by himself, approximated the neurological basis of habit formation.[62] James built up to this conclusion through a series of articles published in the 1880s.[63] What he expressed in *The Principles of Psychology*, with this and that additional flourish, was the result of these earlier cumulative efforts.

A fundamental distinction that James made was between instinctual reflexes, associated with the lower brain stem, and learned habits, associated with the cerebral hemispheres. All of scientific psychology, he felt, was developing, in the wake of evolutionary science, on the model of reflex action. The pivotal fact was that, in humans, the evolution of the hemispheres has allowed not only the emergence of full-blown consciousness but also higher orders of habit formation than we see in organisms with less developed and more rigid nervous systems. The evolutionary advancement represented by the hemispheres resides in their "plasticity," which facilitates the establishment of new or altered neural pathways through which electrophysiological currents pass on the way from sensory input to motor output.[64] For James, electrophysiological currents always underlie conscious awareness, emotional feeling, and behavioral action, but the particular pathways by which these currents travel from the point of input to the point of output can be modified or even created anew. (This is what is made possible by the "plastic" nature of the hemispheres.) There is nothing mysterious about this, James felt: "The currents, once in [the hemispheres], must find a way out."[65] If a pathway is blocked, some other "channel" will have to be found. Paths taken by electrophysiological currents may be either built-in or accidental, but they never come about *initially* as the result of conscious intent or willful effort.[66] Nonetheless, once a pathway has been made, consciousness can enter into the picture, ex post facto. This contention was central to James's understanding of both habit and will, and it made good on his earlier claim that consciousness, as something that has evolved, must have some practical utility.

James's classic illustration of habit formation was a child who has touched a lit candle and subsequently remembers the pain (in James's term, the "image") of having done so. He or she will then associate, by means of their neural connection, "the original tendency to touch" with the image of pain, and this association will inhibit "the touching tendency" the next time the child perceives a lit candle.[67] This inhibition of the electrophysiological impulse in turn will necessitate the traversing of a new pathway—a different route for the current to find its way out of the cerebral hemisphere. With repetition, as the current flows more and more readily down this new route, the initially conscious withholding of the hand from the lit candle will become unconscious and habitual.[68] In this way, humans—and to the extent that their lesser brain capacity allows, other animals—learn both what *not* to do and what *to* do when excitation enters the cerebral hemispheres from this or that internal or external source. And what can and cannot be done—as well as what habits are formed—depends upon the extant evolution of physical structure and the associated degree of consciousness. The important thing is that, whatever happens, whether habitual or non-habitual, there will always be a specific neurological substrate, and both consciousness and habits will remain firmly rooted in neurology.

In this scheme—and thus in James's proposed physiological psychology as a whole—consciousness itself is now a causal factor. Images, or ideas in classical terminology, are posited as factors in the transmission or inhibition of neural impulses, acting now to keep the path open to action (when they prefigure desirable outcomes), acting at other times to close it (when they prefigure undesirable ones). And since "what is early 'learned by heart' becomes branded-in (as it were) upon the Cerebrum" so that "it becomes part of the normal fabric,"[69] it is crucial, James concluded, for each of us "to make our nervous system our ally instead of our enemy" by making "automatic and habitual, as early as possible, as many useful actions as we can."[70] Reflecting the hard-earned lessons of his own life, James added that "there is no more miserable human being than one in whom nothing is habitual but indecision,"[71] and then he proceeded to list a series of maxims that in his view would help to assure the establishment of "moral habits."[72] He drew these lessons in large part from Bain, but he grounded his support of them on his preceding analysis of the plastic nature of neural structures, noting that "the physiological study of mental conditions is thus the most powerful ally of hortatory ethics."[73]

Although James admitted that many habits in humans as in other animals are built upon instinctual tendencies, his primary concern was with those habits, especially in humans, that are unique to the individual and instrumental to living a good life. Striving for the latter, as we have seen, raised for James the conundrum of the will. He addressed this conundrum at length in his *Principles*, basing his proposed solution of it—a solution that satisfied both his scientific and moral inclinations—upon the same neurological structures and other factors encountered earlier in his analysis of habit.[74] In particular, he reached back to a basic premise of his chapter on habit: that a potential "innervation" of human conduct is sometimes associated, through experience, with an "image" of how we would feel "when the innervation [i.e., conduct] is over."[75] If this "anticipatory image" provides no hindrance, the action will take place more or less automatically. But if it arouses resistance, the action will occur only if sufficient will is summoned. Such summoning occurs typically when the individual has an *interest* in the imagined outcome. That interest directs and sustains the individual's conscious *attention* to the outcome, thereby triggering the action whose end has come to dominate consciousness. This directing and sustaining of attention to a desired end is, for James, equivalent to a willful assertion that it occur. As he put it in his Latinate terminology, it is the *fiat* (the decision to "let it be") that constitutes "the essence of the voluntariness of the act."[76] Intentionally affirming a mental idea or wish of this kind, James noted, "is the only psychic state which introspection lets us discern as the forerunner of our voluntary acts."[77]

The key hypothesis underlying this account of willful action—action caused by conscious and even effortful attention to the idea of its consequences—is provided by James's "ideo-motor theory," which he elaborated upon Maudsley's more restricted clinical observations of "ideo-motor action."[78] According to Maudsley's observations, the idea of an action, barring effective resistance, brings about that action. James may have been attracted to this premise, initially, because it represents consciousness—and more specifically, particular conscious ideas—as effectual, but he was probably persuaded that the premise is true by his reading about and experimental duplication of various phenomena associated with hypnotic states, in which an idea (i.e., a "suggestion") is implemented without hesitation, unless some inhibitory obstruction takes place.[79]

However ironic it may seem, habit is important in James's treatment of will. Once established, James argued, a habit can be triggered by "the idea of the end," which "tends more and more to make itself all-sufficient." So if the initiating idea is held long enough in consciousness, James continued, "the whole chain [of associated connections and final action] rattles off *quasi*-reflexly," as described in his earlier chapter on habit.[80] Although in some cases "the bare idea of a movement's sensible effects" is a sufficient "mental cue" to action, in other cases "an additional mental antecedent, in the shape of a *fiat*, decision, consent, volitional mandate, or other synonymous phenomenon of consciousness" must intervene "before the movement can follow."[81] But when it follows, it tends to trace the path that has been established in the past, both by its electrophysiological current and by the behavioral outcome to which it has led. Though James gave only a single example of his own before referring the reader to relevant examples provided by Bain, he insisted that "it was in fact through meditating on the phenomenon in my own person that I first became convinced of the truth of the doctrine which these pages present."[82] We have seen earlier some of the personal experiences that fed his meditations. In fact, it is noteworthy that his explanation of the will in 1890, wedded now to speculative yet experimentally grounded neurology and to the clinical observations of a leading psychiatrist, is amazingly consonant with Renouvier's definition of free will as "the sustaining of a thought *because I choose to*," which James had accepted as he struggled with the implications of scientific analysis and skepticism, way back in 1870.[83]

In the next pages in his chapter on the will, James went from a discussion of simple yes-no decision-making to more complex situations in which actions result from "deliberation" over multiple, often conflicting ideas about possible actions. He also discussed five types of decision, the feeling of effort, and two kinds of "unhealthy will": the "obstructed will" that makes normal actions impossible and "the explosive will" that makes abnormal ones irrepressible. These are interesting and relevant discussions, as are his subsequent critique of pleasure and pain as "springs of action" and his philosophical ruminations on "free-will" and "the education of the will," which include further neurological speculations. But we have covered enough to document our central contention that habit is at the foundation of James's thought, providing a means for the emergence of distinctly human, purposeful behavior while also playing an essential role in other aspects of psychological functioning, including the will. All that remains to underscore is James's contention that neither habit nor will creates options out of thin air; they can only tip the balance to or from one or the other extant idea by selecting or not selecting it for attention from among "the theatre of simultaneous possibilities" for human action.[84] But though the range of potential habits is constrained and the will is not *radically* free, both being dependent on material conditions and their conscious representation, they are nonetheless indelibly individual and consequential. Each person, as James had hoped to show, is in the game, each can make a difference, and each can leave a nick in the universe by the cultivation of his or her own habits and the assertion of his or her own will.

## 5. CONCLUSION

In subsequent works after the publication of *The Principles of Psychology* in 1890, James continued to direct attention to the importance of habit, most notably in his popular textbook on psychology (*Psychology: Briefer Course* [1892], an abbreviated version of his *Principles*) and in his *Talks to Teachers* (delivered throughout the 1890s and then published in 1899). In the former work, besides treating habit itself in a thorough manner, he emphasized that "what is called our 'experience' is almost entirely determined by our habits of attention,"[85] and he discussed a number of ways in which "the law of neural habit" has an impact on human thought, feeling, and behavior.[86] In the latter work, he hit many of the same notes, after defining education as "the organization of acquired habits of conduct and tendencies to behavior"[87] and before concluding with a Spinozistic plea that "you [should] make freemen of your pupils by habituating them to act, whenever possible, under the notion of a good," which is to say, according to the idea of what, first, teachers and later the students themselves take to be good.[88] To the considerable extent that humans are "bundles of habit,"[89] he argued, their moral character will consist in "an organized set of habits of reaction."[90]

At the same time, over the final decades of his life, a counterpoint to the positive representation of habit became increasingly apparent in James's thought and work. This counterpoint had always been a feature, though a much less prominent feature, of his work. For instance, in his very first publication on philosophy, James contrasted philosophical thinking with common ways of thinking, saying that the philosophical student had to get into the *habit* of thinking *unhabitually*! As he put it, "philosophic study means the habit of always seeing an alternative, of not taking the usual for granted, of making conventionalities fluid again, of imagining foreign states of mind. In a word, it means the possession of mental perspective,"[91] by which he clearly meant the possession of a *different* perspective from that of common sense. This accorded with his understanding of "genius," which he defined early on as the ability to make *atypical* analogical connections.[92] He repeated this definition in *Principles*[93] and expressed it two years later when he wrote that "genius, in truth, means little more than the faculty of perceiving in an unhabitual way."[94] In contrast, said James, most of us "have no eyes but for those aspects of things" which we have "already been taught to discern"—things that "have been labeled for us," the labels then being "stamped into our mind."[95] Thus, "most of us grow more and more enslaved to the stock conceptions with which we have once become familiar," leading to a kind of "old-fogyism" in which our thinking and behavior are all too conventional.[96] So, while it may simplify and organize life to have routine ways of perceiving, thinking about, and responding to the stream of experience, James realized that there is a potential downside to this economy of habit. Hence, he felt that *some* individuals, at least, need to see and think and act outside the box, for the sake of others as well as themselves, lest habit become too much of a good thing, stultifying and routinizing rather than freeing and guiding us.

Perhaps it was James's increasing dismay at the political and social conventions of the 1890s and early 1900s that aroused him, as it seems, to seek more pointedly *new* ways of thinking and acting after 1890.[97] But in any case, in his initial discussion of pragmatism, he represented the pragmatic philosopher as a "path-finder," even a "trail blazer," who sets out to identify new ways of trying to get to the "center" of the forest of experience.[98] It is probably relevant too that, after focusing on establishing psychology on a *scientific* basis over the preceding decades, James was now concerned, in his initial presentation on pragmatism, with making room for *religious* as well as scientific modes of understanding and living. Only a few years later, in

*Varieties of Religious Experience* (1902), he discussed "the hot spot in a man's consciousness" that constitutes "the habitual centre of his personal energy"[99] and explored how this habitual center of energy might be "converted" to another set of ideas (e.g., religious ideas) by that individual's "growth into *new* habits."[100]

Similarly, James expressed an increasing desire to break other kinds of barriers to innovation and revivification, such as restraints placed on the inner "energies" and "powers" of human beings.[101] Liberating and expressing those powers, he hoped, would free himself and others from being "victims of habit-neurosis" and from "habituation" to "literality and decorum."[102] In sum, then, James seemed to be saying, in a variety of venues, that if habit can help us feel comfortable in a world of change, there are times when breaking habits, challenging beliefs, trying out new perspectives—and feeling *un*comfortable—is more likely to prompt major advancements in knowledge, custom, and goodwill.

Perhaps James's pragmatism can best be seen, in this context, as a way of moving from resting point to resting point along the path to fuller knowledge, more confident beliefs, and a better world. "A pragmatist turns his back resolutely and once for all upon a lot of inveterate habits dear to professional philosophers," said James.[103] "Pragmatism unstiffens all our theories" while allowing enough lingering, if loosely held, "loyalty" to "older truths" to keep us sufficiently steady for the next step into a newer and better world.[104] As "mediator and reconciler," pragmatism has "no prejudices whatever, no obstructive dogmas, no rigid canons. . . . Her only test of probable truth is what works best in the way of leading us" ahead, toward the goal of ever more useful thought and ever more satisfying life.[105] Perhaps it is useful to think of James urging us to develop a new habit of proceeding pragmatically, keeping one hand on the relatively known past as we reach for the relatively unknown future, striving for what is beyond our grasp but not beyond our hope.

Whether that is a useful thought or not—whether James's pragmatism represents a blending of the habitual and unhabitual in a productive alliance—is an issue for another time. *This* chapter has been concerned primarily with exploring the role of habit in William James's life and thought, and how it allowed him to mediate between his physiological studies, psychological speculations, philosophical conclusions, and moral aspirations. Though typically passed over as one of his more popular and least original contributions to psychology and philosophy, in fact his treatment of habit was crucial in allowing him to walk a fine line between scientific analysis (and objective determinism), on the one hand, and moral advocacy (and subjective indeterminism), on the other. It also allowed for the imposition of order upon relatively unstructured human experience (as readily illustrated in his own personal life), while providing a place, even if an admittedly small place, in which human will (considered in a new way) could be seen as playing a crucial role in the midst of an apparently all-too-material universe. And although James spent the rest of his career, after 1890, searching for a compelling articulation of a new metaphysics that would eliminate the chasm between mental and bodily processes—maybe it would be a new kind of materialism that was somehow *aufgehoben* to incorporate consciousness as a natural, evolved, and efficacious part of nature[106]—in the meantime his approach to habit and to the closely associated processes of cognition, feeling, volition, and action would have to "stand in," however awkwardly at times, for this needed, eagerly anticipated, but indefinitely deferred conceptual and theoretical breakthrough.

James was not alone—and was far from the first—to show such interest in or to make extensive use of habit. He was well aware of earlier treatments by Aristotle, Augustine, the Scholastics, Jonathan Edwards, and Jean-Jacques Rousseau, and he was intimately familiar with the relevant philosophical ideas of Alexander Bain and Herbert Spencer, the physiological speculations of Thomas Laycock and William Carpenter, the psychiatric observations of Isaac Ray and Henry Maudsley, and the innovative thought of his own friends Chauncey Wright and Charles Sanders Peirce. He was also well informed about the recent results of experimental physiology and neurology in England, France, Germany, and elsewhere, including the research of David Ferrier, John Hughlings Jackson, and Theodor Meynert. His travels, studies, and reading—as random as they may have seemed to others—provided an unusually broad and solid framework for his creative thinking. It is probably safe to say that few twenty-first-century psychologists or philosophers, aside from a rather small group of dedicated James scholars, realize how deep as well as wide his reading, conversations, correspondence, and reflections were in the decades leading up to the publication of his *Principles of Psychology*, which in various ways provided the foundation for his subsequent work in philosophy as well as psychology. Everyone knows that *Principles*, his first book, was published relatively late in his career (he was forty-eight when it appeared), but a careful review of the preceding development of his thought has revealed how early he came to his basic ideas and how thoroughly he worked through their implications over the subsequent decades. In addition, tracing the development of James's thinking has highlighted his intentions, the obstacles he met, and how he dealt with them. Seemingly simple ideas—even ones that he took directly from someone else—were often made to do distinctive work within the economy of his own evolving system of thought. This fact has often been missed by those who analyze elements of his thinking without sufficient understanding of their role within the entire corpus of his thought.

Hilary Putnam has remarked that "William James is a figure who simply won't go away."[107] One reason, as the neuropsychologist Richard F. Thompson has noted, is that "his views remain astonishingly contemporary."[108]

Regarding habit, for instance, James's emphasis on plasticity "has only recently regained popularity in study of the neurobiology of learning and memory," and his neurological speculations are now seen as advocating a "kind of connectionist machinery," akin to contemporary theorizing. Indeed, so much is now going the way of James's hypotheses—for instance, regarding the localization of functions and the basic structure of the brain as "a circuit, albeit an immensely complicated one"—that Thompson is confident that "James would be very pleased" by the recent body of neurological literature. Similar things have been said, from time to time, about James's ideas in other areas of psychology and in philosophy as well. Bruce Wilshire is only one among many who have called for "a serious reconsideration of William James," despite the "mixed bag" of "strengths" and "defects" that he sees in James's work.[109] Even regarding the controversial topic of free will, anathema in scientific psychology and much of philosophy over the past century, James's ideas and near analogues are once again receiving close, sympathetic, even appreciative attention.[110]

Further consideration of James's views, then, can advance not only our knowledge of history but also our understanding of where matters currently stand and where they might be heading in the future. With regard to the topic of habit, in particular, this chapter has clarified and expanded upon some of the basic claims that James made: claims that have sometimes been simplified by others to the point of travesty. As Charlene Haddock Seigfried has said, rephrasing what John McDermott said before her, "James is delightfully easy reading the first time around, but gets more difficult with each successive reading."[111] Unfortunately, few people bother to read James a second time, if they read him at all, and the vast majority of those who read him at all, read only selected portions of well-known classics, whether *The Principles of Psychology*, *The Will to Believe*, *The Varieties of Religious Experience*, *Pragmatism*, *A Pluralistic Universe*, *The Meaning of Truth*, or *Essays in Radical Empiricism*. Far fewer know about, much less read, the documents and other works (letters, diaries, notebooks, unpublished drafts, and early articles) that have made possible this reconstruction of his views on habit and associated matters and their relation to his views on science and morality as well as psychology and philosophy. With their aid we have seen how James used habit to mediate between scientific determinism and moral freedom, and thus to establish psychology and philosophy on a new foundation.

The philosopher Stephen Toulmin (1922–2009), a beloved teacher and dear friend to whose memory I dedicate this chapter, once observed that "philosophy has always flourished on half-fledged sciences."[112] The still-fertile philosophical contributions of William James, emerging as they did from the half-tilled soil of new scientific research in anatomy, neurology, and psychology, provide as compelling an illustration as one could wish.

# NOTES

1. William James, Letter to Catherine Elizabeth Havens, 23 March 1874, in *The Correspondence of William James*, 12 volumes, eds. Ignas K. Skrupskelis and Elizabeth M. Berkeley (Charlottesville: University Press of Virginia, 1992–2004), vol. 4, 486.

2. James, Letter to Catherine Elizabeth Havens, 13 July 1874, in *Correspondence*, vol. 4, 499.

3. James, Letter to Catherine Elizabeth Havens, 13 July 1874, 499.

4. James, Letter to Charles Augustus Strong, 21 October 1889, in *Correspondence*, vol. 4, 541.

5. William James, "Are We Automata?", in *Essays in Psychology*, ed. Frederick Burkhardt (Cambridge, MA: Harvard University Press, 1983), 58.

6. See, for example, Gay Wilson Allen, *William James: A Biography* (New York: Viking, 1967); Daniel W. Bjork, *William James: The Center of His Vision* (New York: Columbia University Press, 1988); Howard M. Feinstein, *Becoming William James* (Ithaca: Cornell University Press, 1984); Alfred Habegger, *The Father: A Life of Henry James, Sr.* (Amherst: University of Massachusetts Press, 1994); Ralph Barton Perry, *The Thought and Character of William James*, 2 vols. (Boston: Little, Brown, 1935); Robert D. Richardson, *William James: In the Maelstrom of American Modernism* (Boston: Houghton Mifflin, 2006); and Linda Simon, *Genuine Reality: A Life of William James* (New York: Harcourt Brace, 1998).

7. Alice James, *The Diary of Alice James*, ed. Leon Edel (New York: Dodd, Mead, 1964), 57.

8. Henry James, *Autobiography*, ed. Frederick W. Dupee (Princeton: Princeton University Press, 1983), 8.

9. William James, "James on Tausch," in *Essays, Comments, and Reviews*, ed. Frederick Burkhardt (Cambridge, MA: Harvard University Press, 1987), 190.

10. James, Letter to Edgar Beach Van Winkle, 1 March 1858, in *Correspondence*, vol. 4, 11–13, and James, Letter to Thomas Wren Ward, 7 January 1868, in *Correspondence*, vol. 4, 248, 250, italics added.

11. James, Letter to Thomas Wren Ward, 7 November 1867, in *Correspondence*, vol. 4, 225, and James, Letter to Thomas Wren Ward, 7 January 1868, 248, 250.

12. See Kim Townsend, *Manhood at Harvard: William James and Others* (New York: Norton, 1996).

13. William James, Diary [1] (1868–1873), in William James Papers, Houghton Library, Harvard University.

14. Perhaps it should be noted that opportunities in philosophy were severely limited and that related scholarly expectations were very different at that time. At Harvard, there was only one professor of philosophy, Francis Bowen, in 1872. Bowen taught from the texts of Scottish philosophers and was one of the exceptions among contemporary academic philosophers in that he produced his own works on metaphysics, logic, and ethics. (Most simply taught from others' texts or from their own commentaries on others' texts.) Of course, there were some instructors who helped Bowen teach philosophy to the approximately 600 undergraduates at Harvard in 1872, but their prospects for advancement were far from good. In fact, only one of the instructors from the entire decade, George Herbert Palmer, ended up becoming a professor of philosophy at Harvard (see George Herbert Palmer and Ralph Barton Perry, "Philosophy," in Samuel Eliot Morison, ed., *The Development of Harvard University since the Inauguration of President Eliot, 1869–1929* (Cambridge, MA: Harvard University Press, 1930), xc, 3; see also Bruce Kuklick, *The Rise of American Philosophy: Cambridge, Massachusetts, 1860–1930* (New Haven: Yale University Press, 1977).

15. James, Diary [1].

16. See, for example, James, Letter to Edgar Beach Van Winkle, 1 March 1858, 14.

17. It is relevant to note that Peirce developed his own views on the importance of habit in the 1860s (see, e.g., Charles S. Peirce, "Some Consequences of Four Incapacities," in *The Essential Peirce: Selected Philosophical Writings*, eds. Nathan Hauser and Christian Kloesel [Bloomington: Indiana University Press,1992]) and further developed those views in his later, more elaborate analyses of the relations among habit, action, doubt, and belief (see, e.g., Peirce,

"The Fixation of Belief" and "How to Make Our Ideas Clear," in *The Essential Peirce*). On Peirce's views, see Sandra B. Rosenthal, *Charles Peirce's Pragmatic Pluralism* (Albany: State University of New York Press, 1994) and Gary Shapiro, "Habit and Meaning in Peirce's Pragmatism," *Transactions of the Charles S. Peirce Society* 9 (1973): 24–40.

18. James, Letter to Thomas Wren Ward, 7 November 1867, 226.

19. James used "mental science" as virtually identical with "philosophy." For him the term covered not only recent and ongoing efforts to integrate scientific research with traditional philosophical concerns about the nature of thought, emotion, will, mind, and consciousness, but also other areas of study that deal with "the Human mind, its laws, its powers & the authority of its conclusions." More specifically, as he wrote to President Eliot in 1875, these other areas of mental science encompassed logic, the history of philosophy, and metaphysics (including epistemology) (James, Letter to Charles W. Eliot, 2 December 1875, in *Correspondence*, vol. 4, 527). In arguing for his appointment in philosophy, primarily to teach the new physiological psychology, James pointed out that he offered what no "mere" philosopher or physiologist could: He had *both* "first hand acquaintance with the facts of nervous physiology" *and* knowledge of "the subtlety & difficulty of the psychologic portions" of the subject (Letter to Charles W. Eliot, 2 December 1875, 528). He soon expanded the argument about the benefit of a scientific background to philosophy *as a whole*, claiming that in the 1870s philosophy must, "like Molière," claim "her own where she finds it," and thus must turn to "physics and natural history" and "educate herself accordingly" (James, "The Teaching of Philosophy in Our Colleges," 6). This obviously expanded the prospects for his own future in philosophy.

20. Charles Darwin, Letter to Chauncey Wright, 3 June 1872, in *The Life and Letters of Charles Darwin*, ed. Francis Darwin (London: John Murray, 1887), vol. 3.

21. See Louis Menand, *The Metaphysical Club* (New York: Farrar, Straus and Giroux, 2001).

22. Charles Eliot, "William James" (1915), in William James Papers, Houghton Library, Harvard University.

23. Charles Eliot, Letter to William James, 20 May 1894, in *Correspondence*, vol. 7, 504.

24. Regarding James's scientific background, see especially Paul Jerome Croce, *Science and Religion in the Era of William James: Eclipse of Certainty (1820–1880)* (Chapel Hill: University of North Carolina Press, 1995) and "William James's Scientific Education," *History of the Human Science* 8 (1995): 9–27. See also Perry, *The Thought and Character of William James*.

25. I emphasize this point, which will be relevant to the argument that follows, because of the repetitious acknowledgment in the literature on James regarding his idiosyncratic formal education and his own typically self-deprecating statements about the negative consequences of not having been sufficiently "drilled" in the sciences and logic in his younger days (see, e.g., James, Letter to Thomas Wren Ward, 7 November 1867, 225). This has led to a vision of James as less directly knowledgeable and less prepared than he actually was to be creative and effective in his chosen line of research (first in "mental science," narrowly defined, and then, by extension, in other areas of philosophy). The relevance of science to his philosophical work *beyond* "mental science" can be underscored by the fact that the first course he taught in philosophy, other than physiological psychology, was "The Philosophy of Evolution" (in 1879). And he approached other philosophical topics, later, with the same scientifically informed consciousness that he brought to his work in psychology. It is relevant to add a word about his background in philosophy, which he had read and discussed with others since at least the early 1860s. It seems clear that he knew a wider range of philosophy, albeit unsystematically, than he would have known by simply following the standard college curriculum. There were, of course, no graduate programs in the subject at that time.

26. In the early 1860s James took Joseph Lovering's physics course, which dealt with electricity among other natural phenomena. He also read William Grove's *Correlation of Physical Forces* (1862), which presented the various natural forces as convertible into each other. And he returned again and again to reports of Michael Faraday's research, including Faraday's own *Experimental Researches in Chemistry and Physics* (1859). In the same period he read and re-read Ludwig Büchner's *Kraft und Stoff* (1858) and found it difficult to shake its central theme that without matter there was no force, and without force there was no matter.

The relevance of these overlapping ideas to his later interest in the electrophysiological research of Du Bois-Reymond, to his subsequent fear "that we are Nature through and through, that we are *wholly* conditioned, that not a wiggle of our will happens save as the result of physical laws" (James, Letter to Thomas Wren Ward, March 1869, in *Correspondence*, vol. 4, 370), and thus to his temporarily held "conscious automaton theory," with its reduction of mental phenomena to physical matter and force, is obvious.

27. Oliver Wendell Holmes, *Mechanism in Thought and Morals: An Address Delivered Before the Phi Beta Kappa Society of Harvard University, June 29, 1870. With Notes and Afterthoughts*, in *Works of Oliver Wendell Holmes* (Boston: Houghton Mifflin, 1891), vol. 8, 261–62 (italics added).

28. See John D. Greenwood, "Whistles, Bells, and Cogs in Machines: Thomas Huxley and Epiphenomenalism," *Journal of the History of the Behavioral Sciences* 46 (2010): 276–99, for details about Huxley and other figures in the subsequent conscious automaton debate.

29. William James, "[Draft on Brain Processes and Feelings]," in *Manuscript Essays and Notes*, ed. Frederick Burkhardt (Cambridge, MA: Harvard University Press, 1988), 253.

30. James, "[Draft on Brain Processes and Feelings]," 252, 255, 256.

31. James, "[Draft on Brain Processes and Feelings]," 253–54.

32. I could have listed Ralph Waldo Emerson as well, but his more general, pervasive, and chronic influence was consonant in this instance with the momentarily more acute impact of William Wordsworth, who had also influenced Emerson himself decades earlier. Still, it is worth noting that Emerson's Americanized version of Wordsworthian ideas, as set forth (among other places) in his 1870 Harvard lectures on the "Natural History of Intellect" (1870), had a significant impact on James, whose familiarity with Emersonian ideas can be traced back to childhood. When James asserted, in 1873, that "I am sure that an age will come . . . when emerson's [*sic*] philosophy will be in our bones," he was acknowledging, he indicated, that Emerson's ideas had already shaped his own "dramatic imagination" of the way things are (James, "[Notes on Art and Pessimism]," in *Manuscript Essays and Notes*, 295).

33. Quoted in Perry, *The Thought and Character of William James*, vol. 1, 340.

34. Whatever the source or sources of his newfound belief in the (at least) potential, relative, or temporary independence of mind from body, James was soon elaborating upon it in two reviews of the physiologist William B. Carpenter's *Principles of Mental Physiology* (1874), which appeared just five months after James published an endorsement of Renouvier's "original and simple" arguments for "the *possibility*" of "free-will" (James, "Renouvier's Contribution to *La Critique Philosophique*," in *Essays, Comments, and Reviews*, 266). While criticizing Carpenter for his "very inadequate" knowledge of recent physiological research as well as for his "descriptive" rather than "analytic" approach (which aligned Carpenter more closely with Bain and Spencer than Wundt and "the immortal Helmholtz"), James nonetheless gave special mention to Carpenter's "copiously and variously illustrated" discussion of "ideo-motor action" (James, "Two Reviews of *Principles of Mental Physiology*, by William B. Carpenter," in *Essays, Comments, and Reviews*, 270, 273). In another review, James outlined the basic premises of this loosely descriptive theory that a "volitional impulse" could assert itself in the natural flow of neural activity and then through repetition—"by virtue of the great law of habit"—bring about an action that becomes "automatic" and "so to speak, second nature." And it could do this, James said, without violating the premise that "all mental action is correlated with brain function" (James, "Recent Works on Mental Hygiene," in *Essays, Comments, and Reviews*, 278). These very general premises, embellished by James's more sophisticated knowledge of neurology and his distinctive understanding of the role of interest-attention-and-selection, would soon define the core of his own views on the physiology of will and habit.

35. Perry, *The Thought and Character of William James*, vol. 1, 339.

36. William Wordsworth, "The Excursion," in *The Poems*, ed. John O. Hayden ( New York: Penguin Books, 1977), vol. 2, 155.

37. Wordsworth, "The Excursion," 152.

38. Wordsworth, "The Excursion," 156.

39. Chauncey Wright, "Evolution of Self-Consciousness," in *Philosophical Discussions*, ed. Charles Eliot Norton (New York: Henry Holt, 1877), 216–17.

40. William James, "*Grundzüge der physiologischen Psychologie*, by Wilhelm Wundt," in *Essays, Comments, and Reviews*, 300.

41. James, "*Grundzüge der physiologischen Psychologie*, by Wilhelm Wundt," 300.

42. For example, in William James, *The Principles of Psychology*, 2 vols., ed. Frederick Burkhardt (Cambridge, MA: Harvard University Press, 1981), vol. 1, 538–41.

43. The year 1878 has been called, with justice, James's *annus mirabilis*. His publications and lectures, drawing upon his evolutionary, physiological, and neurological knowledge, conveyed a distinctive understanding of sensation, perception, and cognition and established him as a significant newcomer in his chosen fields. Also, in June, he signed the contract that led, twelve years later, to the publication of his magisterial *Principles of Psychology*, and in July he married Alice Howe Gibbens, signaling the beginning of a considerable moderation if not a once-and-for-all end to his various nervous conditions. Finally, late that year, he submitted three additional articles for publication, including the article (published in January 1879) that explained his opposition to conscious automaton theory.

44. William James, "Remarks on Spencer's Definition of Mind as Correspondence," in *Essays in Philosophy*, ed. Frederick Burkhardt (Cambridge, MA: Harvard University Press, 1978), 21.

45. James, "Brute and Human Intellect," in *Essays in Psychology*, 15.

46. William James, Lowell Lectures on "The Brain and the Mind," in *Manuscript Lectures*, ed. Frederick Burkhardt (Cambridge, MA: Harvard University Press, 1988), 27.

47. James seems to have been the first individual to extend selectionism (which was still, then and for a good while longer, a highly debated characteristic of Darwinian evolutionary theory) from the domain of Nature in general to that of Mind in particular, which was still typically seen as somehow different from Nature. He first expressed his thoroughgoing selectionist view of mental processing in the late 1870s: "The highest and most elaborated mental products are filtered from the data chosen by the faculty next beneath out of the mass offered by the faculty below that" (James, "Are We Automata?", 51). Hence, ideas and feelings regarded as ethically salient were selected from among aesthetically selected ideas and feelings, which were derived, in turn, from those ideas and feelings that were abstracted from the wide array of perceptions, which in turn were selected from among the mass of constituent elements produced by the senses, which had, after all, responded only to a rather narrow range of the full spectrum of ambient stimuli. At each level some *possible* sensations, perceptions, ideas, feelings, and reactions had been selected while others went unnoticed or ignored.

48. James, "Are We Automata?", 41.

49. James, "Are We Automata?", 51.

50. James, "Are We Automata?", 51; repeated in James, *Principles of* Psychology, vol. 1, 277. Although James *mentioned* his famous analogy between the mind and a sculptor in the sentences following this passage in his 1879 article, he *elaborated* upon it in his *Principles*, creating another classic passage that helps to explain his thought on the role of consciousness: "The mind, in short, works on the data it receives very much as a sculptor works on his block of stone. In a sense the statue stood there from eternity. But there were a thousand different ones beside it, and the sculptor alone is to thank for having extricated this one from the rest. Just so the world of each of us, howsoever different our several views of it may be, all lay embedded in the primordial chaos of sensations, which gave the mere *matter* to the thought of all of us indifferently" (James, *Principles of Psychology*, vol. 1, 277). This passage makes it clear that James was a realist, though one (like Wordsworth) who felt that reality results from a productive interaction of mind and matter.

51. James, "Are We Automata?", 58.

52. James, "Are We Automata?", 59.

53. I should note that although James felt that he had shown that consciousness matters—that it can exert causal force—he admitted to a friend that "free-will is . . . no necessary corollary of giving causality to consciousness." Someone who has a "fatalistic faith," he said, is no more compelled to change his or her mind because of his (James's) argument than a person who has a "freewill faith" is compelled to give it up because of a compelling argument in favor of non-conscious causality (James, Letter to James Jackson Putnam, 17 January 1879, in *Correspondence*, vol. 5, 34; see also James, *Principles of Psychology*, vol. 2, 1173–1182). In

the end, as Renouvier said, the belief in free will is a matter of voluntary faith. James had addressed this issue, obliquely, five years earlier, when he argued in a letter to an editor that scientists like Huxley who claim to *know* what they can only *assume* are as much swept up in "the mood of Faith" as persons who do the same thing on behalf of religious beliefs or "moral speculation" (James, "The Mood of Science and the Mood of Faith," in *Essays, Comments, and Reviews*, 115). James signed this letter "Ignoramus." He had, of course, staked his own faith on free will and felt his belief was consonant with, if not a mandatory conclusion from, coherent principles and apparent facts. He similarly foreswore any possibility of giving "a coercive demonstration" in his extensive defense of his belief in indeterminism and free will in "The Dilemma of Determinism" (1884).

54. James, Lowell Lectures on "The Brain and the Mind," 19.

55. James, Lowell Lectures on "The Brain and the Mind," 18–19.

56. James's originality, especially when it comes to his views on habit, has often been underestimated (see, e.g., John C. Malone, "William James and Habit: A Century Later," in *Reflections on* The Principles of Psychology*: William James After a Century*, eds. Michael G. Johnson and Tracy B. Henley [Hillsdale, NJ: Lawrence Erlbaum Associates, 1990], which is otherwise a useful and informative source). Because James drew upon the work of Bain, Carpenter, and Maudsley, among others, it is often thought that he was simply repeating what others had said. But in fact he brought to his reading of their works—and to his selective adoption of some of their ideas—a much more sophisticated understanding of evolution, physiology, and neurology than they possessed. Bain, for instance, had only a schematic knowledge of recent scientific advances, and his lack of facility in German blocked his access to the most recent literature, including the literature on the cerebral hemispheres, that was important in James's assimilation and reformulation of his views on habit. Similarly, Carpenter's knowledge of the body was based on old-fashioned empirical anatomy rather than the new experimental physiology. And Maudsley's research was largely clinical in origin and nature. See Kurt Danziger, "Mid-Nineteenth-Century British Psycho-Physiology: A Neglected Chapter in the History of Psychology," in *The Problematic Science: Psychology in Nineteenth-Century Thought*, eds. William R. Woodward and Mitchell G. Ash (New York: Praeger, 1982), and Lorraine J. Daston, "The Theory of Will versus the Science of Mind" (in *The Problematic Science*) and "British Responses to Psycho-Physiology," *Isis* 69 (1978): 192–208, for useful historical background. James adopted their ideas only if they were compatible with the most recent experimental research, and only to the extent that their adaptation made sense within the context of this research and his own analysis of the facts presented in their works and in the general literature. More specifically, although he took descriptive examples and practical maxims regarding habits from Bain and Maudsley, he turned elsewhere when he was concerned about explanation rather than description. And in the same way, he took Carpenter's description of "ideo-motor *action*," purportedly involved in *some* "curiosities of our mental life," and expanded it into a generalized "ideo-motor *theory*" that he (James) embedded, as Carpenter had not, within a contemporary neurological framework (see James, *Principles of Psychology*, vol. 2, 1131). Finally, with regard to Bain (and also to Spencer), it is worth noting that James's critique of traditional utilitarianism, especially its emphasis on pleasure as the primary motive for human action, was but one source of the important conceptual distance James created between his views and theirs. This separation was apparent as early as James, "Two Reviews of *Principles of Mental Physiology*."

57. James, *Principles of Psychology*, vol. 1, 38. On Meynert and James's use of "the Meynert scheme," see Frank Sulloway, *Freud, Biologist of Mind* (New York: Basic Books, 1979) and William R. Woodward, "William James's Psychology of Will: Its Revolutionary Impact on American Psychology," in *Explorations in the History of Psychology in the United States*, ed. Josef Brožek (Lewisburg, PA: Bucknell University Press, 1984), each of whom emphasizes how James modified Meynert's account—at once too mechanical regarding reflexes and too purposive regarding mental processes (James, *Principles of Psychology*, vol. 1, 80)—from a more up-to-date evolutionary perspective. What I wish to emphasize, in addition, is how James used his "correction of the Meynert scheme" (James, *Principles of Psychology*, vol. 1, 79) to change, in fundamental ways, previous associationist accounts of habit from which he retained much of his basic psychological vocabulary. The fact that his account

*sounded like* earlier accounts by Spencer, Bain, Carpenter, and others has obscured the degree to which it was significantly different. For one thing, it attempted a causal *explanation* of association rather than a verbal *description* of it (James, *Principles of Psychology*, vol. 1, 566). For another, it switched pleasure or satisfaction from a *motivation* to a *consequence* of behavior (*Principles of Psychology,* vol. 2, 1156–64). Besides inspiring John Dewey's (1896) classic discussion of "the reflex arc" and Edward L. Thorndike's (1898) studies leading to "the law of effect" as well as anticipating B. F. Skinner's (1938) operant psychology and later social learning theory (see William R. Woodward, "The 'Discovery' of Social Behaviorism and Social Learning Theory, 1870–1980," *American Psychologist* 37 [1982: 396–410]), this provided a neurological basis for the kind of trial-and-error learning that Peirce and James saw as essential to pragmatic notions of progressive truth-approximating.

58. James, Lowell Lectures on "The Brain and the Mind," 17.

59. James, *Principles of Psychology*, vol. 1, 36–39.

60. James, *Principles of Psychology*, vol. 1, 39–87.

61. James, *Principles of Psychology*, vol. 1, 84.

62. Another advantage of this scheme was that it also provided the basis for non-habitual thought, feeling, and behavior as well as the operation of the will, as we shall see.

63. Including, for example, James, "The Feeling of Effort" and "What the Will Effects," in *Essays in Psychology*.

64. "Plasticity" was a term that James took from Darwin, who used it in reference to the modifiability of the *entire* physical organism (Darwin, *On the Origin of Species*, 12, 31, 80). This is relevant to note, given the evolutionary perspective from which James approached habit formation.

65. James, *Principles of Psychology*, vol. 1, 112.

66. James, *Principles of Psychology*, vol. 1, 113.

67. James, *Principles of Psychology*, vol. 1, 86.

68. James, *Principles of Psychology*, vol. 1, 119.

69. James, *Principles of Psychology*, vol. 1, 117.

70. James, *Principles of Psychology*, vol. 1, 126, italics omitted.

71. James, *Principles of Psychology*, vol. 1, 126.

72. James, *Principles of Psychology*, vol. 1, 127–131.

73. James, *Principles of Psychology*, vol. 1, 130. At the head of his chapter on habit in his own personal copy of the abbreviated version of *Principles*, James epitomized his argument and its moral significance by inserting this handwritten summary: "Sow an action, and you reap a habit; sow a habit and you reap a character; sow a character and reap a destiny" (James, *Psychology: Briefer Course*; see Richardson, *William James*, 315).

74. Just as habit is the subject of a fundamental chapter (ch. 4) toward the beginning of James's *Principles*, so is will the subject of what is, in many respects, the culminating chapter (ch. 26) of this masterwork. Between these two chapters, which form virtual bookends that support and justify his psychological system, James frequently noted ways in which "the great law of habit" (James, *Principles of Psychology*, vol. 1, 521) plays a significant role in a wide variety of psychological phenomena, ranging across association (ch. 14), memory (ch. 16), sensation (ch. 17), perception (ch. 19), belief (ch. 21), reasoning (ch. 22), and the modification and elaboration of instincts (ch. 12). Most crucial to James, however, were phenomena associated with voluntary vs. involuntary action (ch. 26).

75. James, *Principles of Psychology*, vol. 2, 1110–1111. In treating the possibility of *voluntary* conduct, James assumed, as a prerequisite, that past *involuntary* movements have left a supply of images in the memory, which are available when the will is called into action (James, *Principles of Psychology*, vol. 2, 1109–1100).

76. James, *Principles of Psychology*, vol. 2, 1111.

77. James, *Principles of Psychology*, vol. 2, 1112.

78. James, *Principles of Psychology*, vol. 2, 1130–1135.

79. See, for example, James, *Principles of Psychology*, vol. 2, 1198–1201, and an early review of Ambrose Liébault's work in James, "*Du sommeil et de états analogues*, by Ambrose Liébault," in *Essays, Comments, and Reviews*.

80. James, *Principles of Psychology*, vol. 2, 1128.

81. James, *Principles of Psychology*, vol. 2, 1130, italics omitted.
82. James, *Principles of Psychology*, vol. 2, 1133.
83. James, Diary [1].
84. James, *Principles of Psychology*, vol. 1, 277.
85. William James, *Psychology: Briefer Course*, ed. Frederick Burkhardt (Cambridge, MA: Harvard University Press, 1984), 156.
86. See, for example, James, *Psychology: Briefer Course*, 225, 243, 254, 286, 278, 345–47, and 352.
87. William James, *Talks to Teachers on Psychology and to Students on Some of Life's Ideals*, ed. Frederick Burkhardt (Cambridge, MA: Harvard University Press, 1983), 27.
88. James, *Talks to Teachers*, 344.
89. James, *Talks to Teachers*, 48.
90. James, *Talks to Teachers*, 108.
91. William James, "The Teaching of Philosophy in Our Colleges," in *Essays in Philosophy*, 4.
92. James, "Brute and Human Intellect," 30.
93. James, *Principles of Psychology*, vol. 1, 500.
94. James, *Psychology: Briefer Course*, 286.
95. James, *Principles of Psychology*, vol. 1, 420.
96. James, *Psychology: Briefer Course*, 286.
97. On James's political and social concerns, see Deborah Coon, "'One Moment in the World's Salvation': Anarchism and the Radicalization of William James," *Journal of American History* 83 (1996): 70–99, and George Cotkin, *William James: Public Philosopher* (Baltimore: Johns Hopkins University Press, 1990). Related expressions of concern were apparent in James's criticism of the "blindness" of human beings to the inner lives of those unlike themselves (James, 1899/1983f), in his negative reaction to the "ice cream soda-water" quality and "irremediable flatness" of Chautauqua gatherings (James, "What Makes Life Significant," in *Talks to Teachers*, 152, 154), and in his objection to the standardization of intellectual activity apparent in what he called "the Ph.D. octopus" (James, "The Ph.D. Octopus," in *Essays, Comments, and Reviews*). And, of course, he was also well aware of the benefits of novel ways of thinking in science.
98. William James, "Philosophical Conceptions and Practical Results," in *Pragmatism*, ed. Frederick Burkhardt (Cambridge, MA: Harvard University Press, 1975).
99. William James, *The Varieties of Religious Experience*, ed. Frederick Burkhardt (Cambridge, MA: Harvard University Press, 1985), 162, italics omitted.
100. James, *Varieties of Religious Experience*, 197, italics added.
101. William James, "The Energies of Men," in *Essays in Religion and Morality*, ed. Frederick Burkhardt (Cambridge, MA: Harvard University Press, 1982).
102. William James, "The Powers of Men," in *Essays in Religion and Morality*, 151, 161.
103. James, *Pragmatism*, 31.
104. James, *Pragmatism*, 32, 35.
105. James, *Pragmatism*, 44.
106. James, Letter to Charles Augustus Strong, 21 October 1889, in *Correspondence*, vol. 6, 541.
107. Hilary Putnam, "The Permanence of William James," in *Pragmatism: An Open Question* (Cambridge, MA: Blackwell, 1995), 5.
108. Richard Thompson, "The Neurobiology of Learning and Memory: William James in Retrospect," *Psychological Sciences* 1 (1990): 172–73.
109. Bruce Wilshire, "William James's Pragmatism: A Distinctly Mixed Bag," in *100 Years of Pragmatism: William James's Revolutionary Philosophy*, ed. John J. Stuhr (Bloomington: Indiana University Press, 2010), 96, 107.
110. The scientific literature on consciousness, plasticity, and free will has exploded over the past decade or two. Jeffrey M. Schwartz and Sharon Begley, *The Mind and the Brain: Neuroplasticity and the Power of Mental Force* (New York: Harper, 2002), and Roy F. Baumeister and John Tierney, *Willpower: Rediscovering the Greatest Human Strength* (New York: Penguin, 2011) are but two of many accessible books, each written by a leading scientist working

with a talented scientific journalist, that survey significant portions of this literature and reach conclusions remarkably consonant with James's basic arguments. Both sets of authors recognize James as a notable predecessor.

111. Charlene Haddock Seigfried, *William James's Radical Reconstruction of Philosophy* (Albany: State University of New York Press, 1990), 173.

112. Stephen Toulmin, "The Logical Status of Psychoanalysis," in Margaret Macdonald, ed., *Philosophy and Analysis* (Oxford: Basil Blackwell, 1954), 132.

# BIBLIOGRAPHY

Allen, Gay Wilson. *William James: A Biography*. New York: Viking, 1967.

Baumeister, Roy F., and John Tierney. *Willpower: Rediscovering the Greatest Human Strength*. New York: Penguin, 2011.

Bjork, Daniel W. *William James: The Center of His Vision*. New York: Columbia University Press, 1988.

Büchner, Ludwig. *Kraft und Stoff*. Frankfurt: Meidinger Sohn, 1858.

Carpenter, William B. *Principles of Mental Physiology, with Their Applications to the Training and Discipline of the Mind, and the Study of Its Morbid Conditions*. New York: D. Appleton, 1874.

Coon, Deborah. "'One Moment in the World's Salvation': Anarchism and the Radicalization of William James." *Journal of American History* 83 (1996): 70–99.

Cotkin, George. *William James: Public Philosopher*. Baltimore: Johns Hopkins University Press, 1990.

Croce, Paul Jerome. *Science and Religion in the Era of William James: Eclipse of Certainty (1820–1880)*. Chapel Hill: University of North Carolina Press, 1995.

———. "William James's Scientific Education." *History of the Human Sciences* 8 (1995): 9–27.

Danziger, Kurt. "Mid-Nineteenth-Century British Psycho-Physiology: A Neglected Chapter in the History of Psychology." In *The Problematic Science: Psychology in Nineteenth-Century Thought*, edited by William R. Woodward and Mitchell G. Ash, 119–46. New York: Praeger, 1982.

Darwin, Charles. *On the Origin of the Species* (The Annotated *Origin*: A Facsimile of the First Edition; James T. Costa, Annotator). Cambridge, MA: Harvard University Press, 2009.

———. Letter to Chauncey Wright, 3 June 1872. In *The Life and Letters of Charles Darwin*. Vol. 3. Edited by Francis Darwin. London: John Murray, 1887.

Daston, Lorraine J. "British Responses to Psycho-Physiology, 1860–1900." *Isis* 69 (1978): 192–208.

———. "The Theory of Will versus the Science of Mind." In *The Problematic Science: Psychology in Nineteenth-Century Thought*, 88–115.

Dewey, John. "The Reflex Arc Concept in Psychology." *Psychological Review* 3 (1896): 357–70.

Eliot, Charles W. "William James" (1915). In the William James Papers, Houghton Library, Harvard University. (A manuscript of reminiscences about James as a student and faculty member at Harvard, sent to Henry James III on 7 September.)

Eliot, George. *Middlemarch: A Study of Provincial Life*. New York: Penguin Books, 1976.

Emerson, Ralph Waldo. "Natural History of Intellect." In *The Complete Works of Ralph Waldo Emerson*, vol. 12, edited by Edward Waldo Emerson, 1–110. Boston: Houghton Mifflin, 1904.

Faraday, Michael. *Experimental Researches in Chemistry and Physics*. London: Taylor & Francis, 1859.

Feinstein, Howard M. *Becoming William James*. Ithaca, NY: Cornell University Press, 1984.

Greenwood, John D. "Whistles, Bells, and Cogs in Machines: Thomas Huxley and Epiphenomenalism." *Journal of the History of the Behavioral Sciences* 46 (2010): 276–99.

Grove, William. *The Correlation of Physical Forces*. 4th ed. London: Longman, Roberts, & Green, 1862.

Habegger, Alfred. *The Father: A Life of Henry James, Sr.* Amherst: University of Massachusetts Press, 1994.

Holmes, Oliver Wendell. *Mechanism in Thought and Morals: An Address Delivered Before the Phi Beta Kappa Society of Harvard University, June 29, 1870. With Notes and After-Thoughts.* In *The Works of Oliver Wendell Holmes*. Vol. 8, 260–314. Boston: Houghton, Mifflin, 1891.

Huxley, Thomas H. "On the Hypothesis That Animals Are Automata, and Its History." *Fortnightly Review*, n.s. 16 (1874): 555–80.

James, Alice. *The Diary of Alice James*. Edited by Leon Edel. New York: Dodd, Mead, 1964.

James, Henry. *Autobiography*. Edited by Frederick W. Dupee. Princeton: Princeton University Press, 1983.

James, William. Diary [1] (1868–1873). In William James Papers, Houghton Library, Harvard University.

———. "The Laws of Habit." *Popular Science Monthly* 30 (1887): 433–51.

———. "Philosophical Conceptions and Practical Results." In *Pragmatism*. Edited by Frederick Burkhardt. Cambridge, MA: Harvard University Press, 1975.

———. *The Meaning of Truth*. Edited by Frederick Burkhardt. Cambridge, MA: Harvard University Press, 1975.

———. *Essays in Radical Empiricism*. Edited by Frederick Burkhardt. Cambridge, MA: Harvard University Press, 1976.

———. *A Pluralistic Universe*. Edited by Frederick Burkhardt. Cambridge, MA: Harvard University Press, 1977.

———. "The Teaching of Philosophy in Our Colleges." In *Essays in Philosophy*. Edited by Frederick Burkhardt. Cambridge, MA: Harvard University Press, 1978.

———. "Remarks on Spencer's Definition of Mind as Correspondence." In *Essays in Philosophy*.

———. *The Will to Believe and Other Essays in Popular Philosophy*. Edited by Frederick Burkhardt. Cambridge, MA: Harvard University Press, 1979.

———. "The Dilemma of Determinism." In *The Will to Believe and Other Essays in Popular Philosophy*.

———. *The Principles of Psychology*. 2 vols. Edited by Frederick Burkhardt. Cambridge, MA: Harvard University Press, 1981.

———. "The Energies of Men." In *Essays in Religion and Morality.* Edited by Frederick Burkhardt. Cambridge, MA: Harvard University Press, 1982.

———. "The Powers of Men." In *Essays in Religion and Morality*.

———. "Brute and Human Intellect." In *Essays in Psychology*. Edited by Frederick Burkhardt. Cambridge, MA: Harvard University Press, 1983.

———. "Are We Automata?" In *Essays in Psychology*.

———. "The Feeling of Effort." In *Essays in Psychology*.

———. "What the Will Effects." In *Essays in Psychology*.

———. *Talks to Teachers on Psychology and to Students on Some of Life's Ideals*. Edited by Frederick Burkhardt. Cambridge, MA: Harvard University Press, 1983.

———. "On a Certain Blindness in Human Beings." In *Talks to Teachers on Psychology and to Students on Some of Life's Ideals*.

———. "What Makes Life Significant." In *Talks to Teachers on Psychology and to Students on Some of Life's Ideals*.

———. *Psychology: Briefer Course*. Edited by Frederick Burkhardt. Cambridge, MA: Harvard University Press, 1984.

———. *The Varieties of Religious Experience.* Edited by Frederick Burkhardt. Cambridge, MA: Harvard University Press, 1985.

———. "*Du sommeil et de états analogues*, by Ambrose A. Liébault." In *Essays, Comments, and Reviews*. Edited by Frederick Burkhardt. Cambridge, MA: Harvard University Press, 1987.

———. "Renouvier's Contribution to *La Critique Philosophique*." In *Essays, Comments, and Reviews*.

———. "The Mood of Science and the Mood of Faith." In *Essays, Comments, and Reviews*.

———. "Two Reviews of *Principles of Mental Physiology*, by William B. Carpenter." In *Essays, Comments, and Reviews*.
———. "Recent Works on Mental Hygiene." In *Essays, Comments, and Reviews*.
———. "*Grundzüge der physiologischen Psychologie*, by Wilhelm Wundt." In *Essays, Comments, and Reviews*.
———. "The Ph.D. Octopus." In *Essays, Comments, and Reviews*.
———. "James on Tausch." In *Essays, Comments, and Reviews*.
———. Johns Hopkins Lectures on "The Senses and the Brain and Their Relation to Thought." In *Manuscript Lectures*. Edited by Frederick Burkhardt. Cambridge, MA: Harvard University Press, 1988.
———. Lowell Lectures on "The Brain and the Mind." In *Manuscript Lectures*.
———. "[Draft on Brain Processes and Feelings]." In *Manuscript Essays and Notes*. Edited by Frederick Burkhardt. Cambridge, MA: Harvard University Press, 1988.
———. "[Notes on Art and Pessimism]." In *Manuscript Essays and Notes*.
———. *The Correspondence of William James*. 12 vol. Edited by Ignas K. Skrupskelis and Elizabeth M. Berkeley. Charlottesville: University Press of Virginia, 1992–2004.
Kuklick, Bruce. *The Rise of American Philosophy: Cambridge, Massachusetts, 1860–1930*. New Haven: Yale University Press, 1977.
Malone, John C. "William James and Habit: A Century Later." In *Reflections on* The Principles of Psychology*: William James after a Century*, edited by Michael G. Johnson an Tracy B. Henley, 139–65. Hillsdale, NJ: Lawrence Erlbaum Associates, 1990.
Menand, Louis. *The Metaphysical Club*. New York: Farrar, Straus and Giroux, 2001.
Palmer, George Herbert, and Ralph Barton Perry (1930). "Philosophy." In *The Development of Harvard University since the Inauguration of President Eliot, 1869–1929*, edited by Samuel Eliot Morison, 3–32. Cambridge, MA: Harvard University Press, 1930.
Peirce, Charles S. "Some Consequences of Four Incapacities." In *The Essential Peirce: Selected Philosophical Writings*. Edited by Nathan Hauser and Christian Kloesel. Bloomington: Indiana University Press, 1992.
———. "The Fixation of Belief." In *The Essential Peirce: Selected Philosophical Writings*.
———. "How to Make Our Ideas Clear." In *The Essential Peirce: Selected Philosophical Writings*.
Perry, Ralph Barton. *The Thought and Character of William James*. 2 vols. Boston: Little, Brown, 1935.
Putnam, Hilary. "The Permanence of William James." In *Pragmatism: An Open Question*. Cambridge, MA: Blackwell, 1995.
Richardson, Robert D. *William James: In the Maelstrom of American Modernism*. Boston: Houghton Mifflin, 2006.
Rosenthal, Sandra B. *Charles Peirce's Pragmatic Pluralism*. Albany: State University of New York Press, 1994.
Schwartz, Jeffrey M., and Sharon Begley. *The Mind and the Brain: Neuroplasticity and the Power of Mental Force*. New York: Harper, 2002.
Seigfried, Charlene Haddock. *William James's Radical Reconstruction of Philosophy*. Albany: State University of New York Press, 1990.
Shapiro, Gary. "Habit and Meaning in Peirce's Pragmatism." *Transactions of the Charles S. Peirce Society* 9 (1973): 24–40.
Simon, Linda. *Genuine Reality: A Life of William James*. New York: Harcourt Brace, 1998.
Skinner, B. F. *The Behavior of Organisms: An Experimental Analysis*. New York: Appleton-Century, 1938.
Sulloway, Frank J. *Freud, Biologist of Mind*. New York: Basic, 1979.
Thompson, Richard F. "The Neurobiology of Learning and Memory: William James in Retrospect." *Psychological Science* 1 (1990): 172–73.
Thorndike, Edward L. "Animal Intelligence: An Experimental Study of the Associative Processes in Animals." *Psychological Review, Monograph Supplements* 2, no. 8 (1898).
Toulmin, Stephen. "The Logical Status of Psychoanalysis." In *Philosophy and Analysis*, edited by Margaret Macdonald, 132–39. Oxford: Basil Blackwell, 1954.
Townsend, Kim. *Manhood at Harvard: William James and Others*. New York: Norton, 1996.

Wilshire, Bruce. "William James's Pragmatism: A Distinctly Mixed Bag." In *100 Years of Pragmatism: William James's Revolutionary Philosophy*, edited by John J. Stuhr, 96–107. Bloomington: Indiana University Press, 2010.

Woodward, William R. "The 'Discovery' of Social Behaviorism and Social Learning Theory, 1870–1980." *American Psychologist* 37 (1982): 396–410.

———. "William James's Psychology of Will: Its Revolutionary Impact on American Psychology." In *Explorations in the History of Psychology in the United States*, edited by Josef Brožek, 148–95. Lewisburg, PA: Bucknell University Press, 1984.

Wordsworth, William. "The Excursion." In *The Poems*, vol. 2, edited by John O. Hayden, 35–289. New York: Penguin Books, 1977.

Wright, Chauncey. "Evolution of Self-Consciousness." In *Philosophical Discussions*. Edited by Charles Eliot Norton. New York: Henry Holt, 1877.

## *Chapter Nine*

# Habitual Body and Memory in Merleau-Ponty

Edward S. Casey

It was Bergson who first attempted to distinguish "habit memory" from "image memory."[1] By the latter he meant any form of representation of past experience, typically via visualization; it is what we normally term "recollection." Before Bergson made the pointed suggestion that there are at least two fundamental forms of memory, it had been widely assumed by philosophers and psychologists alike that there is only one basic kind of remembering, namely, recollecting. This was the case whether recollection is conceived in a transpersonal setting (as by Plato, who made it essential to all eidetic knowledge) or in a strictly personal context (which is how we tend to think of it today). Either way, recollection is considered to be reproductive in operation, proceeding by isomorphism—whether this be an isomorphism between *dianoetic* diagrams in the soul and the Forms, or between "ideas" that resemble "impressions," or between mind and its own past being. The premise at work throughout this redoubtable tradition is that remembering, if it is to work at all, must replicate past events in an explicitly representational format. These events in turn make up the life history of the individual rememberer (this holds true even for Plato insofar as the history of a given soul includes episodes of viewing the Forms in a previous life). From the standpoint of this premise, it does not matter whether the replicative representations are mental in status (e.g., the notion of "ideas" in Locke, Hume, and Berkeley) or physiological in being (as Descartes was tempted to think and as "trace" theories have presumed from the nineteenth century onward). These options complement and mirror each other, and they accomplish essentially the same work.

Bergson's recognition of habit memory in *Matter and Memory* put this whole tradition on notice in one stroke. It did so on two basic counts. First, the idea that there might be *another* fundamental type of remembering places in jeopardy the presumed primacy of recollection. It thus anticipated Husserl's strikingly similar move of a decade later when "primary memory" was made more *ursprünglich* than recollection, revealing renamed "secondary memory" in Husserl's lectures on internal time-consciousness.[2] Second, habit memory resists construal in the usual Cartesian alternatives of matter *or* mind. For the habitual in matters of memory is neither strictly mental (as in the case of "image memory") nor entirely physical (as in trace theory). It is *both at once*, thoroughly mental and yet wholly bodily—as Aristotle first realized in linking *hexis* with character and virtue, neither of which is reducible to mind or to body.[3] At this point in time, we might be more inclined to cite *style* as the most revealing instance in which the habitual comes to concretion in a form belonging neither to *res cogitans* nor to *res extensa*. It is not therefore surprising to find Merleau-Ponty turning to style increasingly in his later writings as an important analogue of what he called the "habitual body" in the *Phenomenology of Perception*. In habit, character, virtue, and style alike, we find an inextricable commixture of intention and behavior, of animation by mind and enactment by body.

The threat to recollection posed by habit memory is thus not only a threat to its uniqueness or power as a prototype for all remembering. It is also a threat to the very idea that memory is either an exclusively mental affair (i.e., a strictly ideational form of re-experiencing the past) or something whose proper preserve is the body alone (e.g., the brain as a storage place for engrammatic traces; or muscle as a concourse of repeated patterns of behavior). Indeed, it even threatens the idea that memory is some admixture of both modes (as in "causal" theories of memory which expressly conjoin bodily and mental elements while keeping them pristinely distinct). Moreover, it acts to undermine the premise that remembering is a replicative replay of the past in some specifically representational guise. It introduces the alarming notion that we can remember the past without reproducing it in *any* identifiable representational format.

What then is habit memory as this was conceived by Bergson in a way that was potentially revolutionary for Western theorizing about memory? I shall sum up his richly detailed analysis in six points, each of which embodies a basic contrast with recollection:

1. It is "acquired by the repetition of the same effort,"[4] where repetition is irrelevant to recollection—which, when achieved, is achieved once and for all—it is essential to the formation of habit memories, which are cumulative and gradual in character and thus thrive on repetition.

2. Habit memory is at least partially dependent on will, that is, on continuing effort on our part: the repetition is typically a voluntary one (e.g., in the interest of learning a certain skill); recollection, in contrast, is "entirely spontaneous" (MM, 77).
3. Despite the willed character of its repetition, habit memory, once attained, takes its course in a strictly consecutive manner: "it is stored up in a mechanism which is set in motion as a whole by an initial impulse, in a closed system of automatic movements which succeed each other in the same order" (MM, 68); recollection, on the other hand, is typically instantaneous—or, if not this, occurs in a duration which is not restricted to any single order of unfolding.
4. As a direct consequence, habit memory becomes increasingly distant from its origin in time and place, which may in fact become altogether forgotten: "a learned recollection [i.e., one which has become habitual] passes out of time in the measure that the lesson is better known; it becomes more and more impersonal, more and more foreign to our past life" (MM, 72); whereas a pure recollection "retains in memory its place and date" (ibid.) and is therefore personal insofar as it reproduces a specific episode of the rememberer's own past history.
5. Closely related to the fourth characteristic is the fact that habit memory does not look backward to the past but ahead to the future; as its past is wholly immanent in it, it tends to be directed at its own accomplishment in the near-term future: its "forward movement bears [it] on to action and to life" (MM, 71); recollections in contrast are exclusively backward-looking and depict the way things were, not as they now are or will be.
6. Most importantly, habit memory is an action, not a representation: "it no longer *represents* our past to us; it *acts* it" (MM, 70; his italics); we realize this in the fact that no special mark "betrays its origin and classes it in the past" (MM, 68); recollections, on the contrary, consist entirely in representing the past by means of such indices as date and place.

In presenting these six points of contrast, I am seeking to endorse Bergson's actual descriptions of the two types of memory. His account of recollection qua "image memory" is highly debatable (for instance, his notion that dates and places serve as inherent *marks* of recollected scenes: enacted bodily[5] is not to be confused with *remembering-how*. This latter term I coin after Ryle's notion of "knowing-how," which has to do with the performance of skilled actions—in contrast with "knowing-that," which concerns propositional knowledge.[6] There certainly is such a thing as remembering how to perform skilled actions—say, doing the breaststroke—and this in fact calls upon habit memory in the Bergsonian sense I have been discussing; but the two forms of remembering are not co-extensive. Skilled actions are only a subset—albeit the most useful and practically valuable subset—of habitual body memories, which also include many unskilled and unuseful actions such as slouching in a certain way, gesturing excessively when speaking, drooling unselfconsciously, or grimacing at insects. The list could go on almost indefinitely: until, finally, one's entire personal being, one's character or style, would be reached. For character and style—perhaps even virtue itself—are very much constituted by habit memories expressed bodily; and they may be more fully revealed in unskilled instances of habitual remembering than efficacious movements done with specific purpose of adapting ourselves more successfully to our ambiance.

A second distinction bears on the difference between "habitual" and "habituated" actions of the body. When I speak of "habitual body memory," I shall be deliberately ambiguous as to which of two things I mean. On the one hand, "habitual" in a narrow sense refers to routinized actions undertaken wholly without premeditation. And, despite his belief that habit memory is situated squarely in the body—that "ever advancing boundary between the future and the past" (MM, 66)—Bergson does not tell us just *how* it is so situated: a task that will be left to Merleau-Ponty. What he does accomplish, however, is to show that there is "a profound difference, a difference in kind" (MM, 69) between habitual and recollective memory and that accordingly, the latter cannot be regarded unthinkingly as "memory par excellence."[7] In spite of the further fact that "the two memories run side by side and lend to each other a mutual support" (MM, 74), their destinies are deeply different and we can no longer assume (as an entire tradition of Western thought has assumed) that one is merely a modality of the other.

I have begun with Bergson not just because of his proto-phenomenological descriptions (themselves based on the strikingly similar sensibilities which he shares with phenomenologists) but mainly because he introduces the topic of habit memory in a way that forms an indispensable prelude to Merleau-Ponty's treatment of body memory in general. Not that this is an isolated case: Bergson is often the most effective escort into Merleau-Pontian reflection on many subjects, as Merleau-Ponty himself acknowledges in his "Eloge of Philosophy," his inaugural lecture upon being appointed to the same chair of philosophy which Bergson had held at the Collège de France.

Before I come to focus closely on Merleau-Ponty's own contributions, I would like to make three basic distinctions. First of all, habit memory is repetitive: not just as steps on the way to learning something (this is the sense of repetition stressed by Bergson) but also as exactly re-enacting earlier performances of the same action. An example would be the habitual action of staring my Honda Civic, an action which since first being learned has become routinized. On the other hand, "habituated" refers specifically to situations of being oriented in a general situation by having become familiar with its particular structure. Both skilled and unskilled actions, as well as routinized and non-routinized ones, contribute to habituation as knowing-your-way-around-somewhere. This latter is a main outcome of habitual body memory, but not the only one and not always the most important one.

The third distinction is that between the actual and the virtual in habitual body memory. Both types of habituality just distinguished bear a significant component of virtuality in their makeup—whether "virtuality" is taken to refer to what Ingarden has called *Parathalthung*, holding-in-readiness.[8] Part of what we mean by the "unconsciousness" of much habitual action in the narrower meaning draws on this sense of being "on tap," of being ready to activate: so ready that conscious deliberation or decision is not called for and would even act to inhibit the action to be undertaken. The virtuality in question also alludes to the marginal position of most habitual body memories: their existence at the edges of our awareness and in a state which Freud would have called "preconscious." It is precisely because of this marginal-yet-available position that so many of these memories arise in an unrehearsed way; we simply snatch them out of the pool of our immediately accessible resources for being-in-the-world in a fully functional way. Contrast this situation with that of recollection, where actuality is the dominant ontic mode: above all in the form of the historical actuality of the scene remembered. In recollecting the virtual is more an obstacle than a resource; it signifies the obscurely remembered, that which complete and veridical recollection attempts to overcome by reproducing an accurate representation of the past event being remembered.

At all times, in many different ways, Merleau-Ponty practices a form of transcendental speleology.[9] His is a philosophy of depths. Two kinds of depth are especially pertinent in the present context. The first is the depth provided by the body itself as it anchors perception and thought, imagination and memory—*and habit*: "habit has its abode neither in thought nor in the objective body, but in the body as mediator of a world."[10] By situating habit in the body, Merleau-Ponty gives to habit a new depth of meaning and function which, though adumbrated by Bergson, is never worked out expressly by the author of *Matter and Memory*. The second kind of depth is that supplied by the past, which serves similarly to anchor our temporal being. In particular it subtends a hectic present and a projected future: a present and a future on which Sartre and Heidegger placed such stress respectively. One way of reading Merleau-Ponty's early work (on which I am mainly drawing in this essay) is to say that it sought to provide past to a distended present and to an anticipatory future: and thus to ground the otherwise unanchored projects of Sartre and Heidegger. But in both cases the grounding is done via the body, which is described at one point as "our anchorage in a world" (PP, 144); for the past is given to us in and through the body as much as habit is. To this it must be added that however much the body is the "general medium" (PP, 146) for habit and the past—the place where they most deeply commingle—still they furnish to it in turn two indispensable dimensions of its own depth. In brief: no habit or past without body; no body without habit or past.[11]

One quite basic way in which this triad of interdependent terms is conjointly active is found in the notion of *sedimentation*, itself a depth-giving process. Sedimentation is implied by my very being-in-the-world, which must be as continually resumptive of acquired experience as it is pro-sumptive of experience still to come. In fact, sedimentation is the necessary complement of spontaneity, since these form the two essential stages of all "world-structure" for Merleau-Ponty.[12] It is revealing that in discussing sedimentation Merleau-Ponty mentions character as a leading example and describes in some detail the experience of knowing your way around a house. Both are aspects of "acquired worlds" which precipitate themselves into my ongoing experience. Even if sedimentation typically begins with a particular person or place, its main tendency is toward depersonalization and generalization (cf. PP, 137, 142). Only thus can we take in new contents of experience without being dumbfounded by them. Only thus too can we develop those patterns of behavior that identify us as continuous persons over time and make meaning possible in our lives. All of this happens inasmuch as in sedimentation—as in habit memory for Bergson—the past is fully immanent in the present, "dovetailed" into it (cf. PP, 140). But the past is not immanent there as an inert mass of accumulated items. The process of sedimentation is ever at work: intentional threads go back and forth between the body and its ever-changing phases, which are continually reanimated by current experience (cf. PP 130). If sedimentation is to be conceived as a precipitation of the past into the present, it is an active precipitation actively maintained.

What sedimentation teaches us, therefore, is that even at a moment of human experience when we might be most tempted to employ terms connoting sheer passivity—for example, as in the locked-in formation of sedimentary rocks, where depth signifies merely greater age or mass—an element of agency is at work, a factor of what Husserl would call "activity in passivity."[13] And if habit memory is a main means of effecting sedimentation, and thus of giving a depth that is not objectively determinable, it cannot be through the working of the strictly habitual in the sense of the routinized: a routine is nothing but an inert pattern of behavior. The working of such memory must be accomplished by an active *habituating*. And this is precisely what the body effects, thanks to its sedimentary powers. Habituation here takes its most concrete form in the body's inhabitation of the world, its active insertion into space and time: "we must therefore avoid saying that our body is *in* space or *in* time. It *inhabits* space and time" (PP, 139). In fact, the habituation which such inhabitation accomplishes involves a delicate dialectic between the implied passivity of enclosure (for space and time undeniably act to contain us) and the activity of getting to know our way around in a given circumstance. This is why it is true to say both that "I belong to [space and time]" and that in turn "my body combines with them and includes them" (PP, 140). Inhabiting, taken as a paradigm of the bodily expression of habit memory, is at once "wholly active and wholly passive" (PP, 428), in the world and *of* it. It is made possible by sedimentation even as it carries sedimentation itself to new depths.

What is habit itself in Merleau-Ponty's view? It is ill conceived, according to him, when we think of it in terms of an association or interpretation of sensations, as an intellectual synthesis or form of knowledge, or as an involuntary action (cf. PP, 142–44, 152). It is always composed of motoric and perceptual elements in an inextricable mixture. Whereas its temporality is most adequately exhibited in the process of sedimentation, its spatiality is best construed in terms of an intuitive incorporation of the space in which it is enacted. Thus a typist employs certain bodily habits (in this case they are skills) so as to modulate manual space in a maximally dexterous manner. Not only is there an intuitive gauging of the positions of the keys on his or her typewriter, but the keys become part of the typist's total intentional arc:

> When the typist performs the necessary movements on the typewriter, these movements are governed by an intention, but the intention does not posit the keys as objective locations. It is literally true that the subject who learns to type incorporates the keybank into his bodily space. (PP, 145)

As a result of this incorporation—which can be considered the converse of the inhabitation effected by sedimentation—the bodily being of this subject is aggrandized: made more capacious because able to undertake a new multiplicity of projects. For this reason Merleau-Ponty maintains that "habit expressed our power of *dilating our being in the world*, of changing our existence by appropriating fresh instruments."[14] But this is so only because habits are themselves "stable dispositional tendencies" (PP 146) whose very regularity and reliability allow them to assume this dilating role. At play here is an implicit spectrum that extends from spontaneity to habit and from habit to custom. A habit is quite settled in comparison with spontaneous action; but it appears itself to be spontaneous when contrasted with custom, which "presupposes the form of passivity derived from nature" (PP, 146). In having a habit (and we should keep in mind that habits are pre-eminently things we *have* as the origin of "habit" in *habere*, reminds us), we possess a world at once sedimented and open to free variation. Beyond the typist there is the organist, who provides Merleau-Ponty with a paradigm case of the creatively habituating: for the organist can adapt himself or herself within an hour to an organ he or she has never played before and differing markedly in structure from one's customary instrument. Habituation of this sort lies on the capital of virtually inherent in all habits that have not degenerated into the strictly habitual—into customary routines. The latter lack the depth of innovating habituation precisely because they are the already fully actualized forms of response that limit adaptation to new circumstances. If the adaptive organist "settles into the organ as one settles into a house" (PP, 145), this is a house whose contents and décor are continually changing. An unadaptive being, delimited by custom alone, is confined to living in a house whose nature never alters. Habit is thus in a middle range position, situated between the very extremes of custom and spontaneity which it nonetheless serves to mediate.

Precisely because of this position, a critique of Bergson begins to emerge. Bergson's two modes of memory need supplementing by a third mode based on an enriched notion of habit. (a) What Merleau-Ponty's predecessor had called "habit memory" would be better entitled "customary memory"; it would include all remembering founded on repetition and lacking in creative habituation. (b) "Image memory" or recollection would remain an antithesis of customary memory; it is at once non-bodily and non-routinized. (c) Habit memory proper—or "habitual body memory" as I prefer to call it—exists *between* (a) and (b) in several ways. It combines repeatability with uniqueness (the organist has played many organs, but is now playing this new organ); permanence with transience (the skill of organ-playing is built into the being of the organist, yet is contingent on the coordinative capacities of his or her hands and limbs); perceptual with motoric action (the same organist sees and touches as he plays);[15] and self with world (the organ player with the music played).[16] Corresponding to this third kind of memory would be a form of being which Merleau-Ponty is at pains to describe at many turns in the *Phenomenology of Perception*: "near-presence" or "ambivalent presence" (PP, 81, 180). Such being is very like virtuality as discussed above, and it is exemplified in such things as horizon, things situated behind me, the imago of a parent, and the phantom limb. All of these call for "a middle term between presence and absence" (PP, 80), and all inhabit the phenomenal field (cf. PP, 80, 81ff., 106). They do so thanks to the role of the lived body in situating us in such a field. This body is therefore a "habitual body" or "virtual body" (PP, 82, 250) which acts to guarantee the actions of my merely momentary body while enlivening my strictly customary body.

It is evident by now that habit, a broadly mediating force, finds it own natural home in the body, itself conceived as the "mediator of a world" (PP, 145). But what does the body contribute specifically to habit—and thus, implicitly at least, to habit memory? At least four things.

1. First, the lived body's prepersonal status facilitates its proclivity for the general, a proclivity crucial to habit as well: as the body "gives to

our life the form of generality" (PP 146), so the full functioning of habits depends directly on their generalizability.

2. Habits take place in an intimate and familiar space which it is the task of the body to delineate. Without the intentional arc effected by the latter, there would be no region within which habits could deploy themselves. Bodily space thus provides "the matrix of habitual action" (PP, 104), a matrix within which virtual as well as actual movements emerge.
3. The body lends itself to habits through the mediation of gesture, which is thus an intermediary of intermediaries. It is as if the body itself were too sullenly permanent to be translated without remainder into habitual action. Much as a cultural tradition requires the medium of spoken or written expressions to come alive for individuals, the body calls for gestures to constitute habits. The organist moves habitually in a series of gestures, not in a set of mechanical movements: his body is an impersonal resource in the creation of the musical work through gesticulations which are the effective expressions of habit (cf. PP, 183).
4. Finally, the body gives to various spontaneities of imagination or thought a subsistence by activity embodying them, bringing them into a consistent core of our being where they can be habitually reenacted:

> At all levels [the body] performs the same function which is to endow the instantaneous expressions of spontaneity with "a little renewable action and independent existence." Habit is merely a form of this fundamental power. (PP, 146)

It is by "absorption" or "assimilation" (ibid.) that the body takes in the spontaneous in such a way as to deliver it over to habit, which mediates it still further in regular patterns of conduct.

Just here we need to pause and ponder a paradox. On the one hand, habit is for Merleau-Ponty a major clue to the nature of the lived body. This is evident, for example, in his interpretation of the phantom limb and of Schneider's various afflictions: in both instances, whose discussion ushers in the very notion of a non-objective body, there is a mismatch between the habitual and the actual body, with bizarre and even devastating consequences. Because of habitual arm movements, I continue to believe in the existence of my actually missing limb; or I am reduced to the actuality of immediate sexual or verbal stimulation when I lack the sense of the virtual required for self-initiated movements of a habituating sort (*not* for those of a customary kind).[17] It is on the basis of observations and interpretations of this type that Merleau-Ponty can conclude that "the phenomenon of habit is just what prompts us to revise our notion of 'understand' *and our notion of the body*" (PP, 144, my italics). Even more generally, habit is a key to the ontology being developed in the *Phenomenology of Perception*: "here, as elsewhere, the relation of *having* . . . is at first concealed by relations belonging to the domain of *being*, or, as we may equally say, by ontic relations obtaining within the world" (PP, 174, his italics).

On the other hand, habit is also held to be "merely a form of [the body's] fundamental power" (PP, 146). Rather than a crucial clue to the nature of bodily being, habit is here regarded as tributary from the body: derivative from it and dependent on it. As such, it is implicitly ranged with other expressive manifestations of the body: for example, style, living speech, and sexuality. With them, it constitutes a middle layer of human being located between the body itself and reflective thought. Although it thus regains its characteristic middle-term position, it loses the distinctiveness and paradigmatic quality which it possessed as the guiding thread for understanding the lived body.

What are we to make of this paradox, which seems to reveal a gaping inconsistency within Merleau-Ponty's thinking? Two resolutions suggest themselves. First, we might say that two sorts of habit are at stake here: one, closer in meaning to the "habitual" in the larger sense discussed earlier, is so encompassing of bodily existence that no part of this existence is *un*habitual; and in this way we would be constrained to approach body from its habituality, while body itself would become fixed at various moments into the habitual in the narrower sense of routinized habits. But this move fails to account for the fact that the freedom possessed by human beings is at once bodily and no habitual in either sense.

A second and preferable resolution is found in the following line of thought: habit is at once primary and secondary in its relation with body, albeit in different senses. Habit is secondary to body insofar as it represents a particularization of the body's generalizing and sedimenting powers; it particularizes by establishing the special ways the lived body comes to inhabit the world in a regular and repeatable (rather than a purely spontaneous) fashion. Put differently: it gives the special depth of virtuality to a body that, lacking it, would be bound forever to the merely episodic and unrepeated. But habit in turn has a twofold primacy. First of all, it is in more intimate connection with the past than is any other power of human nature. If it is true that the past forms a permanent background of all my action and thought (cf. PP, 395); if the unreflective source of all experience, including bodily experience, is to be conceived as an "original past" (242, 280); if human "existence always carries forward its past, whether it be by accepting it or disclaiming it" (393); if "each present reasserts the presence of the whole past which it supplants" (42); and if, in short, "I belong to my past" (422)—then habit will have a privileged place in human experience, for it is at once the most pervasive and subtle way in which we are in touch with the past that we bear and that bears us. No wonder then that it can be exemplary of bodily being, which is wholly and yet nonspecifically rooted in the past. The specification begins with habit; and it is furthered by the habitual body memory which habit brings with it. In this way habit takes the lead over the very body which it requires for its own realization.

A second primacy of habit over body is located in the relationship between habit and the other so-called expressive phenomena with which Merleau-Ponty implicitly aligns it. Style, living speech, and sexuality, far from being simply coeval with habit, all presuppose it and employ it actively. For this role, "habitude" might be a more lucid term than "habit." The former means "a settled practice or usage" (OED), and it connotes an ongoing activity whose reliability makes it indispensable to the pursuit of such things as speaking or making love. Consider only the way that everyone falls into characteristic speaking patterns, whether those of a dialect or idiolect, and how these are not merely matters of facilitation (which "habit" and especially "skill" are often taken to provide) but indicate the positive presence of a linguistic style that aids in recognition and understanding. Similarly, habitudes underlie erotic play: not just in enabling such play in some minimal sense but in making it distinctive of oneself in interaction with others. And style, in all of its many avatars, has a habitudinal basis, which subtends not just its identifiability over time or space but its ability to act as a unique mark of the being or thing which exhibits it ("that's the way that Miró paints," we say, wishing to capture the essence of his particular form of painting as well as its flair). Here the habitual is once more in the middle position: now between the body in its anonymous generality and the unique and highly personal expressiveness manifest in manners of speaking, in modes of sexual activity, and in matters of style.

It is time to return to the topic of memory now that we have an enriched sense of the role of habit and body in relation to each other. Merleau-Ponty himself singles out the past as an "inalienable dimension"[18] of body and habit alike. Indeed, given his preoccupation with the past in general and with the habitual body in particular, we should expect him to have presented us with a theory of habitual body memory. Yet we look in vain for any such theory—or even the sketch of one. A strange lacuna looms large in the very center of the *Phenomenology of Perception*. This is all the stranger in that this book contains a number of passages expressly critical of recollection as a paradigm for remembering (cf. PP, 19ff., 83, 180, 275, 393, 418–19). Taken together, these passages compose a veritable leitmotif of the book as a whole: just as we are told in the Introduction that the "projection of memories" through recollection cannot begin to explain ambiguous figures or perceptual illusions, so we are told near the end of Part Three that:

> If the past were available to us only in the form of express recollections, we should be continually tempted to recall it in order to verify its existence, and

> thus resemble the patient mentioned by Scheler, who was constantly turning round in order to reassure himself that things were really there—whereas in fact we feel it behind us as an incontestable acquisition. (PP, 418–19)

Since the past exists for us as an "incontestable acquisition" largely because of the actions of our own habitual body, it would be only natural to think that Merleau-Ponty would have developed a notion of habitual body memory to fill the gap left by the diminution of recollection's role in recapturing the past. That he did not do so is not likely to have been the product of a mere oversight. It testifies, rather, to a source of tension within his reflections on memory and the past which we must now confront.

The tension exists between two directions of thought. The first we are by now quite familiar with. This is the view that the past is deeply ingredient in the present—so much so that we can say (in a passage cited above) that "each present reasserts the immanence of *the whole past* which it supplants" (PP, 420, my italics). The only plausible receptacle for the past as an entire unit—in contrast with episodic details of it—is found precisely in the habitual body. Where else, how else, could the past effect such a subtle and complete ingression than in our bodily habits and habitudes? Part of the very meaning of embodiment is the capacity to incorporate items (whether they be thoughts, emotions, or other residua of the past) so thoroughly that they become one with the body, yet do not require auxiliary acts of cognition or recollection. The organist absorbs and assimilates the whole of his musically relevant past into his habitual body; as he tries out a new organ, he has this past literally in his hands and feet—and in such a way that their operative intentionality calls for no "interposed recollection."[19] Indeed, on the basis of such an example as this one could go on to build a coherent notion of habitual body memory which might point to its specific forms of incorporation, its particular efficacy, and its own ways of being rule-bound.

Yet Merleau-Ponty does not go on to build any such notion. The reason why he does not—in the face of a manifest need to do so—is to be found in a second direction of his thought. This is a commitment to a direct realism of the past as given in memory. He comes to this from an admirable critique of the idea that the past must appear to us borne by intermediaries such as mental representations or physiological traces:

> Psychology has involved itself in endless difficulties by trying to base memory on the possession of certain contents or recollections, the present traces (in the body or the unconscious) of the abolished past, for from these traces we can never come to understand the recognition of the past as past . . . memory can be understood only as a direct possession of the past with no interposed contents. (PP, 265)

But does this last sentence follow strictly from the preceding remarks? Granting the problematic character of the intermediaries (how do we know that they are *of* the past in the first place?), is it necessary to conclude that we directly possess the past? Are there not other ways of possessing it which convey it to us more subtly than do representations or traces—yet no less surely? The habitual body is itself one such vehicle. Tradition as conceived by Gadamer is another. (Indeed, as I have hinted, the body in its habitual being constitutes a personal tradition in its own right.)

In any case, Merleau-Ponty does not follow up on these possibilities because of his bedrock belief in the directly given character of the remembered past. In terms of this belief, the role of memory is to *reopen time*: a theme which is reiterated at several points in the text (cf. PP, 22, 85, 181, 265, 393). It does not matter that, at one late point, he draws misleadingly on Husserl's notion of primary memory—in which the *immediate* past is directly given—as testimony for the unmediated givenness of the remote past as well.[20] What does matter is that the conception of the entire past as directly given forces Merleau-Ponty to look elsewhere than the habitual body or cultural tradition for the means of reopening time. The body in particular cannot effect such a reopening since its access to the past is inherently indirect; it is precisely as habit-bound that it gives us not the past per se (which, in the case of habits, would be the moments in which the habits were first learned) but the past as presently efficacious in habitual actions of all kinds. To borrow a metaphor which both Bergson and Proust employ: in the embodiment of the past in habits we witness the tip of an enormous pyramid whose total bulk is the past itself. Moreover, the tip is moving in a way the past is not: hence the effect of the past's receding from us, a phenomenon which Merleau-Ponty can hardly deny. In fact, not only does he acknowledge that the past is "a mobile setting which moves away from us" (PP, 149), he also avers that the past is a "dimension of escape and absence" (413). Such admissions create problems enough for a direct realism of past existence. Compounding them is an equal insistence on the desirability of actively assuming the past and thereby *transforming* it in the present: "by taking up a present, I draw together and transform my past, altering its significance, freeing and detaching myself from it" (PP, 455). If we transform the past in the very act of taking it up to the present, it is difficult to see how we are ever in contact with an unadulterated, directly given past.

But let us keep our focus on the body—or more exactly, on its failure to serve as an adequate vehicle of a past which is supposedly given without mediation. The reason for this failure is straightforward: what the past as directly given calls for is *contemplation*, not action. As Bergson made abundantly clear, habit memory eventuates in actions: precisely in contrast with recollections, which are contemplative in nature (cf. MM, 66–70, 220). One might grant that there are contemplative modes of direct access to the past other than recollection—a possibility which neither Bergson nor Merleau-Ponty seriously considers—but that one has to insist that the habitual body is not such a mode; indeed, the latter even obstructs direct access while being nevertheless an effective indirect avenue. Thus it is in vain that the following passage struggles to make the body essential to the reopening of time:

> The part played by the body in memory is comprehensible only if memory is, not just the constituting consciousness of the past [i.e., in recollection], but an effort to re-open time on the basis of the implications contained in the present, and if the body, as our permanent means of "taking up attitudes" and thus constructing pseudo-presents, is the medium of our communication with time as with space. (PP, 181)

But the body is engaged—as Merleau-Ponty himself shows so eloquently elsewhere in the *Phenomenology of Perception*—not in the construction of pseudo-presents but of massively layered and richly overladen actual presents show through with virtualities. If the body living this present is for the most part a habitual body, then the issue is not that of reopening the past (which would be retrogressive in character) but of carrying it forward into the future of eventual accomplishment. Just *this* action is the habitual body's way of being memorious: incorporating the past and carrying it on in concrete action. No claim as to the past's direct givenness needs to be made in order to support this view; in fact, making this puts us considerably off track, since it impels us to move beyond the body in its felt density into a contemplative mode in which clarity is a primary value: the body as we live it is anything but pellucid. In the circumstance, it is not at all surprising that Merleau-Ponty, divided against himself as to the nature of the past, should have no theory of habitual body memory. This is so in spite of the fact that, more than any philosopher since Descartes (and more even than Bergson), he has furnished a wealth of insight into habit, body, and memory. His masterful treatment of this august triad of terms taken separately masks, however, a lack of insight into their concatenation as "habitual-body-memory."

I want to make two remarks in conclusion, one quite general and the other pertinent to this particular occasion:[21]

The first is that, beyond the question as to the character of habitual body memory itself, there is the question of whether this latter exhausts the types of body memory on which we can and do draw. My own recent work on this subject has led me to believe that traumatic body memory, erotic body memory, the body memory of being with others in various non-erotic ways, and still other types are all valid forms of bodily remembering. In this spectrum of types, habitual body memory and traumatic body memory stand out as extremes between which the other types are ranged. While habitual body memory is characterized by traits such as repeatability and virtuality, its traumatic counterpart manifests itself as characteristically unique (just *this* episode of pain is remembered) and as actual (otherwise the pain would have no continuing "sting"). It remains true, nonetheless, that habitual body memory overlaps the other types—with the normal exception of remembered trauma—and may even facilitate these others: much as we have seen bodily habitudes to act as enablers of style, sexuality, and *la parole parlante*. And when this is so, it is not merely a matter of providing these other kinds of body memory with substructures of skilled actions but of allowing them to be more innovative and less circumstance-bound than they would otherwise be. In short: habitual body memory is habituating as well as habituated in its operations and in its effects.

The second remark bears on the issue of depth in body memory. Here I only want to suggest that Merleau-Ponty's views of body, habit, and memory are all concerned with depth in one form or another. Body is the main provider of depth to consciousness, and it does so through its anchoring and sedimenting activities. These latter are in turn borne forward by the infusion of habits, which lend a special depth of assurance, regularity, and scope. As for memory: it is a depth phenomenon through and through, a way to the depths of our being—as both Merleau-Ponty and Freud would affirm, though for different reasons. It is striking that at one point Merleau-Ponty develops his argument for a direct grasp of the past by analogizing non-recollective remembering to the perception of depth: neither is mediated by contents, both involve continued transitions, and in each something comparatively remote is made present (PP, 264–66, 423). If depth is defined as "the dimension in which things or elements of things envelop each other" (PP, 264–65), then remembering is ineluctably depth-drawn and depth-drawing. This is above all evident in the manner in which the past is said to encircle the present like an atmosphere or horizon:

> To remember is not to bring into the focus of consciousness a self-subsistent picture of the past; it is to thrust deeply into the horizon of the past and take apart step by step the interlocked perspectives until the experiences which it epitomizes are as if relived in their temporal setting. (PP, 22; cf. also 264–66)

Remembering, in other words, is not only very *like* perceiving objects in depth: it *is* grasping objects in depth, only in the depth that time rather than space provides. Depth itself, as Erwin Straus demonstrated in *The Primary World of Senses*,[22] is spatio-temporal in character. Thus the depth of perception and the depth of memory are more than merely parallel; they are in the end the same depth, that of our being-in-the-world. But they are such, Merleau-Ponty would insist, only as experienced by the lived body and more particularly by the habitual body, which ties us to space as well as to time. Habits are movements in space even as they are amassments of their own repetition and deployment. This is why it could be claimed that habits "*dilate* our being in the world" (PP, 143) and why they are the very basis of our inhabiting the world. Such inhabiting is in turn something more than habitual just as it is something more than bodily; it is also profoundly memorial. The depth of familiarity which human inhabitation brings with it is a depth made possible by a habitual body memory whose full significance we are only beginning to fathom.

## NOTES

1. This chapter originally appeared in *Man and World* 17 (1984): 279–97.

2. The terms "primary memory" and "secondary memory" were first coined by James in his *Principles of Psychology* in 1890; but James refused to make one form of memory more basic than the other.

3. See *Nicomachean Ethics*, 1103a and 1114b–1115a. Aristotle is also notable for having distinguished two forms of remembering, not "primary" vs. "secondary" but "*memoria*" vs. "*reminiscentia*." See Richard J. Sorabji, *Aristotle on Memory* (Providence: Brown University Press, 1972).

4. Henri Bergson, *Matter and Memory*, trans. N. M. Paul and W. S. Palmer (New York: Doubleday, 1959), 68. (Hereafter referred to as MM.)

5. I say "as enacted bodily" since it cannot be denied that mental operations may also be fully habitual.

6. See Gilbert Ryle, *The Concept of Mind* (New York: Barnes & Noble, 1949), ch. 2.

7. Bergson, MM, 72. In the passage from which this phrase is taken, the expression is nonetheless applied to recollective memory alone.

8. See Roman Ingarden, *The Literary Work of Art*, trans. George G. Grabowicz (Evanston: Northwestern University Press, 1973), 265–67, 330–31.

9. Merleau-Ponty himself speaks of "transcendental geology" (*The Visible and the Invisible*, trans. Alphonso Lingis [Evanston: Northwestern University Press, 1968], 258–59).

10. Maurice Merleau-Ponty, *Phenomenology of Perception*, trans. Colin Smith (New York: Humanities Press, 1862), 145. (Hereafter referred to as PP.)

11. Consciousness projects itself into a physical world and has a body, as it projects itself into a cultural world and has its habits: because it cannot be consciousness without playing upon significances, given either in the absolute past of nature or in its own personal past" (PP, 137).

12. Cf. Merleau-Ponty, PP, 130. The mention of spontaneity reminds us that Merleau-Ponty is also seeking to counterbalance the predilection for spontaneity so evident in Kant and Sartre, neither of whom has an adequate notion of the concretely sedimented foundations of human experience.

13. Edmund Husserl, *Experience and Judgment*, trans. James S. Churchill and Karl Ameriks (Evanston: Northwestern University Press, 1973), 108.

14. Merleau-Ponty, PP, 143, my italics. For a strikingly similar view of habit, see John Dewey, *Human Nature and Conduct* (New York: Random House, 1950), 41–45, 66–67.

15. "Every habit is both motor and perceptual because it lies . . . between explicit perception and actual movement" (PP, 152).

16. "The analysis of motor habit as an extension of existence leads on, then, to an analysis of perceptual habit as the coming into possession of a world" (PP 153).

17. For the discussion of the phantom limb in the context of habituality, see PP, 76ff.: and for Schneider, see esp. 135.

18. This phrase is applied to consciousness at PP, 266, but it applies even more convincingly to body and habit—as well as to thought (cf. 137) and to time itself (cf. 395).

19. The passage from which this phrase comes reads as follows: "I still 'have in hand' the immediate past without any distortion and without any interposed 'recollection'." (PP, 265; the phrase 'have in hand' is Husserl's from *The Phenomenology of Internal Time-Consciousness.*)

20. Cf. PP, 416ff., where "transition synthesis" are held to like the two kinds of past; this overlooks their difference in kind: a difference explicitly pointed to by Husserl himself in his 1905 lectures.

21. The present chapter was first delivered as a lecture at a symposium on "Body, Depth, and Memory" held at the annual meeting of the Merleau-Ponty Circle in the fall term of 1982. The other speaker was Glen Mazis of Northern Kentucky University.

22. See Erwin Straus, *The Primary World of Senses*, trans. Jacob Needleman (Glencoe: Free Press, 1963), 379ff.

## BIBLIOGRAPHY

Bergson, Henri. *Matter and Memory*. Translated by N. M. Paul and W. S. Palmer. New York: Doubleday, 1959.

Dewey, John. *Human Nature and Conduct*. New York: Random House, 1950.

Husserl, Edmund. *The Phenomenology of Internal Time-Consciousness*. Edited by Martin Heidegger. Translated by James Spencer Churchill and Calvin O. Schrag. Bloomington: Indiana University Press, 1964.

———. *Experience and Judgment*. Translated by James Spencer Churchill and Karl Ameriks. Evanston: Northwestern University Press, 1973.

Ingarden, Roman. *The Literary Work of Art*. Translated by George G. Grabowicz. Evanston: Northwestern University Press, 1973.

Merleau-Ponty, Maurice. *Phenomenology of Perception*. Translated by Colin Smith. New York: Humanities Press, 1962.

———. *The Visible and the Invisible*. Translated by Alphonso Lingis. Evanston: Northwestern University Press, 1968.

Ryle, Gilbert. *The Concept of Mind*. New York: Barnes & Noble, 1949.

Sorabji, Richard J. *Aristotle on Memory*. Providence: Brown University Press, 1972.

Straus, Erwin. *The Primary World of Senses*. Translated by Jacob Needleman. Glencoe: Free Press, 1963.

# *III*

# The Application of Habit in Contemporary Theory

*Chapter Ten*

# The Fly Wheel of Society

## *Habit and Social Meliorism in the Pragmatist Tradition*

Terrance MacMullan

While habit has an ancient philosophical lineage stretching back at least as far as the work of Aristotle, it only achieved the apex of its philosophical impact in the nineteeenth century within North American pragmatism. From Peirce's Darwinian reconstruction of belief and science to the social meliorism of W. E. B. DuBois, habit receives its most thorough and convincing philosophical treatment within the pragmatist tradition. This chapter explores the role of habit within the American philosophical tradition in two ways.[1] First, it offers a historical overview of the role of habit in works of some of the most notable pragmatist philosophers, including C. S. Peirce, William James, and John Dewey. Second, it demonstrates the past and continuing meliorist potential of the doctrine of habit by surveying works by pragmatist intellectuals in the twentieth century—like Jane Addams and W. E. B. DuBois—and twenty-first century—like Shannon Sullivan—who use the pragmatist concept of habit to address particular lived problems including sexism, racism, and homophobia.

The doctrine of habit is the pragmatist framework par excellence, as no other concept so thoroughly and ably serves as the "happy harmonizer," to use James's phrase, of so many apparently disparate elements of our experience.[2] While each pragmatist philosopher uses the theory slightly differently, they all use habit in a way that emphasizes its relational holism and naturalism. The doctrine of habit emerges organically from pragmatism's relational holism—the quintessential pragmatist metaphysical and epistemological premise—that counters the reductionism of the modern period by positing that all the features of our experience—cause and effect, knower and known, self and society, mind and body—are best understood as transactional, fluid, and mutually constitutive. Habit helps us understand this relational holism by showing, among other things, that the self is less the regal and detached knower who only intentionally acts in the world, but is instead a dynamic porous self—as much imprinted *by* the world as it is an actor *within* the world—whose habits are in turn liberating wings and constraining bonds.

When pragmatist philosophers speak of naturalism they are referencing the belief that Michael Eldridge once summarized as, "[i]n short, nature, which is inclusive of humanity, is all there is, and that's okay."[3] Habit is one of the primary ways that naturalism is manifested within the realm of human ethics and behavior. James finds it moving our very flesh, guiding arcs of electricity through our nerves in patterns that make our movements and reactions not just possible but smooth, effective, and joined. Peirce finds habit in the deepest recesses of our mind, a set of heuristics that enable fluid action in the world by creating patterns of thought and behavior, much as patterns of attack and defense enable a chess player to see the whole board as a unified game and not hundreds of individual interactions.

However, habit plays its greatest role in the works of John Dewey, who sees habit as the proper seat of not just moral philosophy (in much the same way as Aristotle) but also as the conduit linking past memories to present experiences to anticipated events, and also as the necessary point of contact between the individual and her society and culture. In the history of pragmatism's unique resolution of (or perhaps evasion of)[4] the metaphysical and epistemological debates within traditional philosophy, habit mediates the idealist/realist debate, by offering a simple yet feasible model for understanding the relationship between the mind and the world: habit is, as Peirce put it, the consequence of a kind of "ideal-realism" which holds that "nature and the mind have such a community as to impart to our guesses a tendency toward the truth."[5] Finally, the great American social critic, political radical and cultural philosopher of the twentieth century, W. E. B. DuBois, critiqued the scourges of poverty, warfare, and racism as habits which persist more through unthinking acquiescence than conscious ill will.

Instead of taking sides on the age-old conflicts of Western philosophy, pragmatist philosophers seek to dissolve or mediate traditional philosophical disputes between, say, determinism and free will, or the negative freedom of individuals and the positive freedom of ordered society. It is no surprise, then, that many pragmatists emphasize the role of habit in their moral or meliorist arguments. By examining the extent to which people act from habit, we are able to harmonize the insights of philosophies that focus on political liberty and individual free will and those from either Hegelian-inspired philosophies that see the state or the *volk* as the natural unit of agency or materialist philosophies that subscribe to forms of biological determinism.

Most of the pragmatists who use the concept of habit in their work agree, at least largely, with Aristotle's famous edict that:

> Moral goodness . . . is the result of habit [ . . . ]. The moral virtues, then, are engendered by us neither *by* nor *contrary to* nature; we are constituted by nature to receive them, but their full development in us is due to habit. (1103a14–16)

However, where Aristotle offers the pessimistic view that our habits are more or less set by the age of twenty, most pragmatists argue that habits, at the individual level, are capable of constant revision and modification. More importantly, they argue that habit functions at the broader, societal level as a kind of societal fulcrum point. Our habits are far from set in stone: they are the ideal target for any project of social meliorism, whether it be Jane Addams's efforts to end war and hunger, John Dewey's efforts to achieve more fully educated and democratic communities, or W. E. B. DuBois's efforts to end racism.

This chapter has three sections. The first section is a historical overview of habit within the works of the two earliest pragmatist philosophers: C. S. Peirce and William James. This section explores the Peircian roots of the view of habit seen in almost all subsequent pragmatist philosophies that use the concept, where habit is a rule of action that emerges from and gives meaning to belief. It will also explore some of Peirce's more enigmatic statements where he seems to indicate that habits are not limited to human belief and behavior, but are instead thick features of the world and can be detected in all phenomena within our ever-emerging cosmos. The section will then examine the work on habit by Peirce's colleague and sometimes friend, William James, who is responsible for taking the kernel of Peirce's idea and cultivating it into a far-reaching and influential idea that would impact not only the popular imagination but generations of philosophers and psychologists alike.

The second section focuses exclusively on John Dewey's detailed examination of habit. In particular, it examines the two most influential Deweyan uses for habit: first, as a means for dissolving many of the purported mind/world, free will/determinism problems of modern philosophy and, second, as a tool for ameliorating the social and cultural problems that stunt our democratic communities.

The third and final section moves from the role of habit within Dewey's political philosophy in general and shows how it can be put to work on the particular social, cultural, and political problems within American society. This final section starts with an overview of how we can use a pragmatist theory of habit to generate an understanding of race that is compatible with the critical conservationist theories advocated by the early DuBois and by contemporary thinkers such as Shannon Sullivan.

## 1. THE ORIGIN OF PRAGMATIST HABITS WITHIN PEIRCE AND JAMES

Habit is more important to the philosophical work of Charles Sanders Peirce than any previous philosopher since Aristotle. Peirce, the enigmatic, querulous, and visionary father of pragmatism, availed himself frequently to the idea of habit as he strove to strike an equilibrium between his commitment, as a philosopher, to make our beliefs clear, certain, and fixed and his realization, as a scientist, that fallibilism is an inescapable feature of any honest approach to belief. The exciting scientific ferment of his day forced him to acknowledge that if for nothing else, the world is not the static Aristotelian world of stable categories each with distinct *teloi*, but is instead a shifting Heraclitean bustle that frequently renders our best theories obsolete. When Peirce brought Darwin into the realm of ontology, he found that we should understand the relationship between the mind and the world not primarily through propositions as in the reductivist modern period, but through the more flexible and responsive notion of habits.

Habits offered Peirce a framework for understanding the fluid and organic relationship between the external world, experiences, inferences, beliefs and, most importantly, actions and their consequences. His groundbreaking work on habit introduced a feature central to all future pragmatist treatments of the subject; namely, its relational holism. As Gary Shapiro writes, "[h]abit is used by Peirce to designate an initially bewildering variety of things, including beliefs, logical principles, dispositions, instincts and personality. It is a broad concept which covers under one umbrella what other philosophers might want to separate as the bodily or the mental, or the rational and the irrational."[6] While we find Peirce's most thorough treatment of habit in his essay "The Fixation of Belief," his single most eloquent description occurs in "How to Make Our Ideas Clear," where he links habit to belief in a way that will set the tone for James, Dewey, and later pragmatists:

> And what, then, is belief? It is the demi-cadence which closes a musical phrase in the symphony of our intellectual life. We have seen that is has just three properties: First, it is something that we are aware of; second, it appeases the irritation of doubt; and, third, it involves the establishment in our nature of a rule of action, or, say for short, a *habit.* It appeases the irritation of doubt, which is the motive for thinking, thought relaxes, and comes to rest for a moment when belief is reached.[7]

Though Peirce makes use of the construct of habit in a great many of his essays, our best introduction to his use of this concept is his essay "The Fixation of Belief," where he revolutionizes the philosophical treatment of belief by rejecting the common view that belief is primarily the product of consciously articulated premises in favor of the view that "belief is of the nature of a habit."[8] In the following quote he argues that the movement from premise to inference to belief is not determined, as we might want to believe, by some careful sorting of the facts or some keen observation of the world, but by habit, a feature of the mind that is flexible (as the point of the essay is to be mindful of which mental habits we use) but not infinitely so (these habits, once set, make the inferences seem necessary and determined).

> That which determines us, from given premises, to draw one inference rather than another, is some habit of mind, whether it be constitutional or acquired. The habit is good or otherwise, according as it produces true conclusions from true premises or not; and an inference is regarded as valid or not, without reference to the truth or falsity of its conclusion specially, but according as the habits which determines it is such as to produce true conclusions in general or not. The particular habit of mind which governs this or that inference may be formulated in a proposition whose truth depends on the validity of the inferences which the habit determines; and such a formula is called a *guiding principle* of inference.[9]

Peirce's revolutionary approach to belief was to move it from the realm of ideas and warrant to the more naturalistic psychological realm of stimulus and habit. A belief for Peirce is not so much the interior recognition that a particular idea is warranted or not. It is instead a sign that the belief holder has a certain predisposition to the world, predisposition that we call a habit. "The feeling of believing is a more or less sure indication of there being established in our nature some habit which will determine our actions."[10] Of course, this does not mean that Peirce sees us as thoroughly conditioned beings whose actions are *determined* by habits. While he acknowledges habit's powerful and translucent pull, he nonetheless shows how doubt and reflection play a decisive role in ensuring as much as possible that our habits work for us and not against us.

> The force of habit will sometimes cause a man to hold on to old beliefs, after he is in a condition to see that they have no sound basis. But reflection upon the state of the case will overcome these habits, and he ought to allow reflection its full weight.[11]

So, despite the irritations that we feel because of them, we are fortunate to have our doubts, those interior experiences or feelings that yield "an uneasy and dissatisfied state from which we struggle to free ourselves and pass into a state of belief."[12] Doubt's function is to jar us out of habit's strong yet resistible pull long enough to have the opportunity to inquire whether or not the habit fits our experiences of the world. The fact that these habits are in place means that, at least to a certain extent, they have "worked": these habits have placed us in some sort of equilibrium or working order within our environment. Doubt is just the feeling that perhaps the habits—the associations between belief and action—are not working and perhaps ought to be replaced. This work on the relation between habit, doubt, and belief shows that Peirce is a logician who nonetheless makes belief seem like an almost entirely physiological affair. Further, Peirce here anticipates the consequentialism that is classically associated with James and Dewey when he writes in "How to Make Our Ideas Clear" that

> [t]he whole function of thought is to produce habits of action and that whatever there is connected with a thought, but irrelevant to its purpose, is an accretion to it, but no part of it. If there be a unity among our sensations which has no reference to how we shall act on a given occasion, as when we listen to a piece of music, why do we not call that thinking. To develop its meaning, we have, therefore, simply to determine what habits it produces, for what a thing means is simply what habits it involves. [13]

Here we see yet another way in which the pragmatist doctrine of habit inaugurated by Peirce functions as a great unifier of human experience. It not only links us as acting and believing things to our environments through our tendency toward habits—rules of actions—that have worked in the past, but it also offers an account of meaning that is anchored in habit. That is, the meaning of a thing—whether it be an idea, an experience, or what have you—is the habits that it involves and nothing else.

While habit plays a prominent role in many of Peirce's works, it receives its grandest and most enigmatic treatment in "A Guess at the Riddle." Here he extends habit beyond the realm of human thought and action and argues that it is a universal force that, like Anaxagoras's *philia*, draws all the disparate entities of the world into an ever more unified whole. As he wrote in "Design and Chance," "[s]ystems or compounds which have bad habits are quickly destroyed, those which have no habits follow the same course; only those which have good habits tend to survive."[14] Here habit functions as the middle category of a triad of cosmic forces he sees moving all things: "three elements are active in the world, first, chance; second, law; and third habit-taking."[15] In this boldest and most confounding work of his scholarly career, Peirce argues that habits are in us only because we are in a universe where everything is subject to a kind of heliotropism that pulls each thing away from chance and closer to law. That pull he names habit.

> The tendency to obey laws has always been and always will be growing. We look back toward a point in the infinitely distant past when there was no law but mere indeterminacy; we look forward to a point in the infinitely distant future when there will be no indeterminacy or chance but a complete reign of law. . . . Moreover, all things have a tendency to take habits. For atoms and their parts, molecules and groups of molecules, and in short every conceivable real object, there is a greater probability of acting as on former like occasion than otherwise. This tendency itself constitutes regularity, and is continually

> on the increase. In looking back into the past we are looking towards periods when it was a less and less decided tendency. But its own essential nature is to grow. . . . We have therefore only to suppose the smallest spur of it in the past, and that germ would have been bound to develop into a mighty and over-ruling principle, until it supersedes itself by strengthening habits into absolute laws regulating the action of all things in every respect in the indefinite future.[16]

If Peirce introduced philosophy to the pragmatist doctrine of habit, William James elevated it to become a central feature of pragmatist philosophy. The doctrine of habit works hand-in-glove with James's radical empiricism as it leads us to focus on relations over objects, the stream of experience rather than the stability of concepts. As Erin Tarver writes, "The notion of habit is, for James, crucial to explaining the continuity of our experiences and the propensity of individuals to engage in certain sorts of behaviors without actively intending to do so."[17] Habits for James are the tell that experience lives in and through us, so much so that it usually moves us without our conscious permission, indeed, sometimes without even our notice. The soldier who rounds each corner in a cautious arc like the parent who quarters and crusts every sandwich long after the last child has grown are like human ponds carrying ripples from experiential stones thrown long ago.

One of the most dedicated and beautifully written analyses of habit within American philosophy occurs within the famous chapter of William James's *The Principles of Psychology,* titled simply "Habit." Ralph Barton Perry gives us a lovely glimpse into habit's importance for James when he tells us that, "[a]t the head of the chapter on habit in his *Briefer Course* [James] wrote with his own hand: 'Sow an action, and you reap a habit; sow a habit and you reap a character; sow a character and you reap a destiny."[18] In James's chapter we find a characteristically eclectic and intimate treatment of this varied and ubiquitous phenomenon that serves as a bridge between Peirce's early analysis of habit and the far more detailed and far-reaching works of John Dewey. James's opening statement posits an essential link between habit and life itself, writing, "[w]hen we look at living creatures from an outward point of view, one of the first things that strike us is that they are bundles of habits."[19]

While most of the chapter examines habit within the realm of human psychology, James starts his discussion of habit evoking Peirce's odd and almost mystical description of habit as one of the three cardinal laws governing and moving all things in the universe when he for his part writes that the "philosophy of habit is thus, in the first instance, a chapter in physics, rather than in physiology or psychology" (*Principles*, 105). He seeks to understand habit at its most minute scale, arguing that "[t]he moment one tries to define what habit is, one is led to the fundamental properties of matter. The laws of Nature are nothing but the immutable habits which the different elementary sorts of matter follow in their actions and reactions upon each other" (*Principles*, 104). He goes on to say that while the habits of the smallest, elemental bodies cannot change because the particles themselves cannot change, everything that is a compound mass can in fact change, and thus its properties can be understood in terms of habit. The most rewarding feature of this early physics discussion is his description of the relationship between habit and *plasticity.*

> *Plasticity*, then, in the wide sense of the word, means the possession of a structure weak enough to yield to an influence, but strong enough not to yield all at once. Each relatively stable phase of equilibrium in such a structure is marked by what we may call a new set of habits. Organic matter, especially nervous tissue, seems endowed with a very extraordinary degree of plasticity of this sort; so that we may without hesitation lay down as our first proposition the following, that *the phenomena of habit in living beings are due to the plasticity of the organic materials of which their bodies are composed.* (*Principles*, 105)

James sets the tone for later pragmatists, especially Dewey, when he uses habit as the bond that links not only the physical to the psychological, but the individual to the environment. It gives us a wonderful description of habit as that part of our behavior that is formed by past experiences and thus offers a degree of rigidity, but also is strong enough to bend in the face of new experience.

James's discussion of the application of plasticity ranges across the human body, from scars to sprained ankles, but ultimately rests within the "bony boxes" that protect the human brain and nervous system (*Principles*, 107). It is here that he transitions from the physical to the anatomical, arguing that in fact any "simple habit . . . is, mechanically, nothing but a reflex discharge" and that even the most complex habits are but "*concatenated* discharges in the nerve-centers" (*Principles*, 108). Again showing that habits emerge naturally from a need for balance and equilibrium, James writes that these habits-as-reflex-arcs only form by virtue of the fact that "a nervous system is a mass of matter whose parts, constantly kept in states of different tension, are as constantly tending to equalize their states" (*Principles*, 109). Having shown that habits emerge of need from our nervous systems, he is ready to posit two significant practical applications for the philosophy of habit.

The first practical application he calls "Economy and efficiency," explaining that "*habit simplifies the movements required to achieve a given result, makes them more accurate, and diminishes fatigue*" (*Principles*, 112). The second, clearly related, application is that habit "*diminishes the conscious attention with which our acts are performed*" (*Principles*, 114). Thus, habits are salutary and even necessary for creatures like us since, once learned, they need only a simple sensory cue to trigger a chain of behaviors with little to no accompanying conscious thought. Anticipating Dewey's later argument that inquiry only begins with the recognition of a problematic situation, James writes that these cues "are *sensations* to which we are *usually inattentive,* but which immediately call our attention if they go *wrong*" (*Principles*, 118). James here draws our attention to the beneficial consequents of this automatic nature of habit—he uses the example of an expert pianist who is only able to play so gracefully because a mere glance at the sheet is sufficient to trigger a flow of musical notes—but also to the deleterious effects. James gives us many funny and embarrassing examples of this, including an anecdote about a person who goes to his room to change for dinner and soon finds himself in bed because the first few movements triggered his nightly habit of preparing for sleep. However, these trivial and embarrassing examples of infelicitous habits gesture toward more serious and damaging habits that live in our bones and muscles, as it were, and hide from conscious recognition.

James summarizes the practical results of habituation by drawing a distinction between habitual behaviors and conscious actions.

> A strictly voluntary act has to be guided by idea, perception, and volition, throughout its whole course. In an habitual action, mere sensation is a sufficient guide, and the upper regions of the brain and mind are comparatively free. (*Principles*, 116)

James's discussion up to this point is a brief but rich treatment of the various ways in which habits mediate our physiological composition and our lived behaviors in the world. In a mere fourteen pages it does as much as any other philosophical treatise to span the Cartesian chasm dividing the mind from the body. Nonetheless, we find the greatest impact of James's early work on habit in the last few pages of this chapter, where he turns his attention "to the *ethical implications of the law of habit*" (*Principles* 120). What follows is a stark and often grim tableau of people and animals staked to set patterns of behavior by the power of long-cemented habits. We see riderless cavalry horses executing movements in the heat of battle described next to beasts of burden who appear to be "machines almost pure and simple" and even "[m]en grown old in prison . . . [asking] to be readmitted after being once set free" (*Principles*, 121). He follows this with one of the most influential yet disturbing passages in philosophy regarding the power of habit:

> Habit is thus the enormous fly-wheel of society, its most precious, conservative agent. It alone is what keeps us all within the bounds of ordinance, and saves the children of fortune from the envious uprisings of the poor. It alone prevents the hardest and most repulsive walks of life from being deserted by those brought up to tread therein. It keeps the fishermen and the deck-hand at

> sea through the winter; it holds the miner in his darkness, and nails the countryman to his log-cabin and his lonely farm through all the months of snow; it protects us from invasion by the natives of the desert and the frozen zone. It dooms us all to fight out the battle of life upon the lines of our nurture or our early choice, and to make the best of a pursuit that disagrees, because there is no other for which we are fitted, and it is too late to begin again. (*Principles*, 121)

This passage is remarkable for many reasons. First, it offers a clear if brutal picture of habit's far-reaching power over our lives. Second, it stands in stark contrast to the largely positive implications of habit from early in the chapter. Where habit earlier freed our minds to think while habits moved our bodies through the world by simple cues, now we find ourselves doomed, nailed by these very habits to our frozen, darkened lots. Third, it gestures—perhaps unwittingly, perhaps intentionally—to the pivotal role of habits in the roiling social revolutions of the twentieth century regarding race, gender, and class. If habit is the ultimate social flywheel that binds us to our various social positions, any effort to change or reform social relations must address the social habits that keep us tethered at least as much as, if not more than, the conscious and explicit ideas and arguments that seek to shore up these patterns of human relation. As we will see later in this chapter, DuBois will cite James's work on habit at the end of his own long fight for racial justice in America when, if you allow me the metaphor, he argues that racism will abide if we merely cut down its visible, that is to say conscious, branches and trunk: instead, we must go further by digging up its roots that lie deep in the recesses of our habits.

Echoing Aristotle's statements regarding one's character being set by early adulthood, James argues that "by the age of thirty, the character has set like plaster and will never soften again" (*Principles*, 121). Also like Aristotle, James's attention to the powers of habit leads him to attend carefully to education, arguing, "the great thing, then, in all education, is to *make our nervous system our ally instead of our enemy*. It is to fund and capitalize our acquisitions, and live at ease upon the interest of the fund. *For this we must make automatic and habitual, as early as possible, as many useful actions as we can*" (*Principles*, 122).

## 2. JOHN DEWEY AND THE CULMINATION OF THE PRAGMATIST THEORY OF HABIT

Just as many commentators on American philosophy summarize pragmatism as a seed sown by Peirce, nurtured by James but only brought to fruition by Dewey, the same general point can be made of the specific pragmatist doctrine of habit. Dewey's doctrine explicitly toes a line drawn by the earlier thinkers, as when in his *Logic: The Theory of Inquiry* (1938) he states:

> I follow in the main the account given by Peirce of "guiding" or "leading" principles. According to this view, every inferential conclusion that is drawn involves a habit . . . in the *organic* sense of habit, since life is impossible without ways of actions sufficiently general to be properly named *habits.*[20]

It is also undeniable that the doctrine of habit as a robust and meaningful feature of pragmatist philosophy only reaches maturity in the far-reaching work of the last thinker of the great triad of American philosophy. Dewey is perhaps the greatest philosopher of habit in that the notion of habit plays a fundamental role in not only his philosophy of education, but also his description of the self, his pragmatist dissolution of the purported problems of modern philosophy and his political meliorism.

Another thinker who offered world-changing ideas in these areas, Karl Marx, emphasized the centrality of labor to human existence by arguing that human beings would be more accurately categorized if we replaced the scientific genus of *Homo Sapiens* ("the knowing human") with *Homo Faber* ("the making human") in order to highlight that what we make defines us more deeply than what we think. Extending this revision, if we were to find a Deweyan alternative to *Homo Sapiens*, it would have to be *Homo Habitus* ("the habituated human") because he argues that they define us more than anything else. As Dewey puts things succinctly, "Man is a creature of habit, not of reason nor yet instinct."[21]

Dewey's much more detailed and thorough scholarship on habit makes explicit many of the consequences of Peirce's psychological treatment of belief and James's holism, but also explores the relevance and power of habits in myriad concrete social and cultural contexts.[22] Nonetheless, habit's role in Dewey's work is also more complex and ambivalent than it was in the works of the earlier two pragmatists. On the one hand, habit finds no greater or more powerful articulation in all of American philosophy than in the work of John Dewey. Yet, at the same time, the dominant theme of Dewey's life work—that we should view ourselves as organisms whose interactions with each other and our environment are marked by novelty, innovation, and evolution—frames habit as less a hero of the human story than as a villain. The dean of contemporary American philosophers, John McDermott, makes just this point when he draws an apt contrast between the first great philosopher of habit and Dewey:

> Happiness, in the Aristotelian sense, is not hereby envisioned by Dewey, whose approach is more empirical, more realistic, more attuned to the crushing sadness which visits most of our lives, most of the time. No, Dewey focuses

> rather on the occasional but crucial moments of celebration, joy, and the ability to break through the ersatz and the habitual.[23]

Just as James's work on habit is concentrated within the chapter on habit in *Principles of Psychology*, Dewey's work on the subject is concentrated within his 1922 work *Human Nature and Conduct*, the first chapter of which starts, "[h]abits may be profitably compared to physiological functions, like breathing [or] digesting . . . in requiring the cooperation of organism and environment."[24] It is important to point out at the outset that Dewey, like the earlier pragmatists who wrote extensively on habit, uses the term in a way that is far more nuanced and far reaching than the colloquial use of the term. Dewey sees habit as being far more than rote or repeated patterns of behavior. He characterizes habit as "an acquired predisposition to *ways* or modes of response."[25] Shannon Sullivan captures nicely the difference between Dewey's use of the term and the common understanding of habit when she writes,

> Habit is not so much the recurrence of particular acts but is instead a style or manner of behaving that is reflected throughout one's being—that is, throughout the way one goes about thinking, as well as acting.[26]

Here we already see Dewey's variation on a theme widely present in earlier pragmatist treatments of habit, namely that it works as a natural bond linking the individual to her environment through her past experiences. However, Dewey's point here is not just to say that living through habits is as natural to us as breathing. Instead, he is more concerned with the interactive features of habit that reach beyond our physiologies to engage our environments. While he first compares habits to physiological functions, he soon attempts to

> convey the same idea by saying that habits are arts. They involve skills of sensory and motor organs, cunning or craft, and objective materials. They assimilate objective energies, and eventuate in command of environment. They require order, discipline, and manifest technique. They have a beginning, middle and end. Each stage marks progress in dealing with materials and tools, advance in converting material to active use.[27]

Habits are crucial to our successful integration within the world because of their transactional and harmonizing roles. They organize the different functions of a single organism into an effective whole, and are further inherently interactional bonds between ourselves and our broader biological, cultural, or social environments. Since human interaction is widely impacted by cultural forces, habit formation is also a function that enables us to make sense of the world. Dewey defines habit as

> that kind of human activity which is influenced by prior activity and in that sense acquired; which contains within itself a certain ordering or systematization of minor elements of action; which is projective, dynamic in quality, ready for overt manifestation; and which is operative in some subdued subordinate form even when not obviously dominating activity.[28]

Dewey's doctrine of habit *temporalizes* our experience in a way that, for example, Hume denied and the Logical Positivists failed to notice. More so than conscious memory or future anticipation, habits mediate the crucial transactions between our past experiences and future actions. What's more, habituation's unification of our experience over time is more than mere repetition. As Dewey says in his *Logic*,

> The view that habits are formed by sheer repetition puts the cart before the horse. Ability to repeat is a result of a formation of a habit through the organic redispositions effected by attainment of a consummatory close. This modification is equivalent to giving some definite direction to future actions.[29]

Echoing insights first articulated by Peirce and James, Dewey argues that habits only form because they work; they become sedimented in a person's behavior because they enable the individual to find equilibrium within the surrounding environment. They only become habitual in the pejorative sense of mindlessly repetitive if they are "the product of conditions that are uniform because they have been made so mechanically—as in much school and factory 'work.'"[30] This point that habits only become stale as a product of a social environment that is itself unduly mechanical and unimaginative underscores Jim Garrison's point about Dewey's doctrine of habits that, "[b]ecause they involve coordinated responses to our habitats, Dewey thought that habits are the means of coordinating self and environment."[31]

Habits become so tightly woven into our sense of self that they become imperceptible until a problem throws one of them into relief.

> No matter how accidental and irrational the circumstances of its origin, no matter how different the conditions which now exist to those under which the habit was formed, the latter persists until the environment obstinately rejects it. Habits once formed perpetuate themselves, by acting unremittingly upon the native stock of activities. They stimulate, inhibit, intensify, weaken, select, concentrate and organize the latter into their own likeness.[32]

Thus, habits are not only interactional but also conservative: once a habit becomes a part of an organism's response to the environment, it is difficult to notice, let alone remove. In most cases this is fortuitous for the organism because the very fact that the habit has taken hold indicates that, at least so far, it fortuitously syncs the organism with its habitat. Of course, Dewey is well aware of the fact that while most of our habits only exist as latent and unremarkable patterns of behavior because of the fact that, to a greater or lesser degree, they succeed at placing us in a beneficial interaction with our environment, not all of our habits bear such flourishing tendencies. This leads to one of the features that distinguishes Dewey's work on pragmatism from that of the earlier pragmatists, namely the attention he pays to the effects of bad—that is to say ill-fitting, infelicitous, and outdated—habits.

Habits, and the problem of bad habits, become the focal point of Dewey's moral philosophy, instead of conscious decisions. James Garrison illuminates clearly habit's value for Dewey's moral philosophy when he points out that, "Dewey thought that habits of intelligent conduct, based on a program of values determined by reflective inquiry and criticism, produce wisdom that goes beyond knowledge of the actual to embrace moral possibilities."[33] Dewey claims we should not so much worry about our conscious responses to moral decisions, but should instead attend to the habits by which we make thousands of unconscious decisions. In particular, we should examine our bad habits: those that continue to function in our behaviors but have somehow fallen out of harmony with their environment.

> A bad habit suggests an inherent tendency to action and also a hold, command over us. It makes us do things we are ashamed of, things which we tell ourselves we prefer not to do. It overrides our formal resolutions, our conscious decisions.[34]

Where older philosophical pictures of the self framed these sorts of ill-fitting, powerful patterns of behavior as somehow external or contrary to our true selves or souls, Dewey claims that "[w]hen we are honest with ourselves we acknowledge that a habit has this power because it is so intimately a part of ourselves. It has a hold upon us because we are the habit."[35]

However, Dewey's main reason for discussing bad habits is that they clarify the role and moral salience of habit within our lives.

> These traits of bad habit are precisely the things which are most instructive about all habits and ourselves. They teach us that all habits are affections, that all have projective power, and that a predisposition formed by a number of specific acts is an immensely more intimate and fundamental part of ourselves than are vague, general, conscious choices. All habits are demands for certain kinds of activity; and they constitute the self.[36]

A common view of habit is that it is often at loggerheads with the will. For example, someone might say that I want to, I will, eat more healthfully, but my bad habits keep *me* from doing so. This assumes that my will can in some meaningful way be understood apart from the habits that actually guide my actions and movements in the world. For example, Augustine develops the most influential Christian narrative about sin, will, and what he takes to be the fallen nature of the flesh when he describes how his lustful habits anchor him like a lodestone to the world he sees as sinful while his will wants to love only God.

> I was astonished that although I now loved [God] and not some phantom in your place, I did not persist in enjoyment of God. Your beauty drew me to you, but soon I was dragged away from you by my own weight and in dismay I plunged again into the things of this world. The weight I carried was the habit of the flesh.[37]

Worse still, Augustine also gives us the classic view of the self as a psychological war zone riven by the conflict between the will and habit.

> From my own experience I now understood what I had read—that *the impulses of nature and the impulses of the spirit are at war with one another.* In this warfare I was on both sides, but I took the part of that which I approved in myself rather than the part of that which I disapproved. For my true self was no longer on the side of which I disapproved, since to a great extent I was now its reluctant victim rather than its willing tool. Yet it was by my own doing that habit had become so potent an enemy, because it was by my own will that I had reached the state in which I no longer wished to stay.[38]

Against all this, Dewey offers a picture of the self and habit that is less dramatic but nonetheless sobering in its view of the power and depths of our habits.

> In any intelligible sense of the word will, [habits] *are* will. They form our effective desires and they furnish us with our working capacities. They rule our thoughts, determining which shall appear and be strong and which shall pass from light into obscurity.[39]

Further emphasizing this idea that we *are* our habits, Dewey argues that all the older notions of self that rest on the image of a wise and judging mind made of ideas fail to understand the mutually constituting relationship between habits and ideas.

> [The] formation of ideas as well as their execution depends upon habit. *If* we could form a correct idea without a concrete habit, then possibly we could carry it out irrespective of habit. But a wish gets definite form only in connection with an idea, and an idea gets shape and consistency only when it has a habit back of it. . . . The act must come before the thought, and a habit before an ability to evoke the thought at will. Ordinary psychology reverses the actual state of affairs.[40]

Dewey argues that we are neither unified, souled essences nor warring mind/body dualisms; instead we are fundamentally dynamic and porous beings that can only be imagined as separate from their environments and actions in the abstract. Shannon Sullivan explains Dewey's transactional, and therefore habituated, view of the self when she writes,

> In contrast to accounts of self as substance, including that of monism as well as that of dualism, Dewey claims that the human organism is characterized by activity, which has physical and mental aspects to it. An organism's activity, in turn, is characterized by a particular style. In an organism's transactions with the world, patterns occur, which is to say that organic activity is characterized primarily by habit.[41]

The moral question is not, therefore, "How can I (as a willing mind) fight my bad habits?" The question is instead, "How can I (as a collection of habits) develop the most intelligent habits possible?" For while it is true that habits work, sometimes, by limiting our attentions and dispositions (Dewey writes that in this regard they "are blinders that confine the eyes of the mind to the road ahead")[42] they also have a second, more dynamic function associated with the fact that they are only capable of limiting our attention because "they are first positive agencies."[43] As James Campbell writes of this liberating function that Dewey sees, "Habits give continuity and stability to our activities; they enable us to act, free from the need to think through and plan our actions at every particular step."[44] Dewey argues that the correct habits enable us to have more open and unfettered actions within our environments because

> the more numerous our habits the wider the field of possible observation and foretelling. The more flexible they are, the more refined is perception in its discrimination and the more delicate the presentation evoked by imagination. For they mean nothing more or less than the habits formed in process of exercising biological aptitudes are the sole agents of observation, recollection, foresight and judgment: a mind or consciousness or soul in general which performs these operations is a myth.[45]

Habits, in Dewey's understanding, perform many of the actions—observing, judging, willing—that have been associated with a unified mind. These actions are not so much features of a unified mind, however, but are in fact features of *unifying habits* that variously function and fail, improve and degrade as we make our way through the world. These habits have enormous social, political, and cultural relevance because they don't just organize an individual's mind across time; they are largely responsible for our social organization, whether for ill or good. This is why Dewey—who urged us continually to recognize the potential of human intelligence and community if only we'd be brave enough to free them from the bonds of tradition and blind habit—went so far as to equate philosophy itself with the search for wiser and better fitting habits.

> The situation defines the vital office of present philosophy. It has to search out and disclose the obstructions; to criticize the habits of mind which stand in the way; to focus reflection upon needs congruous to present life; to interpret the conclusions of science with respect to their consequences for our beliefs about purposes and values in all phases of life.

This idea that a vital philosophy must, among other things, concern itself with the correction of ill-fitting habits and the establishment of better ones leads us to our final section on the pragmatist doctrine of habit and its application within various forms of pragmatist meliorism.[46]

## 3. HABIT AND POLITICAL MELIORISM

In the previous two sections we saw how the pragmatist doctrine of habit was articulated during the late nineteenth and early twentieth centuries. In this section we will see some of the ways in which it has been applied, in true pragmatist fashion, to lived problems affecting the lives of real people. In particular, this section will examine the value of the pragmatist doctrine of habit for the goal of meliorism. Colin Koopman explains meliorism, the quintessential pragmatist political goal, thus

> Meliorism, holding together pluralism with humanism, is the thesis that we are capable of creating better worlds and selves. Pluralism says that better futures are possible, humanism that possibilities are often enough decided by human energies, and meliorism that better futures are made real by our effort. Meliorism, then, is best seen as humanism and pluralism combined and in confident mood. Melioristic confidence offers a genuine alternative to both pessimism and optimism. These two moods, almost universally proffered by modern philosophers, share a common assumption that progress or decline is inevitable. Meliorism, on the other hand, focuses on what we can do to hasten our progress and mitigate our decline.[47]

The pragmatist belief in meliorism navigates a path between revolutionary utopianism and the cynical acceptance of the status quo as intractable, just as the pragmatist doctrine of habit finds a middle ground between radical free will and behaviorized conditioning. Instead of trying to address a social problem by developing a radically new framework or social arrangement, most pragmatist political thinkers hope to improve lived conditions mindful of the limits imposed by present social conditions.

The first American philosopher to use the doctrine of habit in order to address lived social and political problems was Jane Addams, the great advocate for women, children, the poor, and global peace. The doctrine of habit is a consistently visible thread that runs throughout her explicitly melioristic political philosophy. Addams first became famous for her work at Hull House in Chicago, where she sought practical ways to help immigrants to the United States best adapt to their new environs and society. Speaking poetically about the incredible skills that these immigrants brought from their older situations, Addams hopes,

> Could we take these primitive habits as they are to be found every day in American cities and give them their significance and place, they would be a wonderful factor for poetry in cities frankly given over to industrialism and absorbed in its activities.[48]

Here she hopes that we might together find an intelligent way to incorporate the value and experience preserved in the habits of the potter's casting and the weaver's weaving in ways that would help offset the increasing mechanization of nineteenth-century America.

Addams also finds melioristic potential within the doctrine of habit in the specific context of her work on pacifism. One of Addams's boldest claims is that peace will be best achieved when men set aside age-old habits of patriarchy and learn to listen to women from around the world who are organizing for global peace. She does not argue that men need to listen to women because women have some sort of essentialist revulsion against warfare or inherent epistemological ability, but because women's social roles as caregivers give them an experientially and habitually broader perspective on the overwhelming waste of war.[49]

Further, she argues that we ought to solve the problem of warfare itself as one of the woefully outdated and ill-adapted habits that has been carried into the industrial age with disastrous consequences. The moralizing and appeals to pity will fail to correct these habits, since only concrete action that starts the process of cementing new habits in their place will effectively address our habitual responses to political disputes through warfare.

> Moralists agree that it is not so much by the teaching of moral theorems that virtue is to be promoted as by the direct expression of social sentiments and by the cultivation of practical habits; that in the progress of society sentiments and opinions come first, then habits of action and lastly moral codes and institutions. Little is gained by creating the latter prematurely, but much may be accomplished to the utilization of human interests and affections. The Advocates of Peace would find the appeal both to Pity and Prudence totally unnecessary, could they utilize the cosmopolitan interest in human affairs with the resultant social sympathy that at the present moment is developing among the nations of the earth.[50]

W. E. B DuBois, arguably the single most visionary and influential philosopher of race, was another American intellectual who, like Addams, looked to the doctrine of habit to effect concrete social change. While his voluminous body of scholarly work evolved to include analyses that stretch beyond pragmatism, his approach to the problem of white racism was marked throughout by his early contact with pragmatist philosophers, especially William James. DuBois explicitly describes himself as working in the same vein, vis-à-vis habit, as the earlier pragmatists, when he writes in *Dusk of Dawn,* which he wrote in his seventy-second year in 1940:

> The meaning and implications of the new psychology had begun slowly to penetrate my thought. My own study of psychology under William James had pre-dated the Freudian era, but it had prepared me for it. I now began to realize that in the fight against race prejudice, we are not facing simply the rational, conscious determination of white folk to oppress us; we were facing age-long complexes sunk now largely to unconscious habit and irrational urge, which demanded on our part not only the patience to wait, but the power to entrench ourselves for a long siege against the strongholds of color caste.[51]

DuBois undoubtedly directed some of his critical powers against the problem of conscious racism on the part of whites. However, he understood that the far more complicated and deep-seated problem of racism dwelled in racist habits that white Americans had learned and preserved, often unawares, that impeded the realization of a truly fair democratic community. After fifty years of continuous work on behalf of racial justice—first in the United States, later around the globe—DuBois diagnoses the continuing and intractable problem of white racism as one of outdated and unjust habits.

> The facts of the situation however as science today conceives it, are clear. The individual may act consciously and rationally and be responsible for what he does; but on the other hand many of his actions, and indeed, as we are coming to believe, most of the actions, are not rational and many of them arise from subconscious urges. It is our duty to assess praise and blame for the rational and conscious acts of men, but to regard the vast area of the subconscious and the irrational and especially of habit and convention which also produce significant action, as an area where we must apply other remedies and judgements if we would get justice and right to prevail in the world. Above all we must survey these vague and uncharted lands and measure their limits.[52]

If Dewey and James were right to say that instead of being people who merely have some habits, we instead *are* our habits, then DuBois was right to say that racial justice would be impossible without examining the "vague and uncharted lands" where these habits dwell. If we recall James's disturbing images of people and other animals locked in fruitless patterns by habits as well as Dewey's exhortation to philosophers to accept the critique of poor social habits as a central duty, then DuBois and Addams alike are paragons of pragmatist meliorism. While Peirce, James, and Dewey undoubtedly created, clarified, and refined the pragmatist doctrine of habit, DuBois and Addams best put the doctrine to work in ways that improved the lives of countless people and communities.

Sadly, the color line, in DuBois's famous phrasing, was not just the problem of the twentieth century. The siege against caste lasted beyond the twentieth century and continues into the twenty-first, where many more pragmatist philosophers and social critics use the pragmatist model of habit to assess and respond to the evolving problematic of racism, as well as sexism and homophobia. Shannon Sullivan is the most prominent contemporary philosopher to methodically use the pragmatist notion of habit, in her case drawn mostly from Dewey's work, to understand and correct problems of racism and sexism. Her essay "Reconfiguring Gender with John Dewey: Habit, Bodies and Cultural Change" (2000) was a milestone for pragmatist philosophy as it was the first time in decades that a pragmatist philosopher did not just discuss the doctrine of habit but actually used an account of habit for meliorist purposes. Her work has been followed closely by a small but growing number of contemporary pragmatists eager to use the pragmatist doctrine of habits to melioristic ends.[53] Sullivan argues that Dewey's "concept of habit helps us both to understand gender as a productive, not just limiting structure of existence that is constitutive of the body, and to explore the co-constitutive relationship of individual gender habits and cultural gender constructs."[54] Sullivan's *Living Across and Through Skins* (2001) expanded on her early work on the meliorist potential of habit and echoed Dewey's call to philosophers to critique habits by arguing that "feminists, pragmatists, and others should seek out the reconfiguration of habit and the configurations of gender, sex, and sexuality that structure human existence. Only by doing so can we free ourselves of the rigidity and stagnation of the self that accompany gender binarism."[55]

While other works by Sullivan focused on race and class, her first book focused primarily, though not exclusively, on discovering ways of correcting and expanding unjust and needlessly constraining constructs of gender and sexuality. One of her greatest achievements in this work was achieving a kind of renaissance of the doctrine of habit by applying it to contemporary problems that were invisible to the early pragmatists but nonetheless well suited for correction through the doctrine of habit.

> How bodies create meaning has implications for the constitution of gender, and Dewey's notion of habit is crucial to understanding gendered existence, including the possibility of its reconfiguration. Thinking of corporeal existence as composed of habit recognizes that the gendered and other habits that structure a person *are* that person. Habit makes human existence possible, as well

> as constrains it to the particular forms of existence that constitute it. . . . The sedimentation of habit does not preclude transformation because the different contexts in which particular habits occur can promote their reconfiguration. Because the relationship between individual habits and the environments in which they are performed is transactional, even relatively fixed habits can be changed.[56]

While her work always maintains a characteristic blend of pragmatism, continental philosophy, and feminist theory, Sullivan later shifted her focus from the transactional nature of gender to the particular problem of unconscious habits of white privilege with the publication of her 2006 work *Revealing Whiteness*. Here Sullivan examines racial whiteness as a network of unexamined habits and reveals some of the most pertinent social and cultural ramifications of the habitual dimension of these habits. While this is a wide-ranging work of scholarship too detailed to fully summarize here, it is worth examining what is likely her most relevant use of the doctrine of habit, namely how she describes, in good Deweyan fashion, the danger of colorblind approaches to racism in light of the habits of whiteness.

> Habits of white privilege support these attempts by making the invisibility of race seem like the goal that all people should aim for. Whiteness and its concomitant privileges tend to operate as invisible, and since whiteness is the standard to which all should aspire, then people of color too should aspire to give up their race and become race-free (= white). The colorblindness that results in turn fuels habits of white privilege by creating a social, political, and psychological atmosphere of racial invisibility in which white privilege can thrive. It is as if, with their style of hidden invisibility, habits of white privilege provide ready-made grooves for colorblindness to slide into, and those grooves in turn are deepened as colorblindness grows.[57]

My own work on the meliorist potential of the doctrine of habit is much like Sullivan's in that I seek to understand, critique, and correct the problems of racial whiteness through a fusion of Dewey's work on the interplay of categories, kinds and habits and DuBois's critique of the habits of white Americans. In *Habits of Whiteness* (2009) I argue that the unconscious manifestations of white racism are ultimately far more privative upon our communities than the less frequent, easily noticed, and almost universally condemned acts of explicit white racism. Where Sullivan's work is characterized by a blend of American pragmatism, feminism and continental phenomenology, and psychoanalysis, I attempt to solve our current problems with whiteness with a detailed application of Dewey's work on habits and ideas as well as a historical genealogy of these habits through American history dating back to Bacon's Rebellion in seventeenth-century Virginia. Regarding the meliorist potential of the pragmatist doctrine of habits for addressing the problem of systematic, white supremacist racism, I wrote,

> a pragmatist model of habit is very useful for addressing this problem because it shows that an individual might have the best of all intentions when it comes to race even as he or she acts on learned and inherited habits that originate from our nation's long and brutal era of legalized white supremacism that formally ended only within the last fifty years. . . . It shows us that we are not at all in the post-racist society many white folk would like to pretend we are in. We are instead in a precarious limbo.[58]

Habit plays a defining role in the formation, evolution, and continuing growth of American pragmatism. It unites disparate elements within the works of pragmatism's founders like Peirce and James. Habit is also like a musical theme that harmonizes the distinct voices of thinkers like DuBois and Dewey into a coherent tradition, even though these thinkers are quite different in terms of tone and focus. It is a theme that works and fits with almost every major philosophical feature of pragmatism: Peirce's pragmatic test of belief would be impossible without it, it is James's holism manifested in the flesh, and it is both the lynchpin of Dewey's educational philosophy as well as the perfect foil and villain to Dewey's heroic vision of human intelligence. However, habit's greatest legacy and future is found in its potential for meliorism, which is after all pragmatism's most definitive and ubiquitous feature. If pragmatism is the commitment that we can always improve our selves and communities by using intelligence to find ever more flourishing and meaningful lives, then pragmatism will always be defined by its ability to refine, reclaim, and refuse the habits through which we actually live our lives.

## NOTES

1. I would like to thank my colleague Kevin Decker for his invaluable insights and advice regarding this chapter.

2. William James, "What Pragmatism Means," in *Pragmatism* (Cambridge, MA: Harvard University Press, 1978), 39.

3. Michael Eldridge, "Naturalism," *The Blackwell Guide to American Philosophy*, eds. Armen Marsoobian and John Ryder (Malden, MA: Blackwell, 2004), 52.

4. Cornel West, *The American Evasion of Philosophy: A Genealogy of Pragmatism* (Madison: University of Wisconsin Press, 1989).

5. C. S. Peirce, "Ideal-Realism" entry in *Century Dictionary* [1911] as quoted in *The Essential Peirce: Selected Philosophical Writings*, eds. Nathan Houser and Christian J. W. Kloesel (Bloomington: Indiana University Press, 1992), xxv.

6. Gary Shapiro, "Habit and Meaning in Peirce's Pragmatism," *Transactions of the Charles S. Peirce Society* 9 (December 1, 1973): 26.

7. C. S. Peirce, "How to Make Our Ideas Clear," in *The Essential Peirce*, 129.

8. Peirce, "The Fixation of Belief," in *The Essential Peirce*, 115.

9. Peirce, "The Fixation of Belief," 112.

10. Peirce, "The Fixation of Belief," 114.

11. Peirce, "The Fixation of Belief," 122.

12. Peirce, "The Fixation of Belief," 114.

13. Peirce, "How to Make Our Ideas Clear," 131.

14. Peirce, "Design and Chance," in *The Essential Peirce*, 553.
15. Peirce, "A Guess at the Riddle," in *The Essential Peirce*, 277.
16. Peirce, "A Guess at the Riddle," in *The Essential Peirce*, 277.
17. Erin Tarver, "Particulars, Practices, and Pragmatic Feminism: Breaking Rules and Rulings with William James," *Journal of Speculative Philosophy* 21, no. 4 (2007): 277.
18. Ralph Barton Perry, [1948] *The Thought and Character of William James* (Nashville: Vanderbilt University Press, 1996), 196.
19. William James, *The Principles of Psychology*, vol. 1 (New York: Henry Holt, 1890), 104. Hereafter, *Principles*.
20. John Dewey, *Logic: The Theory of Inquiry*, in *The Later Works, 1925–1953*, ed. Jo Ann Boydston (Carbondale: Southern Illinois University Press, 1980), 9:19.
21. John Dewey, *Human Nature and Conduct*, in *The Middle Works, 1899–1924*, ed. Jo Ann Boydston (Carbondale: Southern Illinois University Press, 1988), 14:88.
22. Selected passages in this section are drawn from my earlier work *Habits of Whiteness: A Pragmatist Reconstruction* (Bloomington: Indiana University Press, 2009).
23. John McDermott, *The Drama of Possibility: Experience as Philosophy of Culture* (New York: Fordham University Press, 2007), 160.
24. Dewey, *Human Nature*, 15.
25. Dewey, *Human Nature*, 32.
26. Shannon Sullivan, *Living Across and Through Skins* (Bloomington, IN: Indiana University Press, 2001), 31.
27. Dewey, *Human Nature*, 16.
28. Dewey, *Human Nature*, 31.
29. Dewey, *Logic*, 39.
30. Dewey, *Logic*, 39.
31. Jim Garrison, "John Dewey's Philosophy as Education," in *Reading Dewey: Interpretations for a Postmodern Generation*, ed. Larry Hickman (Bloomington: Indiana University Press, 1998), 74.
32. Dewey, *Human Nature*, 88.
33. Garrison, "John Dewey's Philosophy as Education," in *Reading Dewey* 64.
34. Dewey, *Human Nature*, 21.
35. Dewey, *Human Nature*, 21.
36. Dewey, *Human Nature*, 21.
37. Augustine, *Confessions*, trans. R. S. Pine-Coffin (London: Penguin Books, 1961), 151.
38. Augustine, *Confessions*, 165.
39. Dewey, *Human Nature*, 22.
40. Dewey, *Human Nature*, 25.
41. Sullivan, *Living Across and Through Skins*, 12.
42. Dewey, *Human Nature,* 121.
43. Dewey, *Human Nature,* 123.
44. James Campbell, "Dewey's Conception of Community," in *Reading Dewey: Interpretations for a Postmodern Generation*, Larry Hickman, ed. (Bloomington: Indiana University Press, 1998), 24.
45. Dewey, *Human Nature,* 123.
46. Dewey, John. *The Question for Certainty*, in *The Later Works, 1925–1953*, ed. Jo Ann Boydstone. (Carbondale: Southern Illinois University Press, 1984) 4:250.
47. Colin Koopman, "Pragmatism as a Philosophy of Hope: Emerson, James, Dewey and Rorty," *Journal of Speculative Philosophy* 20, no. 2 (2006): 107.
48. Jane Addams, *Newer Ideals of Peace* (New York: Macmillan, 1907), 64.
49. Terrance MacMullan, "War as Waste: Jane Addams' Pragmatic Pacifism," *Journal of Speculative Philosophy* 15, no. 2 (2001): 86–104.
50. Addams, *Newer Ideals of Peace*, 8.
51. W. E. B. DuBois, *Dusk of Dawn* (New York: Schocken, 1968), 296.
52. DuBois, *Dusk of Dawn*, 171.

53. Lara Trout, "Attunement to the Invisible: Applying Paulo Freire's Problem-Posing Education to "Invisibility," *Pluralist* 3, no. 3 (Fall 2008): 63–78; Tarver, "Particulars, Practices, and Pragmatic Feminism: Breaking Rules and Rulings with William James," 275–90.

54. Shannon Sullivan, "Reconfiguring Gender with John Dewey: Habit, Bodies, and Cultural Change," *Hypatia* 15, no. 1 (Winter 2000): 24.

55. Sullivan, *Living Across and Through Skins*, 110.

56. Sullivan, *Living Across and Through Skins*, 9.

57. Sullivan, *Revealing Whiteness* (Bloomington: Indiana University Press, 2006), 191.

58. MacMullan, *Habits of Whiteness*, 6.

# BIBLIOGRAPHY

Addams, Jane. *Newer Ideals of Peace*. New York: Macmillan, 1907.

Augustine, *Confessions*. Translated by R. S. Pine-Coffin. London: Penguin Books, 1961.

Campbell, James. "Dewey's Conception of Community." In *Reading Dewey: Interpretations for a Postmodern Generation*, edited by Larry Hickman. Bloomington: Indiana University Press, 1998.

Dewey, John. *Logic: The Theory of Inquiry*. In *The Later Works, 1925–1953*, edited by Jo Ann Boydston. Carbondale: Southern Illinois University Press, 1980.

———. *Human Nature and Conduct*. In *The Middle Works, 1899–1924*, edited by Jo Ann Boydston. Carbondale: Southern Illinois University Press, 1988.

Dewey, John. *The Quest for Certainty*, in *The Later Works, 1925–1953*, edited by Jo Ann Boydstone. Carbondale: Southern Illinois University Press, 1984.

DuBois, W. E. B. *Dusk of Dawn*. New York: Schocken, 1968.

Eldridge, Michael. "Naturalism." In *The Blackwell Guide to American Philosophy*, edited by Armen Marsoobian and John Ryder. Malden, MA: Blackwell.

Garrison, Jim. "John Dewey's Philosophy as Education." In *Reading Dewey*.

James, William. *The Principles of Psychology*. Vol. 1. New York: Henry Holt, 1890.

———. "What Pragmatism Means." In *Pragmatism*. Cambridge, MA: Harvard University Press, 1978.

Koopman, Colin. "Pragmatism as a Philosophy of Hope: Emerson, James, Dewey and Rorty." *Journal of Speculative Philosophy* 20, no. 2 (2006): 106–16.

MacMullan, Terrance. "War as Waste: Jane Addams' Pragmatic Pacifism." *Journal of Speculative Philosophy* 15, no. 2 (2001): 86–104.

———. *Habits of Whiteness: A Pragmatist Reconstruction*. Bloomington: Indiana University Press, 2009.

McDermott, John. *The Drama of Possibility: Experience as Philosophy of Culture*. New York: Fordham University Press, 2007.

Peirce, Charles S. "Ideal-Realism." In *Century Dictionary* [1911], quoted in *The Essential Peirce: Selected Philosophical Writings*, edited by Nathan Houser and Christian J. W. Kloesel. Bloomington: Indiana University Press, 1992.

———. "Design and Chance." In *The Essential Peirce*.

———. "The Fixation of Belief." In *The Essential Peirce*.

———. "A Guess at the Riddle." In *The Essential Peirce*.

———. "How to Make Our Ideas Clear." In *The Essential Peirce*.

Perry, Ralph Barton. *The Thought and Character of William James*. Nashville: Vanderbilt University Press, 1996.

Shapiro, Gary. "Habit and Meaning in Peirce's Pragmatism." *Transactions of the Charles S. Peirce Society* 9 (December 1, 1973): 24–40.

Sullivan, Shannon. "Reconfiguring Gender with John Dewey: Habit, Bodies, and Cultural Change," *Hypatia* 15, no. 1 (Winter 2000): 23–42.

———. *Living Across and Through Skins*. Bloomington: Indiana University Press, 2001.

———. *Revealing Whiteness*. Bloomington: Indiana University Press, 2006.

Tarver, Erin. "Particulars, Practices, and Pragmatic Feminism: Breaking Rules and Rulings with William James." *Journal of Speculative Philosophy* 21, no. 4 (2007): 275–90.

Trout, Lara. "Attunement to the Invisible: Applying Paulo Freire's Problem-Posing Education to "Invisibility." *Pluralist* 3, no. 3 (Fall 2008): 63–78.

West, Cornel. *The American Evasion of Philosophy: A Genealogy of Pragmatism.* Madison: University of Wisconsin Press, 1989.

## *Chapter Eleven*

# Oppression in the Gut

## *The Biological Dimensions of Deweyan Habit*

Shannon Sullivan

> To understand the existence of organized ways or habits we surely need to go to physics, chemistry and physiology rather than to psychology.
>
> A morals based on study of human nature instead of disregard for it . . . would thereby ally ethics with physics and biology.
>
> —John Dewey, *Human Nature and Conduct*

John Dewey's concept of habit has proven to be a powerful tool for understanding the embodied self in transaction with its environment. As a predisposition for taking in and responding to the world in particular ways, habit is composed of the dynamic, co-constitutive relationship between bodies and their physical, social, political, economic, and other surroundings. In particular, in a world characterized by sexism and white racism, this dynamic composition means that a person's habits will tend to be shaped by and in response to male privilege and white domination. This shaping can be and has been well understood both phenomenologically and psychoanalytically: phenomenologically in that habit concerns the lived experience of embodiment, which includes unreflective bodily knowledge that lends people their distinctive bodily comportments.[1] And psychoanalytically in that some embodied habits are not merely unreflective or non-conscious, but unconscious. Habits that are unconscious don't just happen to go unnoticed at a particular moment; instead they actively obstruct attempts to bring them to conscious awareness and deviously thwart efforts to transform them.[2]

What has tended to be neglected in scholarly accounts of Deweyan habit, however, are its biological dimensions, especially those of sexist and white racist habits. How do sexism and racism help constitute the embodied habits of both dominant and subordinate groups: men and women, and white people and people of color? And how can understanding the bodily aspects of sexist and racist habits help support their transformation? As Dewey suggests in the epigraphs above, to best tackle these questions, we need an understanding of habit that pays attention to what the "hard" sciences of physics, biology, chemistry, and physiology tell us about human bodies. Doing so, moreover, is not merely for the sake of developing an adequate understanding of habit. It also can be important for the way that we grapple with ethical and political problems, such as sexism and white racism.

Let me be clear that this turn to biology and physiology is not a rejection of phenomenological and psychoanalytic understandings of embodied habit. Especially when pragmatically appropriated, phenomenology and psychoanalytic theory can be important tools for understanding the transactional relationship of bodily self and world. But in that relationship, especially when focusing on politically charged issues such as sexism and white racism, biology has tended to be overlooked or dismissed. More precisely, because biology historically was (and often still is) used to justify and explain the alleged inferiority of women and people of color, the hallmark of much feminist and anti-racist theory has been a fierce opposition to the biological sciences.[3] In critical philosophy of race, contemporary appeals to biology tend to be considered exclusively as the methodology of racist pseudoscience, such as that found in Richard Herrnstein and Charles Murray's notorious book *The Bell Curve*.[4] For its part, even when examining the materiality of the gendered body, contemporary feminist philosophy and theory tends resolutely to avoid biology, except to criticize the biological reductionism into which all appeals to biology supposedly collapse.[5]

While mindful of the sexist and racist abuses of the biological sciences, I disagree that all appeals to biology inevitably result in biological reductionism or necessarily support social oppression and domination. I think that by exploring the transactional relationship between the biological body and the world, feminists and critical philosophers of race can learn something useful about how sexist and racist habits operate and thus how they might be transformed. For that reason, I examine here the biological processes of the human enteric nervous system—the stomach and intestines, or more succinctly, the gut—to understand them as a site of Deweyan habit. I choose the gut because it is one of the most significant places in which the "external" world transacts with the "inside" of the body, and because it has been called "the second brain" due to its independent ability to regulate fundamental modes of engagement with the world, such as mood.[6] As we will see, the gut is a site of complex co-constitutive relationships between bodily organism and environment that can help us understand how gendered and raced habits are not merely phenomenologically and psychoanalytically, but also biologically embodied.

Somewhat ironically, an obstacle to understanding the gut as a site of Deweyan habit might appear to be Dewey himself. Even though Dewey instructs his readers to turn to physics, chemistry, biology, and physiology to understand habit, he has been described as discontent with the physiological account of habit that William James provided in *The Principles of Psychology*.[7] In his landmark work on psychology, James explains habit as a feature of the nervous system: the brain and spinal cord. For James, habits are discharges in the nervous system, and their "anatomical substratum must be a path in that system."[8] While part of human psychology, habit also is necessarily bodily and must be understood in terms of the anatomy of neural firing and muscular contractions: either a "reflex discharge" in the case of a simple habit, or "concatenated discharges in the nerve-centres, due to the presence there of systems of reflex paths" in the case of complex habits.[9] James's account of habit emphasizes its unreflective dimensions and brings out the ethical implications of habit on character, both of which are important to Dewey's later development of habit. But James's psychology of habit remains focused on its physiology in a fairly isolated way. When discussing habit, James tends to concentrate solely on the nervous system and the economization of nervous and muscular energy that habit provides, as if habit, including its neural firings and muscular contractions, could be properly understood apart from its social and other environments.

As this last comment suggests, it ultimately isn't James's attention to biology and physiology per se that troubles Dewey. It is the subjectivism that James's psychology retains. As Dewey charges, "the point of view [in James's *Psychology*] remained that of a realm of consciousness set off by itself," and that, rather than James's use of biology, is Dewey's basis for criticism.[10] In fact, Dewey praises James's "return to the earlier [e.g., Aristotelian] biological conception of the psyche," explaining that it—and not the more recent and popular works *The Will to Believe*, *A Pluralistic Universe*, or *Pragmatism*—was the "one specifiable philosophic factor which entered into my [Dewey's] thinking so as to give it a new direction and quality."[11]

The nature of Dewey's appreciation of, as well as dissatisfaction with, James's psychology becomes apparent in Dewey's primary work on habit, which is a book on psychology as well. But Dewey's version of psychology more strongly emphasizes the social than does James's. As Dewey's subtitle indicates, *Human Nature and Conduct: An Introduction to Social Psychology* unequivocally presents habit as a social function and mind as a product of engagement with its social surroundings. And yet, when explaining the book's subtitle in the preface, Dewey also brings out the importance of biology to his social psychology, describing mind "as a system of beliefs, desires, and purposes which are formed in the interaction of biological aptitudes with a social environment."[12] In the first sentence of the first chapter, furthermore, Dewey compares habit to the physiological functions of respiration and digestion, a topic to which I will return shortly.[13] Even though he may have been dissatisfied with the particular physiological account of habit provided by James because of its isolated character, Dewey clearly did not reject physiology. While I agree that Dewey's account of habit is richer than James's because of Dewey's phenomenological analysis,[14] the significant accomplishment of *Human Nature and Conduct* is that it successfully combines the physiology and sociality of habit in its phenomenology.

As Dewey indicates in chapter one of *Human Nature and Conduct*, the central point of comparison between habit and physiological function is that both are transactional: they are constituted in and through a dynamic relationship with their environment. Breathing cannot take place by means of lungs alone; it requires air (or oxygen, more precisely). Likewise, digestion only occurs when the stomach and intestines have food to process and absorb. Respiration and digestion are made up of a cooperative, active relationship between organism and environment. The "between" here is important: even though the lungs are crucial to respiration, respiration cannot be located inside the human body considered sharply distinct from the air that is "outside" it. Nor is digestion complete within the human body, as if the stomach and intestines owned the process apart from food on which it works. Rather than describe respiration and digestion as activities done by the human body by means of air and food, we just as accurately could depict them as "things done *by* the environment by means of organic structures."[15]

Likewise, habit is transactional. To take a wide assortment of quick examples, whether the activity is riding a bicycle, walking in high-heeled shoes, or interrupting people while they talk, habits are constituted in and through a dynamic relationship with the world "outside" them: bicycles, sidewalk pavement, shoes, societal expectations of femininity, and other people. Walking in high-heeled shoes, to stick with one example, isn't an activity that is contained within a person's feet and legs. It is located, so to speak, between feet, legs, shoes, floors, and gendered expectations. In fact, on Dewey's account, we could go so far as to describe walking in high-heeled shoes as an activity done by a gendered and male privileged world by means of a woman's comportment of her feet and legs. The habit of walking in high heels is a "wa[y] of using and incorporating the environment in which the latter has its say as surely as the former."[16]

In the case of both physiological functions and habit, their transactional relationship with the world means not only does the environment help constitute the function or habit, but also the function or habit helps constitute, and possibly change, the world. The relationship between function and habit and their environments is non-viciously circular. As the environment helps form the physiological functions and habits a person has, her physiological functions and habits enable her to take up and respond to the world in particular ways, which then alter her environment and thus indirectly affect both her and other people's physiological functions and habits. In the case of digestion, the introduction of food to the stomach and intestines allows the body to digest it, which enables a person to respond to the world with the output of waste matter, which alters the environment for good (fertilizer) or ill (toxic sewage) in ways that feed back into her and other people's food sources and prospects for future digestion. Likewise, as a gendered world shapes a woman's (and men's) habits of walking and occupying space, those habits both enable and constrain the way that she might respond to the world, perhaps maintaining gendered expectations regarding shoes and locomotion and perhaps challenging or transforming them. Either way, her response helps (re)constitute the environment that then feeds back into expectations for both her and other women's (and men's) footwear habits.

The cyclical relationship between physiological function and habit and their environments demonstrates their plasticity, which means that function and habit are simultaneously durable and corrigible. Plasticity does not mean that something is extremely flexible or supple or that it can easily or quickly be changed into a new shape. As William James clarifies in his account of habit, plasticity "means the possession of a structure weak enough to yield to an influence, but strong enough not to yield all at once."[17] Through their plasticity, physiological functions and habits help constitute the self, and their constitution makes the self something that endures over time as the particular, recognizable self that it is. In the case of habit, one way to put this point is to say that habits are ontological, providing a person with her character. Character is the interpenetrated collection of habits that gives a person coherence and prevents her from being, as Dewey says, "a juxtaposition of disconnected reactions to separated situations."[18] At the same time, however, the ontological status of habit does not mean that it is static or fixed. Habits are always in principle capable of change even if in practice they sometimes become rigid and inflexible. Since habits are formed in transaction with different environments and since those environments inevitably overlap, habit, and thus human ontology, is always potentially modifiable. A live organism only stays alive by means of an active relationship with its environment: when environments change or conflict with each other, then the habits—the selves—built in transaction with them are disrupted and must change too.

While we usually don't speak of physiological functions as having a character, like habits they are simultaneously durable and corrigible. Digestion, for example, is a way of responding to food that allows the organism to endure over its lifespan as the particular being that it is. The reliable consistency and ongoing durability of processes of digestion help keep an organism *this* organism and not decaying organic matter returning to the soil. At the same time, if they are to keep an organism alive, processes of digestion must be somewhat flexible and capable of change. When the environment changes—for example, when spoiled food is ingested—the stomach and intestines usually do not, and should not, engage in their typical process of digestion, for to do so would be to absorb poisonous matter. In that case, the gut responds to its environment in a different manner: through diarrhea or vomiting.

I want to press the question of the relationship between physiological functions and habit further than Dewey does in his discussion of digestion and respiration. As noted above, Dewey introduces digestion and respiration as points of comparison with habit. We can learn about habit by recalling how digestion and respiration work since they are alike one another in significant ways. The comparison of habit with digestion and respiration in *Human Nature and Conduct* is merely that, however: a comparison. Dewey never makes the stronger claim that digestion or respiration is itself an instance of habit. For that reason, we might conclude that while physiological examples help illuminate the salient features of habit, they are merely analogies or metaphors that could be replaced by a host of others. After all, on the first page of *Human Nature and Conduct,* Dewey himself quickly switches from physiological examples to comparisons of habit with the arts.[19]

But recent biological research focusing on gastrointestinal disorders suggests that physiological functions such as the digestion and absorption provided by the stomach and intestines can be considered *to be*—not just *be like*—a habit. To begin, the gut is transactional: the food that comes "inside" the body helps constitute the body, and the body in turn helps constitute the world "outside" it with its waste matter, which in turn helps constitute the next round of food that enters the body, and so on. In this cyclical relationship, the gut is an ontological site and could be considered the most significant place "inside" the body with which the "outside" world comes into contact. Or rather, as the scare quotes around "inside" and "outside" indicate, perhaps the gut shouldn't be thought of as inside the body at all. In fact, biologists John B. Furness and Nadine Clerc will claim "the lining of the gastrointestinal tract is our largest *external* surface."[20] Neurogastroenterologist Michael D. Gershon elaborates:

> The space enclosed within the wall of the bowel, its *lumen*, is part of the outside world. . . . The gut is a tunnel that permits the exterior to run right through us. Whatever is in the lumen of the gut is thus actually outside our bodies, no matter how counterintuitive that seems. The body proper stops at the wall of the gut. Nothing is truly in us until it crosses that boundary and is absorbed; moreover, anything that moves across the intestinal wall in the reverse direction, into the lumen, is gone.[21]

These ways of putting the point about the gut's relationship with the outside world helpfully disrupt customary and misguided assumptions about the stomach and intestines. But we might better think of the gut as in-between the inside and outside, where sharp boundaries between inside and outside break down into a dynamic relationship. Neither wholly contained inside the body nor wholly outside it, the gut is the place "inside" the body where the "outside" world is most intimately engaged. The wall of the gut, in particular, is a site of dynamic co-constitution in which what is "properly" body and what is "properly" world is necessarily and productively indeterminate.

The gut's engagement with the world takes the complicated form of simultaneously absorbing nutrients into the body and defending the body against bacteria and toxic substances that might have been ingested. To absorb nutrients, the gut must be welcoming and open to the "external" world, and for that reason it is lined with a highly permeable epithelial membrane.[22] But at the same time, its welcoming, permeable nature makes it extremely vulnerable, and so the gut must have a complex mechanism for monitoring and responding to its contents. "More extensive than those of any other organ" including presumably the brain, the gut has three control systems that determine how it should engage with the "external" world: "the gut immune system, in which 70 percent of the body's immune cells are found; the gastroenteropancreatic endocrine system, which uses more than 30 identified hormones; and the enteric nervous system, which contains of the order of $10^8$ neurons."[23] One of those identified hormones is the neurochemical serotonin, which regulates mood and plays a significant role in depression and its relief. Over 95 percent of the body's serotonin is found not in the brain, but in the gut.[24] (I'll return to the issue of depression and visceral serotonin below.)

Here we can begin to see what we could call the character of the gut, which helps highlight the gut's function and status as a habit. A person's gut immune, endocrine, and enteric nervous systems predispose a person to take up and respond to the world in particular ways. Of course, broadly considered the gut does the same sort of thing for all people: digesting and absorbing food, and excreting the waste products it cannot use. But different guts can have different styles of doing this, different manners of welcoming (or not) the external world they take in. Some guts can be more and others less receptive of the outside world, or receptive and responsive to the world in different ways, and this can mean more than the obvious and simple fact that some gastrointestinal systems tolerate a broader range of foods than others. Take the example of bowel dysfunctions such as Irritable Bowel Syndrome (IBS). IBS is a functional disorder, which means that there is no damaged or diseased organ to account for its symptoms of abdominal pain, diarrhea, constipation, bloating, and/or urgency.[25] IBS is associated with life stress (as distinct from physical stress, such as trying to lift an object too heavy to carry), and for that reason, until recently it was marginalized and dismissed by the medical community as a psychological, rather than medical, problem.[26] I suggest that guts with IBS have a distinctive character, a particular way of responding to—digesting and excreting—the food that they ingest that is simultaneously psychological and biological. More specifically, I suggest that guts with IBS are marked by a character that is uneasy with (some aspect of) the world. Furthermore, as we will see, this particular gut disposition is more characteristic of women than men due to the disproportionate harmful effects of sexism and male privilege on girls and women.

To make sense of these claims, two additional and related facts about IBS are crucial. First, there is a high prevalence of a history of sexual abuse with the occurrence of gastrointestinal disorders.[27] In a pioneering 1990 study of the connections between bowel dysfunction and a history of sexual abuse, 44 percent of patients with gastrointestinal disorders (constipation, diarrhea, and abdominal pain) reported a history of sexual abuse in childhood. "Patients with functional disorders were twice as likely as those with organic disease to report a history of forced intercourse, and more than ten times as likely to report a history of frequent physical abuse," including ongoing sexual abuse in adulthood for half of the abused patients.[28] Perhaps then the second relevant fact will come as no surprise: gastrointestinal disorders such as IBS are prevalent in women on a ratio of about 2:1, and this ratio holds up "even after accounting for potentially confounding psychological and health care seeking gender differences."[29] Girls and women are more often the victims of sexual abuse than boys and men, and the rate of their abuse is higher than often is acknowledged. For example, the U.S. Department of Justice reports that approximately 25 percent of college women have been victims of rape or attempted rape but that fewer than 5 percent of those women report the assault to the police.[30] Similarly, in the 1990 study mentioned above, "almost one-third of the abused patients had never discussed their experience with anyone, 60 percent had not discussed it with their family, and only 17 percent had informed their gastroenterologist."[31] A recent review of all research articles and observational data on the topic produced a clear scientific conclusion: "an abuse history is associated with gastrointestinal illness and psychological disturbance, appearing more often in women and patients with functional rather than organic, gastrointestinal disorders, is not usually known by the physician, and is associated with poorer adjustment to illness and adverse health outcome. Women are more often victims than men."[32]

Women can and sometimes do have different gastrointestinal habits than do men, and this is a biological, ontological detail that is inseparable from the political, historical, social, and other details about the contemporary world. Women's guts often have a different character or style of taking in and responding to the world because the world includes a "rapist culture" that valorizes male sexual aggression and normalizes the sexual abuse of girls and women.[33] It is important, of course, to remember that cultures, rapist or otherwise, differ from place to place and nation to nation and also to note that rates of gastrointestinal disturbance vary across different countries.[34] The situation is never as simple as a universal equation in which women + sexual abuse = gastrointestinal dysfunction. Nevertheless, the claims that women confront a sexist world and that social and cultural factors affect the frequency of gastrointestinal symptoms generally hold true. We thus could plausibly say that women's guts often have difficulty digesting and absorbing a sexist world that tends to be hostile to them, and this difficulty is as much a biological matter as it is a psychological one. "Digestion" and "absorption" are not metaphors in this claim, in other words. The type of gut in question literally will not digest and absorb its food without abdominal pain, diarrhea, and/or constipation because it does not want to be constituted by a world that includes its (her) sexual abuse.

Take the example of constipation and suppressed anger. As feminists and critical race theorists have documented, oppressed groups such as women and people of color are forbidden to express anger and/or their anger is dismissed as irrelevant or irrational.[35] Their anger tends to be seen as an intolerable act of insubordination, and so it often is suppressed by the oppressed person who feels it. Suppression of any emotion has consequences, and one doesn't have to be a devotee of Freud to say that the suppressed anger of an abused woman can be as much of a visceral as a psychological phenomenon. Constipation has been associated with the predominance of the sympathetic limb of the autonomic nervous system and with vagal suppression, which is suppression of the vagus nerve that innervates the muscles of the abdominal viscera.[36] So too has the suppression of anger been associated with reduced vagal activity and sympathetic dominance. (Reduced vagal activity also has been documented in patients with functional dyspepsia and gastro-esophageal reflux.) As physiologist N. W. Read concludes, "these data suggest that symptoms indicating a psychovisceral attitude of resistance and hold-up are associated with sympathetic dominance."[37] An angry body that isn't allowed to express its anger can manifest its resistance to the world through its gut reactions. It can withhold itself, its contributions to the world, by withholding its feces. This withholding is a gut judgment of the world that something is wrong with it—with both the world and thus also with the gut (person) who is transactionally constituted in relationship with it.

Of course, not every angry person or every abused woman is constipated. Positing an uncomplicated causal relationship between sexual abuse, suppressed anger, and constipation would be woefully simplistic. People's lives and patients' symptoms are too specific and individual to be fully captured by broad characterizations of gut habits, and any generalization about women, sexual abuse, and gastro-intestinal dysfunction is only that—a generalization that admits of many exceptions. But as neurobiologists, colorectal physicians, and gastroenterological specialists are documenting, there nonetheless remain "different styles of psychovisceral expression that are observed clinically," and given the importance of embodiment to human experience, we may ask "why shouldn't the body (and particularly the gut) be able to express more subtle aspects of personality and feelings?"[38] (Indeed, one scientific study suggests that the effects of personality are greater than the intake of fiber in determining bowel functions.[39] ) As an expression of a person's feelings and personality, gut function thus can be considered a Deweyan habit. Gut function is a predisposition to transact with the world in particular ways that contribute to a person's style, manner, and character of being.

Depression offers another example of gut character, one that has a gendered association as well. Depression can be described both as an isolating breakdown of relationships with the world and other people and a biochemical imbalance (depletion) of neurotransmitters such as serotonin.[40] Women suffer depression more often than men, tend to develop depression at an earlier age than men, and tend to have longer lasting and more frequently recurring episodes of depression.[41] Depression typically is marked by symptoms that include problems with eating: most often a loss of interest in food, although sometimes an inability to stop eating. When a person is depressed, she becomes disconnected with the world, and that disconnection tends to be manifest in a gut refusal to take the world in. The depressed person has little interest in the "outside" world, one manifestation of which can be her body's having little interest in its largest "external" surface: the lining of the gastrointestinal tract.

As we have seen in the example of gastrointestinal disorders such as IBS, the gut can be a key site for the working-through, both physiologically and psychologically, of a person's relations with others. We might say that relationships with other people become internalized in the habitual ways that the gut responds to the world it ingests. This phenomenon of transactional internalization also can be seen in the depressed person's refusal or failure to eat. A person's willingness or inability to put part of the world (food) in her mouth to digest and absorb is a form of her relationship with the world (other people). As feminist Elizabeth Wilson has argued, this description of eating is not a mere metaphor for internalization of social relationships, as if eating represented relationships with others and depression represented their interruption. Rather, Wilson suggests, "gut pathology doesn't stand in for ideational disruption, but is another form of perturbed relations to others—a form that is enacted enterologically."[42] In that case, the result is "a schema of depression in which the failure to eat doesn't represent a breakdown of connection to others, but is seen as a direct interruption to the process of remaining connected to others. The struggle to eat (or to stop eating) when depressed is a struggle to mediate difficult, attenuated, or lost relations to others and the outside world."[43]

This bodily form of perturbed relationships is not psychosomatic in the dismissive way that the term sometimes is used. To call a bodily ailment "psychosomatic" can be to brush it off as imaginary or—to say the same thing from some perspectives—as an offshoot of a psychical problem. As colorectal physician Ghislain Devroede explains, "the medical community, in general, has a tendency to confuse imaginary diseases, i.e., fictitious disorders, with somatization disorders, which [are] really in the body."[44] In the case of depression, perturbed relationships with other people really are in the body, just as reduced serotonin levels really are in the gut (and, secondarily, the brain). So too are the feelings of sadness and dejection that are the subjective hallmark of depression. We could say that disturbed social relationships, low serotonin levels, and feelings of sadness are the very same thing considered from three different angles: social, biological, and psychological. All three considerations are functional, not substantive distinctions regarding depression. Thus each consideration is inaccurate if it is thought to be ontologically separate or separable from the other. Depression is a biopsychosocial phenomenon in which low serotonin levels, feelings of profound sadness, and disconnected social relationships help constitute each other in an ongoing transactional spiral.

This explains why successful treatment of depression often depends on addressing multiple aspects of the syndrome at once. This usually takes the form of therapy combined with serotonin-selective reuptake inhibitor (SSRI) medications, addressing the psychological and biological dimensions of depression. But it also can take the form of working directly on the social, interpersonal relationships that the gut has with the world, namely through the act of eating with others. For example, in one man's account of his episodes of major depression, Andrew Solomon documents how he became emotionally frail, unable to sleep, disinterested in food, and increasingly isolated. Retching in the bathroom, Solomon felt as though his "acute understanding of [his] loneliness were a virus in my system. . . . I thought that the normal and real world in which I had grown up, and in which I believed other people lived, would never open itself up to receive me."[45] As Wilson explains, through its refusal to eat and vomiting when he did eat, Solomon's gut was "unable to take in the world, to let others pass through him and be absorbed."[46] Finding a way to get Solomon to take in the world was integral to his recovery. This happened when Solomon's father canceled all other plans to sit with his son at the dinner table, cut up his food, and talk and joke with Solomon as he fed him. Solomon was able to eat, which is to say that he was able to begin repairing broken social connections with the world. While Solomon also used SSRI antidepressants and psychotherapy to facilitate his recovery, his father's love expressed through acts of feeding and eating was crucial to changing the way that Solomon's gut worked, and thus also to changing his body's serotonin and other hormone levels.

A final example of gut character that I will offer here also involves eating and focuses in particular on some of the visceral effects of white racism. The example I have in mind concerns white people's general refusal to eat with

African Americans during the period of legalized racial segregation in the United States. This example is different from the above examples of sexism in that the latter examples explored how women's gut dysfunction could be a manifestation of gendered oppression. In contrast, white people's gut-level refusal to eat with people of color was not a manifestation of the oppression of white people. White people's gut reaction to interracial eating instead was a gastrointestinal enactment of white people's racist domination of others. Systems of oppression can and do have (often different) physiological effects on the oppressor as well as the oppressed, in other words. This fact does not mean that the oppressor has now become the oppressed, a fellow victim of some impersonal system of oppression. In the case of white racism, white people are not victims of white domination just because their guts were involved in their attempts to establish and maintain white superiority. But the point is that their guts *were* involved: white people's physiological bodies historically have been involved in their attempts to dominate and degrade people of color, and this fact needs to be recognized if we are to adequately address white racism's operation outside of conscious beliefs.

Like interracial sex, interracial dining has long been a concern of systems of white domination (and the two practices aren't unrelated from that perspective).[47] In antebellum and especially Jim Crow United States, who ate with whom was a matter of much attention and grave concern. More specifically, white people's eating with black people was a serious violation of the racial etiquette of white domination. Interracial eating was not allowed on pain of severe physical punishment, perhaps even lynching, in the case of black people. In Jim Crow America, black people might purchase food from the same restaurants and drugstores as white people, but they were expected to stand at the rear of the counter and take their food outside (or perhaps into the restaurant kitchen) to eat it.[48]

Codes of racial etiquette were (and are) binding on the dominant as well as the subordinate,[49] which meant that white people who violated interracial eating taboos were subject to significant social censure. But the taboo against interracial eating was not solely enforced from without. It was so deeply ingrained in the habits of white lives that many white people experienced intense revulsion at the thought of eating with African Americans. As one white woman wrote in 1947 when reflecting back on her childhood, "often we spoke of the sin it would be to eat with a Negro. Next to 'intermarriage' this was a most appalling thought. It was an unthinkable act. . . . In the whole roster of Southern taboos ['eating with Negroes'] was nearly the most sacred. It was a grievous Southern sin for which were allowed no mitigating circumstances."[50] Another white woman explained in 1904 that "if anything would make me kill my children, it would be the possibility that niggers might sometime eat at the same table and associate with them as equals."[51] And a white woman living in Mississippi in the 1890s explained that, "the colored people all love me where I live. Some would almost give their right hands to help me if I asked them. But I would starve to death before I would eat a crust of bread at a table with one of them."[52]

It is indisputable that the essence of Jim Crow etiquette was the unrelenting demonstration and enforcement of black people's alleged inferiority.[53] But the question remains, why was interracial eating central to this demonstration? Why did white people so vehemently reject the idea of eating with black people? After all, the taboo against interracial eating was highly hypocritical: white people were fully aware and accepting of the fact that black people prepared and served the food that white people ate, both at home and in restaurants.[54] How could white people say they preferred their own death and the death of their children to the act of eating with black people? The answer I propose is that a white person's refusal to eat with a black person was part of her racist rejection of black people's constitution of herself. The segregation enacted in restaurants, dining cars, and dining rooms and kitchens in white homes was not merely geographical. Nor was it only political, in terms of the socio-legal-political question of whether black people were treated as equal or inferior to white people. It also was ontological: it was a matter of what parts of the "outside" world would be taken into white bodies to help constitute them. Of course, this refusal failed: black people and other people of color do help constitute who and what white people are. But its failure does not change the fact that white people have tried mightily to convince themselves that they are ontologically separate from people of color, and taboos against interracial eating historically were a significant part of that effort. Ironically, while white people long have been "eating the other" in terms of culturally appropriating and commodifying their music, clothing, dance, food, and more, white people historically have been unwilling to eat *with* the other.[55]

The white refusal to be constituted by black people was not merely a conscious decision. Especially as this refusal concentrated on the question of interracial eating and drinking, it also was a visceral habit, a biological manifestation of racism in the gut that wouldn't allow interracial eating on (stomach) pain of nausea, loss of appetite, and related symptoms. This suggestion admittedly is speculative. I am unaware of any medical research on white people's gastrointestinal reactions to racial situations, culinary or otherwise. (There does exist research on the cardiovascular system and cognitive control brain regions of white people with high levels of racial bias, who tend to experience interracial interactions as distressing and threatening.)[56] But as one historian of the Jim Crow South has argued, white people's belief in white superiority "may have operated at a visceral level, [a white person's] gut reaction telling him that [eating or] drinking after a black person was somehow dirty and defiling."[57] Given that the gut is a key site for the transaction of body and world, of biology and psychology and society, then white people's racism and their racist habits of engaging with the world can be found in their guts. White racism does not merely take the form of thoughts and ideas, such as the thought that black people are inferior and dangerous to white people. It is not only found in unreflective and/or unconscious bodily behaviors, for example, as in "the elevator effect" when a white woman's body tenses and she clutches her purse when alone on an elevator with a black man.[58] It also can be found in the elevator-bound white woman's gastrointestinal tract: the "difficulty swallowing, . . . dry mouth, [and] nausea,"[59] as well as the eventual constipation (from the digestion-slowing effects of adrenaline on the stomach and intestines)[60] that her racist fear and anxiety can produce. The character of the gut can be racist, and white people's racist guts have contributed to their habitual ways of engaging with the world, with black people and other people of color in particular.

Let me address a possible misunderstanding of my claim that human biology is implicated in white racism. This claim does not justify or defend white racism by means of biology's alleged inevitability. Put another way, this claim not does mean that white racism—or racial categories, which I do not address here but often are tangled up in discussions of biology and race—is determined by biology (e.g., a person's genes) such that racism can never be eliminated. It is not the case, as sometimes is mistakenly thought, that culture is malleable and biology is irrevocably fixed. For one thing, culture and other "non-biological" aspects of the human world can become quite sedimented such that they are very difficult to change. And on the flipside, understanding human biology as habitual means recognizing that changes to an individual's biological character can and do occur through its relationship with its environment. This doesn't necessarily make change easy. Change often is difficult to achieve no matter which aspect of human existence—cultural or biological, to oversimplify—is in question. But the hard problems of changing human behavior and beliefs are not reserved for the biological aspects of human life. They are shared across the board of human existence, even as different tactics for change might be in order depending on whether the more cultural or biological aspects of human existence are at stake. Because bodily habits are transactionally constituted by the world around them, work to eliminate societal problems, such as sexism and white racism, needs to address all aspects of that transaction, including the biological.

I know that invoking biological habits in the context of race and racism, perhaps even more so than in the case of gender and sexism, will alarm some readers. A long and destructive history of using biology to justify white domination—Nazi Germany is the prime example, but it is important to remember that the United States and many other countries were engaged in eugenics in the first half of the twentieth century[61]—has tended to make considerations of biology out of the question for critical philosophy of race. I am cognizant of that history, but I am concerned that out of fear of appearing to be a neo-Nazi or a racist, contemporary critical philosophers of race might avoid examining the role that human biology plays in white domination or restrict that role to the relatively safe terrain of phenomenology. The body surely is phenomenological, and understanding the embodied phenomenology of race is important to racial justice movements.[62] But the body also is biological, neurochemical, and physiological, and critically understanding those aspects of human embodiment is important as well. Leaving out the biological dimension of bodily habits misunderstands them and thus impedes attempts to change them, and this is as true of white racist habits as of less politically charged ones.

Let me close where I began, with the two epigraphs from Dewey. I have been emphasizing Dewey's inclusion of biology in his account of habit, but his dismissal of psychology does not mean that his account of habit is narrowly physiological. When Dewey dismisses psychology in his claim that we should turn to physics, chemistry, and physiology to understand habit, he rejects a very particular kind of psychology that treats individuals as prior to and independent of society and then tries to solve the artificial problem of how individuals come together to form society. This is the same sort of wrongheaded psychology that treats mind as independent of body and then tries to figure out how minds and bodies interact. It is this "orthodox" or "traditional" psychology that Dewey's social psychology rejects for an understanding of mind, body, and society as transactionally constituted.[63] As Dewey claims, "there is doubtless a great mystery as to why any such thing as being conscious should exist at all. But *if* consciousness exists at all, there is no mystery in its being connected with what it is connected with."[64] Mind, or consciousness, is intimately connected with its social and material environments, and it is this basic fact about human nature that physics, chemistry, and physiology understand better than orthodox psychology does.

I have argued that we do not have to read Dewey's use of biological functions, such as digestion, as a mere metaphor. Gastrointestinal functions are instances of Deweyan habit, not merely analogies for it. This understanding of habit does not amount to biological reductionism. Put another way, if not just critically but also sympathetically considering biological detail makes an understanding of habit reductive, then I think feminists and critical philosophers of race should tolerate the risk of biological reductionism.[65] Because Dewey's concept of habit is transactional, his appeal to biological data and processes understands them as always and necessarily informed by social and psychological realities.[66] The flipside is true as well. Following Dewey in understanding habit as transactional, we should not disregard what biology and other "hard" sciences tell us about human embodiment. We can and need to go all the way down, so to speak, to the level of the gut's lumen, epithelial membrane, and endocrine and enteric nervous systems to understand the bodily aspects of human beings' habits of engaging with the world.

Doing so could make a meaningful and positive difference to our ethical and political approaches to important social problems, such as sexism and white racism. As the second epigraph from Dewey attests, biology does not have to be the enemy of an ethics of social justice. It can be an ally. It can help us understand that bodies, not just conscious beliefs, need to be changed in order for oppression and domination to be eliminated. It can help us better hear when bodies are crying out in pain from oppressive situations, as in the case of gastrointestinal dysfunction and the sexual abuse of women.[67] And as in the case of the dry-mouthed, nauseous white woman in the elevator, it can help us perceive ongoing, subterranean white privilege in a post–Jim Crow era when most "good" white people would never openly endorse white racism and often claim not to even see race at all. Biology certainly will not and cannot solve every problem having to do with sexism and white racism. And given the past (and present) uses of biology to support oppression and domination, biology, like all sciences of human life, needs to be approached not just sympathetically, but also critically. With the help of Deweyan habit, however, rather than disregard what biology and other "hard" sciences tell us about human embodiment, feminist and critical philosophers of race can draw on biological knowledge to build an ethics of social justice. Doing so would be to the benefit of both.[68]

## NOTES

1. Victor Kestenbaum, *The Phenomenological Sense of John Dewey: Habit and Meaning* (Atlantic Highlands, NJ: Humanities Press, 1977). See also Kestenbaum, *The Grace and Severity of the Ideal: John Dewey and the Transcendent* (Chicago: University of Chicago Press, 2002); and Shannon Sullivan, *Living Across and Through Skins: Transactional Bodies, Pragmatism, and Feminism* (Bloomington: Indiana University Press, 2001).
2. Shannon Sullivan, *Revealing Whiteness: The Unconscious Habits of Racial Privilege* (Bloomington: Indiana University Press, 2006).
3. Claire Blencowe tracks the anti-biologism of 1970s and 1980s feminist discourse in "Biology, Contingency, and the Problem of Racism in Feminist Discourse," *Theory, Culture and Society* 28, no. 3 (May 2011): 3–27.
4. Richard Herrnstein and Charles Murray, *The Bell Curve: Intelligence and Class Structure in American Life* (New York: Free Press, 1996).
5. Elizabeth A. Wilson makes this point in *Psychosomatic: Feminism and the Neurological Body* (Durham, NC: Duke University Press, 2004), 3.
6. Michael D. Gershon, *The Second Brain: A Groundbreaking New Understanding of Nervous Disorders of the Stomach and Intestines* (New York: Harper Paperbacks, 1999).
7. Kestenbaum, *The Grace and Severity of the Ideal*, 66.
8. William James, *The Principles of Psychology*, vol. 1 (New York: Dover, 1950), 108.
9. James, *Principles*, vol. 1, 108.
10. John Dewey, "From Absolutism to Experimentalism," in volume 5 of *John Dewey: The Later Works, 1925–1953*, ed. Jo Ann Boydston (Carbondale: Southern Illinois University Press, 1988), 157.
11. Dewey, "From Absolutism to Experimentalism," 157.
12. John Dewey, *Human Nature and Conduct: An Introduction to Social Psychology* (Carbondale: Southern Illinois University Press, 1988), 3.
13. Dewey, *Human Nature and Conduct*, 15.

14. Kestenbaum, *The Grace and Severity of the Ideal*, 70.
15. Dewey, *Human Nature and Conduct*, 15, emphasis in original.
16. Dewey, *Human Nature and Conduct*, 15.
17. James, *Principles*, vol. 1, 105. See also chapter 1 of Catherine Malabou, *What Should We Do with Our Brain?*, trans. Sebastian Rand (New York: Fordham University Press, 2008).
18. Dewey, *Human Nature and Conduct*, 29.
19. Dewey, *Human Nature and Conduct*, 15.
20. John B. Furness and Nadine Clerc, "Responses of Afferent Neurons to the Contents of the Digestive Tract, and Their Relation to Endocrine and Immune Responses," in vol. 122 of *Progress in Brain Research*, eds. E. A. Mayer and C. B. Saper (Elsevier Science, 2000), 159, emphasis added.
21. Gershon, *The Second Brain,* 84.
22. Furness and Clerc, "Responses of Afferent Neurons," 159.
23. Furness and Clerc, "Responses of Afferent Neurons," 159.
24. Gershon, *The Second Brain,* xii.
25. Bruce B. Naliboff et al., "Towards an Integrative Model of Irritable Bowel Syndrome," in vol. 122 of *Progress in Brain Research*, eds. E. A. Mayer and C. B. Saper (Elsevier Science, 2000) 413.
26. Naliboff et al., "Towards an Integrative Model of Irritable Bowel Syndrome," 413.
27. Ghislain Devroede, "Early Life Abuses in the Past History of Patients with Gastrointestinal Tract and Pelvic Floor Dysfunctions," in vol. 122 of *Progress in Brain Research*, eds. E. A. Mayer and C. B. Saper (Elsevier Science, 2000) 131.
28. Devroede, "Early Life Abuses," 144.
29. Naliboff et al., "Towards an Integrative Model of Irritable Bowel Syndrome," 414.
30. U.S. Department of Justice, "Acquaintance Rape of College Students," accessed January 7, 2013. http://www.cops.usdoj.gov/ric/ResourceDetail.aspx?RID=6
31. Devroede, "Early Life Abuses," 144.
32. Devroede, "Early Life Abuses," 145.
33. See Andrea Dworkin's "Women in the Public Domain," in *Women and Values: Readings in Recent Feminist Philosophy*, ed. Marilyn Pearsall (Wadsworth Publishing, 1986), for a powerful account of the rapist culture in the United States.
34. Douglas A. Drossman, ed., *The Functional Gastrointestinal Disorders: Diagnosis, Pathophysiology, and Treatment—A Multinational Consensus* (New York: Little, Brown, 1994), 119.
35. See Marilyn Frye, "A Note on Anger," in *The Politics of Reality: Essays in Feminist Theory* (Freedom, CA: The Crossing Press, 1983) and Elizabeth Spelman, "Anger and Insubordination," in *Women, Knowledge, and Reality: Explorations in Feminist Philosophy*, eds. Ann Garry and Marilyn Pearsall (New York: Routledge, 1992).
36. N. W. Read, "Bridging the Gap between Mind and Body: Do Cultural and Psychoanalytic Concepts of Visceral Disease Have an Explanation in Contemporary Neuroscience?" in volume 122 of *Progress in Brain Research*, eds. E. A. Mayer and C. B. Saper (Elsevier Science, 2000), 435. See also Emeran A. Mayer, Bruce Naliboff, and Julie Munakata, "The Evolving Neurobiology of Gut Feelings," in volume 122 of *Progress in Brain Research*, eds. E. A. Mayer and C. B. Saper (Elsevier Science, 2000), 197.
37. Read, "Bridging the Gap between Mind and Body," 435.
38. Read, "Bridging the Gap between Mind and Body," 434, 436.
39. Cited on page 436 of Read, "Bridging the Gap between Mind and Body."
40. Wilson, *Psychosomatic,* 45.
41. Roxann Dryden-Edwards, MD, and William C. Shiel Jr., MD, FACP, FACR, "Women and Depression," http://www.medicinenet.com/script/main/art.asp?articlekey=18987. Accessed January 5, 2011.
42. Wilson, *Psychosomatic,* 45.
43. Wilson, *Psychosomatic,* 45.
44. Devroede, "Early Life Abuses," 151.
45. Quoted in Wilson, *Psychosomatic*, 46.
46. Wilson, *Psychosomatic*, 46.

47. Jennifer Ritterhouse, *Growing Up Jim Crow: How Black and White Southern Children Learned Race* (Chapel Hill: University of North Carolina Press, 2006), 30.
48. Bertram Wilbur Doyle, *The Etiquette of Race Relations in the South: A Study in Social Control* (Chicago: University of Chicago Press, 1937), 146.
49. Doyle, *The Etiquette of Race Relations in the South*, xx.
50. Katherine Du Pre Lumpkin, quoted in Fred Hobson, *But Now I See: The White Southern Racial Conversion Narrative* (Baton Rouge: Louisiana State University Press, 1999), 45, 49.
51. Ritterhouse, *Growing Up Jim Crow*, 42.
52. Doyle, *The Etiquette of Race Relations in the South*, 150.
53. http://www.jimcrowhistory.org/resources/lessonplans/hs_es_etiquette.htm. Accessed January 7, 2011.
54. Ritterhouse, *Growing Up Jim Crow*, 42.
55. bell hooks, "Eating the Other," in *Black Looks: Race and Representation* (Boston: South End Press, 1999). See also Greg Tate, *Everything but the Burden: What White People Are Taking from Black Culture* (New York: Harlem Moon, 2003).
56. Jennifer A. Richeson and Sophie Trawalter, "Why Do Interracial Interactions Impair Executive Function? A Resource Depletion Account," *Journal of Personality and Social Psychology* 88, no. 6 (2005): 934–47.
57. Ritterhouse, *Growing Up Jim Crow*, 127.
58. George Yancy provides an excellent account of what he calls "the elevator effect" in *Black Bodies, White Gazes: The Continuing Significance of Race* (Lanham, MD: Rowman and Littlefield, 2008), 5.
59. Yancy, *Black Bodies, White Gazes*, 5.
60. http://digestive.niddk.nih.gov/ddiseases/pubs/yrdd/. Accessed January 7, 2011.
61. Ladelle McWhorter, *Racism and Sexual Oppression in Anglo-America: A Genealogy* (Bloomington: Indiana University Press, 2009).
62. Linda Martín Alcoff provides an excellent account of the phenomenology of race in "Toward a Phenomenology of Racial Embodiment," *Radical Philosophy* 95 (1998): 15–26.
63. Dewey, *Human Nature and Conduct*, 60.
64. Dewey, *Human Nature and Conduct*, 46.
65. Cf. Wilson, *Psychosomatic*, 3 and 14.
66. Perhaps even transcendent ones too. While it is beyond the scope of this chapter to address Kestenbaum's refreshingly original analysis of Deweyan habit as "the transcendentals of experience" (*The Grace and Severity of the Ideal,* 2), let me note that I don't see a necessary conflict between our two accounts. Understood as a kind of hermeneutic horizon, as "the source of what comes into view and . . . the limiting condition of what is viewable, that is, of what transcends my view" (3), transcendence can be found in bodily existence.
67. As Read claims, gastrointestinal dysfunction "may require us to look at symptoms, not [merely] as components of a medical diagnosis, but as highly individual expressions of emotional conflict. In other words, the symptom carries a meaning; it is a body language that needs to be understood" ("Bridging the Gap between Mind and Body," 432).
68. Many thanks to Cameron O'Mara and Cori Wong for their research assistance and feedback on this chapter.

## BIBLIOGRAPHY

Alcoff, Linda Martín. "Toward a Phenomenology of Racial Embodiment." *Radical Philosophy* 95 (1998): 15–26.

Blencowe, Claire. "Biology, Contingency, and the Problem of Racism in Feminist Discourse." *Theory, Culture and Society* 28, no. 3 (May 2011): 3–27.

Devroede, Ghislain. "Early Life Abuses in the Past History of Patients with Gastrointestinal Tract and Pelvic Floor Dysfunctions." In *Progress in Brain Research*. Vol. 122. Edited by E. A. Mayer and C. B. Saper. Elsevier Science, 2000.

Dewey, John. "From Absolutism to Experimentalism." In *John Dewey: The Later Works, 1925–1953*. Vol. 5. Edited by Jo Ann Boydston. Carbondale: Southern Illinois University Press, 1988.

———. *Human Nature and Conduct: An Introduction to Social Psychology*. Carbondale: Southern Illinois University Press, 1988.

Doyle, Bertram Wilbur. *The Etiquette of Race Relations in the South: A Study in Social Control*. Chicago: University of Chicago Press, 1937.

Drossman, Douglas A., ed. *The Functional Gastrointestinal Disorders: Diagnosis, Pathophysiology, and Treatment—A Multinational Consensus*. New York: Little, Brown, 1994.

Dryden-Edwards, Roxann, MD and William C. Shiel Jr., MD, FACP, FACR, "Women and Depression." Accessed January 5, 2011. http://www.medicinenet.com/script/main/art.asp?articlekey=18987.

Dworkin, Andrea. "Women in the Public Domain." In *Women and Values: Readings in Recent Feminist Philosophy*, edited by Marilyn Pearsall. Wadsworth Publishing, 1986.

Frye, Marilyn. "A Note on Anger." In *The Politics of Reality: Essays in Feminist Theory*. Freedom, CA: The Crossing Press, 1983.

Furness, John B. and Nadine Clerc. "Responses of Afferent Neurons to the Contents of the Digestive Tract, and Their Relation to Endocrine and Immune Responses." In *Progress in Brain Research*. Vol. 122.

Gershon, Michael D. *The Second Brain: A Groundbreaking New Understanding of Nervous Disorders of the Stomach and Intestines*. New York: Harper Paperbacks, 1999.

Herrnstein, Richard, and Charles Murray. *The Bell Curve: Intelligence and Class Structure in American Life*. New York: Free Press, 1996.

hooks, bell. "Eating the Other." In *Black Looks: Race and Representation*. Boston: South End Press, 1999.

James, William. *The Principles of Psychology*. Vol. 1. New York: Dover, 1950.

Kestenbaum, Victor. *The Phenomenological Sense of John Dewey: Habit and Meaning*. Atlantic Highlands, NJ: Humanities Press, 1977.

———. *The Grace and Severity of the Ideal: John Dewey and the Transcendent*. Chicago: University of Chicago Press, 2002.

Lumpkin, Katherine Du Pre. Quoted in Fred Hobson, *But Now I See: The White Southern Racial Conversion Narrative*. Baton Rouge: Louisiana State University Press, 1999.

Malabou, Catherine. *What Should We Do with Our Brain?* Translated by Sebastian Rand. New York: Fordham University Press, 2008.

Mayer, Emeran A. et al. "The Evolving Neurobiology of Gut Feelings." In *Progress in Brain Research*. Vol. 122.

McWhorter, Ladelle. *Racism and Sexual Oppression in Anglo-America: A Genealogy*. Bloomington: Indiana University Press, 2009.

Naliboff, Bruce B. et al. "Towards an Integrative Model of Irritable Bowel Syndrome." In *Progress in Brain Research*. Vol. 122.

Read, N. W. "Bridging the Gap between Mind and Body: Do Cultural and Psychoanalytic Concepts of Visceral Disease Have an Explanation in Contemporary Neuroscience?" In *Progress in Brain Research*. Vol. 122.

Richeson, Jennifer A., and Sophie Trawalter. "Why Do Interracial Interactions Impair Executive Function? A Resource Depletion Account." *Journal of Personality and Social Psychology* 88, no. 6 (2005): 934–47.

Ritterhouse, Jennifer. *Growing Up Jim Crow: How Black and White Southern Children Learned Race*. Chapel Hill: University of North Carolina Press, 2006.

Spelman, Elizabeth. "Anger and Insubordination." In *Women, Knowledge, and Reality: Explorations in Feminist Philosophy*, edited by Ann Garry and Marilyn Pearsall. New York: Routledge, 1992.

Sullivan, Shannon. *Living Across and Through Skins: Transactional Bodies, Pragmatism, and Feminism*. Bloomington: Indiana University Press, 2001.

———. *Revealing Whiteness: The Unconscious Habits of Racial Privilege*. Bloomington: Indiana University Press, 2006.

Tate, Greg. *Everything but the Burden: What White People Are Taking from Black Culture*. New York: Harlem Moon, 2003.

U.S. Department of Justice. "Acquaintance Rape of College Students." Accessed January 7, 2013. http://www.cops.usdoj.gov/ric/ResourceDetail.aspx?RID=6.

Wilson, Elizabeth. *Psychosomatic: Feminism and the Neurological Body*. Durham, NC: Duke University Press, 2004.

Yancy, George. *Black Bodies, White Gazes: The Continuing Significance of Race*. Lanham, MD: Rowman and Littlefield, 2008.

*Chapter Twelve*

# Conceiving Things

## *Deleuze, Concepts, and the Habits of Thinking*

Jeffrey Bell

In *Difference and Repetition* Gilles Deleuze makes the provocative claim that "To think is to create—there is no other creation—but to create is first of all to engender 'thinking' in thought."[1] What immediately stands out in this claim is the strong qualifying statement that "there is no other creation" than thinking. This might on first reading appear to be a philosophical misstep for Deleuze, a return to the consciousness-focused phenomenological tradition Deleuze sought to move beyond. Moreover, if we are to take the claim seriously, then what are we to make of the myriad other forms of creation besides thinking that proliferate throughout Deleuze's and Deleuze and Guattari's books? In *Anti-Oedipus*, for example, Deleuze and Guattari stress that they "make no distinction between man and nature," to which they add, "Not man as the king of creation, but rather as the being who is in intimate contact with the profound life of all forms or all types of beings. . . ."[2] In refusing to make a distinction between man and nature, therefore, they refuse as well to place them into bipolar opposition with one another; rather, man and nature are, as Deleuze and Guattari put it, "one and the same essential reality, the producer-product" (AO, 5). So it would seem, then, that the creation associated with thinking is not that of "man as the king of creation" but is merely a part of a more essential reality—the producer-product, or the "profound life" of all forms and types of beings.

With this move to the reality of the producer-product we come to a central concern of Deleuze's thought; namely, how to understand the relationships between different identifiable terms—for example, an identifiable producer and its identifiable product, a thinker and its thought, et cetera—without making these relationships subservient to the identity of these terms. This effort is what Deleuze understands to be the attempt to think difference in itself rather than doing what we tend to do, which is "to subordinate difference to identity in order to think it," and think it, Deleuze claims, parenthetically, "from the point of view of the concept or the subject" (DR, xv). In short, Deleuze is attempting to think the "profound life" of things.

We can now begin to see that when Deleuze claims there is no other creation than thinking he is not isolating creation within the purview of human thought but is rather extending thought itself to being simply the profound life of things. This profound life of things, however, involves the problematics of an Idea, with a capital "I," in what Deleuze admits is a form of Platonism.[3] This is not the standard, Introduction to Philosophy reading of Plato, however, the reading of Platonism whereby one "subscribes to a simplicity of the essence or an ipseity of the Idea," as Deleuze puts it. If this is instead the Platonism of the later dialogues (in particular the *Philebus*) which involves the assertion that "Ideas are a little like multiplicities which must be traversed by the questions How? How much? In what case?, then yes," Deleuze claims, "everything that I am saying seems to me in effect to be Platonic." To think the essence of things, therefore, or to conceive the "profound life" of things, entails a "thinking"—the "thinking" in thought—that is itself one and the same with the "profound life" or Idea of things. In consonance with Deleuze's efforts to think difference in itself, a difference that is not subordinate to any identity, a Deleuzian attempt to think the nature of thinking itself will similarly not reduce this thinking to being nothing more than the relationship between a thinker and her thoughts. Again, it will be a matter of thinking the Idea of thinking itself, where Idea is understood as a dramatization, which Deleuze defines as follows:

> what I have in mind are dynamisms, dynamic spatio-temporal determinations, that are pre-qualitative and pre-extensive, taking "place" in intensive systems dramatization where differences are distributed at different depths, whose "patients" are larval subjects and whose "function" is to actualize Ideas.[4]

Instead of attempting to understand the nature of thinking by detailing how a thinking subject is related to an object that is thought, Deleuze turns to an account of the relationship between differentiated multiplicities—that is, Ideas—and their differenciated, bifurcated actualizations. The differenciation of Ideas becomes actualized as bifurcations since the "two aspects of differenciation" are already present within the content of the differentiated. As Deleuze put this in an early essay on Bergson, he claims that "what is differentiating itself in two divergent tendencies is a virtuality" (DI, 42), and this "virtuality exists in such a way that it actualizes itself as it dissociates itself; it must dissociate itself to actualize itself" (DI, 40). To understand the nature of thought, therefore, involves detailing the relationship between a differentiated multiplicity—an Idea—where the two divergent tendencies then come to be actualized as the bifurcated dissociation between a thinker and her thought, a producer and its product, and so on.

To clarify the relationship between differentiated multiplicities and differenciated actualities, we must turn to metaphysics, which Deleuze, of course, never shied away from. In particular, I will argue that for a Deleuzian metaphysics of becoming the real is a double movement, a double articulation; or, as Deleuze and Guattari put it in *A Thousand Plateaus*, "God is a lobster." The two movements of this double movement I will call the *movement of indetermination* and the *movement of determination*. This should come as no surprise to those familiar with Deleuze, for in *Logic of Sense* Deleuze argues on the very first page (in the "First Series of Paradoxes of Pure Becoming") that there is a "simultaneity of becoming" that "eludes the present" and does not "tolerate the separation of the distinction of before and after, or of past and future. It pertains," Deleuze concludes, "to the essence of becoming to move and pull in both directions at once."[5]

The movement of the double movement, however, requires a further distinction, or else it risks being thought of as the movement of a determinate, identifiable thing, and hence Deleuze would have failed in his efforts to think the difference in itself that is the profound life of things. Deleuze thus distinguishes between a determinable sense or direction, a movement that can be identified, and the double movement that is the paradoxical "affirmation of both senses or directions at the same time." To illustrate this distinction by way of example, Deleuze turns to Plato. For Plato there is both the dimension of "limited and measured things, of fixed qualities, permanent or temporary which always presuppose pauses and rests, the fixing of presets, and the assignation of subjects," and then there is the dimension of "a pure becoming without measure, a veritable becoming-mad which never rests" (LS, 1–2). It is the former dimension that is generally identified with the Platonism of eternal Ideas, the fixed forms that are impressed upon a passive matter, but it is the Platonism of the later Dialogues that recognizes the "pure becoming without measure." In the *Philebus*, for example, and in a passage cited by Deleuze, Socrates notes that "'Hotter' never stops where it is but is always going a point further, and the same applies to 'colder,' whereas definite quality is something that has stopped going on and is fixed" (24d). The double movement, therefore, is not the dual movement of actualities but is what Deleuze calls a "subterranean dualism" between "that which receives the action of the Idea and that which eludes this action." The first is what we call the *movement of determination*. It is the movement whereby a determinable process leads to a determinate result which exemplifies an Idea. This movement is integral to the standard dualism of model and copy, intelligible and sensible, Idea and matter, mind and body, and so on. That which eludes this movement is what we call the *movement of indetermination*. This is the movement of becoming that eludes the present and the bifurcated actualities and dualisms that come with it. The double movement we will use to understand the nature of thought is precisely the paradoxical affirmation of both the movement of determination and indetermination. There can be no determinate and determinable process or Idea that does not simultaneously involve the indeterminate, problematic Idea.

To begin to situate this double movement within philosophy, and in particular within the philosophical tradition's attempt to think the nature of thought itself, let us turn first to Frege. Frege's theory of sense and reference exemplifies the double movement but Frege resists the movement of indetermination. In accounting for the fact that two things may be equal in that they refer to the same thing, for instance that Clark Kent and Superman are the same in that they each refer to the same human being, just as the morning star and the evening star each refers to Venus, and yet to say that Clark Kent *is* Superman is not the same as saying Clark Kent is Clark Kent. Lois Lane, for instance, did not take it to be the case that Clark Kent is Superman, and for a long time many thought the evening star and the morning star were distinct entities. It is to account for this fact that Frege draws upon his distinction between sense and reference (*Bedeutung*). Although Clark Kent and Superman, morning star and evening star, each have the same referent, they each have a different sense. As Frege puts it, and as is obvious with the case of Lois Lane, in "grasping a sense, one is not thereby assured of a *Bedeutung*,"[6] or, to state it more precisely in the case of Lois Lane, one is not assured of recognizing that two distinct senses have one and the same *Bedeutung*. In fiction, however, one may grasp the sense without the *Bedeutung*. In most cases one can read a fictional tale and not even assume that there is a *Bedeutung*. In a state of what Frege calls "aesthetic delight," one can read the story of the sacking of Troy, following all along the details of the narrative—the places, times, and people involved—and never once wonder or even consider whether there actually is or was such a city as Troy. When we move from the perspective of "aesthetic delight" to one of "scientific investigation," however, we move in turn from a stance wherein one is only concerned with the sense of what is said to the stance where one is interested to know whether there is a referent (*Bedeutung*) that corresponds to this sense. When Heinrich Schliemann set out to discover whether there was once a city of Troy that was sacked at the place and time as discussed in Homer's epic, he sought to discover the *Bedeutung*, in this case the physical object, that corresponded to the sense of Troy.

Things become more complicated for Frege as he turns to discuss concepts which are, as both Frege and Deleuze admit, integral to what is going on when one is thinking or conceiving things. In our previous examples of Troy, Clark Kent, and morning star the sense of the word corresponded to a distinct and determinate object (or thing) as its referent (*Bedeutung*), whereas a concept word (Frege's term) such as planet, superhero, and city does not refer to a singular object but instead refers to a functional relationship between a concept and the differentiated "set" of determinate and determinable objects that are correctly identified by the concept word. Frege thus recognizes that "objects and concepts are fundamentally different."[7] Whereas the *Bedeutung* of a proper name such as Clark Kent, et cetera, is an object, the *Bedeutung* of a concept word is not an object, nor is it a plurality of objects, but it is a concept; and a concept, for Frege, is what he calls an unsaturated function, an incompleteness that waits upon the determinate objects to complete or saturate the concept. For Frege this is essential to the nature of thought itself, which includes both the predicative nature of the concept as unsaturated and an object which completes this unsaturated function; and the referent (*Bedeutung*) of the thought itself is its truth value. To express the thought that "The morning star is a planet," we relate the unsaturated function of the concept word planet to the object that is the *Bedeutung* of morning star, and if the object is indeed that which the concept maps on to then the reference of the thought is its truth value—in short, one has expressed a truth. What is critical here for Frege is that every thought has an element that is incomplete, an unsaturated concept that is not to be confused with an object, and yet at the same time a concept must for Frege be fully determinate and determinable. As Frege puts it, "It must be determinate for every object whether it falls under a concept or not; a concept word which does not meet this requirement on its *Bedeutung* is *bedeutunglos* [that is, meaningless]."[8]

We can now begin to see the necessary double movement of Deleuzian metaphysics come to the surface in Frege. On the one hand, Frege is quite clearly in line with the movement of determination. For one to express a meaningful thought, even in the context of fiction, it "must be determinate for every object whether it falls under a concept or not." In understanding the manner in which an Idea is "fully differentiated in itself," there is the Fregean (traditional Platonic) understanding of an Idea (or concept for Frege) where it is fully determinate whether or not an object falls under an Idea or not. The second movement, as we saw, eludes the movement of determination, the stasis of present, determinate and determinable objects and things. For Frege this movement appears as he discusses the nature of concepts themselves—in short, when the concept word becomes the object referred to by another word, such as when one expresses the thought, "a planet is a concept word." In this thought the unsaturated component is the concept, and hence "it must be," according to Frege, "determinate for every object whether if falls under a concept or not." We have encountered what Graham Priest has referred to as a limit of thought, meaning that there are certain aspects of thought itself that cannot themselves be thought.[9] In the case of Frege, while concepts are integral to thought, they themselves cannot be the object of a thought. As Frege argues, "we really should outlaw the expression 'the *Bedeutung* of the concept word' because the definite article before '*Bedeutung*' points to an object and belies the predicative nature of the concept"; and Frege will add that we need to take our language and its references to concepts as if they were objects with a grain of salt and recognize that concepts are not objects. Stated baldly, although it "must be determinate for every object whether it falls under a concept or not," if a concept is not going to be a meaningless one (*bedeutunglos*), a concept is itself one of the determinate objects that fall under another concept (although concepts can be in nested relationships to other concepts, they are nonetheless not objects). Concepts thus elude the fully determinate presence of objects. As Priest points out, however, in making this claim about concepts being that which cannot be thought by thought—in other words, in encountering the limit of thought—Frege has nonetheless paradoxically thought that which cannot be thought. To state this in terms of the double movement, there is a subterranean dualism at the center of Frege's efforts to think the nature of thought itself: on the one hand there is the relationship between determinate concepts and the fully determinate objects that fall under these concepts, and on the other hand there is that which, as Deleuze put it, "eludes this action." As "hotter" and "colder," on Deleuze's reading of Plato, elude the determinate state or quality of being hot or cold, so too does the "thinking" that Frege seeks to understand elude the determinate thoughts that are expressed within and by determinate relationships between concepts and their objects. It is this "thinking" that Deleuze seeks to engender in thought, and this involves the paradoxical double movement of determinate thought and that which eludes thought and which is the power of creation, the profound life, essential to what it is to think.

Let us turn now to Hume for another example of the double movement that is essential to what it is to think, and for there to be creation in thought. This will also bring to the fore key affinities between Hume's philosophy and the philosophical project of Deleuze—namely, Deleuze's effort to think difference in itself. For Hume the problem of conceiving things is very different from what it was for Frege. For Frege the referent (*Bedeutung*) of a thought is its truth value, and hence the task and problem associated with thinking becomes one of determining the truth value of the thought. For Hume, by contrast, the problem becomes one of determination itself. In other words, Frege presupposes the possibility of determining an object that will give a thought a truth value (movement of determination), whereas for Hume determination itself is undermined by the sheer excess of possibilities. For any thought where there is a determinate object that saturates the thought and gives it a truth value the determinateness of this object is undermined by the fact that for Hume anything we can conceive is possible.[10] For example, the thought that "this is a nice glass of red wine" that follows my having taken a sip of a nice red wine from a glass can be conceived to be another liquid that tastes as such because of a neurological disorder; or it can be conceived to be colored water that changes tastes randomly and it just happens to taste like wine when I drink it; and so on. In a famous passage from his *Enquiry*, Hume argues:

> When I see, for instance, a Billiard-ball moving in a straight line towards another; even suppose motion in the second ball should by accident be suggested to me, as the result of their contact or impulse; may I not conceive that a hundred different events might follow from that cause? . . . Why then should we give the preference to one, which is no more consistent or conceivable than the rest? All our reasonings a priori will never be able to show any foundation for this preference.[11]

Now, it might seem we are conflating an epistemological skepticism with a metaphysics of modality—that is, with Hume's metaphysical critique of a priori necessity. For Frege we clearly begin with a determinate sense which then enables us to determine whether there is a reference which satisfies it. As we saw, for Frege a thought has a determinate sense that selects which objects do or do not fall under the concept which is the unsaturated, predicative aspect of the thought. Similarly for Hume, it would seem, there is the relationship between the impressions and the ideas which are their less lively copies. Thus a thought we have is merely the less lively copy and/or assemblage of impressions—such as the thought of a pink elephant, a billiard-ball leaping off the table after a straight shot, and so on. But now we can begin to see the becoming-mad nature of the movement of indetermination. The reason we come to have the preference we do for a certain connection and association of ideas is habit and custom, which gives us through repetition the strength and liveliness that results in the preference for one over another. For a madman, however, as Hume points out, they may have the same force and vivacity from a single exposure. What narrows down the "hundred different events [that] might follow" from any particular cause is habit, and yet these habits may be undermined and are forever threatened by madness and delusion, or the movement of indetermination that can either keep our thoughts from settling on one preference or indiscriminately moving from preference to preference, where we again fail to settle on an established habit and preference.

But do we not begin, at the very least, with the determinate impressions and their faithful copies, the ideas? As I have argued elsewhere, it would be a mistake to think so.[12] Rather than think of the multiplicity of impressions and ideas as a collection of determinate identities, it is best understood along the lines of Deleuze's reading of the late Plato where the Idea is a multiplicity, with multiplicity not being understood, as in the conventional reading of Plato, as a set of determinate identities gathered under the aegis of an Idea that is the model of which the determinate identities are copies. Instead, the very nature of determinate self-identity through time needs to be accounted for, and as I argue in *Deleuze's Hume*, this identity is fictioned, or created, and with this move we come to the necessary double movement, the profound life that is the essential nature of determinate things. Thus for Deleuze to understand the nature of thinking as an Idea is not, therefore, a matter of epistemology, of detailing how a thinking subject comes to have the thoughts they do and how these thoughts in turn give us access to a world that consists of everything that is thought and known; rather, for Deleuze we begin with metaphysics, with the double movement that is the very reality of determinate things.

To clarify this metaphysics further, and more precisely to understand its relationship to Deleuze's claim that the task of philosophy is to create concepts, we will first situate our account of a Deleuzian metaphysics of double movement relative to recent debates concerning ontological realism, nihilism, and anti-realism. More to the point, this discussion will allow us to account for the relationship between the differentiated content of the Idea and its bifurcated, dissociated actualities.

To account for the differentiated content of the Idea relative to a Deleuzian metaphysics, it is necessary first to note the importance of two traditional concepts in Deleuze's thought: the univocity of being and the principle of sufficient reason. In affirming the univocity of being, Deleuze maintains the traditional position that "Being is said in a single and same sense" (DR, 36) of all that is, but it is univocal, however, not of the determinate, identifiable beings that are, but "of all [their] individuating differences" (DR, 36). In other words, when it comes to differences, Deleuze is clear that "it is not the differences which are and must be; it is being which is Difference . . . we and our individuality . . . remains equivocal in and for a univocal Being" (DR, 39). Put in other words, rather than differences being understood in terms of the Being they speak, it is Being itself that is to be understood in terms of the difference it speaks univocally—being is difference, or the individuating differences of the Idea. As Deleuze puts it, the "Univocity of being, in so far as it is immediately related to difference, demands that we show how individuating difference precedes generic, specific and even individual differences within being" (DR, 39). This brings us to the principle of sufficient reason. As traditionally understood, the principle of sufficient reason (attributed to Leibniz) states that for every entity, event, or proposition there is a sufficient explanation as to why the entity exists, the event occurs, or the proposition is true. What provides for such a sufficient explanation, however, has traditionally been thought to be another being or state of affairs. There is another entity, an unmoved mover perhaps, that is the sufficient explanation for the fact that other entities exist; another determinate event or conjunction of events is the sufficient explanation for a particular event; and a state of affairs in the world, a truth-maker, provides the sufficient explanation for the truth of a given proposition. For Deleuze, by contrast, what provides the sufficient explanation for determinate entities, events, and propositions is not another determinate entity or being but difference itself, the individuating differences that precede "generic, specific and even individual differences within being." This is what Deleuze will also call the "field of individuation," and it is this field of individuating differences that constitutes the differentiated content of the Idea, the problematic dimension or horizon that "designates," Deleuze claims , "precisely the objectivity of Ideas" (DR, 280). It is this problematic dimension of the Ideas, with their individuating differences, that provides for Deleuze the sufficient explanation for "generic, specific and even individual differences within being."

But what is this differentiated content of the Idea, these individuating differences that are not to be confused with the determinate, individual differences within being—that is, the differences between identifiable, determinate things? In a privileged example within Deleuze's work, Deleuze draws from the example of an egg, going so far as to claim that "The world is an egg" (DR, 251). The example of the egg, moreover, provides an excellent example and model for what Deleuze sees as the "order of reasons" in providing a sufficient explanation for what is, in the generic, specific and individual sense of is—this is the order of "differentiation-individuation-dramatization-differenciation" (DR, 251). For Deleuze there are differences of intensity with respect to the relations between the content of the egg, its nucleus, genes, cytoplasm, and the numerous proteins. This constitutes the "virtual matter to be organized," according to Deleuze, or this is the differentiated content of the egg. As Deleuze points out, however, the "nucleus and the genes designate only the differentiated matter—in other words, the differential relations which constitute the pre-individual field to be actualized; but their actualization is determined only by the cytoplasm, with its gradients and its fields of individuation" (DR, 251). The cytoplasm initiates the next step of the order of reasons—individuation—and it does so through intensive gradients. For example, when the concentration of a certain protein achieves a particular gradient-threshold, what Deleuze and others will call a singular point, then it signals to a target gene to continue or discontinue with its processing. In the case of the widely studied fruitfly, the protein bicoid is more highly concentrated toward one end of the embryo, and this signals the genes to produce the head and thorax of the fruitfly. In experiments where the gradient was extended the result was a much larger head and thorax relative to the rest of the body, and in mutations where there is no bicoid gradient the embryo will not develop a head or a thorax.[13] What is important here is not the particular protein but the concentration gradient, the field of intensive, individuating differences that, when combined with other gradients, provides the signals that trigger genetic processes and account for the development of complex organisms.

An important point to stress is that the differentiated content of the egg, and this is true for the differentiated content of Ideas as well, is, as Deleuze argues, "perfectly determinable"[14]—and the fruitfly studies are further evidence for this as well. It is the intensive field of this perfectly determinable, differentiated content that is crucial in understanding the processes of individuation, as the example of the egg shows. Moreover, we could understand the determinate, individuated content of the egg itself along similar lines. Take the bicoid protein, for instance. As with other proteins, carbon is one of the essential elements, but as I have argued elsewhere, carbon itself depends upon particular individuating processes with threshold gradients—in this case the heat and pressure of large stars—that result in the fusion of the atoms that constitute carbon. The point, in other words, is not that we are reducing individuation to a difference of degree between a determinate and determinable content such as bicoid protein; rather, it is intensive, individuating difference all the way down; or being is difference.

The third step in the order of reasons is dramatization. Deleuze refers to this as the step where the intensive field, such as the threshold gradients of bicoid in the case of the fruitfly, become "incarnated in spatio-temporal dynamisms," meaning that the intensive field becomes the process of a fruitfly embryo developing a head and thorax, along with the other spatio-temporal dynamisms that similarly incarnate various intensive fields. These spatio-temporal dynamisms, or this dramatization, in turn become actualized as the individual fruitfly, or this is where the differenciation that results in the mutually exclusive differences between genera, species, and individuals arises. As Deleuze argues, "differenciation is always simultaneously differenciation of species and parts, of qualities and extensities . . . ," and yet, as Deleuze makes clear in his "Method of Dramatization" talk, these constituted entities, species and parts, et cetera, are where illusion comes in. Whereas the differentiated content of the idea is perfectly real and determinable, the "illusion . . . appears afterwards, on the side of the constituted extensions and the qualities which fill these extensions." This is much like the play of differences in the game of life, where constituted patterns such as the glider emerge and take on causal efficacies of their own. Do we have, then, a Deleuzian mereology? The differentiated content of the egg becomes, through the order of reasons sketched above, the individual fruitfly of a particular species and with numerous parts that constitute the individual (e.g., head and thorax, etc.); and the differentiated content of the embryo itself, such as bicoid, for instance, is itself a constituted pattern of spatio-temporal dynamisms, including carbon, which in turn is a constituted pattern of spatio-temporal dynamisms that include the furnaces of stars, gravitational pressure, and other intensive fields. Can we say, then, that carbon is a necessary part of bicoid which in turn is a necessary part of the fruitfly? For Deleuze the answer is no. For Deleuze, what is primary are the individuating factors, or the univocity of Being as difference, and when it comes to "species and parts" they, as Deleuze puts it, "cover over the preceding factors" (DR, 278), factors, as we saw, that are the sufficient reason for the determination of species and parts in the first place.

Understood in this way, Deleuze does not adopt the traditional mereological position with respect to the composition of individuals, whereby one individual is composed of many parts. David Lewis, for example, adopts a fairly standard mereological position—namely, there is a relationship of whole to parts wherein the whole is composed of the parts. Where Lewis breaks with the standard view is in adopting what he calls the principle of Unrestricted Composition, which for him entails that "whenever there are some things, no matter how many or how unrelated or disparate in character they may be, they have a mereological fusion."[15] There is thus, to use Lewis's example, a "trout-turkey" fusion, a "salt beef sandwich" fusion, and unrestricted others. Whenever and wherever there are things, no matter how many, then we have a mereological fusion. Lewis's position regarding composition is known as universalist. Simply put, a universalist believes that mereological sums and fusions exist. By contrast, a nihilist with respect to composition of parts believes that mereological sums never exist. As Ted Sider puts it, nothing is a proper part of anything else. For Deleuze, however, the universalist approach of Lewis is inadequate for it assumes from the start that "there are some things" when it is precisely the identity of individuals that it is the effort of Deleuze's philosophy of difference to account for, and he does this through the order of reasons which begins with pre-individual singularities and the intensive field. At the same time, however, Deleuze is not a nihilist, for as we have seen carbon *is* a part of bicoid which *is* in turn a part of the embryonic processes of the fruitfly. The best term to account for Deleuze's position is one he offers himself—a concrete universal. As Deleuze defines it,

> Ideas are concrete universals in which extension and comprehension go together—not only because they include variety or multiplicity in themselves, but because they include singularity in all its varieties. They subsume the distribution of distinctive or singular points; their distinctive character—in other words, the *distinctness* of Ideas—consists precisely in the distribution of the ordinary and the distinctive, the singular and the regular, and in the extension of the singular across regular points into the vicinity of another singularity. (DR, 176)

Deleuze would be best described then as a concrete universalist. As an example of a concrete universal, Deleuze gives "white light." In an early essay on Bergson, Deleuze claims that white light, as a concrete universal, "gives us an understanding of the particular because it is the far end of the particular. Because things have become nuances or degrees of the concept, the concept itself has become a thing" (DI, 43)—hence a concrete universal. When one thinks of white light, however, and especially when one thinks of white noise in the context of music, one tends to think of chaos or of the absence of music. White noise thus cannot form the basis of any aesthetic judgments regarding music other than the perhaps the judgment that "it's not music." What seems to drive such criticisms is the presupposition that white noise cannot justify any aesthetic taste for as chaos, as information theorists might tell us, it entails an excess of information to the point that nothing can be discerned with any predictable regularity. Or as Ladyman and Ross might say,[16] white noise harbors no trackable patterns and hence lacks reality if we take, as Ladyman and Ross do (following Dan Dennett), the real to be real patterns. One with a fondness for white noise is in effect one with a fondness for nothing at all.

At the basis of the criticism of white noise as I've sketched it here is a premise that Deleuze challenges, and challenges from an admittedly Platonic perspective. The premise is that to be fully real is to be determinate and identifiable, in the sense that Platonic Ideas are traditionally thought to be simple essences that serve as models for the numerous copies and instantiations we see around us. Deleuze rejects this view of Plato, however, but if one has the Platonism of the later dialogues in mind, which involves the assertion that "Ideas are a little like multiplicities which must be traversed by the questions How? How much? In what case?, then yes," Deleuze claims, "everything that I am saying seems to me in effect to be Platonic." Interestingly, Donald Davidson was drawn, both early and late in his career, to the late dialogues of Plato, and the *Philebus* in particular. As Davidson understands the Ideas of Plato, they no longer represent the simple essence or truth such that one can, on grasping this truth, proceed to live the good life. By the time of the *Philebus*, however, Davidson claims that

> The study of the good life develops from a manifest exchange of originally opposed opinions. The goal is not fixed in advance, for the goal is not represented as a matter of finding the nature of some single idea, but rather as knowing the art of discriminating, judging, selecting, and mixing the appropriate elements of a life in a way that exhibits measure, proportion, and stability.[17]

We begin, in short, with "originally opposed" and identified positions and then move, with the goal "not fixed in advance" in an effort to select, mix, and discern the "appropriate elements of a life." As Deleuze understands this effort, we move from a position of intellectual bifurcation, from an either/or of mutually exclusive positions, to a multiplicity of selecting, mixing, and composing a multiplicity of the "appropriate elements of a life." It is this sense of Idea (and with a capital I), the Ideas that "swarm in the fractures" of the originally opposed, bifurcated positions, that Deleuze will use repeatedly throughout *Difference and Repetition.*[18]

Let us return then to the example Deleuze offers of an Idea—the Idea of color—which he claims "is like white light which perplicates in itself the genetic elements and relations of all the colours, but is actualized in the diverse colours with their respective spaces; or the Idea of sound, which is also like white noise" (DR, 206). What we are to make of this, put briefly, is that the Idea as a concrete universal is not a predetermining identity that in effect preforms the determinate identities that come to instantiate the Idea (on the model-copy reading of Plato, for instance); rather, Ideas are what we get as the intensive variations of colors come to be condensed into a single field of intensive variations—that is, white light. But to think of it this way is not quite right if we take the field of intensive variations to be the result of this condensation rather than the condition for differentiating between different colors in the first place. Deleuze makes this point quite clearly in an early essay on Bergson when discussing how white light is what we get when "we send the colors through a convergent lens that concentrates them on the same point: what we have then is 'pure white light,' the very light that 'makes the differences come out between the shades.' So, the different colors are no longer objects *under* a concept, but nuances or degrees of the concept itself" (DI, 43). The point is worth repeating: white light is what "makes the differences come out between the shades," and with this move we return to the core of Deleuze's project, as discussed above: an affirmation of the univocity of Being as Difference. White light is thus not the combination of all the colors that fall under the concept or Idea of color, but it is the very real and concrete condition for the differences between colors.

We can now clarify how Deleuze's metaphysics is neither universalist in the manner of Lewis nor nihilist in the manner of Sider and Cian Dorr. Like Lewis, for Deleuze the concrete universal color—that is, white light—is necessarily related to the many instances of color that can be differentiated from one another. However, this concrete universal is not an already composed and constituted identity that enables us to then group the particular colors "under" the abstract universal, nor is it a unity composed of the many instances through mereological fusion. White light instead "gives us an understanding of the particular because it is the far end of the particular," or it is what "makes the differences come out between the shades," and what this means is that white light does not predetermine which particular colors will be identified as colors, but when such colors are identified it will be by virtue of the differences "between the shades" that white light makes possible. As with Davidson, the Idea of color is not fixed in advance but is continually composed as we discern the differences between the shades. This is what Deleuze will refer to as the power of AND, the power of creativity between the determinate and identifiable; and it is not surprising, but to be expected, that creative efforts are first judged to be white noise—the power of AND, of white noise between the shades, awaits its determinate place before it comes to be identified as the creative product that it is.

We can now return to the metaphysics of the double movement in light of what we have set forth. There is the movement of determination, the movement of indeterminate white noise or virtual multiplicity to determinate colors. This movement involves, as Deleuze (and Guattari) argue, and as I have shown elsewhere, a double articulation. In the context of this essay we have discussed this as the order of reasons, but the two key aspects of the double movement are differentiation and differenciation. In expanding upon the notion that "white light perplicates in itself the genetic elements and relations of all the colours," referring to these elements as the virtual content, or the first of the order of reasons, Deleuze then claims that "We call the determination of the virtual content of an Idea differentiation; we call the actualization of that virtuality into species and distinguished parts (e.g., different colors and their distinguished and distinguishable shades) differenciation" (DR, 207). The processes of individuation and dramatization (the second and third orders of reason) were part of Deleuze's efforts to detail how a virtual multiplicity of elements and reciprocal relations between elements (e.g., the reciprocal relation between the bicoid protein and the targeted gene of the fruitfly) becomes, through intensive fields and gradients and the spatio-temporal dynamisms, the determinate, identifiable individual exhibiting species and parts. Similarly for white light, it too contains, as we have seen, the elements and reciprocal relations of all the colors—this is the first articulation of differentiation—and then the distinct colors become actualized as determinate and distinct colors as the intensive field of white light becomes spatially separated by way of differing intensity gradients (wavelengths) and then a distinct color such as blue emerges (species) and its corresponding shades (parts).

As for the second movement, the movement of indetermination, this is the movement associated with the power of AND. This is the movement from mutually opposed and determinate positions, or from the fracturing and bifurcation of identity, into the multiplicities and concrete universals that made the determinate and distinct positions themselves possible. To return us to where we began, I would now like to call this movement the movement of thought, thought taken in its broadest sense as thinking matter, or conceiving things (emphasis on the things). Where thought enters is with the difference between things. It is at this point where Ideas enter, or what Deleuze will call problems, and with this as well comes the possibility for something new. Deleuze will frequently discuss this process as the process of learning. In "learning to swim or learning a foreign language," for example, Deleuze argues that this

> Means composing singular points of one's own body or one's own language with those of another shape or element, which tears us apart but also propels us into a hitherto unknown and unheard-of world of problems . . . the Idea and "learning" express that extra-propositional or sub-representative problematic instance: the presentation of the unconscious, not the representation of consciousness. (DR, 192)

The key phrase in that passage, at least as this relates to the arguments that have been set forth here, is that learning is something that "tears us apart." In other words, learning creates the fractures, the splits between identifiable elements, individuals, positions, such as a body in the water which "tears us apart" from our accustomed bodily habits, or being in contact with a foreign language that "tears us apart" from the language we speak in order to learn to speak the other language, or to swim. The process of learning, therefore, is a movement of thought, a movement from a determinate encounter (body in water) to an indeterminate, "hitherto unknown and unheard-of world of problems," and from here we may begin the first movement again and actualize a new habit such as swimming or speaking a foreign language. This movement of thought, however, is to be extended beyond merely the human encounter but is, writ large, how things become other and how something new is created. For Deleuze, therefore, it is indeed the case that to think is to create and that "there is no other creation" than the movement of thought.

## NOTES

1. Gilles Deleuze, *Difference and Repetition*, trans. Paul Patton (New York: Columbia University Press, 1995), 147. Hereafter cited as DR.
2. Gilles Deleuze and Félix Guattari, *Anti-Oedipus*, trans. Robert Hurley (Minneapolis: University of Minnesota Press, 1983), 4. Hereafter cited as AO.
3. See "The Method of Dramatization," in *Desert Islands*, trans. Mike Taormina (New York: Semiotext(e), 2004), 116. Hereafter cited as DI.
4. Deleuze, "The Method of Dramatization," 108.
5. Gilles Deleuze, *The Logic of Sense*, trans. Mark Lester and ed. Constantin Boundas (New York: Columbia University Press, 1990), 1. Hereafter cited as LS.
6. Gottlob Frege, "On Sinn and Bedeutung," in *The Frege Reader*, ed. Michael Beaney (London: Blackwell Publishing, 1997), 153.
7. Frege, "On Sinn and Bedeutung," 174–75.
8. Frege, "On Sinn and Bedeutung," 178.
9. See Graham Priest, *Beyond the Limits of Thought* (New York: Oxford University Press, 2003).
10. David Hume, *A Treatise of Human Nature*, ed. L. A. Selby-Bigge (Oxford: Clarendon Press, 1978), 32: "an established maxim in metaphysics is: 'whatever the mind clearly conceives includes the idea of possible existence or in other words, that nothing we imagine is absolutely impossible.' And again from the Abstract to the Treatise: 'The mind can always conceive any effect to follow from any cause, and indeed any event to follow upon another: whatever we conceive is possible, at least in a metaphysical sense: but wherever demonstration takes place, the contrary is impossible, and implies a contradiction.'" Ibid., 650.
11. David Hume, *An Enquiry Concerning Human Understanding*, ed. Tom Beauchamp (Oxford: Oxford University Press, 2000), 27.

12. See Jeffrey Bell, *Deleuze's Hume* (Edinburgh: Edinburgh University Press, 2009).

13. See Christiane Nüsslein-Volhard, "Gradients That Organize Embryo Development," Max Planck Institute for Developmental Biology. Accessed January 11, 2013. http://www.eb.tuebingen.mpg.de/departments/3-genetics/christiane-nusslein-volhard/gradients-that-organize-embryo-development.

14. Deleuze stresses this point in his "Method of Dramatization" talk as well, in response to one of Philonenko's questions. Deleuze argues that "it seems to me that we have the means to penetrate into the realm of the sub-representative, to reach right into the root of spatiotemporal dynamisms, into the Ideas which actualize themselves in them: ideal elements and events, relations and singularities, are perfectly determinable."

15. David Lewis, *Parts of Classes* (Oxford: Wiley-Blackwell, 1991), 8.

16. See James Ladyman, Don Ross et al., *Every Thing Must Go* (Oxford: Oxford University Press, 2009).

17. Donald Davidson, *Truth, Language, and History* (Oxford: Oxford University Press, 2005), 267.

18. Deleuze, *Difference and Repetition*, 170: "Ideas are exactly the thoughts of the Cogito, the differentials of thought. Moreover, in so far as the Cogito refers to a fractured I, an I split from end to end by the form of time which runs through it, it must be said that Ideas swarm in the fracture, constantly emerging on its edges, ceaselessly coming out and going back, being composed in a thousand different manners." By arguing that Ideas are "composed in a thousand different manners," we have further evidence that Deleuze is not a nihilist with respect to composition.

## BIBLIOGRAPHY

Bell, Jeffrey. *Deleuze's Hume*. Edinburgh: Edinburgh University Press, 2009.

Davidson, Donald. *Truth, Language, and History*. Oxford: Oxford University Press, 2005.

Deleuze, Gilles. *The Logic of Sense*. Translated by Mark Lester. Edited by Constantin Boundas. New York: Columbia University Press, 1990.

———. *Difference and Repetition*. Translated by Paul Patton. New York: Columbia University Press, 1995.

———. "The Method of Dramatization." In *Desert Islands*. Translated by Mike Taormina. New York: Columbia University Press, 2004.

Frege, Gottlob. "On Sinn and Bedeutung." In *The Frege Reader*, edited by Michael Beaney. London: Blackwell, 1997.

Hume, David. *A Treatise of Human Nature*, edited by L. A. Selby-Bigge. Oxford: Clarendon Press, 1978.

———. *An Enquiry Concerning Human Understanding*, edited by Tom Beauchamp. Oxford: Oxford University Press, 2000.

Ladyman, James, Don Ross et al., *Every Thing Must Go*. Oxford: Oxford University Press, 2009.

Lewis, David. *Parts of Classes*. Oxford: Wiley-Blackwell, 1991.

Nüsslein-Volhard, Christiane. "Gradients That Organize Embryo Development." Max Planck Institute for Developmental Biology. Accessed January 11, 2013. http://www.eb.tuebingen.mpg.de/departments/3-genetics/christiane-nusslein-volhard/gradients-that-organize-embryo-development.

Priest, Graham. *Beyond the Limits of Thought*. New York: Oxford University Press, 2003.

*Chapter Thirteen*

# Pierre Bourdieu's *Habitus*

Nick Crossley

The term *habitus* has been used by a number of key sociological thinkers, often loosely and usually to denote shared ways of life or a national (or group specific) character. In contemporary sociology, however, the term is strongly identified with the work of Pierre Bourdieu. Bourdieu gives "habitus" a more technical meaning or rather, over time and in different projects, he gives it several such meanings. The variations in his usage reflect a gradual refinement and development of his thinking and an engagement with criticisms of his early work. They reflect the different weaknesses he perceives in the work of whichever "sparring partner" he is engaging with at the time and a corresponding strength which he wishes to claim for his own work. In addition, they reflect the different questions that he is addressing and, as both a theorist and an empirical researcher, the different contexts that he is researching. To name only four such contexts, Bourdieu has explored: 1) the reproduction of inequality through the French educational system (e.g., *Reproduction in Education, Society and Culture* and *The State Nobility*); 2) social variations in taste and consumption (e.g., *Distinction* and *The Love of Art*); 3) the construction of both philosophical and literary texts (e.g., *The Political Ontology of Martin Heidegger* and *The Rules of Art*); and 4) the practical logic of everyday forms of action in Kabyle society (e.g., *Outline of a Theory of Practice* and *The Logic of Practice*). He uses "habitus" in each of these contexts and while there is a strong common thread running through his usage he adapts the concept in each case to meet the different intellectual demands made upon him.

In this chapter I will try to capture both the common thread and the variations in Bourdieu's use of "habitus." I begin with a brief reflection upon the contrast that some sociologists, including Bourdieu, have drawn between "habitus" and the more widely used concept of habit.

## 1. HABITUS AND HABIT

The concept of habit has a long history and it has acquired quite different meanings at different points in this history. As Charles Camic observes, however, it fell out of favor in sociology during the twentieth century on account of its appropriation within crude forms of psychological/physiological behaviorism.[1] The behaviorists applied it to very basic behaviors and interpreted it mechanically, in terms of conditioned (stimulus-response) reflexes. With its concern for more complex and purposive action sociology had little use for "habit" understood thus.

The use of "habitus" by Bourdieu and others must be understood in light of this. "Habitus" is intended to capture all that is useful, indeed sociologically indispensable, in the concept of "habit," while simultaneously rejecting the more problematic connotations (and denotations) that "habit" acquired from behaviorism. As Bourdieu explains in a footnote to one of his earlier discussions of habitus:

> One of the reasons for the use of the term habitus is the wish to set aside the common conception of habit as a mechanical assembly or preformed programme, as Hegel does when in the *Phenomenology of Mind* he speaks of "habit as dexterity."[2]

More positively, Marcel Mauss, whose work influenced Bourdieu, comments:

> I have had this notion of the social nature of "*the habitus*" for many years. Please note that I use the Latin word—it should be understood in France—*habitus*. The word translates infinitely better than "*habitude*" (habit or custom), the "*hexis*," the "acquired ability" and "faculty" of Aristotle. . . . These "habits" do not vary just with individuals and their imitations; they vary between societies, educations, proprieties and fashions, prestiges. In them we should see the techniques and work of collective and individual practical reason rather than, in the ordinary way, merely the soul and its repetitive faculties.[3]

There are three key points in this passage. The first is Mauss's reference to Aristotle. "Habitus," for him, is an attempt to restore a specifically Aristotelian sense to "habit." Second, integral to this, he rejects a mechanistic interpretation, conceiving of habitus as ability and as a facet of practical reason. Habitus belong to the realm of intelligent, moral and rational action. They are not stimulus-response pathways nor should we associate them exclusively with simple behaviors. Third, habitus are defined in social terms. They are "social facts," in Durkheim's sense,[4] varying between social groups and historical eras and thereby characterizing those groups and eras. Individuals may have their own distinctive habitus but Mauss's interest is focused on the collective, social level.

The above passage, for example, is taken from a discussion of "body techniques," wherein Mauss describes how different social groups manifest different "uses" of the body. He claims to find some techniques which are exclusive to specific societies. Some societies have a stock of hunting techniques, for example, and others do not. Other techniques, including walking, dancing, speaking and sexual intercourse, are universal. They exist in every society. But their form varies. These types of variation are often found within societies, moreover, between the genders and other status groups. Social elites are often distinguished, for example, by their way of speaking and comporting themselves. This is not affected, at least not usually and not in the case of those born to privilege. It is just how they speak and act. It is a matter of habitus.

As the reference to "body techniques" suggests, Mauss's concept of habitus invokes a sense of embodied and practical activity. Although he does not elaborate, his account alludes to forms of knowledge and understanding which operate at a pre-reflective, pre-conceptual level, consisting entirely in an embodied mastery of particular types of situation and a capacity to do certain sorts of things. Hunting techniques embody a particular understanding and knowledge of the prey and its environment, for example, and the know-how to trap and subdue it. But this knowledge and understanding are not and often cannot be articulated in discourse. They consist entirely in the ability to hunt effectively and they are indissociable from this embodied ability.

These same themes are important in Bourdieu's version of "habitus." We have already seen that he rejects the idea of habit as a "mechanical assembly" or "pre-formed programme." Habitus, for Bourdieu, involve "dexterity," a form of competence or mastery which affords social actors a capacity to act and react to particular types of situation. Mauss is an influence in this respect but so too is Merleau-Ponty—who, in contrast to Bourdieu, Mauss, and also Husserl, chose to rehabilitate "habit" rather than developing a concept of habitus.[5] Merleau-Ponty's critique of mechanical forms of behaviorism and his phenomenological exploration of embodied knowledge and understanding are taken up, albeit tacitly, in Bourdieu's various discussions of habitus (and the body). Indeed, Dreyfus and Rabinow have argued that Bourdieu's habitus renders the wider existential notion of being-in-the-world, which Merleau-Ponty borrowed from Heidegger's *Being and Time*, and even Heidegger's "Dasein," into a social scientific form.[6] "Habitus," for Bourdieu, denotes the practical understanding and embodied grasp upon the world that constitutes our primordial relation to and manner of being-in it.

This is a far cry from the behaviorist's reflex arcs. However, Bourdieu's earlier uses of habitus often have a more mechanistic feel than his later uses.[7]

One of the ways in which the concept evolves over time is that it loses its residual mechanistic overtones and is increasingly conceived in terms of its flexibility and capacity for adaptive change. This no doubt reflects a response, by Bourdieu, to charges of determinism leveled at his earlier work and related claims that he pays insufficient attention to agency.

At the same time, Bourdieu consistently makes the social and collective nature of habitus central too. He uses the concept to mark differences between different national societies, different types of society (agrarian and industrial), between genders, generations, and professions. He is best known, in sociology, however, for his various investigations of class habitus. This point is central to Bourdieu's conception of habitus and I will return to and elaborate it at various points.

Although he never acknowledges the Aristotelian root of habitus, Aristotelian language is common in Bourdieu's work, such that it is reasonable to assume that his "habitus," again mirroring Mauss, has an Aristotelian root. Somewhat confusingly, for example, in addition to his use of (the Latin) "habitus" he also sometimes uses the Greek term, "hexis," from which it derives and which Aristotle elaborates in the *Nicomachean Ethics*. Moreover, again hinting at an Aristotelian influence, he makes reference to both "ethos" and "doxa," using them in a manner consistent with that of Aristotle. Why he sometimes uses "hexis" and other times "habitus" is never made clear. If there is a difference in use/meaning it is perhaps that he reserves "hexis" specifically for stylistic variations in bodily comportment (sometimes referring specifically to "bodily hexis"). This is speculation, however, in relation to what may be no more than inconsistency.

Finally, again in parallel to Mauss, Bourdieu uses "habitus" to capture the practical and embodied nature of human being. Following Marx's *Economic and Philosophical Manuscripts of 1844*, Merleau-Ponty's *Phenomenology of Perception*, Heidegger's *Being and Time*, and Wittgenstein's *Philosophical Investigations*, each of which influenced him in some ways, he resists Cartesian understandings of the human subject as a disembodied mind whose primary relation to the world consists in reflective thought. The human actor is irreducibly embodied for Bourdieu; located within the world and attached to it, in the first instance, by way of practical mastery. "Habitus" captures this mastery and the various schemas of embodied knowledge and understanding that it involves.

## 2. HABITUS AND SOCIAL PRACTICE

In his more anthropologically driven works Bourdieu uses the habitus concept to steer a path between what he takes to be the equally problematic approaches to the study of social practice represented by (the early) Sartre and Lévi-Strauss.[8] As Bourdieu reads him, Sartre fails to recognize the extent to which actors are shaped by both their own individual biographical trajectories and by the broader, socio-historical context to which they belong. Sartre puts the individual in society but fails to put society "in" the individual; that is, he fails to recognize that and how individual desires, perception, cognition and action are shaped by social experience and by the internalization of collectively shared schemata.[9] Habitus is intended to correct this problem. It captures the way in which the individual is shaped by their own history which, in turn, is shaped by the wider historical process to which they belong:

> Since the history of the individual is never anything other than a certain specification of the collective history of his class or group, *each individual system of dispositions* may be seen as a *structural variant* of all other group or class habitus, expressing the difference between the trajectories and positions inside or outside the class. "Personal" style, the particular stamp marking all products of the same habitus, whether practices or works, is never more than a deviation in relation to the style of a period or class.[10]

Agency is not denied in this account, but it is a situated form of agency which emerges from and draws upon a collective history. It takes shape within the context of pre-existing dispositions or schemata which, contra Sartre, the agent cannot be said to have freely chosen for herself.

Lévi-Strauss, as Bourdieu reads him, is at the opposite extreme to Sartre. He eliminates agency by reducing action to a set of underlying rules which actors are said to (often unconsciously) follow, thereby reproducing enduring patterns or structures. Bourdieu is not averse to the idea that action, or practice, is structured. This is another reason for his opposition to Sartre. Sartre's position, on some interpretations, reduces society and history to an aggregate effect of the free actions of multiple individuals and, as such, is poorly placed to explain the enduring patterns that sociology, anthropology and history reveal within the social world. The concept of "rules" is inadequate to the job too, according to Bourdieu, however.

In part his opposition centers upon agency. Bourdieu opposes the "death of the subject" and "dissolving of man" (by recourse to rules and structures) celebrated by Lévi-Strauss and other structuralists, with its dire consequences for agency. A strong concept of agency is necessary for both political and sociological reasons and the concept of habitus is intended to facilitate this. Habitus are the forms of competence, the schemata of practical understanding and the preferences that make agency possible and meaningful. They reflect the social location of the actor (society, era, generation, gender, class, etc.), situating her within the evolving socio-historical world, but not dissolving her into her position as structuralism sought to do.

Bourdieu also has a number of more specific objections to the idea of rules, as posited both within Lévi-Strauss's structuralism and Parsons's "normative" functionalism, however.[11] Some accounts, he argues, focus upon explicit rules that social agents talk about in research interviews: for example, "oh, we always do this" or "we never do that." This is just an official picture of the social world, he objects, which often belies a more complex and conflict-ridden reality. Defined thus, he argues, rules are bent in practice as people pursue their own strategic ends. They are contested and fought over. As such they do not suffice for an explanatory sociological account.

A further problem with "rules," in this sense, is that they only provide a very broad parameter for containing behavior which agents can strategically maneuver within. A society's rules may stipulate how marriage partners are to be selected, for example, but they do not stipulate whom a person should marry, and that leaves considerable room for decision and "strategy." A sociology which focuses only on the rule, to the detriment of the strategy, misses all of this.

However, where rules are not formulated by lay actors themselves, where they are inferred by the social scientific observer on the basis of regularities in conduct, they are only descriptive devices and cannot be invoked in causal accounts. Such rules do not exist for the lay actors whose conduct is under scrutiny and it makes no sense, therefore, to suppose that they are following such rules. I may describe regularities in actors' conduct by formulating those regularities as rules—for example, if *x* then *y*, never *z*, et cetera—but those are *my rules*, they have nothing to do with the actor and I cannot invoke them to explain her conduct, as the structuralists are inclined to do.

Some structuralists proleptically challenge such objections by arguing that their rules are real but unconscious. It is not clear what sense it makes to talk of actors unconsciously following rules, however, and Bourdieu prefers to say that action is guided by a practical sense or "competence": a "feel for the game." I am able to speak and write intelligible English, for example, not because I follow rules (either consciously or unconsciously) but because I have acquired a practical grasp of the language: a linguistic habitus.

Finally, rules must be applied appropriately, at the right time, in the right way and in the right place, which begs the question whether rule following itself requires rules. This raises the possibility of an infinite regress in which each set of rules presupposes a prior set. We avoid this pitfall, in Bourdieu's view, if we replace rules with habitus; that is, with practical sense and a "feel for the game."[12]

Habitus qua "feel for the game" corresponds in some part to "understanding" as rendered by Merleau-Ponty in the *Phenomenology* or Wittgenstein in the *Investigations*. Insofar as habitus are adjusted to "the game," the actor is able to "go on"; to act appropriately. They also incorporate a focus upon strategy, however, such as Bourdieu believes is missing in the structuralist's rule-governed universe. In virtue of her habitus the actor is able to act "instinctively" in ways which are advantageous to her; "advantage," in this respect, meaning that she accrues "capital" (see below) which has value in whatever "game" she is playing, or to introduce another concept of Bourdieu's, whatever "field" she is involved in. Sport provides good examples of this. The pace of sport is often such that actors have no time to think reflectively about their next move. They rely upon "instinct." Such "instinct" is social; it inclines the athlete to act in ways which accord with the arbitrary conventions of whatever game they are playing. But it is not mechanical. It is intelligent and strategic. Where not countered by the intervention of another player or beset by unforeseeable contingencies it puts the actor in an advantageous position, manifesting both an understanding of the game and a strategic capacity to succeed within it. The soccer player who spontaneously launches into a run, heading for an empty space and arriving there just as the ball does, in time and at the right angle from which to take a shot at goal, captures this.

"The game" is a long-standing metaphor in social science, not least in game theory. Bourdieu doubtless takes something from game theory in his appropriation of this metaphor but he purports to be a critic. On one level, for example, his "feel for the game" is posited as an alternative to the notion of rational calculation presupposed in most forms of game theory. Actors do not think reflectively (athletes do not have time). They are guided by a socially acquired intuitive sense. On another level, his games, or "fields," involve culturally arbitrary elements. Even their ends are in some part conventional, such that actors must learn to "believe in the game" and invest, emotionally, in it before it will mean anything to them and they will be inspired to play. As such they are a far cry from the "state of nature" beloved of many game theorists.

Fields are "serious" games which, in contrast to soccer or chess, we do not see as games. They are games "in" but not "for themselves." But they are games. And the social world comprises multiple such games; tournaments in which actors, equipped to varying degrees by their habitus, pursue different forms of economic and cultural advantage (capital). From politics to science, literature to fashion, social life is a complex of games whose players act on the basis of a deep rooted "practical sense"; a "feel for the game" or habitus.

In opposing "habitus" to the conscious calculation invoked in some forms of game theory Bourdieu also allows for a degree of self-deception or Sartrean "bad faith." Habitus operate at a pre-reflective level, "below the level of consciousness or language, beyond the reach of introspective scrutiny,"[13] such that actors are not always aware of the strategic adaptation of their activities to "games" which, again, they may not be aware of as such. Social life sometimes requires that actors disavow selfish motivations which nevertheless do and perhaps must steer their conduct, Bourdieu believes, and habitus afford this insofar as strategy becomes "instinctive" and need not be reflected upon. This claim is clearly highly contentious and Bourdieu never addresses the many questions which it begs.

## 3. STRUCTURES AND FIELDS

Bourdieu's opposition to structuralism is not an opposition to the concept of structure itself. He sometimes describes habitus as structures and he believes that they have a crucial role in the reproduction of wider social structures (much as rules do for Lévi-Strauss). They are shaped by social structures external to them and they shape such structures, in a recursive manner, reproducing the abovementioned patterns of the social world. In a somewhat convoluted passage, for example, he argues that habitus are:

> systems of durable, transposable dispositions, structured structures predisposed to function as structuring structures, that is, as principles which generate and organise practices and representations that can be objectively adapted to their outcomes without presupposing a conscious aiming at ends or an express mastery of the operations necessary in order to attain them. Objectively "regulated" and "regular" without being in any way the product of obedience to rules, they can be collectively orchestrated without being the product of an organising action of a conductor.[14]

One's linguistic habitus, for example, is formed through internalization of linguistic structures, which is itself an effect of engagement with such structures through participation in a linguistic community. However, the survival of linguistic structures depends upon correct speech and thus upon habitus. There would be no social structures without habitus. Adapting this same point to fields, we acquire a "feel for the game" by playing it and internalizing its constitutive structures. But those constitutive structures only survive in virtue of actors continuing to play the game. Players exist only in virtue of the game and the game exists only in virtue of players. This circle is broken by time. Older generations of players draw newer players into a game that is already ongoing.

Importantly, this entails that "the game" itself is often taken for granted and remains unquestioned. Bourdieu makes this point in relation to politics and the state in particular. Arguing against contractarian, Weberian, and Marxist theories, which each suppose that social and political order rests upon conscious (albeit in some cases manipulated) consent, Bourdieu argues that political order is maintained because its premises are not in question; because they are taken for granted at a pre-reflective level and are seldom brought into discourse. He often conceptualizes this in terms of doxa rather than habitus; doxa is that which is not brought into question, what we accept without reflection. Doxa is conceived in a way which overlaps with habitus, however, emphasizing embodiment and practice. Bourdieu claims, for example, that adherence to political order is achieved not by "forms of consciousness but *dispositions of the body*."[15] Social order is maintained to the extent that we continue to do whatever we do without giving it much thought.

In a similar vein, Bourdieu notes that habitus can act as a censor, shaping discourse to fit particular fields and removing that which would be deemed inappropriate. In a discussion of the fit between Heidegger's politics and his philosophy, for example, he argues that Heidegger's practical mastery of the philosophical field allowed him to sublimate political sentiments into it which could not be stated in their raw political form because they would not be recognized as philosophical.[16] Heidegger instinctively edited those of his utterances intended for the philosophical field in accordance with demands of the field, perhaps suppressing some sentiments that he expressed in other contexts but also translating others into a philosophical idiom.

Similarly, in a brief and polemical critique of the media Bourdieu claims that journalists learn to anticipate the objections of their editors (who learn to anticipate the objections of their proprietors) such that they effectively censor themselves, sometimes to the point where they no longer realize what they are doing.[17] This is in a context, moreover, where the relative autonomy of the "journalistic field," relative to the economic field, is diminishing. Journalists are experiencing a loss of their freedom of expression but at the same time accommodating to that loss and gradually losing sight of it.

## 4. TASTE AND DISTINCTION

Bourdieu uses the concept of fields to gain an analytic purchase upon the differentiation of society. Any society, or at least any modern, complex society, comprises multiple fields within which actors compete for and struggle over resources (capital) of various kinds. Participation in any of these fields presupposes a "feel for the game" which is inculcated by means of participation and also perhaps by means of earlier formative experiences. Each field presupposes a "feel" and thus habitus.

Society is differentiated in another way too, however. It is unequal. Actors have different amounts of what Bourdieu refers to as "capital"; that is, goods and resources which have exchange value in one or more fields. He identifies a variety of forms of capital across his various works but the main two are economic capital, which is self-explanatory, and cultural capital, which involves objects and abilities with a cultural value, not least educational qualifications which can be used to procure further goods, such as economic capital or status (symbolic capital), within particular fields. The social world is differentiated according to the distribution of these two forms of capital, he argues. Actors vary in terms of their overall wealth (economic and cultural combined) or *volume* of capital, and they vary in terms of the *composition* of their capital; that is, the relative weighting of economic and cultural capital in their portfolio.

Detailed statistical analysis in his most famous study, *Distinction*, indicates that habitus are shaped by these inequalities: clusters of actors defined by different volumes and compositions of capital, that is to say, *social classes*, manifest different habitus. More specifically, they have different tastes. A preference for avant-garde art is more likely among the culturally wealthy, for example, while the economically wealthy might prefer more conservative artistic forms, such as classical ballet. Meanwhile, those poor in both forms of capital shun either alternative in preference to the objects and pursuits of popular or folk culture. Such aesthetic differences, as applied to both art and lifestyle, have been a major focus of sociological interest in Bourdieu and his habitus concept, and a source of many efforts at (partial and in some cases complete) empirical replication of his now somewhat dated study.

There is a potentially confusing overlap here between habitus and cultural capital, especially as the latter is said, in some cases, to assume an embodied form—it may also assume an objectified form (i.e., ownership of cultural objects) or an institutionalized form (e.g., educational qualifications). For example, Bourdieu argues that the bourgeoisie are distinguished by a peculiar "use of the mouth." They speak from the front of their mouths, which gives them a distinctive accent, and they also eat and laugh in this "tight lipped" way:

> Language is a body technique, and specifically linguistic, especially phonetic, competence is a dimension of bodily hexis in which one's whole relation to the social world, and one's wholly socially informed relation to the world, are expressed. [ . . . ] The most frequent articulatory position is an element in an overall way of using the mouth (in talking but also in eating, drinking, laughing etc.) [ . . . ] in the case of the lower classes, articulatory style is quite clearly part of a relation to the body that is dominated by the refusal of "airs and graces" [ . . . ] Bourgeois dispositions convey in their physical postures of tension and exertion . . . the bodily indices of quite general dispositions towards the world and other people, such as haughtiness and disdain.[18]

Is this use of the mouth an instance of habitus or of embodied cultural capital (Bourdieu confuses matters further here by reverting to the Greek *hexis*)? The answer, I suggest, is a matter of function. Insofar as a "use of the mouth" belongs to a general manner of being-in-the-world, projecting the actor into social relations and orienting them therein, then it is a facet of habitus. Insofar as it procures them advantage (e.g., social recognition and whatever further advantage that affords) then it is embodied cultural capital. As noted, however, this is potentially confusing and it poses a problem when Bourdieu seeks to explain habitus by reference to capital. In some cases habitus and (embodied) cultural capital are only analytically and not substantively distinct.

Bourdieu has less to say about how habitus are shaped in these ways than one might expect. He loads most of the weight of explanation onto the various constraints and opportunities associated with a given volume and composition of capital. The habitus of those lacking in all forms of capital, the working class, for example, are said to be shaped by their proximity to "necessity"; that is, by their struggle to provide the basics of survival and their relative lack of options:

> The adjustment to objective chances which is inscribed in the dispositions constituting the habitus is the source of all the realistic choices which, based on the renunciation of symbolic profits that are in any case inaccessible, reduce practices or objects to their technical function. . . . Thus nothing is more alien to working class women than the typically bourgeois idea of making each object in the home the occasion for an aesthetic choice, of extending the intention of harmony or beauty even into the bathroom or kitchen, places strictly defined by their function.[19]

This is not only a matter of external constraint, however. The fact that the poor do not typically visit the opera is not only a function of the fact that opera is expensive and they cannot afford to go. The relation between constraint and practice is mediated by habitus. In part this is a matter of lifestyles becoming habitual and shaping desires and expectations. Having never been to the opera the poor have acquired no taste for it, no desire to go, and even if they won the lottery such that they could afford to go, therefore, they would be unlikely to do so. In part, however, it is a function of a psychological response to social conditions. The poor "make a virtue of necessity," Bourdieu insists. They value the way that they are, in effect, constrained to live. And they reject that which, to paraphrase Bourdieu, rejects them. Invoking Nietzsche's concept of *ressentiment*, he notes that the working class refuse the lifestyle "frills" of the middle classes, deeming them "not for the likes of us" and perhaps putting a positive spin upon their own, more "grounded" approach to life.

It is evident in this line of argument that habitus are not identical with practices but rather comprise an underlying attitude or ethos which informs their appropriation and stylization. This becomes most evident when Bourdieu discusses homology. Not all individuals in a given social position have a taste for exactly the same things, he notes, and each individual has a range of likes and activities. This diversity is relatively superficial, however. Practices and tastes located at a similar position in social space express the same underlying ethos (habitus) and therefore resemble one another, structurally. They are homologous.

The association between social position and lifestyle preferences is not fixed, however. It varies across societies and within societies over time. Bourdieu notes, for example, that boxing began as a bourgeois sport, practiced in British public schools, but subsequently moved downward in social space, becoming the preserve of the working class and ethnic minorities.[20] Similarly, a typically working class pursuit in the U.S. may have a middle class connotation in Japan and vice versa. How and why this variation is achieved is never fully addressed by Bourdieu and it is clearly a question begging in relation to some of his claims.

Bourdieu draws two key implications from his reflections upon taste. First, he posits his analyses as a critique of both Kantian aesthetics and more recent "deconstructions" of Kant. The precise claims of the critique are not spelled out but the point appears to be that taste has social conditions of existence not identified by Kant. This points to a blind spot in Kant's critique and also allows Bourdieu to claim that Kantian theory falsely universalizes bourgeois standards of taste, contributing to a process whereby that taste and the practices associated with it are consecrated as official social values.

This leads on to Bourdieu's second key point. Tastes and lifestyles are not only different. They are ranked in social hierarchies. Furthermore, the contingency of this process is masked to some degree by habitus, which tend to naturalize differences. Differences in taste and lifestyle which sociological analyses reveal to be contingent upon social and historical situation feel natural because they are internalized as habitus and therefore function below the level of reflective awareness and choice. Some people, specifically the bourgeoisie, seem, paradoxically, to be naturally more cultured than others.

## 5. EDUCATION

The ranking of cultural differences is achieved, to some extent, through the education system. Schools and universities bestow legitimacy upon certain cultural forms, converting them into an institutionalized form of cultural capital (qualifications), which in turn allows their holder to secure better jobs, with a higher income. Bourdieu conducted many studies of the French education system, which explore this and related themes and argument.[21] Much of his work in this area, moreover, reflecting a key theme in the sociology of education, explores the inequality of educational outcomes; that is, the fact that middle class children do better at school than working class children. He explains this, in part, by reference to habitus. Not only do working class children and parents have different values and expectations from their middle class counterparts, deep rooted in habitus, he argues, but the culture of the school is middle class. Teachers, because middle class, identify with middle class pupils and identify middle class behaviors with academic aptitude. Furthermore, middle class kids are often in possession of the cultural capital that the school rewards and "converts" into qualifications. The patterns of linguistic usage expected and rewarded by the school are those of the middle class, for example, such that middle class kids are advantaged in the school by the culture of their home life. The same applies to the literature read at home, music listened to, topics discussed around the tea table, and so on.

The theme of naturalization is important again here because, in Bourdieu's view, teachers systematically misperceive such social differences as natural differences, with great consequences. If differences in working and middle class "linguistic codes" are interpreted as innate differences in ability and intelligence, then working class students are not only disadvantaged by their lack of access to the official, sanctioned culture but also by a system of negative expectations which numerous studies have shown to be a significant factor explaining poor educational outcomes. Moreover the consequent inequality of outcomes, the reproduction of inequality through the school, is itself naturalized and legitimated. Hierarchies are perceived to be the outcome of natural differences in ability.

## 6. BOURDIEU ASSESSED

Bourdieu has been one of if not the most influential sociologist and social theorist of the twenty-first century so far. Consequently his work has been subject to extensive commentary, much positive but inevitably also involving a great deal of critique. His empirical claims have been tested and retested in new studies and his theoretical claims have been inspected and dissected with a fine-tooth comb. I cannot hope to summarize this wealth of discussion here. I will limit myself to five brief points which bear specifically upon "habitus."

My first point bears upon the merits of the concept relative to that of rules. Bourdieu is not the only theorist to question the adequacy of the concept of rules. It is flawed. However, as Winch notes in an earlier version of the habit vs. rule debate, "rule" captures a normative element that is evident in social life but missing in "habit" (and, I would add, in "habitus").[22] Social practice has a normative aspect. Actors judge actions right and wrong in both moral and technical senses. This normative aspect does not belong to the grammar of "habit," however. Habits qua habits cannot be right or wrong. They simply exist or they do not. When we say that an actor has a "feel for the game" we mean, among other things, that they understand the game, which implies that they understand it correctly; that there is a rule or norm against which their understanding can be judged correct or not. Even simple competence implies such normativity. To say that I can play the guitar, that I have the basic know-how, is to suggest that my playing accords with certain standards and benchmarks. Habitus, at least as Bourdieu develops it, doesn't quite capture this.

This, in turn, points to a further problem. "Habitus" tends to individualize social structure, locating it within the individual rather than where it should be, in my view: between them. As Wittgenstein argued in *Philosophical Investigations*, the "rules" that allow us to judge understanding, game playing, and so on as "correct" (or not) consist in agreement in "forms of life."[23] I understand the guitar to the extent that my playing accords with that of a wider community of musicians, audiences, and so on. Moreover, what counts as correct playing may change over time because forms of life themselves evolve as a function of interaction between members of this community—in which new agreements are arrived at. Bourdieu's habitus doesn't capture this sense of practical agreement—indeed he is often hostile to approaches which emphasize interaction. For all of its sociological credentials Bourdieu's habitus tends to atomize social and cultural life.

Furthermore, "playing the game" will involve interacting and "negotiation" with others, both to establish the competence of those involved, in some cases, and also to facilitate coordination. Barry Barnes has criticized Bourdieu on these grounds, noting that his tendency to explain action in terms of habitus ignores the ongoing processes of interaction by which actors fit their actions with those of others.[24] Referring to the musical analogy invoked by Bourdieu in the above-cited passage on "structuring structures" Barnes notes that Bourdieu theorizes action as if it were a virtuoso solo performance, guided entirely by internalized structures, where in fact much action is in "the ensemble" and requires that "players" constantly monitor one another in an effort to achieve something together.

None of this suggests that we could or should reverse Bourdieu's judgment and reinstate "rules" over habitus, but it suggests perhaps that we need a concept more sensitive to the tacit agreement and negotiation entailed in action—elsewhere I have suggested the concept of "convention" and we might also return to take a closer look at Aristotle's treatment of "hexis"—or perhaps that we should not try to load too much onto any one concept.[25] Indeed, there are several ways in which Bourdieu might be said to overload the concept to the point where its function becomes unclear and its usage inconsistent.

There is also a danger in Bourdieu that habitus is conflated with agency. Bourdieu objects to the dissolving of "man" (*sic*) in Lévi-Strauss's structuralism but in some ways his own account does the same by substituting "habitus" for "actor." This substitution does not work because we can only explain the acquisition, formation, and modification of habitus if we also have an actor who acquires them and initiates their formation and modification. Habitus are traces or sediments of actions which pre-exist them. We ignore this and reify them if we allow them to substitute for agency itself. I do not mean to suggest that habit formation is an activity as such. As both Husserl and Merleau-Ponty stress, habit formation is a tendency of the organism which eludes reflective choice and agency, even if it can be enlisted for reflective purposes, but it presupposes agency. I can only acquire a "feel for the game" if I can first play the game in the absence of such a feel—albeit not in the absence of any habits altogether—and I can only modify the game and my feel for it to the extent that my habits are integrated into an organic system that is not entirely reducible to them, however dependent it may be upon them. Accounts such as that of Merleau-Ponty and Dewey, which analyze and locate habit within the context of a wider account of embodied agency, are more persuasive in my view.[26]

Finally, there is a danger in Bourdieu's account that social actors are reduced to stereotypes or caricatures: "the working class are like this" or "women do that." Of course any empirical discipline generalizes from specific cases and requires tools that allow it to do this. Different social groups do sometimes have some distinctive traits, statistically, and it is important to draw these out and analyze them. There are dangers, both analytical and political, in overstating these group characteristics, however, and the more reified the concept of the habitus becomes the more real those dangers are. In-group variations can be interpreted as mere "surface" variations upon a hypothesized deeper structure, for example, while tastes and behaviors which do not fit an obvious class or gendered pattern are ignored, obscuring a level of concrete detail that is important to a proper grasp of social practice.

Whatever the shortcomings of the concept, however, Bourdieu's "habitus" has served an important function in bringing dispositional concepts back to the forefront of sociological thought. It is a useful tool both to think and to probe the empirical social world with. For this reason it is destined to be maintained by sociologists for some time to come.

## NOTES

1. Charles Camic, "The Matter of Habit," *American Journal of Sociology* 91 (1986): 1039–1087.

2. Pierre Bourdieu, *Outline of a Theory of Practice*, trans. Richard Nice (Cambridge: Cambridge University Press, 1977), 218.

3. Marcel Mauss, "Techniques of the Body," in *Sociology and Psychology: Essays*, trans. Ben Brewster (London: Routledge and Kegan Paul, 1979), 101, emphasis in original.

4. See Emile Durkheim, *The Rules of Sociological Method*, trans. W. D. Halls (New York: Free Press, 1982).

5. See Maurice Merleau-Ponty, *Phenomenology of Perception*, trans. Colin Smith (London: Routledge, 1926) and *The Structure of Behaviour*, trans. Alden Fisher (London: Methuen, 1965); Edmund Husserl, *Experience and Judgment*, trans. James Spencer Churchill and Karl

Ameriks (Evanston: Northwestern University Press, 1973) and *Cartesian Meditations*, trans. Dorion Cairns (The Hague: Martinus Nijhoff, 1990).

6. Hubert Dreyfus and Paul Rabinow, "Can There Be a Science of Existential Structure and Social Meaning?" in Craig Calhoun et al., *Bourdieu: Critical Perspectives* (Cambridge: Polity Press, 1993), 35–44.

7. Compare Pierre Bourdieu and Jean-Claude Passeron, *Reproduction in Education, Society, and Culture*, trans. Richard Nice (London: Sage, 1996) with Pierre Bourdieu, *Pascalian Meditations*, trans. Richard Nice (Cambridge: Polity Press, 2000).

8. Jean-Paul Sartre, *Being and Nothingness*, trans. Hazel E. Barnes (London: Routledge, 1969); Claude Lévi-Strauss, *Structural Anthropology*, trans. Claire Jacobson (New York: Basic Books, 1963).

9. But see Nick Crossley, "Body and Society: Sartre and the Sociologists," in *Sartre on the Body*, ed. Katherine Morris (London: Palgrave, 2010), 215–30.

10. Bourdieu, *Outline of a Theory of Practice*, 86.

11. Talcott Parsons, *The Social System* (New York: Free Press, 1951).

12. See also Charles Taylor, "To Follow a Rule . . . ," in Calhoun et al., *Bourdieu: Critical Perspectives*, 45–60.

13. Pierre Bourdieu, *Distinction: A Social Critique of the Judgement of Taste*, trans. Richard Nice (London: Routledge, 1984), 466.

14. Pierre Bourdieu, *The Logic of Practice*, trans. Richard Nice (Cambridge: Polity Press, 1992), 53.

15. Pierre Bourdieu, *Practical Reason*, trans. Randall Johnson (Cambridge: Polity Press, 1998), 54, emphasis in original.

16. Pierre Bourdieu, *The Political Ontology of Martin Heidegger*, trans. Peter Collier (Cambridge: Polity Press, 1991).

17. Pierre Bourdieu, *On Television and Journalism*, trans. Priscilla Parkhurst Ferguson (London: Pluto Press, 1998).

18. Pierre Bourdieu, *Language and Symbolic Power*, ed. John Thompson, trans. Gino Raymond and Matthew Adamson (Cambridge: Polity Press, 1992), 86–87.

19. Bourdieu, *Distinction,* 379.

20. Pierre Bourdieu, "Sport and Social Class," *Social Science Information* 17 (1978): 819–40.

21. See, for example, Pierre Bourdieu, *The State Nobility*, trans. Lauretta C. Clough (Stanford: Stanford University Press, 1996) and Bourdieu and Passeron, *Reproduction.*

22. Peter Winch, *The Idea of a Social Science* (London: Routledge and Kegan Paul, 1958).

23. Ludwig Wittgenstein, *Philosophical Investigations*, 3rd ed., trans. G. E. M. Anscombe (Oxford: Blackwell, 1953).

24. Barry Barnes, *Understanding Agency: Social Theory and Responsible Action* (London: Sage, 2000).

25. Nick Crossley, *Towards Relational Sociology* (London: Routledge, 2011).

26. See Merleau-Ponty, *Phenomenology of Perception* and *The Structure of Behavior*; John Dewey, *Human Nature and Conduct* (Carbondale: Southern Illinois University Press, 1988).

## BIBLIOGRAPHY

Aristotle. *The Ethics*. Translated by J. A. K. Thomson. Harmondsworth: Penguin, 1955.

Barnes, Barry. *Understanding Agency: Social Theory and Responsible Action*. London: Sage, 2000.

Bourdieu, Pierre. *Outline of a Theory of Practice*. Translated by Richard Nice. Cambridge: Cambridge University Press, 1977.

———. "Sport and Social Class." *Social Science Information* 17 (1978): 819–40.

———. *Distinction*. Translated by Richard Nice. London: Routledge and Kegan Paul, 1984.

———. *The Political Ontology of Martin Heidegger*. Translated by Peter Collier. Cambridge: Polity, 1991.

———. *The Logic of Practice*. Translated by Richard Nice. Cambridge: Polity, 1992.

———. *Language and Symbolic Power*. Edited by John Thompson. Translated by Gino Raymond and Matthew Adamson. Cambridge: Polity, 1992.

———. "Social Space and the Genesis of Classes." In *Language and Symbolic Power*, 229–51. Cambridge: Polity, 1993.

———. *The Rules of Art*. Translated by Susan Emanuel. Cambridge: Polity, 1994.

———. *The State Nobility*. Translated by Lauretta C. Clough. Cambridge: Polity, 1996.

———. *Practical Reason*. Translated by Randall Johnson. Cambridge: Polity, 1998.

———. *On Television and Journalism*. Translated by Priscilla Parkhurst Ferguson. London: Pluto, 1998.

———. *Pascalian Meditations*. Translated by Richard Nice. Cambridge: Polity, 2000.

Bourdieu, Pierre and Jean-Claude Passeron. *Reproduction*. Translated by Richard Nice. London: Sage, 1996.

Bourdieu, Pierre et al. *The Love of Art*. Translated by Caroline Beattie and Nick Merriman. Cambridge: Polity, 1991.

Camic, Charles. "The Matter of Habit." *American Journal of Sociology* 91 (1986): 1039–1087.

Crossley, Nick. "Body and Society: Sartre and the Sociologists." In *Sartre on the Body*, edited by Katherine Morris, 215–30. London: Palgrave, 2010.

———. *Towards Relational Sociology*. London: Routledge, 2011.

Dewey, John. *Human Nature and Conduct*. Edited by Jo Ann Boydston. Carbondale: Southern Illinois University Press, 1988.

Dreyfus, Hubert and Paul Rabinow. "Can There Be a Science of Existential Structure and Social Meaning?" In *Bourdieu: Critical Perspectives*, edited by Craig Calhoun et al., 35–44. Cambridge: Polity, 1993.

Durkheim, Emile. *The Rules of Sociological Method*. Translated by W. D. Halls. New York: Free Press, 1982.

Husserl, Edmund. *Experience and Judgment*. Translated by James Spencer Churchill and Karl Ameriks. Evanston: Northwestern University Press, 1973.

———. *Cartesian Meditations*. Translated by Dorion Cairns. The Hague: Martinus Nijhoff, 1990.

Lévi-Strauss, Claude. *Structural Anthropology*. Translated by Claire Jacobson. New York: Basic Books, 1963.

Marx, Karl. *The Economic and Philosophical Manuscripts of 1844*. Translated by Martin Mulligan. Moscow: Progress Publishers, 1959.

Mauss, Marcel. "Techniques of the Body." In *Sociology and Psychology: Essays*. Translated by Ben Brewster. London: Routledge and Kegan Paul, 1979.

Merleau-Ponty, Maurice. *Phenomenology of Perception*. Translated by Colin Smith. London: Routledge, 1962.

———. *The Structure of Behavior*. Translated by Alden Fisher. London: Methuen, 1965.

Nietzsche, Friedrich. *The Genealogy of Morals*. Translated by Walter Kaufmann. New York: Vintage, 1967.

Parsons, Talcott. *The Social System*. New York: Free Press, 1951.

Sartre, Jean-Paul. *Being and Nothingness*. Translated by Hazel E. Barnes. London: Routledge, 1969.

Taylor, Charles. "To Follow a Rule . . . " In *Bourdieu: Critical Perspectives*, 45–60. Cambridge: Polity, 1993.

Winch, Peter. *The Idea of a Social Science*. London: Routledge and Kegan Paul, 1958.

Wittgenstein, Ludwig. *Philosophical Investigations*, 3rd ed. Translated by G. E. M. Anscombe. Oxford: Blackwell, 1953.

# Index

# About the Contributors

**Jeffrey Bell** is professor of philosophy at Southeastern Louisiana University. He is the author and editor of numerous books, including *Philosophy at the Edge of Chaos: Gilles Deleuze and the Philosophy of Difference* (Toronto, 2006), *Deleuze's Hume: Philosophy, Culture and the Scottish Enlightenment* (Edinburgh, 2009), and, with Claire Colebrook, *Deleuze and History* (Edinburgh, 2009). In addition to working and writing on Deleuze, Bell has written articles and chapters on Spinoza, Whitehead, intellectual history, and Nietzsche. He is currently at work on a manuscript on metaphysics and the principle of sufficient reason.

**Clare Carlisle** is lecturer in philosophy of religion at King's College London. She studied philosophy and theology at Trinity College, Cambridge, between 1995 and 2002. She is the author of three books on Kierkegaard, and the translator of Félix Ravaisson's *De l'habitude*. Her next book, *On Habit* (Routledge), is forthcoming in 2014.

**Edward S. Casey** is distinguished professor of philosophy at SUNY, Stony Brook. A recent president of the American Philosophical Association, Eastern Division, he is the author of ten books. He has written copiously on the relation between body, memory, place, and habit in such books as *Remembering, Getting Back into Place*, and *The Fate of Place*. He recently published *The World at a Glance*. Forthcoming are *The World on Edge* and (with Mary Watkins) *Up Against the Wall: Re-imagining the U.S.-Mexico Border*.

**Nick Crossley** is professor of sociology at the University of Manchester (UK). He has published widely on issues of embodiment and habit. His latest book is *Towards Relational Sociology* (Routledge, 2011).

**Dennis Des Chene** is professor of philosophy at Washington University. He is the author of *Physiologia* (Cornell, 1996), *Life's Form* (Cornell,

2000), and *Spirits and Clocks* (Cornell, 2001), and of articles on mechanism, Suárez, Régis, Bayle, and late Aristotelianism. In 2007 he was awarded fellowships by the John Simon Guggenheim Foundation and the American Philosophical Society. He is now working on seventeenth-century theories of emotion and on the history and philosophy of mathematics.

**Peter S. Fosl** is professor of philosophy at Transylvania University in Lexington, Kentucky, where he is chair of both the Philosophy and the PPE (Philosophy, Politics, and Economic) programs. Co-author of *The Philosopher's Toolkit* with Julian Baggini (Wiley-Blackwell, 2011), Fosl's articles on Hume, skepticism, philosophy of religion, and ethics have appeared in *Hume Studies*, *Journal of the History of Philosophy*, and *1650–1850.* His essay on military suicide, "American Despair in a Time of Hope," appears in the Fall 2012 issue of *Salmagundi Magazine.*

**Adam Hutchinson** is a PhD candidate in philosophy at Duquesne University. He works mainly in American pragmatism, the history of materialism, and critical theory (especially questions of race). Currently he is completing a manuscript on the body, materiality, and force in the writings of Newton, Kant, and Fichte.

**David E. Leary** is former co-director of the History and Theory of Psychology Graduate Program at the University of New Hampshire, where he also served as professor of psychology, history, and the humanities and chairperson of psychology. He is fellow and past president of the Society for the History of Psychology. From 1989 to 2002 he was Dean of Arts and Sciences at the University of Richmond, where he is currently university professor.

**Thornton C. Lockwood** is assistant professor of philosophy at Quinnipiac University. He has published articles on Aristotle's *Nicomachean Ethics* and *Politics* in *Phronesis*, *Journal of the History of Philosophy*, *History of Political Thought*, *Ancient Philosophy*, and *Oxford Bibliographies On-line.* He is the associate editor (book reviews) at *POLIS: The Journal of Ancient Greek Political Thought.*

**Terrance MacMullan** is professor of philosophy and honors at Eastern Washington University. His essays on pragmatism, the philosophy of race, and the relationship between public intellectuals and democracy have been published in the *Journal of Speculative Philosophy*, *Philosophy and Social Criticism*, and *Transactions of the Charles S. Peirce Society*. His book *The Habits of Whiteness: A Pragmatist Reconstruction* was published by Indiana University Press in May 2009. He is currently researching a book on the affinities between pragmatism and Latin American philosophy.

**Robert C. Miner** is associate professor of philosophy in the Honors College at Baylor University. He is the author of *Thomas Aquinas on the Passions: A Study of* Summa Theologiae *1a2ae qq. 22–48* (Cambridge University Press, 2009), as well as articles on Nietzsche, Vico, Hobbes, Pascal, and Suárez.

**Tom Sparrow** teaches in the Department of Philosophy at Slippery Rock University, Pennsylvania, where he works primarily in continental and modern philosophy. He is the author of *Levinas Unhinged* (Zero Books, 2013) and *The End of Phenomenology: Metaphysics and the New Realism* (Edinburgh University Press, forthcoming).

**William O. Stephens** is professor of philosophy and classical and Near Eastern studies at Creighton University in Omaha, Nebraska. He has published articles on topics in Stoicism, Epicureanism, ecology and vegetarianism, ethics and animals, sex and love, and the concept of a person. His books include an English translation of Adolf Bonhöffer's work *The Ethics of the Stoic Epictetus* (Peter Lang, 1996), the edited collection *The Person: Readings in Human Nature* (Prentice Hall, 2006), *Stoic Ethics: Epictetus and Happiness as Freedom* (Continuum, 2007), and *Marcus Aurelius: A Guide for the Perplexed* (Continuum, 2012). He is currently working on a manuscript titled *Lessons in Liberation: Epictetus as Educator.*

**Shannon Sullivan** is head of the Philosophy Department and professor of philosophy, women's studies, and African American Studies at Penn State University. She teaches and writes at the intersections of feminist philosophy, critical philosophy of race, American pragmatism, and continental philosophy. She is author of *Living Across and Through Skins: Transactional Bodies, Pragmatism and Feminism* (Indiana, 2001) and *Revealing Whiteness: The Unconscious Habits of Racial Privilege* (Indiana, 2006). She is coeditor of *Race and Epistemologies of Ignorance* (SUNY, 2007), *Difficulties of Ethical Life* (Fordham, 2008), and *Race Questions, Provincialism, and Other American Problems: Expanded Edition* (Fordham, 2009). She is currently finishing a book on transforming whiteness.

**Margaret Watkins** is assistant professor of philosophy at Saint Vincent College in southwestern Pennsylvania. After graduating from the College of William and Mary, she earned her PhD in philosophy at the University of Notre Dame. Her research focuses on ethics and early modern philosophy, with a particular emphasis on the moral philosophy of David Hume. She has published several articles on the relationship between literature and philosophy, exploring the resources of Jane Austen's novels for questions in ethics generally and virtue theory in particular. She is currently working on a book on Hume's *Essays Moral, Political, and Literary.*